THE BLUE
PERIOD

D1528586

THINKING LITERATURE
A series edited by Nan Z. Da and Anahid Nersessian

The Blue Period

BLACK WRITING IN
THE EARLY COLD WAR

Jesse McCarthy

The University of Chicago Press
Chicago and London

The University of Chicago Press, Chicago 60637
The University of Chicago Press, Ltd., London
© 2024 by The University of Chicago
All rights reserved. No part of this book may be used or reproduced
in any manner whatsoever without written permission, except
in the case of brief quotations in critical articles and reviews. For
more information, contact the University of Chicago Press, 1427
East 60th Street, Chicago, IL 60637.
Published 2024
Printed in the United States of America

33 32 31 30 29 28 27 26 25 24   1 2 3 4 5

ISBN-13: 978-0-226-83037-7 (cloth)
ISBN-13: 978-0-226-83217-3 (paper)
ISBN-13: 978-0-226-83218-0 (e-book)
DOI: https://doi.org/10.7208/chicago/9780226832180.001.0001

The University of Chicago Press gratefully acknowledges the
generous support of Harvard University toward the publication of
this book.

Library of Congress Cataloging-in-Publication Data

Names: McCarthy, Jesse, author.
Title: The blue period : black writing in the early Cold War / Jesse
     McCarthy.
Other titles: Thinking literature.
Description: Chicago : The University of Chicago Press, 2024. |
     Series: Thinking literature | Includes bibliographical references
     and index.
Identifiers: LCCN 2023037530 | ISBN 9780226830377 (cloth) |
     ISBN 9780226832173 (paperback) | ISBN 9780226832180 (ebook)
Subjects: LCSH: African American authors—20th century. |
     American literature—20th century—History and criticism. | Cold
     War in literature.
Classification: LCC PS153.B53 M33 2024 | DDC
     810.9/8960730904—dc23/eng/20230816
LC record available at https://lccn.loc.gov/2023037530

♾ This paper meets the requirements of ANSI/NISO Z39.48-1992
(Permanence of Paper).

Contents

INTRODUCTION · Black and Blue at Midcentury 1

CHAPTER 1 · James Baldwin's Revelations 18

CHAPTER 2 · Édouard Glissant's Relocations 42

CHAPTER 3 · Vincent O. Carter's Exiles 69

CHAPTER 4 · Gwendolyn Brooks's and Paule Marshall's Elusions 104

CHAPTER 5 · Richard Wright's Negations 143

CONCLUSION · Writing for a Future World 188

ACKNOWLEDGMENTS 211

NOTES 213

BIBLIOGRAPHY 271

INDEX 293

Black and Blue at Midcentury

The period through which we are living is characterized by a double failure: one which has been evident for a long time, that of capitalism. But also another: the dreadful failure of that which for too long we took to be socialism, when it was nothing but Stalinism.

The result is that, at the present time, the world is at an impasse.

This can only mean one thing: not that there is no way out, but that the time has come to abandon all the old ways, which have led to fraud, tyranny, and murder.

Suffice it to say that, for our part, we no longer want to remain content with being present while others do politics, while they get nowhere, while they make deals, while they perform makeshift repairs on their consciences and engage in casuistry.

Our time has come.

AIMÉ CÉSAIRE, "Letter to Maurice Thorez," October 24, 1956

What happens to literary expression when belief in the available forms of political and social struggle, the ideological horizons in every direction, are suddenly foreclosed? In 1956 the Martinican poet Aimé Césaire wrote to Maurice Thorez, the leader of the French Communist Party, publicly announcing his break with the political and ideological family that had nurtured him. He had been elected in 1945 as the first black mayor of Fort-de-France (and a deputy member of the French National Assembly for Martinique) on a Communist Party ticket. Like most black writers who began their careers in the interwar years, Césaire had been formed by the communist left; to break with it was no small gesture. What had changed? One striking aspect of Césaire's argument is its insistence upon the notion of period, his conviction that something about the historical conjunction of the postwar years presents itself as a historical "impasse." He connects this to a discrediting of the Cold War's ideological binary, viewing both sides as equally unable to address the needs and aspirations of black lives. This situation does not prompt in Césaire a sense of hopelessness, nor does it imply a renunciation of political struggle or commitment. Elsewhere in the letter, he states, "It is neither Marxism nor communism that I am renouncing." The issue is how these forces relate, or fail to relate, to the experience of black oppression and the agency of black communities: "What I want is that Marxism and communism be placed in the service of black peoples, and not black peoples in the service of Marxism and communism."[1]

The "Letter to Maurice Thorez" is, of course, only nominally episto-lary. Its declamatory tone and liberal use of nominative and genitive plu-ral pronouns betray its generic indebtedness to the political manifesto, in this case one with anticolonial and Pan-Africanist orientations that are the logical extension of Césaire's *Discourse on Colonialism*, his seminal 1950 manifesto published in a freshly revised version in 1955.[2] These rhetorical markings place "Letter to Maurice Thorez" rightfully among those cele-brated documents of black midcentury resistance announcing the nascent struggle for decolonization.

But can we read it as a *literary* manifesto?[3] Should it not, by corollary, announce the opening of a new period for black literature? If Césaire is right that "our time has come," does it not imply a fortiori that a new kind of writing must accompany this shift in paradigm? What are the impli-cations of this break for black writing? These are reasonable questions to ask given the importance of Césaire's voice as a flag bearer for black poetry. Césaire's mayorship was an impressive feat in the 1950s, but his real force (at once cultural and political) accrued from his landmark poem *Notebook of a Return to the Native Land* (1939). His open letter to Thorez—again, only the nominal addressee of its contents—carried the imprimatur chiefly of its author's literary authority, a beacon recognized by his read-ership throughout the Francophone diaspora and beyond.[4] Was Césaire responding to a feeling that was shared within the wider world of black letters? If he was, we should expect to find other voices confirming his sen-timent and his diagnosis. The main argument of this book is that we can answer that hypothesis in the affirmative: there is a discernible common sensibility that enters black literature in the early years of the Cold War, and the examples of it are numerous and compelling enough to warrant the discrete periodization of the two decades following the end of World War II, an era I propose calling the Blue Period.

Indeed, we find an argument remarkably like Césaire's emerging al-most a decade earlier. On December 16, 1948, an essay written by an American living in self-imposed exile in Paris appeared on the front page of the French newspaper *Franc-Tireur*. Under its grandiloquent title, "Our Humanity Is Greater Than America or Russia," appeared the byline and photograph of—in the words of the editors—"a great American writer" and "a representative of a race crushed in its soul and destiny." The essay opens with a sentence whose chiasmus emphasizes the divided, unhappy consciousness of its author: "My body was born in America; my heart was born in Russia, and today I stand contritely ashamed between my two par-ent countries."[5] This figure, with its split anatomy of melancholy, is at once a stateless exile, driven by choice and conviction to a radical departure from his native grounds, and the isolated voice of a black writer holding fast in the midst of an engulfing totalitarian night of the soul.

He declares allegiance to a *patria* of the mind and, like Césaire, condemns the stifling imperialisms of the two postwar superpowers vying at the dawn of the Cold War for global supremacy:

> The hysterical political atmosphere, in America and in Russia, already has removed from man the means of objectively and reasonably resolving the problems of food and shelter. The present nationalism, in America and in Russia, forces a man to abandon his human heritage. America and Russia pretend that their action is in defense of the lives of their people; but in truth, it kills the life of man on earth. In rejecting all this, what can we do? Fortunately, the situation is not completely desperate. I believe that we still have a chance. It is not a question of our fighting these national giants on their own ground. Our weapons are not their weapons. For us there still exists room for liberty, and that room is your spirit and mine, your ability to speak and write the words which hold attention and make men stop, look and listen. For some time yet, we shall have this liberty; for how long? We don't know.

To be a black writer in the middle of the twentieth century—to be Richard Wright, the author of *Native Son* and *Black Boy*, penning this essay just two years after immigrating to Paris in 1946—was to face a stark predicament.

On the one hand, the political and intellectual force of revolutionary communism had unquestionably galvanized the energies of change, launched the promise of egalitarianism and brotherhood, and lit the sparks of anticolonial struggle. But the same forces had proved quick to instrumentalize racial strife for the ends of that geopolitical struggle. As was particularly clear after the rise to power of Stalin in the Soviet Union, those forces were also inclined to pursue their ends in a fashion inimical to conceptions of personal freedom—which were precisely those felt to be most necessary to black writers and thinkers, who were still seeking to self-fashion independent voices out of experiences that for centuries had been relegated to racist caricature for the purposes of crude entertainment or political expediency. On the other hand, the great force opposing the Soviets at midcentury was itself the fountainhead of racial prejudice, emblematized in the social and cultural logic of the United States: Jim Crow.

For Wright, the choices on the menu of Cold War politics amount to what Césaire in 1956 still called an "impasse," that is, no choice at all. As scholars of the cultural and literary life of this period have shown, the specter of totalitarianism and the immediate backdrop of the Holocaust raised the stakes to an almost unbearable pitch. "They are guilty of degrading humanity," Wright writes of the dueling Soviet and American camps, "guilty of debasing the culture of our times, guilty of replacing the value of quality by the value of quantity, guilty of creating a universe which, little by little, is revealed as the gas chamber of humanity." Wright had come to France seeking a reprieve from the racial antagonisms that he experienced at home. But the direction of his fiction and the remainder of his all-too-brief life would betray the inevitability of confrontation with the global reach of the Cold War's ideological constrictions and his own failure to fall in line with any of them. Indeed, Cross Damon, the lone-wolf hero of *The Outsider* (1953), Wright's most ambitious philosophical novel from this period, mirrors the radical isolation of his creator.

Despite Césaire's famous defection from the Communist Party and Wright's plea for a nonaligned literature, studies that read black writers as dissenting equally from the political Left and Right are surprisingly rare in histories of the period. This is because the logics of the Cold War have, perhaps inevitably, dominated the past half century or so of criticism, repeatedly recruiting major figures like Wright, Ralph Ellison, James Baldwin, and Gwendolyn Brooks into political arguments and affiliations that their work itself persistently and, as I will show, necessarily confounds. *The Blue Period* argues that what is so distinctive, compelling, and politically potent about black writing from this era is its dissent from both of the hegemonic Cold War ideological blocks: a radical dissatisfaction, a double negative that produces, as a remainder, an extraordinary effort to self-authorize an art capable of capturing the needs, hopes, fears, and despairs—that is, the affective dimensions—of a black experience of modernity that the dominant frameworks of politics and literary criticism could not, and did not, address.

In the decades immediately preceding this period, traditional forms of literary realism, incorporating the tropes of proletarian literature, documentary fiction, and Popular Front poetics, had been the predominant literary norms for black writers. The mistake has been to assume that black writers' turn away from a leftist literary aesthetics during the Cold War must imply an endorsement of centrist, liberal, or even reactionary politics. But these experiments in dissent are woefully misrepresented when they are relegated to a dematerialized category of "the universal" or the rubric of an abstracted liberal individualism.[6] On the contrary, as this study shows, the writings from this period persistently take up radical perspectives on the meaning and possibilities of freedom, and they conceive new aesthetic strategies for connecting ideas about power to the authority of lived experience, to alternative or subversive epistemologies, and to alternative conceptions of community. My claim is not that black writers or artists were the only ones to tackle these kinds of problems; but the specific conditions of the postwar ideological landscape threw experiential and affective aspects of blackness into relief for black writers in an unprecedented way. Their synchronic response to these conditions left a discernible pattern, a "blue" literature, produced by black writers at the dawn of what Alan Wald calls "Cold War modernity."[7]

The Blue Period asks how and why the texts and contexts of postwar black writing shaped each other and makes an argument for how best to interpret the significance of those relations. The specter of geopolitics is not of primary interest, but it is never far off either. The evolution of the second half of the twentieth century was determined by the confrontation between the superpowers that emerged from the rubble of World War II. The contest between the Soviet Union and the United States was global and subsumed the rest of the world into two opposed and expansionist blocs. "Locked in conflict over the very concept of European modernity—to which both states saw themselves as successors," the historian Odd Arne Westad has written, "Washington and Moscow needed to change the world in order to prove the universal applicability of their ideologies, and the elites of the newly independent states proved fertile ground for their competition."[8] This pitched ideological battle dominated almost every aspect of the social, political, and cultural agenda between 1945 and 1965. The Cold War created a set of conditions wherein, as Louis Menand has written, the arts and the realm of ideas were taken seriously in a way that was responsive to these geopolitical pressures, "the way people judged and interpreted paintings, movies, and poems mattered" to a degree that appears distinctly historically bounded from our present vantage point.[9]

There could be no "outside" to this all-encompassing conflict, but there were many "outsiders," the vast majority of the world's inhabitants—the so-called darker nations or Third World that had assembled at Bandung, Indonesia, in 1955 and would come to assert themselves in wars for independence and decolonization across Africa, the Middle East, South East Asia, the Caribbean, and those "nations within a nation," in the United States itself, during the height of the Black Nationalist moment.[10] Indeed, for the decolonial movement, these decades were some of the harshest and most eventful of all.[11] Yet, as Raymond Williams once said, whenever we encounter such totalizing conditions, it is necessary to remember that "however dominant a social system may be, the very meaning of its domination involves a limitation or selection of the activities it covers, so that by definition it cannot exhaust all social experience, which therefore always potentially contains space for alternative acts and alternative intentions which are not yet articulated as a social institution or even project."[12] There were enormous constraints on where and how the visions, ideas, and affective experiences of black literary outsiders could enter the hegemonic discourses and ideologies of the Cold War, yet these very constraints also permitted a special kind of opportunity. This book argues that black writers during the Cold War seized on the "Negro Problem," as it was then called, not as sociological fact for one ideological school or the other to address through redistribution or formal recognition, but as *lived experience*—as phenomenology and interiority, what the title of the fifth chapter of Frantz Fanon's *Black Skin, White Masks* (first published in 1952) calls "L'expérience vécue du Noir," properly rendered in the Richard Philcox translation as "The Lived Experience of the Black Man."[13] Falling back in this way served them precisely because it put into focus what remained insoluble, what could not be contained by the Cold War anticommunism's "containment culture," that degree of freedom that the system could not regulate or effectively address and that therefore contained within it the seeds of "alternative acts and alternative intentions."[14]

The alienated quality of this lived experience required an expressive form that reflected what Louis Althusser has called "an internal distance," immanent to the writing itself. Indeed, the passage in which this phrase arises is powerfully suggestive of the notion of alienation that I am interested in tracking through the authors discussed in this book. "I believe that the peculiarity of art," says Althusser, "is to 'make us see' (*nous donner à voir*), 'make us perceive,' 'make us feel' something which *alludes* to reality."[15] In so doing, he goes on to say, they "give us a 'view' of the ideology to which their work alludes and with which it is constantly fed, a view which presupposes a *retreat*, an *internal distantiation* from the very ideology from which their novels emerged. They make us 'perceive' (but not know) in some sense *from the inside*, by an *internal distance*, the very ideology in which they are held."[16] In a time of unprecedented ideological pressure bearing down upon the function of the black writer and the presuppositional environment for the reception of their work, this internal retreat, and whatever remaining affordances could be invented and conceived there, became all the more essential to probe.

The persistent illegibility of this affective and aesthetic remainder has had consequences for how we read and understand black writing produced in the two decades following the end of World War II. To properly grasp them, we have to consider the singular position from which they addressed, and understood themselves to be implicated in, what Du Bois called "the problem of the future world."[17] We need to resituate ourselves in that moment and see it from the inside, as it were: a time of hollow liberalism and racist backlash in the United States, collapsed moral and colonial authority in Europe, compromised communism devoured by state-capitalist dictatorship, the prospects of revolutionary action grumbling but not yet fully legible as writing on the wall.[18] How did black writers forge new perspectives out of their position of deep alienation? Can we understand certain formalist aspects of these texts as strategies for incorporating newly emergent relationships between affect, aesthetics, and politics? These are the kinds of questions the framing of a literary period can supply answers for.

Why Periodize?

I have sketched some of the attractions and motivations for a periodizing project, but one might still ask: Why make an argument for periodization *now*? It is a fair question. A growing chorus of voices object to historicism and its associated pedagogical methods as démodé or, worse, reactionary. Isn't periodization inherently a social, institutional, and disciplinary construct in need of wholesale reform?[19]

It is tempting in a first instance to return to Fredric Jameson's famous injunction to "always historicize!"[20] Indeed, Jameson's contention that ideology always works upon literary texts through "strategies of containment" that attempt to normalize and suppress their irruptive and utopian impulses is irresistibly consonant with my period's aforementioned cultural scripts.[21] Against this background, black writers necessarily turned to *strategies of evasion*—an aesthetic of fugitive dissent from the hegemonic ideologemes of that historical conjunction. But besides this overarching theme, to the questions about methodology, I offer three answers.

The first is that within African American literary studies, Kenneth Warren's pressing inquiry into the nature and scope of the field has returned the issue of periodization to center stage.[22] Warren has argued that "African American literature itself constitutes a representational and rhetorical strategy within the domain of a literary practice responsive to conditions that, by and large, no longer obtain."[23] In the aftermath of this polemical challenge there has been a healthy debate about whether or not the relevant "conditions" do or do not obtain. What Warren, I think uncontrovertibly, gets right is that African American literature is a representational and rhetorical strategy that necessarily responds to conditions that change, according to what Stuart Hall calls the different "conjunctures" and historical "articulations" of blackness.[24] Mores and political attitudes, fashion and taste, idiom and vocabulary—most notoriously the very words black people use to describe themselves—what it means and how it feels to be black in the modern world have swung wildly, radically, and unpredictably, sometimes over the course of more than a decade, sometimes seemingly overnight. What is needed, then, is not necessarily a postmortem on the category of African American literature as such but a finer-grained and discretely periodized assessment of it.

This leads directly to my second answer, which is that, while the utility of periodization debates may differ in other subfields, within black literary studies the need for a framework to address the midcentury has repeatedly resurfaced. Stacy Morgan cites Ellison's *Invisible Man* (1952), Brooks's *Annie Allen* (1949), and the paintings of Charles Alston and Hale Woodruff as "signposts that African American literature and visual art were gravitating in a qualitatively new direction—one still vastly understudied but clearly stemming from a heightened engagement with American high modernism and 'universalist' impulses."[25] Similarly, Vaughn Rasberry points to "formal shifts in black literary production at midcentury—a still undefined interregnum (in the dual sense of 'any period of freedom from the usual authority' and 'any pause or interruption in continuity') between the canonized Harlem Renaissance and Black Arts movement—as writers experimented with 'raceless' fiction, tempered earlier radical tendencies, and adopted various idioms of liberal individualism."[26] Both scholars, publishing more than a decade apart, agree that a "vastly understudied" period, an "interregnum" of black art, exists in the early years of the Cold War. Cedric Tolliver has also recently argued for revising this literary history to account for those "African diaspora radicals of the postwar period" who launched "a political-cultural movement that refused the ideological limits imposed by the East-West binary."[27] These assessments point to a cohering strand of scholarship that is producing an ongoing transformation of our understanding of this period.[28]

Alongside these two theoretical and historical arguments, this book also suggests a third answer: periodization can reconfigure and rebalance how we teach and study the canon of black literary texts. When Henry Louis Gates Jr. said in 1992 that "the particular burden of scholars of Afro-American studies is that we must often resurrect the texts of our tradition before we can even begin to analyze them," he had in mind both the acrimonious "culture wars" then raging and the painstaking task of excavating the archive of slave narratives, a groundbreaking recovery that he has, famously, undertaken.[29] We know now that these efforts cannot be confined to uncovering lost writings from the eighteenth and nineteenth centuries. As Jean-Christophe Cloutier's discovery in 2009 of Claude McKay's manuscript from 1941 for the novel *Amiable with Big Teeth* and Glenda Carpio and Werner Sollors's publication of previously unpublished short fiction by Zora Neale Hurston have shown, there are still surprising gaps in our knowledge even of purportedly well-established figures.[30] These discoveries, alongside pioneering work being done by scholars like

Brent Edwards, Kinohi Nishikawa, and Britt Rusert, have led to talk of an "archival turn" in African American literary studies: both a return to the archive as a source and a change to our understanding of what counts as an archive, of how it relates to the texts that live in its shadows.[31]

These questions of canonicity come to the fore in my chapter on Vincent O. Carter, whose work, absent intervention, would have been entirely lost. This anachronic reception history has become part of the story of Carter's work, but it also creeps up as a spectral feature that limns many published works from this period that have completely fallen out of scholarly conversations, to say nothing of syllabi. This certainly seems to be the fate of John A. William's icy first novel, *The Angry Ones* (1960), whose protagonist integrates the world of allegedly liberal postwar New York City publishing only to find it a harrowing cesspool of racist fantasies and resentments.[32] Or Julian Mayfield's *The Grand Parade* (1961), which casts a jaundiced eye on the small-town Southern politics of school integration efforts, and whose protagonists are disillusioned black ex-communists who appear poised to turn either to radical Black Nationalist militancy or to writing novels. Feminist scholarship has thankfully recovered novels like Paule Marshall's *Brown Girl, Brownstones* (1959), Gwendolyn Brooks's *Maud Martha* (1953), and Ann Petry's *The Narrows* (1953) from decades of neglect.

Yet even these works are still marginalized in accounts of this amorphous midcentury period, which still gravitate heavily around Ellison's *Invisible Man*. Therefore, I deliberately avoid a chapter dedicated solely, or principally, to *Invisible Man*, even though it is arguably one of the most emblematic examples of the literature of the period I seek to define. By decentering Ellison, I emphasize another advantage of a periodizing framework: it evens the playing field among the plurality of texts that vie for our attention, without denying any their respective achievement. Shades of Ellison nonetheless hover over every chapter. I would like the reader to think of him as an ever-present guide, a Virgil to this blue underworld, whose presence need not eclipse the other works that demand our attention.

Indeed, many of the themes and questions this book addresses are ones that lie at the heart of Ellison's novel. What is the connection between politics, ideology, and being forced into a state of isolation underground? How should one think about the politics of hibernation and strategic retreat? Why is black interiority so prominent in Ellison's novel, and why did the *blackness* of that experiential representation prove so illegible to some of his critics?[33] Why does Ellison's narrator linger upon Louis Armstrong's disembodied voice playing on the phonograph, as if the novel wanted to insist upon something that has become detached and ambient, the correlative for a feeling that is also expressly a condition? Why is the record that "colors" the period when he is underground "(What Did I Do to Be So) Black and Blue," a title itself metonymic for a racialized affect? What is it about this time, this place, this "structure of feeling," to use Raymond Williams's phrase? What makes it "so black and blue"?[34]

Defining the Blue Period

By any reasonable measure, 1953 ought to be recognized as the annus mirabilis of twentieth-century black literature. That year, James Baldwin published his first novel, *Go Tell It on the Mountain*, announcing a major new voice in American letters; Gwendolyn Brooks, already winner of the Pulitzer Prize for poetry, published her singular experimental novel, *Maud Martha*; Ann Petry published her second and most ambitious novel, *The Narrows*; Richard Wright published *The Outsider*; the Barbadian George Lamming published his first novel, *In the Castle of My Skin*; and Ralph Ellison won the National Book Award for *Invisible Man*, which catapulted the novel and its author into the highest ranks of literary fame. Yet despite this impressive constellation, a coherent critical framework connecting these various texts is strikingly absent from prevailing narratives of twentieth-century literary history.[35]

This book addresses this lacuna by proposing that we demarcate a literary period on either side of this pivotal year, one that spans the twenty years between 1945, the end of World War II, and 1965, the year Malcolm X was assassinated; the year LeRoi Jones changed his name to Amiri Baraka and founded the Black Arts Repertory Theatre/School; the year of the Watts rebellion; and the year "Black Power"—as a politics and a discourse—broke onto the common tongue, becoming explicit and made politically potent through Stokely Carmichael's intervention in the Meredith March against Fear during the summer of 1966.[36]

Part of the difficulty in generating a coherent framework for black postwar literature is that the critical vocabulary applied to it has been beholden to a fossilized vocabulary. The two most flagrant offenders are the terms *protest* and *universal* (or *universalism*).[37] The terms *maturity* and, closely associated with it, *technique*, are thankfully no longer in vogue, but Warren rightly points out that they played a key role in defining the attitude of black midcentury literary criticism, notably in the 1950 special issue of *Phylon* magazine devoted to the symposium "The Negro in Literature."[38] Warren argues that black literary criticism essentially leveraged racial particularity as a liability at midcentury, only to reverse course in the Black Arts era by inverting the value of this same quality to make it a virtue; in both cases, African American literature remained a prospective project whose promise had yet to be fulfilled.[39] Where Warren contends that this provides reason to doubt the very category of African American literature, I see an old-fashioned imaginative failure—one that I suspect has to do with the ideological pressures that overdetermined critical discourse then, and latently, even now. The answer to this impasse is to freshen the critical lenses we apply to these works, not to retreat into skepticism.

One of those lenses key to *The Blue Period* is the scholarship that has examined the relationship between black writers and communism—the red and the black. Behind these arguments about the shape of literary history, there is an implicit argument about the shape (and destiny) of American leftist politics, and of black politics as a special case within it. Literary scholars and cultural historians like Barbara Foley, Bill V. Mullen, James Smethurst, and Mary Helen Washington have resisted the notion of a radical shift in aesthetics during this period because, for at least a generation, liberal-leaning critics have martialed it to discredit or disparage the Popular Front and leftist commitment of its writers. If, for example, you are inclined to see a welcome evolution in this period away from explicitly Left-engaged aesthetics and politics, then to some extent you are committed to endorsing the liberal position, as incarnated in the work of, say, Lionel Trilling, one of the most emblematic critics of the Cold War era. In this view, literature is engaged in a struggle against ideology, supporting formal equality and justice but advocating for it primarily by appealing to sentiment, empathy, and imagination.

This liberal reading has been historically and historiographically dominant. This is in part because during the Cold War, the repression and harassment of writers with ties (or merely sympathies) to the Communist Party of the USA was so relentless and often effective, placing a sinister veil of silence and invisibility over leftist works—and effectively imposing a collective historical amnesia. Thanks to the work of William J. Maxwell, we now have an unprecedented view into the scope and intensity with which black writers came under surveillance by the federal government, acting in the name of J. Edgar Hoover's Federal Bureau of Investigation.[40] But even when overt intimidation or covert spying is not necessarily in evidence, we know that black writers may have censored themselves to protect others. Mary Helen Washington makes a compelling case that Gwendolyn Brooks scrubbed her memoirs for this reason, eliminating, or referring only obliquely to her many communist friends and acquaintances from the South Side Community Arts Center.[41] Studies by influential critics, like Alfred Kazin's *On Native Grounds* (1942), Lionel Trilling's *The Liberal Imagination* (1950), and Walter Rideout's *The Radical Novel in America* (1956), played a major role in discrediting novelists associated with literary naturalism and the proletarian novel, and coupled with a weaponized reading of James Baldwin's dissent against "protest fiction," they helped to cement a liberal reading of the prewar years that would endure for at least a generation.[42]

Liberal literary historians have noticed and welcomed the aesthetic evolution of the time but have typically evacuated its radical political intent by implicitly or explicitly using it as evidence of an endorsement of liberalism. For literary historians on the Left, the seeming evidence of continuity in thinking and aesthetics from the 1930s to the 1960s has played into a narrative of a long civil rights movement, essentially subtending a Marxist view that literature must either be engaged or reactionary, and that the advance of substantive equality can be met only by overt resistance and class-conscious affirmation. But both arguments have underplayed overwhelming evidence of a significant shift in the relationship of aesthetics and politics during the period. Are these positions and their commitments themselves necessary? Or do they reflect lingering Cold War antinomies, battle lines that were inescapable for an earlier generation of critics but that we need not endlessly reproduce?

As recent work by Peter J. Kalliney and others shows, even the well-documented and now openly acknowledged covert patronage of Cold War literary magazines and institutions by the intelligence services of the rival superpowers could not, and did not, guarantee that the writings funded by those institutions conformed to ideological diktats. As Kalliney notes, "It is not at all clear that the United States or the Soviet Union successfully created partisan intellectual networks among writers of the decolonizing world. The presence of competing cold war programs and the willingness of canny, nonaligned intellectuals to be courted by multiple interests while remaining uncommitted complicates such a narrative."[43]

Reimagining and rebuilding a canon around the midcentury that does justice to the aesthetics and the politics these texts evince doesn't require us to deny or diminish the Left's literary culture, only to recognize that it underwent an experimental phase when it could no longer be equated with the rhetorical strategies that had seemed obvious to an earlier period's overt proletarian engagement. But nor can we merely subsume these works into ideal exemplars of the liberal imagination or anticommunist tracts. Indeed, precisely this failure to please any of the preconceived public attitudes of the time explains why (apart from Ellison) the reception of these works was so often muted, hostile, or simply deferred.

This book shows how black writing in the postwar decades dissented from the pressures of political ideology by leveraging black interiority as a challenge to conventional representational strategies. Making that case has always required a theoretical vocabulary and a critical attitude capable of discerning the qualities of friction and fugitivity in black subjectivity, or what Elizabeth Alexander calls "the black interior."[44] Thankfully, over the past two decades, a growing body of interdisciplinary work at the crossroads of black studies, affect theory, poetics, musicology, and aesthetics has supplied a rich vein of scholarship for mining the complicated intersection of race, aesthetics, and politics, especially within formally innovative or experimental art, a body of work that my own insights are greatly indebted to.

That said, *The Blue Period* does not establish a chronology or sequence within which works from this period must necessarily be read. The chapters are arranged to give a rhythmic effect of departure and return with respect to the many transatlantic crossings undertaken by the authors under consideration. I like to think of this as a call-and-response across Paul Gilroy's Black Atlantic, yet I must emphasize that exile and expatriation are *not* central to my argument. They are symptomatic of this era, but they are not nearly as important as the deliberate undertaking of strategic isolation—whether metaphorical or literal—and their capacity to represent or induce affective dissonance and alienation. These shades of blue can take hold just as surely on the South Side of Chicago as in the mountains of Switzerland. What these writers have in common is a sense that the black interior is an unknown country, more a spell than a space, to be explored and only sometimes returned from. As those who did take the path of expatriation inevitably discovered, the black interior has no borders and requires no passport.

Why the Blue Period?

John Akomfrah's documentary film *The Stuart Hall Project* (2013) opens with a fixed shot of a record player bathed in blue light. The song that is playing is Miles Davis's "Blue Room" (composed by Rodgers and Hart), a track that appeared on the B side of an LP released by Prestige Records in 1953 entitled *Blue Period*. Over the record we hear Stuart Hall say: "When I was about nineteen or twenty, Miles Davis put his finger on my soul. The various moods of Miles Davis matched the evolution of my own feelings."[45] At one point, Hall speaks of a possibility in his life that he could have pursued but never did. He doesn't say what the untested vocation was, but his later account of driving through France, reading James Joyce's *Ulysses*, makes one wonder. Had Stuart Hall dreamed of becoming a novelist? If he did, he did not feel comfortable saying so—or only indirectly, by letting Miles imply it, as though he trusted his audience to read between the lines, to hear in "Blue Room" the obvious correlative for a submerged subjectivity.

In his 1996 essay "Blue in Green: Black Interiority," Nathaniel Mackey argues that this era of Miles's recording history is distinctive because his aesthetic introduces and makes room for thought within the musical phrasing itself.[46] Of listening to this music, Mackey writes: "Just as a certain withholding we hear in Billie Holiday's voice heightens, by way of contrast, the emotional extremity her lyrics announce, Miles's less-is-more approach appears to make deliberative thought audible, palpable—deliberative thought itself, not simply the decisions at which it has arrived."[47] Miles's favorite koans from this time—"playing what isn't there," "space breathing through the music," "a round sound, with no attitude in it"—reflect an affect that is *cool* with respect to its content, an expressive grammar shunning emotiveness in favor of, "analysis, dissection, the act of selection, discernment, choice."[48] In these records, Mackey argues, negative space, absence, and silence express cognition as much as emotion—or, as it were, they express the emotion of cognition, "the sound of consciousness being caressed," as Mackey puts it.[49] The central insight of the essay is that Miles invented a sound that "made music more palpably a vehicle for thinking out loud, though the 'out loud' was in fact an effect of his use of silence."[50]

Tellingly, there is a description of this very sound in Richard Wright's *The Outsider*. Shortly after arriving in Harlem, where he moves into a single room, Cross Damon, a black man who has severed all connections to his past and is fleeing toward an unknown destination while philosophizing on the nature and fate of Western civilization, finds himself to be connected to the world solely through a blue sound: "the raucous blue-jazz welling up from the downstairs was his only emotional home now."[51] This "blue-jazz" is as an objective correlative for Damon, but it can't simply be a matter of his personal emotional state and ruminations; it is an expression of his Weltanschauung, his posture vis-à-vis the world, one that we are to understand as belonging to a type of alienated black consciousness.

There is a long tradition of binding black literary expression to its musical counterpart. If there is a pervasive affect coloring black expression in the decades I am interested in, then the specific blue sound of Miles Davis that emerges in the 1950s seems to me its logical touchstone. It is in effect the color of an affect: isolated, estranged; cool without, fiery within. Davis famously liked to turn his back on his audience when he played, as if signaling that, even in performance, he was privately at home, in his own world. The paradox of this kind of blue is that its "raucousness" can emerge from a deliberate reserve, inwardness, and even reticence. Blue is the color of a flame at its hottest point but also its most focused.

Think of Roy DeCarava's hushed and private photographs of midcentury black life, scenes of ordinary people imbued with an aura of intense concentration. The instantly recognizable chiaroscuro tones in a DeCarava, Teju Cole has said, were his way to go against the grain of conventional photographic wisdom: "Instead of trying to brighten blackness ... he went against expectation and darkened it further. What is dark is neither blank nor empty. It is in fact full of wise light, which, with patient seeing, can open out into glories."[52] DeCarava's portraits of black life "insisted on finding a way into the inner life of his scenes."[53] In her book *Harlem Crossroads*, Sara Blair captures what distinguished DeCarava in a passage that could apply to the writers I consider in *The Blue Period* equally well: "[He was] creating a new aesthetic with and for the camera, one that combined meditative distance with palpable intimacy. With this complexly wrought stance, DeCarava evaded the programmatic thrust of postwar cultural politics centered in Harlem. Drawing on realism and expressionism, referentiality and abstraction, formalism and vernacular codes, DeCarava amalgamated and transformed them, and in the process expanded the possibilities for the camera as an instrument of cultural response."[54] This expansion of aesthetic possibility in a moment of political and ideological evasion is precisely what Gwendolyn Brooks, Vincent O. Carter, James Baldwin, Richard Wright, Paule Marshall, and Édouard Glissant were realizing in their own way—only their jazz club, their darkroom, was the novel, the essay, the lyric, the bildungsroman, and the epic poem.

I find these cultural coordinates of "blue" from the musical and visual arts suggestive for describing what Moten has called "the crawlspace" between freedom and unfreedom, the powerful crosscurrents of a particular world-historical moment that black writers active in this period were navigating.[55] Of course, the labels we attach to periods are always a combination of convenience and cultural cachet. One advantage to the relatively abstract and capacious umbrella of a color, as opposed to a proper noun for a place-name, or a famous author, is that, should my Blue Period be taken up by others, it keeps the field of incorporation open and neutral with respect to all kinds of works, in genres high and low, popular and rarefied, best-selling and obscure. My purpose is not to confine works or restrict those that "count"; it is to throw the contours of a moment into relief precisely so that we can better see how much is still there to be discovered, juxtaposed, or reconsidered in a new light.

I said that Ellison will accompany this study rather than loom at its center. It is useful, nevertheless, to begin with one of his most powerful symbols, a metaphorical architecture that evokes many of themes that we will return to throughout the chapters that follow.

Every reader of *Invisible Man* is likely to remember, if nothing else, the image of the narrator in his underground retreat beneath the streets of Harlem. What does this image mean? What does it stand for? By the end of the novel, he has abandoned the ranks of the Brotherhood, is hounded by Ras the Exhorter, and cannot hold a job at the Liberty Paints factory or in the world of white-collar employment where Mr. Emerson will not have him. He is forced into a space without horizons, forced to adopt a strategy that none of the social and political actors has anticipated or pre-scripted for him. What is the affordance of that strategic retreat? In the closing pages, the narrator insists that "in going underground, I whipped it all except the mind, the *mind.*"[56] The repetition and emphasis are not un-important. Ellison's *cogito* is more than just a philosophical *ergo sum.* It is a declaration of independence—always a political act. In an era of rigid and powerful ideas, appropriating the time to determine one's own, the value of articulating an independent perspective that can speak to a condition confined to the margins, is itself a powerful act of dissension. Our narra-tor hints that the time of his underground alienation will soon come to an end. Yet it was a necessary passage, a productive interregnum—a spell of being "black and blue"—without which any plans for challenging the rag-ing world above could not have been formulated.

Ellison's underground man concentrates into a symbolic image, the specific predicament of the black writer in the postwar years. Kenneth Warren's study of Ellison, *So Black and Blue: Ralph Ellison and the Occa-sion of Criticism* is arguably one of the finest—and most finely attuned—assessments of this predicament. Warren shows how closely Ellison him-self understood his great novel to be an "occasional piece," a term Ellison applied to his own pathbreaking essays.[57] In reconstructing the affective contours of this era, my aim is not to show how ours and every period in the future can see itself in the same light. On the contrary, I share War-ren's view that "the goal must be to understand these feelings in order to loosen their grip on the levers that control the present and the future" and to clarify for ourselves "the *problématique* that gave rise to the artis-tic, political, philosophical, and intellectual concerns that made possible the phenomenon of *Invisible Man* as well as our liking of *Invisible Man*" in the first place.[58]

To do so, however, requires that we plunge fully into the mood of those times and acknowledge too, the ruminative power that these writings—and not only Ellison's—were capable of generating. For then, as now, the problems of racial antagonism, political manipulation, and geopolitical tension were permanently threatening to boil over. But in that uncertain and foreboding postwar period, a distinctive aesthetic power arising from the very tension and alienation that had crept into black writing in concen-trated form prompted a flourishing of new aesthetic variations: coolness and strategic retreat, new attention to the representation of phenomenological interiority and private experience, exilic consciousness and archival impulse. In artistic terms, the value of this time, full of covert signals and new experiments, was hardly marginal. At a remove from hegemonic ideologies, it kept alive a blue flame and bequeathed its meanings to the future.

James Baldwin's Revelations

[CHAPTER ONE]

This world is white no longer, and it will never be white again.

JAMES BALDWIN, "Stranger in the Village," 1953

In 1997, the painter Glenn Ligon began working on a series of large mono-chromatic paintings—mostly black or white—using a mix of oil paints, acrylics, glue, coal dust, and inked stencil blocks. The paintings were meant to reproduce excerpted passages from James Baldwin's celebrated 1953 essay "A Stranger in the Village." Ligon had first encountered the text as an undergraduate at Wesleyan, where he studied African American literature under Robert O'Meally.[1] Although Ligon shares with Baldwin a common biographical background as an artist and as a black, gay New Yorker, he has made clear that his interest in this particular essay is tied to conceptual concerns about aesthetic form and historical period. Many have taken this stance to be characteristic of Ligon's artistic practice, one that "has consistently looked back to earlier moments for its historical and formal articulations."[2] Other sources (notably Zora Neale Hurston's 1928 essay "How It Feels to Be Colored Me" and skits by Richard Pryor) crept into this conceptual matrix, but Baldwin's essay continued to command Ligon's attention.

In a 2001 interview with Hilton Als at the Studio Museum in Harlem, much of it devoted to discussing the "Stranger" paintings, Ligon gives an extended account of the stakes of his project:

> There are several ways to view the paintings, and I feel that when I started doing these paintings that people's relationship to Baldwin's writing was one of just celebration, that there was this uncritical relationship to him, and they weren't looking at the essays anymore and weren't diving into them in the way that I thought they should. I didn't want my paintings just to be re-presenting the text, saying "Baldwin is important, here's the text, read it again." I wanted to explore the more abstract level of why do certain things disappear or how have they become so known that they're not

visible anymore, and pushing the viewer to think about this visual object, and in that way I've rendered the text in terms of these more abstract questions that the paintings ask.[3]

These "abstract questions" led Ligon to revisit his source repeatedly, eventually producing nearly two hundred pieces over thirteen years.[4]

The "Stranger" paintings stand out immediately for the way the textual elements on the canvas are made nearly illegible by superimposition and crosshatching, especially when set against the work's defiant monochromatism. Individual words become glyphs, as if inscribed on an ancient obsidian stele. Fragmented phrases ripple over the surface of the painting, presenting a barnacled texture. It is as though Baldwin's words were corroded over time and must be recovered in our viewing. Ligon has said of the "Stranger" paintings that "the gravity and weight and panoramic nature of that work inspired me"; of his choice to use coal dust in these works, he said that he "wanted a material that was very visceral and bumped up the physicality of the text, but at the same time obscured the text even more."[5]

As Ligon's exchange with Als suggests, one way of describing the effect of these paintings is to say that they return Baldwin to first interpretation; they reestablish something vital and radical as already present in his early works; they restore to him an originating opacity that his later canonization has ignored; they make visible an aesthetic of negation that does not accede to an absence but rather operates as a force. Was there always a better way to read early Baldwin? To restore to a text the fieriness and resolute iconoclasm that Ligon implies we have lost? How ought a theoretical recontextualization of this crucial moment in Baldwin's career proceed?

The View from the Mountain

In "A Word from Writer Directly to Reader" (1959), James Baldwin wrote: "The world has shrunk to the size of several ignorant armies; each of them vociferously demanding allegiance and many of them brutally imposing it. Nor is it easy for me, when I try to examine the world in which I live, to distinguish the right side from the wrong side. I share, for example, the ideals of the West—freedom, justice, brotherhood—but I cannot say that I have often seen these honored; and the people whose faces are set against us have never seen us honor them at all." The passage is a prefatory response included in the short-story anthology *Fiction of the Fifties: A Decade of American Writing*, edited by Herbert Gold and including stories by Baldwin, John Cheever, Saul Bellow, and Anatole Broyard. It is the answer to a question posed by the editor: "in what way—if any—do you feel that the problems of writing from the Fifties has differed from the problems of writing in other times?" In his remarks, Baldwin goes on to emphasize certain existentialist and aestheticizing notes about the importance of the "private life." He insists that the key test of the age lay in the writer's ability "to resist at whatever cost the fearful pressures placed on one to lie about one's own experience."[6]

And yet the thrust of the passage is distinctly geopolitical, suggesting that for Baldwin, the writer's tasks and constraints were framed by the tensions of the antagonistic blocs and ideological constructs of the Cold War. The position sketched out here is, with respect to that field of contest, decidedly nonaligned. Indeed, it is no stretch to read in between these lines a not-so-veiled critique of American midcentury liberalism, which does not, by the logic of Baldwin's phrasing, escape the category of "ignorant armies" and, worse, suffers the burden of hypocrisy. Nested more subtly in this barb is a further mark of dislocated experience, what Glissant in his own idiom called a "cross-cultural poetics."[7] For when Baldwin speaks of "the ideals of the West—freedom, justice, brotherhood," he is invoking not American liberalism, which does not typically invoke the last term, but rather the French republican trinity that it nearly perfectly transposes: *liberté, égalité, fraternité.*

This is, in other words, a perspective informed by Baldwin's decade of experience in France, and especially Paris, where he had spent the majority of the 1950s and embarked upon the first major phase of his literary career. Baldwin's retrospection draws together two key lessons from his Parisian Blue Period: the power of a privately sovereign and independent vision of the world and the historical and political panorama that such a vision must rise to encompass. It is a potent dialectical formula that the twenty-four-year-old Baldwin didn't possess when he abruptly left the United States in 1948; by the time he returned at the end of the decade, it had become the admired hallmark of a mature style.

For him, the world had "shrunk" in the sense that the Cold War's opposing blocs dominated the globe, but also because he was looking down on it from a greater height: he had built a loyal audience in the highest perches of the postwar American public sphere. How did Baldwin attain that sense of authority? And how did his looking-glass vision of self and world get constructed? How was it possible for Baldwin to single-handedly do the work of "provincializing Europe," Dipesh Chakrabarty's phrase for a proleptic project that was still provocative half a century later at the turn of the millennium.[8]

It is from the margins of Baldwin's writings, in certain overlooked pieces, that we can best see how that sense of authority came into being and how its political valences became sublimated and increasingly central to Baldwin's aesthetics, eventually culminating in his essay "Stranger in the Village" (1953) and his novel *Go Tell It on the Mountain* (1953).[9] These two mountaintop works evince the desolation and the potency of rising above the fray—the arcing, sometimes arch, point of view that was so politically necessary for the black writers of the Blue Period. It demonstrates the self-imposed discipline necessary for a black thinker to hold an independent perspective and speak truthfully, not only against the powers that be but also to the ambivalent truths of one's own experience.

From Harlem to Paris

After Baldwin first arrived in Paris in November 1948, he spent his first years enjoying a bohemian lifestyle focused on a loose group of expatriates lodged at a cheap hotel on the rue de Verneuil. Many black writers— most famously Richard Wright—were already in Paris, constituting what Michel Fabre called the "rive noire."[10] But Baldwin chose to immerse himself in alternative, adjacent spaces. When the essay "Everybody's Protest Novel" appeared in the spring 1949 issue of *Zero* magazine, its argument against *Native Son*, linking the racial sentimentality of Wright's novel back to *Uncle Tom's Cabin*, necessarily distanced Baldwin from the core of the black expatriate literati. But its tone, decidedly more serious and ambitious than the vision of *Zero*'s editors, also signaled a move away from the bohemian party.[11] This double disaffiliation is characteristic, as we will see, of black writers active in this era.

On his own, Baldwin made what José Muñoz has called a queer practice of "disidentification" by exploring and cruising the North African neighborhoods of the capital. In so doing, Baldwin was deliberately and relentlessly positioning himself as an outsider, even to the rarefied circles he was already in. As Muñoz argues, "the importance of such public and semi-public enactments of the hybrid self cannot be undervalued in relation to the formation of counterpublics that contest the hegemonic supremacy of the majoritarian public sphere."[12] This self-fashioning, strategic disaffiliation remains an underappreciated contextual aspect of Baldwin's rebuke of Wright, which has typically been framed along Bloomian lines as an Oedipal resistance catalyzed by a novice writer's anxiety about the influence of an elder rival.

There are other ways of thinking about the function of this "cutting away from the scene" that are not any less political for it; on the contrary, they help to clarify Baldwin's infusion of the personal and political into his aesthetic and fictional constructions. "Disidentification," as Muñoz rightly notes, "is not an apolitical middle ground," and in Baldwin's *parcours*, it always leads from experience to imagination, which is why his "non-fiction, or more nearly, autobiography, is a rehearsal for fiction."[13] For Baldwin, the essay acts like a literary waystation, a testing ground for new social, sexual, and racial appreciations and the new perspectives these confer upon the writer as a reader of his own transformations in tandem with those of the Zeitgeist. They are blueprints for the fiction in the sense that they furnish the organizing pattern for the hypothetical existence and significance of the characters that will live there—but also because they give Baldwin a chance to practice his creolized voice, to test the limits of its authority and plausibility, the racial plasticity of the essayist's first-person singular and fraught implications of its plural.[14] Baldwin's essays, then, are not intended merely to explain cultural and racial differences to US readers; they are autotelic experiments in the invention of a prose style. Baldwin transmutes his insights about his disidentifications, his social outsiderness, into a form, a new aesthetic meant to convey the strangeness of being a stranger to one's own racialized experience, as that experience is actively (perhaps willfully) being altered by a new set of contours whose fluidity and parameters are not yet entirely known—or even perfectly knowable—to the author himself.

This alignment of form, method, and intention did not arise spontaneously. Lawrence Jackson has located the origins of Baldwin's mature essayistic style in the articles and reviews he produced for the small magazine circuit in New York in the late 1940s, specifically his work in the *New Leader*, the *Nation*, and *Commentary*.[15] Jackson singles out "The Harlem Ghetto," a piece commissioned for *Commentary* in 1948 by its editor Robert Warshow, in which Baldwin for the first time "started to speak for his audience in the first person plural," embodying a racially amphibious "we" that effectively produced "a new kind of essay for liberal American readers."[16] "The Harlem Ghetto" had the limitation of belonging to a suffocating and clichéd form of native reporting on an uptown world for a downtown audience that Jackson compellingly argues amounted almost to a genre unto itself.[17]

Still, it set up a new template for Baldwin's essays, one that wedded an ethnographic authority on a particular place (the neighborhood) to a larger geography of imagined community (the nation). In the process, this template assumed an arbitrage that confounded long-established precincts of ethnic and literary authority. What's striking is Baldwin's personal conviction that even this was not enough: his success in New York circles was still too stifling, and his sense of outsiderness demanded both a wider view and an even sharper alienation. It wasn't just that American racism didn't disappear below 110th Street. For the kind of writer Baldwin wanted to become, Greenwich Village was, in a sense, still too provincial.

When Jackson follows Baldwin across the Atlantic, out of the 1940s and into the 1950s through his relationships to his literary patrons, "Everybody's Protest Novel" comes into focus. The essay was a declaration of independence that also captured something of the rapidly shifting Zeitgeist and, with it, a changing of the guard, "a kind of 'Blueprint for Negro Writing' breaking ground for the Eisenhower 1950s."[18] For Jackson, Baldwin's essay is aimed not so much at Richard Wright, although it uses him somewhat cruelly as an anvil, but at "the eminent dean of American cultural criticism," Edmund Wilson, who had argued in a 1948 essay in the *New Yorker* for the neglected literary merit of Harriet Beecher Stowe's *Uncle Tom's Cabin*. On this reading, Baldwin was using "Everybody's Protest Novel" as a tool to assert a kind of one-upmanship over the New York literary world he saw himself as having graduated from.

But Jackson also suggests that Baldwin himself was being used, by Philip Rhav, the ambitious and dashing editor of *Partisan Review*, and by Mary McCarthy (who had divorced Wilson in 1946), each of whom had stakes—social status and personal, respectively—in swiping at Wilson.[19] This is confusing not least because Baldwin went ahead and published the essay in Themistocles Hoetis's tiny avant-garde Paris magazine *Zero*, even though he knew he was supposed to give *Partisan Review* first rights per his contract (*Partisan Review* amicably settled with *Zero* and quickly republished the piece).[20] If Baldwin were so determined to sting the old éminence grise of the *New Yorker*, why, with the contacts that he had, did he publish the piece in a magazine they would so easily miss it in?

Jackson's argument in effect downgrades the agency of the writers involved so that the history eventually starts to look like a parable about how black writers are pawns on the chessboard of white liberal publishers. Jackson is right to be skeptical of the notion that the essay was intended primarily as a takedown of Wright, but what he suggests in its place is a kind of formalist proxy war. He takes Baldwin's adoption of the new critical register of Lionel Trilling's *Liberal Imagination* and Cleanth Brooks's *The Well-Wrought Urn* as evidence that Baldwin was being (wittingly or unwittingly) dragooned into the American establishment's shadow war with the cultural capital of communist-affiliated intellectuals and in particular its desire to target and tarnish the prestige of Sartre. But if Wilson and Wright were (at best) secondary targets, and Trilling's "liberal imagination" was (at best) a proximate influence, what was really driving the essay?

One answer, often held at some distance, is that it reflects Baldwin's decisive encounter with Henry James.[21] There is by now a copious literature on the Jamesian line in Baldwin; I won't dwell here on what "Everybody's Protest Novel" owes to James's "The Art of Fiction" (1884), an essay that likewise affirms that a writer's authority need lie only in the fullness of the writer's experience and takes aim at sentimentality, overly rigid moralism, and devotion to plot. Instead, the extant description of Baldwin's unrealized study of James is an overlooked piece of evidence that ought to inform our understanding of Baldwin's development of his style in the Blue Period.

The Self as Journey

In the early 1960s, as Baldwin was initiating the second phase of his expatriation in Istanbul, he started work on an article about James's "late phase" novel *The Ambassadors* (1903). Baldwin called it "The Self as Journey," and he never finished it. His biographer David A. Leeming reminded him of the essay in an interview conducted at Baldwin's home at Saint-Paul-de-Vence that was published in the fall 1986 issue of the *Henry James Review*.[22] In his prefatory remarks to the interview, Leeming recalls how Baldwin had joined his classes at Robert College in Istanbul and "lectured several times on *The American, The Portrait of a Lady*, and *The Ambassadors*."[23] In the interview Baldwin describes the article he never finished, sketching out what might have been: a rich account of the parallels between James's fiction and his own, and the importance James held for him in his years in Paris in the early 1950s. In his closing remarks, he tells Leeming: "In France I had to live in a kind of vacuum, absolute silence. I didn't speak French, and I couldn't understand a word. So I had to listen to what I had been avoiding. I had to start facing where I really came from, the speech I really spoke, which is much closer to Bessie Smith than it is to Henry James. But as a writer I needed a box to put thoughts in—a model.... James was my key."[24] The Jamesian model of consciousness, obsessed with perspectival difference (in James, the difference between Europe and America; in Baldwin, the difference race makes when overlaid and expanded upon the same), offered a means to test perception against reality, to check sentimentality, and to disarm conceptual binaries.

But the real key to the Jamesian model for Baldwin is evident in the essay's proposed title: the metonymic conjunction of *self*, indicating an inward orientation, and *journey*, implying a movement outward. What Baldwin took from James was first and foremost a model for a voice, a consciousness, that could move through and across the subtlety of those experiential differences without being locked into any one political, ideological, social, or racial identity. That is, by tracking psychology inward to the core of his racially conditioned experiences while simultaneously pushing geographically outward to encompass new kinds of difference and sources of authority, Baldwin was, in Glissantian terms, "creolizing" Henry James.[25]

For Baldwin, James was the escape hatch. He stood in Baldwin's mind for the aesthetic primacy of an overflowing subjectivity whose porous interpenetration with the world, and with the consciousness of others, as emblematically represented by Lambert Strether's journey through Paris in *The Ambassadors*, could not be reductively accounted for or, as the same protagonist is at pains to insist, be used as a source of "profit."[26] Superficially, this sounds like the interest in James propounded by Trilling and the critics associated with *Partisan Review*. But in substance, and sensibility, it was not, making their eventual disappointment in Baldwin a matter foreordained.

As a literary mantra, "The Self as Journey" describes what Baldwin's rejection of *Native Son* in "Everybody's Protest Novel" implied. Baldwin specifically wanted a new paradigm for African American writing, one that would self-consciously remain open-ended, refusing to be enlisted in superficial or sentimental instrumentality, whether in the service of racial innocence and damnation or of the pieties of progressive political expediency. "One is told to put first things first, the good of society coming before niceties of style or characterization," Baldwin complains, in a dig at the diktats of proletarian realism or "protest fiction" that Wright is alleged to have too faithfully followed.[27]

But it is notable that when Baldwin further describes the protest novel as "a mirror of our confusion, dishonesty, panic, trapped and immobilized in the sunlit prison of the American dream," he is co-indicting the conflation of the leftist political correctness of the form with the core ideological promise of US liberalism. The black novelist ought to reject and dissent from both, and for the same reasons, insofar as they share a "passion for categorization, life neatly fitted into pegs."[28]

The Negro at Home and Abroad

In *The Totalitarian Century*, Vaughn Rasberry rejects the old critical reflex that tends to use Baldwin as "an index of black artistic maturation or as a capitulation to what Thomas Schaub calls the 'liberal narrative of the Cold War.'"[29] Rasberry reinserts Baldwin instead into the matrix of thinkers attempting to grapple with the global significance of totalitarianism, thereby foregrounding the important political thinking that he was doing even in work that may appear to be more personal. One of Rasberry's keen insights here is that "Baldwin's essays relentlessly disrupt liberalism's construction of the Negro as an object of sympathy and sociology's fixation on the Negro as an object of knowledge."[30] An excellent example of just such a disruption in the "Paris Essays" is "The Negro at Home and Abroad,"

Baldwin's 1951 review in the *Reporter* of Roi Ottley's book *No Green Pastures*.[31] This apparently negligible review of a mostly forgotten author has an important relationship to "Stranger in the Village."

Roi Ottley is a lost figure of midcentury black letters, exemplifying the fickleness of premature fame. A native of Harlem, of West Indian descent, he studied journalism in Michigan and spent the Depression years working for the *Amsterdam News* before taking up a stint with the Harlem branch of the Federal Writers' Project, where he encountered Dorothy West, Richard Wright, and Ralph Ellison. In 1944, he joined the army as a commissioned captain and during the last years of the war covered events in Europe, North Africa, and the Middle East for a variety of outlets, especially the *Pittsburgh Courier*.[32] He first made a name for himself in 1943 with *New World A-Coming: Inside Black America*, a study of Harlem based on his years of experience reporting for the *Amsterdam News* (some of it drawn directly from his columns) and another typical example of the "native report on Harlem" genre.

Drawing on his travels, his wartime reportage, and a recently discovered diary, Ottley put together *No Green Pastures*.[33] It was supposed to be a comparative study of racism in European countries as viewed by a black American, but Ottley turned it into an unrelenting indictment of Europe as hypocritical and ridden with racial discrimination. That conclusion wasn't entirely against the grain or unexpected, but Ottley, perhaps for rhetorical effect (it's unclear how deeply he believed what he was saying), drew up a contrasting portrait of the United States as a paradise where blacks were able to attain material prosperity and thrive so long as they worked hard. This take, in 1951, in a still legally segregated America, was predictably cheered by several white reviewers and just as immediately condemned by Ottley's peers—many of them his former colleagues in the black press.[34]

Baldwin reviewed *No Green Pastures* for the *Reporter*, the magazine in which the year before he had published "The Negro in Paris," which was later included in *Notes of a Native Son* as "Encounter on the Seine."[35] The *Reporter*, which ran biweekly from 1949 to 1968, was the flagship of the midcentury liberal intelligentsia (and, as it turned out, of American intelligence agencies).[36] While mostly forgotten today, the magazine (founded and edited by Max Ascoli, a Jewish Italian legal philosopher and émigré who had fled Mussolini's Italy), stood at the center of American political and intellectual life where those Washington insiders whom C. Wright Mills in 1956 memorably described as the nation's "power elite" lived within an area known colloquially to us as "the Beltway," the capital's ring road, then under construction.[37] One of the *Reporter*'s Washington staff writers described it as "a magazine so significant that nearly every important government official reads it himself or assigns it to an underling."[38] Among those who praised its first issue in 1949 were Hubert Humphrey and Nelson Rockefeller, and at the height of its influence, in 1966, it could claim as paid subscribers "the President and Vice President, seven members of the Cabinet, and one-third of the Senate."[39]

Ascoli saw his magazine as a rival to the *New Yorker*, and it's reasonable to imagine that Baldwin wrote for them mainly because Ascoli coveted cultured respect and the magazine paid writers relatively well; but he was no novice when it came to the cultural politics and influence of the American elite's public sphere. He would not have failed to notice the pedigree of the paper, the kinds of issues debated in its columns and the names under letters to the editor indicating the nature of its readership. The jarring quality of the unrelenting fury in Baldwin's review can properly be understood only when one resituates it within this staid liberal elite atmosphere where it originally appeared. Baldwin's rhetorical posture is a choice: he perfectly understood how to calibrate his voice for a liberal audience. "The Negro in Paris," the piece he had published with the *Reporter* the year before, for instance, invites the reader in with a genteel paragraph full of suave evocations of the Roaring Twenties. By contrast, the opening of the Ottley review, entitled "The Negro at Home and Abroad," directly evokes the specter of a "black skeleton in the Old-World closet." This seems merely a trite figure of speech until Baldwin asserts that it won't "impress the Europeans, who have lived for generations on a continent absolutely phosphorescent with dry bones."[40] For a black writer to open an essay by evoking the still vivid carnage of World War II and the Holocaust would be fair enough, but Baldwin's gothic image of Europe as generational charnel house, recasting it as a boneyard of warring tribes rather than the center of civilization he knows his readers believe it to be, is a provocative and even hostile maneuver.

The main thrust of the review that follows aims to peg Ottley as a writer out of his depth, a naïf whose "journalist method" schtick is not up to the task he has set for himself. A shorter piece might have left it at that. But one of Ottley's anecdotes retains Baldwin's interest: the practice in the Netherlands of corking up at Christmas and impersonating the black servant of Sinterklaas. "No one, I suppose, will seriously suggest," Baldwin snaps, "that because we in America no longer blacken our faces with burnt cork—to impersonate, say, Sambo—we are freer from racial prejudice than the Europeans."[41] Setting aside the dubious assertion that Americans no longer cork up, this slices fairly harshly at both sides, insofar as it removes wholesale a plank of progress not infrequently leaned upon by liberal progressives—that we can bury regrettable behaviors of the past and move on. But this episode also finds echo in the Swiss mountain village where Baldwin invokes the similar practices of "the natives" in "Stranger in the Village."

And this is the strange thing about this review of *No Green Pastures*. Even as Baldwin faults the quality of the writing, he basically doubles down on Ottley's thesis, castigating him for *not going* far enough. Baldwin restates Ottley in his own high tone: "[Ottley] means that white men harbor, in relation to black men, a certain unconscious assumption of superiority, and that they look upon black men as travelers from another world. This is, indeed, one of the causes of the bottomless anger of black men: that they have been forced to learn far more about whites than whites have ever found it necessary to learn about them."[42] We can overhear in this passage the dry run for the magisterial modulations that will come in the Swiss mountains. But if these seem stark enough, Baldwin goes further: "The questions that the Negro lives with are how not to hate the white man, or, otherwise, how to hate him most effectively; how to fool him, cheat him, use him; how in short, failing the possibility of a general overturn, to wrest for himself in the white man's world an honored place, or at any rate a bearable Lebensraum."[43] Even if one grants, as I would, that these passages still have the tone of an appeal to the better angels of white liberal readers, the invocation of Hitlerian racial doctrine against the master race is incontestably vitriolic.[44]

Rasberry's contention that Baldwin's thinking must be understood in the framework of midcentury fears and fantasies of totalitarianism acquires a spectral force in these lines, which are from 1951—at least fifteen years before the bitter, angry Baldwin is conventionally said to begin alienating liberals. In fact, Baldwin's thinking runs culverted throughout the 1950s and evolves far less than is sometimes supposed. Almost every major theme of "Stranger in the Village" is brought out in this review from two years earlier. The core argument is identically expressed: "The black man exists for Europe almost entirely in the mind, in which cage he is, not surprisingly, a kind of archetypal Noble Savage, exotic, childlike, backward."[45]

Baldwin scornfully demolishes Ottley's enthrallment with the United States' superficial and cheap materialism. But he also looks past it to notice a wider implication with which he is in deep sympathy. Ottley concludes that "what America has learned about race relations is of vital importance to a multicolored world."[46] To which Baldwin retorts: "This is perfectly true and yet the reader feels by the time he has reached it, that all Mr. Ottley means to say is that America has learned that, given education (and the possibility of Cadillacs), American whites and Negroes can be polite to one another."[47] This tartness hurt Ottley (if not his feelings, then certainly his career), but it can't have been too reassuring to the liberal readers of the *Reporter* either. One also guesses that Ottley's last sentence stuck with Baldwin because its echoes are in the last lines of "Stranger in the Village," a book reviewer's barb transformed into a prophet's freighted charge and verdict.

"Stranger in the Village"

The personal origins of "Stranger in the Village" are in the winter trips of 1951–1952 that Baldwin made to his lover Lucien Happersburger's chalet in Switzerland at Loèche-les-Bains. The plan was to retreat there periodically so Baldwin could complete the manuscript for *Go Tell It on the Mountain*, eventually published by Knopf in 1953. His biographer David Leeming describes a domestic and romantic getaway from bohemian Paris that "was the closest Baldwin ever came to his dream of domestic life with a lover. […] Lucien painted and Jimmy wrote during the day. Bessie Smith was constantly on the small portable Victrola. In the evening the couple strolled through the village to the local café."[48] On the one hand, Baldwin was in a strategic retreat, a kind of queer marronage; on the other hand, this site of secluded intimacy was unarguably the whitest place he had ever set foot in. These contradictions became the structuring premise for a catalytic piece of writing and a pivot in Baldwin's career.

"A Stranger in the Village" marked Baldwin's debut appearance in the pages of *Harper's*, a publication he would keep up a relationship with until the end of his life.[49] His essay was the cover story. The illustrator, who may or may not have actually read the story, depicted a rather quaint (or eerie, depending on how you look at it) scene of a wiry black figure guiding the hand of little girl in skirts toward a flight of winter chalets winding up a mountainside (fig. 1). One guesses that they chose the figure of a girl to foreclose unwelcome associations with the author's sexuality. The magazine added a biographical notice presenting what to many of its readers would have been a complete unknown (Baldwin's fame wouldn't be widespread until *Notes* appeared in 1955): he is described as the author of a novel, *Go Tell It on the Mountain*, "living abroad and working on a second novel. He here contrasts the present status of the American Negro at home and abroad." This is word for word what Roi Ottley's book was intended to do, and it seems plausible that the idea for the *Harper's* piece had its origins in Baldwin's earlier review. Taken together, these elements give us the contours for how American liberals sought to package Baldwin: the whiff of fairy tale, travel literature, and exoticism would preemptively prime *Harper's* readers for a soothing and quintessentially belletristic narrative. What the cover literally illustrates is the gulf between how the liberal presentation of Baldwin understands "the view from the mountain"—an

OCTOBER 1953
FIFTY CENTS

Harper's
MAGAZINE

Why Did They Fight? . . . .
Eric Sevareid

We've Found a Substitute
for Income . . . .
Darrell Huff

The Decay of
State Governments . . . .
Richard L. Neuberger

You, too, Can Write
the Casual Style . . . .
William H. Whyte, Jr.

Stranger in the Village
by James Baldwin

1 *Harper's Magazine*, October 1953 (front cover). Copyright © 1953 Harper's Magazine. All rights reserved. Photograph: *Harper's Magazine*, reproduced from the October issue by special permission.

exteriorized and exotic travel narrative with a kindly black chaperone who will take the reader by the hand and make his own blackness familiar and graspable—and Baldwin's "view from the mountain," what his text actually delivers, which is at the polar opposite, concerned primarily with the consciousness, interiority, and affective impact of black alienation, understanding the mountain as a metaphorical, symbolic, and prophetic site, indelibly linked to theo-political augury. Baldwin's mountaintop is always hermeneutically that of the Black Church, a site that exists even, and most especially, when there are no good secular alternatives to turn to: a site from which one might, indeed, glimpse the end of one world and the beginning of another, where one receives and relays messages of hope that can sustain the will an oppressed people.

Seemingly aware of the need to navigate this enormous gulf, Baldwin's essay begins smoothly before swerving into its more jarring counterpoints and oracular pronouncements. "Stranger in the Village" opens by modulating between a note of ironic astonishment and a kind of cultivated incredulity: "It did not occur to me—possibly because I am an American—that there could be people anywhere who had never seen a Negro."[50] Baldwin emphasizes that he expects his own exoticism for the inhabitants of Loèche, that he knows he "would probably be a 'sight' for the village."[51] He is aware of arriving on a stage with prescribed roles. This sense of reenactment is made possible by the racial scripts that are essentially the hand-me-down inheritance, as Baldwin points out, of its Swiss inhabitants.

In the very next paragraph, however, Baldwin ironically inverts this ethnographic gaze. The black specimen under intense ocular scrutiny, whose color is magnified by contrast with his surroundings, assumes the position and authority of the metropolitan explorer or midcentury ethnographer who takes stock of how limited the inroads of civilization have really been: "In the village there is no movie house, no bank, no library, no theater; very few radios, one jeep, one station wagon; and at the moment, one typewriter, mine, an invention which the woman next door to me here had never seen."[52]

This list is not arbitrary, nor is the stress on the possessive qualifier *mine* accidental. Baldwin famously taught himself at the 135th Street Branch of the New York Public Library; as a child he went to the movies and to the theater—sparking a lifelong passion and critical interest in both; cars and radios were a ubiquitous presence, even in Harlem. In sum, the white village is more provincial than the black ghetto, which Baldwin has crossed an ocean to escape. But there is a special valence, of course, to the list's last object: the typewriter.

In Loèche, Baldwin is in a position of unrivaled literacy. The villagers possess a power invested historically in them and projected superstitiously upon him. But as a published American writer from New York, Baldwin can leverage the power of the word to frame these people in ways entirely beyond their control or even comprehension. As he says in a later interview, "We who have been described so often are now describing [you]."[53]

We will later see that this reversal of the gaze and play on the ethnographic discourse is even more in evidence in Glissant, as though both writers had, independently of each other, discovered the same formal solution to the same problem of positionality as a black author seeking to reorient the currents of cultural authority for their own use.

I stress this underlying power dynamic in part because it occasions the writing but also because it makes legible the essay's concluding sentence, which famously declares: "This world is white no longer, and it will never be white again."[54] Cheryl Wall observes that this statement is prophetic in that it "foretells not only the emergence of postcolonial nations but the emergence of a multiracial Europe."[55] I agree, but I caution us not to undervalue the use of the present tense in "this world is white no longer." "Stranger in the Village" first appeared in October 1953, six months before *Brown v. Board of Education*, two years before the Bandung Conference of 1955, and three years before the Conference of Negro-African Writers and Artists of 1956 that Baldwin would cover in "Princes and Powers" for *Encounter* magazine (or for the CIA, as he later drily noted).[56] In other words, although this essay speaks to a larger Cold War and decolonial context, we must not lose sight of its more proximate genesis and meanings. To wit, how can the white world be said to have ended *within* the horizon of this essay?

In a well-known passage, Baldwin takes in a sweeping canonical panorama of the West and considers his relation to it vis-à-vis the people of Loèche: "The most illiterate among them is related, in a way that I am not, to Dante, Shakespeare, Michelangelo, Aeschylus, Da Vinci, Rembrandt and Racine; the cathedral at Chartres says something to them which it cannot say to me, as indeed would New York's Empire State Building, should anyone here ever see it. Out of their hymns and dances come Beethoven and Bach. Go back a few centuries and they are in their full glory—but I am in Africa, watching the conquerors arrive."[57] Throughout his career, Baldwin would rehearse this list with different effects. For the introductory "Autobiographical Notes" to *Notes of a Native Son*, he doubles down, explaining of these monuments that he "might search in them in vain forever for any reflection of myself; I was an interloper ... I would have to appropriate these white centuries, I would have to make them mine."[58]

In 2014, in the pages of the *New Yorker*, the Nigerian American writer Teju Cole described making a kind of literary pilgrimage to Loèche. His essay understandably takes issue with Baldwin's devaluation of the African's position and suggests—pointing to the breadth and beauty of African art as but one example—that "the distant African past has also become much more available than it was in 1953" and that "we know better now."[59] The perspective available to almost anyone today is indeed far richer than what Baldwin could have expected half a century ago. But part of Baldwin's complicated relationship to Africa, as Douglas Field has shown, is his troubled relationship to his father and to the Black Church—that is, to his overarching skepticism about patrilineal inheritance and identity, a skepticism that should put this list into perspective.[60]

Take Chartres. Baldwin isn't merely citing Chartres as a well-known architectural icon. He finished writing "Stranger" quite literally in the shadow of the cathedral itself, during a stay in a nearby village. And as Leeming notes, he was reading Henry Adams's *Mont-Saint Michel and Chartres*, a politically reactionary elegy for a lost medieval spirit of European unity that Baldwin is countering with his own vision of a spiritually integrated modernity.[61] What of the Bard? In his 1964 essay "Why I Stopped Hating Shakespeare," Baldwin observed that he came to understand Shakespeare during his time in France, in part because of his need to speak and think in French.[62] His very estrangement made a deeper connection with his own language possible. Moreover, he connected Shakespeare's bawdiness to Bessie Smith's; he would later write that he arrived in Loèche "armed with two Bessie Smith records and a typewriter."[63] What he was really armed with was a new cast of mind bold enough to shade in areas Shakespeare had left out.

Baldwin's survey of Western greatness appears, at first, to be about the diremption of black subjectivity from its civilizational matrix.[64] But to read it this way misses the passage's strategic and rhetorical effect, unfolded within the narrative and symbolic context of the broader essay. In this light, it is really about what Dipesh Chakrabarty calls "the problem of asymmetric ignorance" or the "inequality of ignorance" between those who can rest comfortably within Western epistemologies and those who cannot.[65] Baldwin's epiphany is not merely about what he *lacks* but about the stunning inequality of ignorance between himself and the inhabitants of the Swiss village (who stand in metonymically here for the European origins of the colonization of the Americas and imperial colonization of non-European peoples), a realization of his own asymmetric relation to the Western sublime. He sees, as if in the black and white of a historiographic X-ray, what Foucault would call "the order of things;" but it is a view made possible only because of this highly unusual journey, this alienating setting that positions him as a black intellectual isolated in a remote and provincialized whiteness.[66]

For Baldwin, experience is a currency more powerful than any cultural inheritance, and it depends very much on how you take in the world. It is precisely Baldwin's journey into what we might call the 'heart of whiteness' that empowers *him*. The Swiss Alps and the "white wilderness" that surrounds him with "ice and snow as far as the eye can reach," provide a prophetic perspective to this pioneer, or reverse-colonist, encountering not the frontier of an undiscovered landscape but that of a new temporality.⁶⁷ Baldwin ironically reappropriates the tropes of the encounter narrative between white explorer settlers and natives, transforming the conditions of his isolation and alienation within overwhelmingly "white" space into a form of power vested in the domain in which he knows his talents give him the upper hand: the space of literature.

I use that phrase deliberately to refer to Maurice Blanchot's book from 1955 *L'espace littéraire*. For Blanchot, another writer and critic contemporaneously grappling with the place of the literary in the postwar landscape, "the space of literature" is produced and distinguished by "the essential solitude" of a work of art. By this, he means that a purely artistic or literary use of language is autarkic, "a monad of words where nothing is reflected but the nature of words," without ends other than in and for itself (his example is Mallarmé).⁶⁸ Baldwin would never go so far. For Baldwin, the risks incurred by writers before the autonomy of their work are structured differently than Blanchot's by virtue of the interposition of race. Baldwin understands (in a way that doesn't arise for Blanchot's consideration) that for the black writer, the autonomy of literary space continues to be strategic and to carry political implications regardless of one's ontological conception of the work of art. The black literary "monad" is impossible, because racialization perforce creates a social identity and imposes a social legibility upon any writing that is identified with it, as Baldwin's obviously is.

And yet under certain conditions, black writing and black literature might well require a drastic solitude—a blue space—that disrupts the preferred channels of instrumentality, advocacy, representativity, or assimilation, that publishers and readers, including black publishers and readers, may desire and demand. In the Blue Period, literary space for black writers is both attractive and made necessary by the ideological pressures and affective dissonances of the moment. The "blue solitude" of black postwar writing may not be Blanchot's "essential solitude," but it is a related form of dehiscence, and it establishes or conventionalizes a solitary position for the black author vis-à-vis the public that is unprecedented and unlike the role of the black writer in the days of abolition, during the Harlem Renaissance, or in the Popular Front years before the end of World War II.

By pressing upon the experience conjurable by these "blue" aesthetics, Baldwin's essay, in fact, mobilizes a formal argument against the scoreboard of cultural accounting, which we must read through the essay's structural irony. What may or may not belong to the villagers or to Baldwin is not as revealing as the fact that a black writer in Switzerland, whose position should be thoroughly marginal, in fact knows more of the West and can speak authoritatively both out of and against it than those who lay claim to it as a birthright. The essay trades on that fact to dissolve the prevailing racial myths that its author invokes; we are made witnesses to how the metascripts that govern Baldwin's entrance to the village singularly fail to capture the reality of the situation. The very existence of the essay utterly shatters them. The white world ends first and foremost on the page.

Lawrence Jackson's assessment that "Stranger" evinces "something like a philosophy of black powerlessness," makes sense only if you read the text with no appreciation for this vividly ironic frame.[69] It seems to me extraordinarily difficult to reconcile an assertion of "black powerlessness" with a piece of writing that authorizes itself, from a remote mountaintop in Switzerland, to declare the end of the white world.

I would venture here to mark a distinction between power and potency. If what we want is for a writer to produce politically effective writing, then we will always, to some extent, consign them to accept and instrumentalize the prevailing ideologies that happen to dominate in the historical period in which they are active. These will, of course, change over time, meaning that a great deal of that work will perforce cease to be "powerful" sooner or later (one can think of countless examples of political writings that are no longer as powerful as they once seemed).[70] Opposed to this would be a writing that may look, and perhaps even sound, powerless in its own time but that retains other ways of mobilizing and charging a reader with ideas that threaten the status quo. We could say of this writing that it is *potent*, and that its potency is likely to reside in precisely that which was not recuperable by the formal and ideological political programs and agendas of its day.

Baldwin's essays are of the potent kind. Their potency is made possible not least because he rejected the assumptions about what a black writer could say and how they could say it. His formal and rhetorical shifts forged a new aesthetic for a new set of historical circumstances. American liberals believed that this powerfully elegant language, with its Jamesian periods, in some sense necessarily sutured his politics to their own. But this was always a delusion. Instead of accepting their arguments around aesthetic merit and decline in Baldwin, we ought to refuse the decoupling of radical politics from Baldwin's style at every point. We ought to reclaim him from the liberal narrative that shallowly takes shelter there.

Set at Naught

Mark McGurl has argued that for the midcentury inheritors of literary modernism, Henry James effectively functioned as one of Bourdieu's badges of distinction, demarcating the art novel from its generic middlebrow cousins. This distinction placed an emphasis on the virtue of intelligence as a reflection of interiority. "What the novelist had, in common with other mental workers," says McGurl, "was his or her *mind*—an entity for which the late novels of Henry James served as advertisements. It was one of the tasks of the novel after James to make the productive force of intellection evident."[71] This highly plausible assessment of the art novel in America must confront, however, the problem posed by the forceful appearance of black intellection. This specific modality has been historically regarded, since at least Thomas Jefferson's dismissal of Phillis Wheatley, as nonexistent, inherently deficient, or worthy only of caricature and satire. The representation of black intellection could therefore never carry the equivalent literary currency of its white counterpart. McGurl also de facto skirts the possibility that certain areas of cognitive experience might be of interest to a writer or a reader whose racialized experience presents a fundamental philosophical quandary.

As it happens, Baldwin constructs just such a scene in "The Threshing Floor," the culminating chapter of his first novel *Go Tell It on the Mountain* (1953), which he was working on during the years of the Paris essays and published the same year as "Stranger in the Village." Prior to this conclusion, the novel unfolds in a series of narrative flashbacks, giving us backstories for the protagonist, John Grimes; his father, Gabriel; his mother, Elizabeth; and his Aunt Florence. The chapter opens on a late evening inside the Temple of the Fire Baptized, the storefront Pentecostal church of Reverend Grimes, where John is lying on the floor before the altar in a stupor—or rather, what Baldwin suggests is something closer to an ecstatic spiritual trance. John has been "moved by the holy spirit," to use the idiom of Brother Elisha, Sister McCandless, and the other parishioners who hover somewhere above John's suspended, visionary state.

This disembodied situation is introduced with two sentences tinged with gothic tropes: "And something moved in John's body that was not John. He was invaded, *set at naught*, possessed."[72] The first sentence suggests the breakdown of a classical model of rationality by mimicking a violation of Aristotelian noncontradiction. The second uses parallelism to heighten dramatic intensity while also suggesting a sluggishness in the rhythm of apperception, the mind slowing as it turns on itself. The terms here are also in tension with each other: to be invaded is to become full of something, whereas to be "set at naught" implies a zero point, an evacuation, an emptying, a yielding kenosis. Yet the middle negating clause stands out; it gives a shuddering effect that comes partly from its archaic diction. What is it doing there?

One answer is that Baldwin has been reading the work of Henry James, where the word *naught* or *nought* in different phrasal varia is used from time to time, although the precise phrase "set at naught" only appears once, in in a letter from his brother William quoted in his memoir *Notes of a Son and a Brother* (1914).[73] Whether the allusion to James was by coincidence or deliberate, Baldwin uses the phrase in an entirely original and unorthodox way by giving it a somatic content. And the Jamesian flavor of these sentences is neither trivial nor accidental. They set a tone that invites us to regard the passages that follow as serious reports on a state of altered consciousness, one capable of delivering self-knowledge and revelation.

Baldwin is aware of the disdain, even disgust, with which rituals of possession in black religious practice have long been held under both the white gaze and that of a black public eager to claim respectability. In *The Souls of Black Folk* (1903), W. E. B. Du Bois uses unflattering and primitivist terms, for example: "Those who have not thus witnessed the frenzy of a Negro revival in the untouched backwoods of the South can but dimly realize the religious feeling of the slave; as described, such scenes appear grotesque and funny, but as seen they are awful."[74] Baldwin, who was raised like John Grimes to be a preacher in the Black Church, knew these rituals intimately. He was deeply acquainted with what Ashon Crawley has called "the irruptive force of Blackpentecostal choreosonic practice," and he decides to treat it seriously.[75]

This decision reveals a lot about Baldwin's attitude toward respectability politics and Afro-diasporic beliefs and epistemologies, but it equally illuminates his approach to literary form. Following James's lead, he makes the narrative climax of his novel take place almost entirely in John's interiority—one can't say *mind*: as we have seen, Baldwin explicitly rejects the Cartesian duality. Baldwin thus inverts one of the central tropes of what Michael Denning calls the "ghetto pastoral" in the proletarian social realism of the thirties. In those fictions, the conditions of oppression are supposed to drive the protagonist to a moment of revolt that merges individual agency with collective action; the hero's trials and tribulations are always prelude to a revolution that satisfactorily releases the narrative tension. But here, John's decisive "actions" and struggles take place within himself:

And he struggled to flee—out of this darkness, out of this company—into the land of the living, so high, so far away. Fear was upon him, a more deadly fear than he had ever known, as he turned and turned in the darkness, as he moaned, and stumbled, and crawled through the darkness, finding no hand, no voice, finding no door.... But he could never go through this darkness, through this fire and this wrath. He never could go through. His strength was finished, and he could not move. He belonged to the darkness—the darkness from which he had thought to flee had claimed him. And he moaned again, weeping, and lifted up his hands.[76]

While these actions, too, are communally mediated through the presence of the praying parishioners around him (especially Brother Elisha), his breakthrough is not an occasion for unity. On the contrary, it is a violent experience of diremption, as befits the biblical overtones of the chapter's title.[77] When John comes to and knows he has been "saved" so that he "moved among the saints," seemingly "one of their company now," the result is not a consolation of community but a confirmation of fear and trembling: "Yes, as he moved among them ... something began to knock in that listening, astonished, newborn, and fragile heart of his; something recalling the terrors of the night, which were not finished, his heart seemed to say; which, *in this company*, were now to begin."[78] John's being "saved" has nothing to do, Baldwin insists, with any reconciliation between him and the church and family that create the conditions through which he has battled on his own to save himself. "The great division between his father and himself," and, indeed, the tears that come down "like a wall between him and his father," are the truth John carries forward *after* he has been saved. He is saved from the ties that bind him to his community; his freedom is forged through and against them.

This aporia of spaceless and timeless "threshing floor" is shot through with splinters of old-time religious song, the voices of the saints, as though John's consciousness were bathed in a lyrical fragmentation. John's agony is not a Romantic poet's encounter with the sublime; there is nothing "natural" about the emotional landscape that terrorizes him. In fact, the terror resides precisely in John's dawning awareness of the socially contingent power of the trinity that holds his life in its hands: patriarchy, racial blackness, and heterosexuality.[79] It is precisely the possible defiance and dispersal of those values at the very instant that he is professing allegiance to them, that makes John's tacit but firm *non serviam* so subversive, both in spite of and because of its defiant alienation of community.

Compare this scene with the climax of Richard Wright's short story "Fire and Cloud," from *Uncle Tom's Children* (1937), a narrative firmly anchored in the ideals and aesthetics of the Popular Front. Like *Go Tell It on the Mountain*, the text tells the story of a man of the church, Reverend Taylor, who, like John Grimes, must pass through a shift in consciousness that will determine his readiness for leadership in his community. In Wright's story, Taylor is initially unsure about supporting a protest movement that is swelling in his town, nurtured by communist activists. But a trial by force (his beating and near lynching) confronts him with the full measure of white oppression. In the final scene, as the white mayor appeals to him to calm the crowd, it is made clear that Taylor is ready for active resistance: "Taylor looked ahead and wondered what was about to happen; he wondered without fear, as though whatever would or could happen could not hurt this many-limbed, many-legged, many-handed crowd that was he."[80] As if on cue, Wright delivers on the political allegory by merging his protagonist's consciousness directly with the crowd.

The link between affect and rhetoric here follows the stated ideals of Wright's "Blueprint for Negro Writing" (1937). By fusing the possibilities of narrative realism and political activism into a unified, ecstatic resolve, it dissolves the barriers that separate the black leadership class and the black working masses while carrying the dream of mobilizing a common front led by black and white communists. The Reverend Taylor's revelation is swift, spontaneous, and essentially frictionless. We are meant to feel the combustible power of its efficacy: "A baptism of clean joy swept over Taylor," we are told, as Reverend Taylor is entranced by "the sea of black and white faces."[81] Wright's story is, in a very direct sense, perfectly suited to the politics of its moment of publication.

In Baldwin's later prose, the interiority of the protagonist is again wedded to the prophetic power of black faith and its communal practice. Here, too, a man is "saved" and the narrative crescendos with epiphany. But John Grimes, by contrast, endures a series of visitations, a private inferno shot through with dissonant and ironic voices. He is plunged into abyssal, gothic darkness. He is also granted meditative retrospection; he comprehends for the first time the meaning of what he calls "this sound," which in its enumerated descriptions is nothing less than the bass note of the black experience in America: "This sound had filled John's life, so it now seemed, from the moment he had first drawn breath. He had heard it everywhere, in prayer and in daily speech, and wherever the saints were gathered, and in the unbelieving streets."[82] Where Wright—writing as a convinced communist—fuses his hero into an expression of the Rousseauean general will of a mobilized community, Baldwin immobilizes the black soul in the throes of a collective unconscious, placing the divisions internal to that experience on raw display and making them unavoidable.

When John is revived, he must still face the force that has been looming over the entire novel and summon "the living word that would conquer the great division between his father and himself."[83] He does find that word and it carries a charge of rebellion that is screened from the man to whom they are addressed. John vows "to stand against the enemy ... and *against everything and everybody* ... that wants to cut down my soul."[84] In doing so, he vows to stand against white oppression but also implicitly, and pointedly, against his own father, the institution of the Black Church that he represents, and the broader community that he loves and that lives under the protection of that institution. John will oppose all of them if they attempt to cut down the truth of his soul, a truth that we know, at least in the present of the novel, they cannot fully accept.

I have drawn attention to how Baldwin deserts the generic expectations of social realism and reimagines the aesthetic uses and possibilities of dramatizing black interiority. Doesn't this retreat into an alienated interiority a fortiori imply a retreat from politics? Does it imply that Baldwin was quietist where his forebear was political? I would answer these questions by taking seriously, as I think Baldwin would want us to, the stylistic qualities of "The Threshing Floor." The tenor of the rhetoric that Baldwin resorts to in this final chapter is most appropriately described as prophetic. Maurice Blanchot, in a remarkable essay on the subject, defines prophetic speech this way: "Prophetic speech announces an impossible future, or makes the future it announces, because it announces it, something impossible, a future one would not know how to live and that must upset all the sure givens of existence. When speech becomes prophetic, it is not the future that is given, it is the present that is taken away."[85] What Baldwin's prophetic speech impresses us with is not a "hope for a better tomorrow," racial liberalism's perpetually vaunted promise of gradual melioration with steadfast effort, that long march through history toward "a more perfect union." The emphasis is rather on what has become irrevocably changed about the present.

When John puts his hand on Brother Elisha's arm and asks for his blessing, he says: "No matter what happens to me, where I go, what folks say about me, no matter what *anybody* says, you remember—please remember—I was saved. I was *there*."[86] The importance of John's journey to the end of the night does not lie in the future, about which the only certainty is that John is ready to face it. An enunciated truth has broken through all the forces arraigned against it, a truth that cannot be denied, because prophetic speech has, at least momentarily, obliterated its temple. When Elisha kisses John on the forehead, "a holy kiss," he seals the truth of a love that is declared in plain sight of his father, Gabriel. At the close of the novel, this father remains in power, but his power to suppress the truth of John's experience, of his life, has been permanently broken.

This, too, is a political allegory (the theme of black leadership runs through the fiction of an astonishingly large number of black male novelists). But it cannot be a socialist one; nor can it conform to a model of liberal assimilation. John could not have attained the insights he needed to achieve anywhere other than in the dark womb of the Black Church from which he will emerge reborn. Baldwin's aesthetic and rhetorical affordances, his signifying markers, are drawn from black oratory, black music, black history, black vernacular, and, of course, from earlier black literature, including the stories of *Uncle Tom's Children* that Baldwin read and knew just as well as his Henry James.

The difference lies in a new affect, a new outlook, one that, from Baldwin's bird's-eye view in the 1950s is perhaps less naive than the spirit of the 1930s about the sources of oppression in society. Baldwin's prophetic speech is willing to say the unspeakable, to make demands that it knows very well cannot be met by a political imagination that can conceive of moral failings only as easily subsumed under the label of "race," of social conflicts that can be accounted for solely under the rubric of "class." The cry in the desert becomes the desert-dry cry of an interiority set at naught— falling back on an experiential truth that is politically unappeasable and ideologically uncontainable, and more powerful and shattering for it.

Baldwin's aesthetic strategies drew on the cultural resources he had at hand: the lesson of Henry James regarding the autonomy of novelistic form, the lessons of his upbringing in the Black Church about the rhetorical power of the sermon and about the construction, and also the subversion, of moral and political authority. And they drew on his discovery and appropriation of a blue space, a weaponized solitude that allowed him to see and say certain things with an authority that proceeded from himself only and on his own terms. On its own, this would be quite significant in black twentieth-century literary history. But we can track a strikingly similar development in the early career of another important black writer from this period. That this is possible even with a vastly different set of cultural inputs supports my central point: there is a pervasive—and more precisely affective—coloring that characterizes black writing in the postwar years.

CHAPTER TWO

Édouard Glissant's Relocations

*L'île est une écharde dans une foudre, que l'arbre partout mène
en lui (The island is a shard in lightning, that the tree everywhere conducts inwardly).*[1]

ÉDOUARD GLISSANT, *Soleil de la conscience* (1956)

In 1953, a twenty-five-year-old Martinican appeared on the Parisian literary scene as the voice behind a slim, delicately bound volume of poetry
bearing the title *Un champ d'îles (A Field of Islands)*.[2] The book included a
frontispiece lithograph printed on a detached flyleaf by Wolfgang Paalen,
an Austrian-Mexican artist who had traveled in the early surrealist circles
and, by the early 1950s, was associated with the nascent abstract expres-
sionists and the French art collective Cahiers d'Art, founded by Christian
Zervos and headquartered at 14 rue du Dragon in Paris.[3] *Un champ d'îles*
was published by Éditions du Dragon, a tiny press operated by the Galerie
du Dragon, an art gallery located on the same street, noted for its interest in Latin American art and surrealism, and for being frequented by a
network of highly influential poets, artists, and literary critics, many also
loosely associated with Cahiers d'Art. Édouard Glissant's second book,
La terre inquiète (The Troubled Earth), was also published by Éditions du
Dragon the following year.[4] Again in a limited edition with a tiny print run,
the book featured a frontispiece by the Cuban artist Wifredo Lam, then at
the summit of his reputation, an artist whose constellation of cosmopolitan influences (including cubism, surrealism and Afro-Cuban folklore), visually articulated a creolized modernist aspiration remarkably consonant
with the ideas Glissant would pursue in his essays and theoretical writings
to come.[5]

Glissant is now considered a major figure within the ambit of those
working on the Caribbean, and he enjoys a major literary reputation, especially in France and the Francophone world. And although he continues
to appear infrequently on the syllabi of African American studies departments, there has recently emerged a rising tide of scholarship pushing back
against such parochial demarcations.[6] There is a growing body of schol-

arship introducing Glissant to a broader audience interested in his writing on race and literature and his project to "creolize philosophy itself."[7] But critics still tend to divide Glissant's oeuvre by foregrounding the later writings, which are deemed useful to poststructuralists, while relegating the early works to a period of sterile aestheticism without theoretical interest.

This is in part because Glissant's writings began circulating in the Anglophone world only in the late 1980s. In 1985, J. Michael Dash translated Glissant's first novel, *La lézarde* (1958), as *The Ripening*, and in 1989 the seminal essay collection *Caribbean Discourse*; Dominique O'Neill published his translation of the epic poem *Les Indes* (1956) in 1992. These translations roughly coincided with Glissant's move to the United States. After a long career divided between Paris and Fort-de-France, Glissant spent his last years teaching at Louisiana State University from 1987 to 1994 and at the CUNY Graduate Center from 1995 until his passing in 2011.

Glissant's reception has relied, then, on a limited number of available translations, including, most influentially, the essay collection *The Poetics of Relation*, translated by Betsy Wing and published by University of Michigan Press in 1997. This collection relied on the republication of Glissant's works by the French publisher Gallimard, which compiled and reissued his essays in three volumes of collected prose between 1990 and 1997. Gallimard didn't reproduce earlier collections in toto; instead, it curated and condensed pieces from the several dozen books Glissant had published between 1953 and 1989. The presentation of the texts in these editions was heavily influenced by a thematic conception of his work (rather than, say, a chronological or bibliographic one).

These circumstances of publication and translation have favored a reading of Glissant, increasingly influential in the 1970s and 1980s, through (and as influenced by) French poststructuralist theory, particularly that of Gilles Deleuze and Félix Guattari, thinkers he was personally and intellectually close to during that period. The reception of Glissant has focused on his later theoretical writings, with the 1981 *Discours antillais* acting as a fulcrum point around which debates swirl over his sufficient commitment to leftist politics, or, as Peter Hallward argues, that signifies a turn to a postmodern aestheticizing gesture and incipient identity politics.[8] The Glissant that has come down to us (especially in the Anglophone world) is thus heavily weighted toward the writings of his later career, where he develops the articulation of his concepts of opacity, creolization, and *antillanité*. In short, we know Glissant as a figure of postcolonial theory.

But there is an early Glissant of the 1950s who remains in the shadows. One of the key texts from this earlier period is the fragmentary *Soleil*

de la conscience, a poetic meditation published in Paris in 1956 and translated into English for the first time only in 2020.[9] In an interesting parallel to Baldwin, a major part of Glissant's writings during his years in Paris
took the form of literary criticism published in various small magazines,
including the influential and prestigious journal *Les lettres nouvelles*, and
the main intellectual organ of the French decolonial movement, *Présence
africaine*. While scholars like Celia Britton and, more recently, Christina
Kullberg, Nick Nesbitt, and Suzy Cater, have drawn attention to this phase
of Glissant's literary production, the full scope of this archive has yet to be
exploited.[10]

Scholars have also tended to neglect Glissant's deep connections to
the transnational art and literary networks of postwar Paris.[11] Yet this
was the world Glissant chose to integrate and where he produced several significant—and mostly unknown or uncollected texts—in which he
set about self-fashioning a new position for black Francophone writing.
Glissant thought it important to distinguish this position and its aesthetics from predecessors like Aimé Césaire; this writing pointed to a future
world and a vastly different landscape for black intellectuals, writers, and
artists.[12]

Glissant's interventions in his manuscripts, his art criticism, his literary
reviews, and especially his early poetry and essays thus constitute a pro-
lific site whose significance remains underexamined. To allow the work
from that period to achieve its rightful significance requires that we redis-
cover him in his synchronic historical context, among a constellation of
black writers across the diaspora. These include Baldwin, but also Aimé
Césaire, Frantz Fanon, Sylvia Wynter, and Maryse Condé, as they experimented with new modes of authority available to black writing in a postwar world in which Europe had for the first time abruptly, but definitively,
become decentered.

By turning to the archive of Glissant's literary criticism and to two of
his works of the 1950s, *Soleil de la conscience* and the long historical poem
Les Indes, I suggest the importance of a decontinentalized Glissant—that
is, the possibility of reading Glissant into an archive of black diasporic
thought responding to the position of the black writer in the early years of
the Cold War. In what follows, I trace a new path for understanding Glissant, one that restores the experimental interest of the works that he produced before the poststructural poetics he developed alongside and in dialogue with the advance of so-called continental theory in the 1970s and
1980s. The "late Glissant" is more familiar to us, but those writings reflect
a background marked by political disappointment and defeat, conditions
radically different from those swirling around the young Glissant in his
student days in the Paris of the 1950s.

The Early Glissant

It is a cliché, but one is tempted to say that Édouard Glissant was born for this moment, coming of age, as he did, under extraordinarily propitious circumstances for a poetic and political initiation into the postwar world order. He was born in 1928 in Sainte-Marie, a rural province of Martinique, then a colonial possession of the French Empire. His father worked as an overseer on a sugarcane plantation, and his mother raised his brother and three sisters.[13] The family moved when he was very young to Lamentin, the main industrialized sector of the island around the capital of Fort-de-France. A gifted student, he passed the exams required to enter the Lycée Schoelcher, the island's premier educational establishment, in 1939, the same year that Aimé Césaire, then returning from studies in Paris, was named professor of modern languages there.

For a brief period, the school effectively became one the intellectual cradles of Caribbean black radicalism. Frantz Fanon, who was three years ahead of Glissant at the same school, was soaking up the philosophical and political views that Césaire had been exposed to in the metropole and brought back with him to Martinique. After the Fall of France in 1940, a swarm of figures connected to and part of the French surrealist movement arrived on the island, including Max Ernst, André Masson, Claude Lévi-Strauss, Michel Leiris, Wifredo Lam, and André Breton. These figures' investment in the Caribbean had been kindled in the early 1930s by Martinican students (most prominently René Ménil) at the Sorbonne who founded a Martinican surrealist group of their own and edited the ephemeral but influential journal *Légitime défense*.[14] During the war years, Césaire and his wife, Suzanne, along with Georges Gratiant, Aristide Maugée, Lucie Thésée and Ménil, essentially the island's most prominent literary figures of the 1930s, collectively founded the Afro-modernist literary journal *Tropiques* (1941–1945).

This period also marks Césaire's turn toward direct politics. World War II had turned the island into a territory of Vichyite Occupation. The Allied Forces blockaded Vichy's colonies, and in Martinique, as elsewhere, the grave economic hardships that ensued helped to fuel social unrest and generate a surge of popularity for communist partisans. Césaire seized the opportunity to prepare an electoral campaign on a Communist Party ticket for mayor of Fort-de-France, which he won in 1945. The end of the war saw the transformation of Martinique from a colony into a new "overseas department," integrated, ostensibly, under equal terms into the French Fourth Republic.

Although Glissant was too young to take classes directly with Césaire at the Lycée Schoelcher, the influence of the Césaires and the energy around their review *Tropiques* was electrifying for him. In a move that prefigures the positioning he would take up in Paris, Glissant founded his own dissident collective, Franc-Jeu, a vanguard artistic-intellectual circle of pamphleteers who organized support for Césaire's political campaign.[15] Glissant described it as "un groupe d'agitation poético-politique" (a poetic-political agitation group), a description that closely resembles the protagonists (Nesbitt calls them "adolescent activists") of his first novel, *La lézarde*.[16] Franc-Jeu published a zine with poetry and reflections on current affairs, printed on gray banana-wrapping paper run through an aging typewriter and distributed by hand and read aloud in the streets of Lamentin.[17]

This biographical background explains why Glissant, when he arrived in Paris in 1946, considered himself (like James Baldwin) not a provincial but already a highly cultured and cosmopolitan emigrant. Writing poetry on the side, he studied philosophy at the Sorbonne, where he obtained his *licence* under Jean Wahl in 1953, as well as a certificate in ethnography under the direction of Michel Leiris at the Musée de l'Homme in 1954. In Paris he lived at 4 rue Blondel in a former brothel; the boarding house was frequented by many of the Antillean students passing through Paris in those years, including his former schoolmate Fanon, with whom he maintained contact until shortly before Fanon's untimely death in 1961.[18]

For Glissant, the 1950s were an intense period of sustained institution building and literary productivity. He was an early member of the circle of black expatriates federated and galvanized around *Présence africaine*, the journal founded by Alioune Diop in 1947, and second, as an executive member of the *Société de Culture Africaine*, which was instrumental in organizing the Congress of Black Writers and Artists, the first of which met in Paris in 1956 and the second in Rome in 1959.[19] His first novel, *La lézarde*, was awarded the Prix Renaudot for 1958. But, as Suzy Cater has argued, his closest personal connections were with the circle of French poets around Henri Pichette, Yves Bonnefoy, and Jean Laude, as well as the young Algerian writer Kateb Yacine, all of whom were collectively seeking to recover a place for poetics in the postwar world. Glissant's most significant literary relationship during this time was with the journal *Les lettres nouvelles*, founded in 1953 by Maurice Nadeau, where he published thirty-four articles and reviews between February 1953 and December 1959.[20] In 1956, he joined the journal's editorial board, where, along with Nadeau, one of his colleagues was Roland Barthes.

That same year, Glissant published his first book of essays, *Soleil de la conscience*, followed quickly by the epic poem *Les Indes*, two key poetic works that help to correct our understanding of the aesthetic and political stakes that shaped his work. *Soleil* is an astonishing essay, reminiscent of the early Baldwin; *Les Indes* supplants the West's authority to tell its own history in a move that prefigures the theoretical challenges that would emerge in *Caribbean Discourse* three decades later. Together, they offer us a picture of the Blue Period Glissant, a figure whose ruminative anomie suggests the restless but tactical intellectual who keeps the flame alive but bides his time.

An Ethnographer of Myself

Soleil de la conscience, like so many of Glissant's writings, is fundamentally transgeneric, a formal hybrid composed of fragmentary and intensely lyric vignettes that are interspersed with more conventionally recognizable verse poems, typically given a year as title—"1948," "1953," and so on—that encrust the text with older material, the earliest dating to 1946, within two years of his first arrival in Paris to study at the Sorbonne. These "prose poems," as Christina Kullberg categorizes them, grant the whole with what could be described as an archipelagic quality, a favored metaphor for Glissant that feels true to the loosely strung net of affinities between these thematically and spatially partitioned islets of text.[21] The geographic metaphor also bespeaks the sense of travel the essay invokes.

Attentive readers of Glissant's *Soleil* have noticed that this germinal text in his oeuvre deploys an intriguing reversal of the ethnographic gaze.[22] It makes sense given his own acquaintance with that tradition in relation to his home island of Martinique and, more immediately, his formal education in anthropology under Michel Leiris at the Musée de l'Homme from 1953 to 1954. He informally assisted Leiris in the landmark survey of Martinique and Guadeloupe produced for the UN Educational, Scientific, and Cultural Organization in 1955, a study Glissant praises in *L'intention poétique*, where he asserts: "L'observateur attentif' qu'est (ou était) l'ethnographe devra s'inscrire au *drame du monde*: par-delà son analytique—en principe "solitaire"—il devra vivre une poétique (un partage). Ainsi Leiris" (The attentive observer that is [or was] the ethnographer will have to subscribe to the *drama of the world*: in addition to any analysis—in principle "solitary"—they will have to live a poetics [a sharing]. Hence Leiris).[23]

Scholars have written convincingly on how Glissant interpolates Leiris in crafting an ethnographic poetics, what one calls his "crossroads poetics."[24] But they tend to skim rather lightly over the astonishing reversal of authority by which Glissant not only answers back to a discipline of which he, for most of his life, has been effectively a subject but also sets the terms for the future of that discipline. His parenthesis (*ou était*) goes so far as to question whether the discipline can even be said to exist anymore, or at least to imply that if it does not evolve, it is bound to obsolescence.

Moreover, Glissant's claim was first published not in 1969 (in *L'intention poétique*) but in 1956—in an article entitled "Michel Leiris, ethnographe," published in *Les lettres nouvelles*, during the high watermark of the French school of ethnography and only three years after Baldwin's "Stranger in the Village."[25] Claude Lévi-Strauss's *Tristes Tropiques* had been published just the year before, in 1955, to wide acclaim. By endorsing Leiris, Glissant's article implicitly rebukes Lévi-Strauss, whose political passivity Glissant calls into question. The phrase "s'inscrire au *drame du monde*" (to subscribe to the drama of the world) is not just an abstract statement. Glissant's readers would have understood exactly what he means, namely, the imperative to involve oneself in the political and historical struggles of others, the drama of decolonization. Leiris had endorsed this position in his 1950 essay "L'ethnographe devant le colonialisme," which first appeared in Sartre's journal, *Les temps modernes*, where he repudiated his earlier lack of engagement as an ethnographer in the 1930s when he was working on *L'Afrique fantôme* (*Phantom Africa*) (1934).[26]

Here, then, is a black Martinican poet declaring the end of white ethnography—the end of an episteme, to borrow Foucault's term—in terms that echo the political critique and the authority Baldwin arrogates to himself in "Stranger in the Village," the essay in which he declares "the end of the white world." Glissant's overturning of authority also employs that reversal of the ethnographic gaze we saw in Baldwin. As Glissant elsewhere puts it, playing on the word *outremer*, the preferred administrative nomenclature for France's overseas colonies (now, territories and departments): "You say: *overseas* (we said it with you), but you too will soon be overseas."[27]

We ought not be surprised, then, to find Glissant in the opening pages of *Soleil de la conscience* interrogating his relationship to the very same European monuments Baldwin cited: "Mais puis-je dire que j'éprouve Racine, par exemple, ou la cathédrale de Chartres?" (But can I say that I bear/feel Racine, for example, or the cathedral of Chartres?).[28] Glissant answers his own question in terms that echo Baldwin's prophecy: "Je devine peut-être qu'il n'y aura plus de culture sans toutes les cultures, plus de civilisation qui puisse être métropole des autres, plus de poète pour ignorer le mouvement de l'Histoire" (My guess is that there will soon no longer be any culture without all other cultures, no civilization that can be the metropole of another, no poet who can ignore the movement of History).[29] Right away, Glissant asserts the decentering of Europe, an end to the authority of the metropole over the periphery, an end to any culture that claims it can segregate itself from other cultures, an end, in Baldwin's terms, to the "whiteness" of the world. Glissant calls himself an "ethnographe de moi-même," "an ethnographer of myself," a description that evokes Du Boisian double consciousness and Baldwin's later self-examining turn, as filtered through the added mesh of colonial (or ex-colonial) subjectivity.[30]

Glissant characterizes this tense interplay between intimacy and alienation as the return of a prodigal son but also of a notorious existentialist antihero. On the first page he writes of holding a gaze that combines "le regard du fils et la vision de l'Étranger," a line that J. Michael Dash translates as "the look of the son and the vision of the outsider."[31] While *outsider* is certainly a fair characterization, Dash has in fact gravely mistranslated by missing out on a contextual literary cue that Glissant's contemporary French readers would not have. Glissant capitalizes l'Étranger. For a reader in 1956 (and even today) this would unmistakably register as a nod to Albert Camus's 1942 novel *L'Étranger* (*The Stranger*). If we are to take this young Antillean man as a black Meursault racked with existential doubts and a jaundiced view of the social mores of the European metropolis he wanders, this allusion takes on far darker associations, and ones of a decidedly more political flavor.

Critics tend to overlook contemporary social and political implications like these to read *Soleil* as a kind of tide-pool laboratory where Glissant is assaying the techniques of ethnographic poetics he would deploy later in (implicitly) more mature works. In my own reading, *Soleil* is already fully formed and announces Glissant's intentions for the future of poetry, an ars poetica steeped in a "blue" affect, the world of the young black student in Paris, moving in artistic circles, negotiating the intense political currents and debates of the time, and trying to find an authoritative footing in a fundamentally alienating and reflexively racist environment.

We can begin to recover these affective and political aspects of Glissant's Blue Period by more closely examining the student milieu itself, the tiny but efflorescent Antillean intelligentsia that was forming in those years.[32] It is no accident, for example, that the book is dedicated to his friends back in Martinique.[33] While there are many pointed reflections in *Soleil* on solitude, some of the more interesting vignettes employ a distanced phenomenological style (probably somewhat indebted to Merleau-Ponty) that give us glimpses of the social world of black student life:

> Des amis sont venus … Ils sont là, sous mon regard … on vit en secret dans l'arène d'une discussion. Il n'y a plus d'individus, mais un seul corps tendu vers son destin. A ce niveau je suis en rien insulaire, je ne représente pas; je suis dans ce café une voix qui s'ajoute aux autres. Mais comme chacun je sens (cependant que le brouhaha des propositions s'épaissit, et que nous voilà tous à tenter la chance du vrai), que le résidu en moi demeure; qu'il est vrai que la littérature désormais ne peut être loge de l'âme; que cette vérité banale dans son éternité nous serons quelques uns à l'avoir vraiment

soufferte. […] Puissance encore de cette ville! Qui abstrait l'être, mais pour le rejeter aussitôt dans sa vérité même.

Some friends have arrived … they are here, in my gaze … we live in secret in the arena of our discussion. There are no more individuals, but one body stretching towards its destiny. In this sense I am not at all insular, I don't represent; I am in this café just one voice joining the others. But like each of us I can feel (as the cacophony of propositions thickens, and we once again try on our truth) that residue in me that remains; that it is true that literature cannot house the soul; that only we few will truly suffer the banality of this truth in all its eternity…. Again the power of this city! To abstract the self, but only to throw it back onto its very truth.[34]

Here the cloister of the Parisian café, where it seems Glissant would retire often to write alone (punning here on his "insular" ways), is interrupted when his friends arrive. The presence of a group of friends creates the "arena of our discussion." One imagines this is for several compounded reasons: the racial divide creates an "island" of blackness in a typically white space; at least some, if not all, of the discussion will be in Creole, a linguistic divide that confers a kind of open secrecy; and finally, some of this discussion may be of sensitive matters touching on explosive political events of great interest to the French authorities, including the intelligence services.

Glissant implies that when the friends get together, discussion naturally turns to politics, the individual aspirations of each forfeited for the common embodied cause they know they must take up. The "propositions" flying around the café table are clearly political ones, turning on the burning question of the place Martinique should have in the Union Française, a debate that consumed black expatriates in these years. Gary Wilder has excavated the stakes of these debates in his study *Freedom Time*, which gives unparalleled insight into the positions on these questions taken up by Aimé Césaire and Leopold Senghor, but only glancingly considers Glissant, whose position was more radical and to the left of theirs.[35] Although they are unnamed here, we can be certain that among the friends Glissant is arguing with at the café are figures like Albert Béville (a.k.a. Paul Niger), Marcel Manville, and Cosnay Marie-Joseph, with whom in 1961 he would eventually found the Front des Antillais et Guyanais pour l'Autonomie, an "independentist" political front that issued the 1961 declaration *Les Antilles et la Guyane à l'heure de la décolonisation*, a rare dissident text recovered for scholarly analysis by Nick Nesbitt.[36]

Glissant, as ethnographer of himself, is essentially describing a life at the intersection of disparate worlds: the tropical Antilles and snow-bound

Paris, the art world and the world of militant anticolonial politics, the arenas of criticism, and prose, and lyrical poetry. *Soleil* is an intimate document but also a political one, a notebook written about these friends in Paris but also for his friends back in Martinique who were part of the artistic-political action front Franc-Jeu. Both groups, like him, could understand the tension, excitement, and alienation of being a young black intellectual at an extraordinary historical crossroads: a world where, for the first time, an end to white European hegemony could be envisaged.[37]

A Hell without Seasons

Although it has gone underexamined in the scholarship, we find in *Soleil* Glissant's scathing indictment of the hypocrisy of the Parisian art world that he has integrated (or, from another point of view, infiltrated) and is, in a sense, spying on for his friends back home. It is in fact from a bitter vignette aimed directly at the art world that the title of the collection is drawn:

> Ils murissent dans cet univers, ils grandissent de cette solitude multipliée. Ils sont, mais oui, dans cet homme qui vous vendrait à seule fin d'occuper l'espace de dix pages de revue; dans cet autre, qui vous flatte, attendant l'heure; dans ce troisième un sourd-muet, dont vous secouez la manchette lustrée. Oui l'ami qui assure que. L'autre qui applaudit, mais. Je ne fais que décrire le cercle, j'y suis moi-même. Grandeur et servitude de Paris, qui enseigne l'art d'être seul. Un enfer sans saisons. D'où il faut pour chacun que lève le Soleil de la Conscience.

> This is the universe that spawns them; they grow up in this multiplication of solitude. They are, oh yes, in this man who would sell you just to fill ten pages in his review; in this other who flatters you, biding his time; in this third, a deaf-mute whose lustrous sleeve you shake. Yes, in the friend who assures you that. Another that applauds, but. I am only describing the circle; I am a part of it myself. Grandeur and servitude of Paris, that teaches the art of being alone. A hell without seasons. Out of which for each the Sun of Consciousness must rise.[38]

The deepest quarrel in Glissant's text is with this infernal circle, the treacherous Balzacian world of *Lost Illusions*, where aspiring writers, critics, and journalists rise and fall, vying with each other in *la vie mondaine* to dominate some clique within it.

Glissant asks his reader to accept this wheel of fortune composed of the white artists, poets, and critics whom the black poet has befriended but also used (and been used by) to embark upon his literary career—to accept it, that is, in order to transcend it by stepping into the essay's titular "sunlight of consciousness." The path into that sunlight, however, must first pass through the vestibular hell where one has practiced "the art of being alone." The alienation of a season in Paris is not a torpor but a tonic; the chrysalis closed on itself today will nurture and produce the radiant power of tomorrow's radical.

The phrase "a hell without seasons" is of particular significance to this prophetic enunciation, which is why it appears in this passage as an isolated sentence. Typical of Glissant's conspicuously allusive style, it condenses a wide foliage of meanings, drawn in sharply like the spray of a palm. It is first and foremost an allusion to Rimbaud's *A Season in Hell* (1873), another poem of the revolted and divided self whose disgust is directed emphatically throughout its opening sequence at the French race ("mes ancêtres gaulois") and the (violently disavowed) history of France. Rimbaud speaks gloatingly of belonging to "an inferior race," by which he means poets, who in his conception are condemned to a permanent state of spiritual combat with a fallen, disenchanted, and philistine world that equally despises them ("le combat spirituel est aussi brutal que la bataille d'hommes").[39]

Through this allusion, Glissant also invokes the most famous Martinican poem, Aimé Césaire's *Cahier d'un retour au pays natal* (1939).[40] The importance of Rimbaud to Césaire and to the poetics that went into his great elegy of exilic *négritude* was well-known to the writers and poets in his circle. André Breton, in his introduction, recalls Césaire teaching Rimbaud to his high school students in Fort-de-France.[41] In Césaire's *Cahier*, the black colonial ghetto is a *paysage moralisé*, a Rimbaldian inferno through which the poet must pass in order to purge his self-hatred and decolonize his mind.

Through this double allusion, Glissant overlays the hell of Paris with the hell of its colonial dependency across the ocean. Up to this point, and throughout his essay, the recurrent image for the alienation of Paris is snow, a commonplace for a metropolitan Frenchman but a surreal encounter, at once enchanting and disenchanting, for the Martinican.[42] That is to say, Paris has seasons; Fort-de-France, the setting of Césaire's poem, does not; but it is the solitude imposed on a black Antillean in Paris that is paradoxically a hell without seasons.

Glissant's line subtly but unmistakably links this alienation to the poetic production of the spirit in revolt—Rimbaud's certainly but, more importantly, if encoded here, Césaire's. This message would be most readily decrypted (in 1956) by a Martinican reader, someone who, say, was a reader of *Tropiques* during the war or a member of Franc-Jeu. In other words, the prophetic line about the sunrise points back to the hell without seasons as the location from which it emerges. The "blue period," the art of being alone, is a stage that cannot be avoided; it precedes the sunrise of consciousness, but it is there in the blue twilight that works of revolutionary potential are forged.

The Light of a Long-Gone Comet

Soleil is an essay about these temptations of solitude and art, about how the complicities of cultural capital conflict with the concrete needs of solidarity and struggle. "One can also say that the primary problem of our time is politics," Glissant asserts; and elsewhere, in the essay's closing paragraph, he insists that one "must attach oneself at once to some square of earth, to problems of the everyday, to the strict measure of sight." Glissant does not say whether artistic commitment and political struggle can ever come into alignment. He refuses to delineate any kind of program for change.

Instead, he repeatedly offers variations on the idea of "a continuous movement of literature," an apt description for the poetic tropes that the essay trades on.[43] Cities, poems, memory—all these, like foam, he says, which is always gathering and being blown off the top of the mind's waves, have in common what Glissant decides is true of the French capital: "Paris is an island, that intercepts from all sides and diffracts forthwith."[44] These synaptic and rhizomatic images of literary and poetic production are an embryonic version of the web of theoretical concepts that will mark the Deleuze-and-Guattari-inflected *Caribbean Discourse* at the beginning of the 1980s. It is hard as a reader who encounters Glissant first through those later writings not to read them back into the earlier ones.

Still, there is something about the tone of this early prose poetry that evinces a more tentative groping toward self-awareness and a more personal reckoning with the conflicting ambitions that attend the awakening of a black artist to the demands of responsibility. A melancholy vulnerability occasionally comes into view, as when, of a morning in Paris, Glissant writes: "Some object of silence rises, but so vast. It is for example the milkman's cart. It is the bus that doesn't stop at this hour, and that I follow on its course: shooting star whose sound diminishes like the light of a long-gone comet." The solitude of this kind of exercise imparts a certain hauteur that stiffens the prose but that also suggests a deep sadness, almost a fragility, that conveys what was in that time (and is often still) the profound isolation of even the relatively successful black intellectual.

In *The World Republic of Letters*, Pascale Casanova takes a dim, near-tragic view of the position on the literary market of writers from France's former colonies. Her Bourdieuian line of argument about the relative cultural capital available to them and the all-importance of Paris as the Greenwich Meridian of literary value leads her to claim that "Paris never took an interest in writers from its colonial territories; or, more precisely, it long despised and mistreated them as a species of extreme provincials, too similar to be celebrated as exotic foreigners but too remote to be considered worthy of interest."[45] The situation of these Francophone writers, Casanova argues, is terrible not only because they are "despised" but also because they are dispossessed.[46] Yet Glissant's case seems to be far more nuanced than this claim would suggest. For one thing, Glissant not only was published but also was given wide berth in Nadeau's *Les lettres nouvelles*, one of the most prominent literary reviews of the period. Ruth Bush's work, a survey of the French publishing industry's relationship to black (albeit primarily African and not Antillean) writers, also puts pressure on Casanova's thesis by revealing how effective ventures like Alioune Diop's *Présence africaine* were in establishing a paradigm for reading and publishing work from the ex-colonies. "The presence of Africa across the literary spectrum was uneven, yet more widespread than has often been presumed," Bush notes, while also providing a fine-grained account of the many tensions that swirled around these projects.[47]

What emerges from a close reading of Glissant's *Soleil de la conscience* is the extent to which writers in his position were exquisitely aware of the ironies and hierarchies of the literary market—indeed, they actively and subversively manipulated them. And not necessarily for the benefit of metropolitan audiences but—at least in the case of *Soleil*—for the educated ex-colonials adrift and alienated in the new reordering of global power, disgusted and disappointed with metropolitan life, and effectively ripe for radicalization. This offers an alternative explanation for why *Soleil* made such a small ripple in what Casanova calls "world literary space." It's not that the power centers neglected and despised it. Simply put, it was never written for them—it was never intended to reach the mainstream French public.

Glissant was writing about and for the coterie he knew and came from, as well as like-minded groups across the diaspora, who would be receptive to its literary brinksmanship and perceive in it the restless spirit of the times. This was always going to be a small readership, but it existed because there was a shared awareness of living through a historical opening, when a new vista for young black writers seemed on the cusp of coming into being. With time, the blue glow of that dawn would fade; friends would die, nations would be born into a costly stillbirth, revolutionary fervor—and its opposite, bitter disillusionment—would demand new and different kinds of writing. The window for Glissant's *Soleil* was bright but brief.

News from the New World

The shelf life of *Soleil de la conscience* was short, perhaps inevitably so. Another work that Glissant published almost simultaneously had a larger impact, although it too has faded from view. This was the ambitious epic poem Glissant composed in the spring of 1955 and published with Falaize in 1956. He called it *Les Indes*.[48] A limited edition run of *Les Indes* was illustrated with engravings by Enrique Zañartu, a Franco-Chilean artist associated with Galerie du Dragon. It was in appearance another art book, but its reception tells another story, one we have failed to see because, like so much else in Glissant's canon, an English translation of the work did not arrive until the 1990s.

Moreover, Dominique O'Neill's 1992 translation of *Les Indes* introduced some errors that have obscured certain aspects of the poem.[49] While O'Neill admirably secures lyrical equivalents for Glissant's often difficult and technically demanding constructions, they nevertheless make two apparently minor but in fact significant errors. The most glaring is the omission of the poem's subtitle "Poème de l'une et l'autre terre" (Poem of the one and of the other land), a formula that insists on the fundamental concept of relation central to Glissantian poetics. The other concerns the dating of the poem's composition. O'Neill places the marker "(April–June 1955)" on the title page.[50] In the original edition published by Falaize, however, Glissant placed the date neither under the title nor, as one might usually do, at the very end of the text but curiously on page 63, beneath the prefatory overture to the last canto, and in the extended form "Avril-mai-juin 1955."[51] This may seem, at first glance, like a trivial detail; to show why it is in fact crucial to reconstructing the political meanings of the poem requires an overview of the epic itself.

The subject of Glissant's poem is the West Indies: its discovery, conquest, colonization, implementation of the triangular trade, and subsequent development. In short, it is an epic poem of the Caribbean since 1492. The epic poems about Caribbean history most familiar to Anglophone readers today are Kamau Braithwaite's *The Arrivants* (1973) and Derek Walcott's *Omeros* (1990). Glissant's *Les Indes* (1956), neglected on account of the language barrier, was composed several decades earlier and is the first epic poem of the Caribbean in the Francophone tradition— indeed, the first in any language by a poet of African descent.[52] Nicolás Guillén's *West Indies Ltd.* (1934) incorporates a self-consciously materialist history of the Caribbean, but his are lyrical poems; Césaire's *Cahier d'un retour au pays natal* (1939) is undoubtedly the seminal text of the modern Francophone Caribbean, a lyrical tour de force that André Breton hailed in *Tropiques* as "the greatest lyrical monument of our time," but it does not attempt to circumscribe a history within the space of a poetic epic.[53] *Les Indes* avowedly is a pioneering epic, albeit in a richly ironic and self-conscious sense, one that ought to be more widely read outside courses devoted to Caribbean studies and diasporic literary history. No less than Maryse Condé, evoking Pablo Neruda, has called it "a Canto General" for the Caribbean.[54]

Les Indes is a poem about the relation of human imagination to historical development. Its voice is oracular, impersonal, and collective, engaged in narrativizing in verse Glissant's "prophetic view of the past."[55] It is composed of six cantos, each representing a movement across space and historical time, a chapter in the imaginative and material construction of the titular "Indies." Glissant's versification in all but one of the lyric cantos varies between the traditional French *alexandrin* (using twelve syllables) and octosyllabic or decasyllabic lines. The verse is thus balanced between an acknowledgment of traditional poetic form (each line preserves the caesura and formal balance of French meter) and a refusal to encase the whole in a regular pattern. This variation suggests the Whitmanian desire for longer lines that change according to sense and breath, fugitive to regimentation and Old World classification alike. The poem is visually stretched open as well. Verse units are constantly separated and dropped down a line so that they cross the page like wavelets heading shoreward.

The first canto describes the departure of the caravels from the point of view of the explorer, in a voice that could be that of Columbus but is impersonally representative of all the European colonizers dreaming of a path to the "Indies." The second canto recounts their voyage across the seas; the third portrays their erotically charged encounter with the indigenous peoples and their conquest. The fourth canto, formally distinct from the rest, is composed in blocks of prose poetry, a *prose dure* (harsh prose), rather than the open lyric line elsewhere used.[56] In effect, the Middle Passage breaks the continuity of form; it forces a generic instability that no stable register or meter can represent. The slave trade is not beyond the scope of the poet's song but belongs to the underworld of the human imagination that erupts into history, a "Song of Death where the Shadow will have reigned."[57] In the fifth canto, a rebellious spirit of freedom and independence rises through the emblematic figures of Caribbean revolt: Toussaint Louverture, Louis Delgrès (who led the resistance to the French reinstitution of slavery in Guadeloupe in 1802), and Jean-Jacques Dessalines. These figures, standing for the historical process of black revolution, are presided over by another figure who is said to embody this new spirit, a dazzling "Woman" who "appears in the morning," and whose ardor, when the "bird of paradise folds its blades of fire," promises a radiant dawn whose full glory is still to come.[58]

Each canto of *Les Indes* begins with a "Péripétie," a vestibular proem giving the argument in italicized prose. In French the intertitle *péripétie* most literally translates as "adventure," especially of an errant kind. One is tempted to connect it etymologically to Ezra Pound's idea (adopted in his own epic *Cantos*) that a poem—in his example, Homer's *Odyssey*—can capture the geographical truth of a perspective as a voyager experiences it, as opposed to the empirical but abstracted truth of the cartographer. This is what Pound calls the *periplum*, a word he defines as not "correct geography ... as you would find it if you had a geography book and a map, but as it would be in 'periplum,' that is, as a coasting sailor would find it."[59] This is especially fitting for a poem like *Les Indes*, filled as it is with seafaring images (Glissant's oneiric diction is steeped in the glistening hyperbole of Rimbaud's *Le bateau ivre*), with rolling swells and shorelines espied at a distance and whose point of view is perpetually given as if from the crow's nest, including in the first line of the sixth canto when the landfall of the return voyage appears on the horizon: "De la proue du navire à la lame de craie, c'est une douve, la dernière" (From the prow of the vessel to the line of chalk, it's a moat, the last).[60]

Glissant's *péripétie* is not entangled with Pound, however, so much as with Aristotle's *Poetics*, where *peripeteia*, the reversal in the plot of a tragedy, is famously connected to both *anagnorisis*, recognition (sometimes also translated as "discovery"), and *pathos*, the occasion and action of suffering.[61] The Aristotelian *peripeteia* refers not to a change of fortunes but to an ironic reversal of expectations. The connection between reversal and recognition is one of ignorance and knowledge. As Malcolm Heath notes, "Both reveal that the situation in which a character has been acting was misinterpreted. Reversal reveals that, because things are not what they seemed, the outcome of a person's actions will be other than what had been expected."[62] The argument of Glissant's poem is that the human imagination and its unconstrained desire for new horizons, symbolized by the Western invention and despoliation of "the Indies," is a tragic force in precisely this Aristotelian sense. The epic of the so-called age of discovery is a suite of actions (one could call it "Errours endlesse traine") that will culminate in a reversal as the ignorance of the "discoverers" ends up producing the unexpected conditions of their rejection and return, including the unforeseen event of the poem itself, which imposes its own narrative logic upon their adventure.[63] Things were never what they seemed, and it is the function of the poem to discover, in the wake (in Christina Sharpe's sense) of all that the discoverers have wrought, a new *gnōsis*.[64]

This is a dialectical knowledge that does not come without a cost, without suffering. The poem insists on weaving together the disastrous dreams of the conquerors and the unheralded dreams of their victims, mourning not only heroic figures of resistance in the West Indies—"Delgrès qui tint trois ans la Guadeloupe" (Delgrès who held for three years in Guadeloupe)—but also the unwritten aspirations of the entire "New World," the repressed "primitives" of Western historiography born on the wrong side of someone else's arbitrary map: "car ils sont morts de ce côté du monde où le soleil decline" (because they died on the side of the world where the sun sets).[65] The paradoxical truth of the Indies ("Les Indes sont vérité") rhymes with their permanence as utopian product of the human imagination ("Les Indes sont éternité").[66] But the concluding couplet of the epic presses home the bitter truth of the condition of perpetual suffering that is the undefeatable historical horizon of the voyage out, the voyage back, and whatever yet may come:

> L'âpre douceur de l'horizon en la rumeur du flot,
> Et l'éternelle fixation des jours et des sanglots.
>
> (The bitter softness of the horizon on the din of the tide
> And the eternal binding of the days and the cries.)

The sixth canto begins with a *péripétie* that sets out a series of questions about the subject who stands at the end of the colonial phase of history and the dawn of a new one whose projects and desires—"What Indies call to him?"—remain unknown and only tentatively conceived:

> The poem is finished when the shore, from which the Discoverers formerly departed, comes into sight … Who returns? And that man there, what does he, in turn covet? … What Indies call to him? Or, if his dream is already no more than an impassioned reason, what ocean yet stands between him and it—? No one can say with certainty; but everyone attempts the new crossing! The sea is eternal.[67]
>
> April-May-June 1955.

Here we find a date formatted to spread over the months of spring and early summer (connoting a return to life and fruition), and the year 1955, only the *second* year to appear anywhere inside the text. Both times a year appears it is, significantly, in the first and last *péripéties*, in other words, in both cases the year is taken as part of the poem's argument and *peripeteia*, its thesis and the reversal of the expectations of that thesis. These two dates are 1492, technically the first "word" of the poem, and 1955, as we see above. This framing, which *Les Indes* presents self-consciously, tells us that it is an epic making an argument for and about periodization. It takes the Columbian year of contact as the inaugural event of modernity as seen from the perspective of the non-European colonized peoples of the world. By bookending 1492 with 1955, Glissant is arguing that the year of his composition of *Les Indes* is the turning point, the hinge that closes the "age of discovery" and opens the door to an entirely new project, a yet-undefined opportunity to decide what we want our dreams of discovery to be, what our desires are for the Earth and the place of human beings in relation to it and to each other. The inscription of the date within the argument (and the stress placed on the duration of composition) implies that the poem is also recording a kind of testament, an act of witnessing, and indeed is even inscribing itself as one of the events contributing to the end of the white world. The importance of the year 1955 and its place within the structure and logic of the poem cannot be stressed enough. In fact, there is still another cardinal reason to attend to this date but to show this we must step back first to examine one of the most pronounced poetic relationships in Glissant's oeuvre: his intricate history of shadowboxing with Saint-John Perse.

Scholars of Caribbean poetry have long recognized the magnetic influence of Saint-John Perse (1887–1975) on Glissant's poetics.[68] Although his reputation has declined in recent years, at midcentury, Perse was considered a hero of Francophone modernism, a major poet whose voice promised to restore a classicizing humanism that had been widely viewed as shattered by the European conflicts of the world wars. Born to plantation aristocracy in the French colony of Guadeloupe, his Caribbean upbringing made him exotic to metropolitan French readers but an enduring source of inspiration to fellow Caribbean poets.[69] Under his real name, Alexis Léger, he was a prominent diplomat in the French civil service between the wars. His strongly anti-Nazi views clashed with the Vichy regime, and in 1940 he went into exile in the United States, where he lived in Washington, DC, and New York from 1941 to 1945. In the postwar period, his influence increased. His poems were published in the United States under the imprint of the Bollingen Series in the 1950s, and in 1960, he was awarded the Nobel Prize for Literature.[70]

Glissant, in an essay contributed to an honorary volume published in 1976 by the *Nouvelle revue française* upon Perse's death, described him as "the most essential poet," admitting he was "souvent présent dans la clairière de mes mots" (often present in the clearing of my words).[71] Bernadette Cailler tentatively made the connection in a 1988 monograph devoted to Glissant and Antillean history.[72] In his 1995 study, Dash collected clues Glissant had himself provided in interviews over the years but generally confined his observations to broad thematic resonances across the two poets' works, including a "marine" or oceanic metaphor, a generative relation between landscape and verb, and a strong interest in the Americas as a counterpresence to the weight of European tradition.[73]

Glissant's *Caribbean Discourse* (*Le Discours antillais*, 1981) includes a section on Perse, significantly under the rubric "A Caribbean Future." Glissant chastises the poet in Hegelian terms for his unmoored pursuit of "universalism" and "totality," a search for "stability" that alienates him from the "tangle of lianas" that is the crucible of Antillean *becoming*.[74] "He is not, after all Caribbean," Glissant argues, because "he is not involved in this history, in that he was free to walk away from it. Perse chose to wander aimlessly, to 'head West,' where the Western world was not only a concrete reality but an Ideal."[75] Yet the poet remains "vital to everyone" and "is Caribbean because of the primal, intertwined density of his style."[76]

One can hear overtones in this of Glissant's chiding of Lévi-Strauss and French ethnographers who remain spectators before the drama of history. But Perse was vital to Glissant in a very specific way and one that he never denied: his appropriation of the epic genre—none of which makes Glissant simply an anxious imitator. In fact, what becomes clear is the extent to which Glissant intentionally set out to answer and subvert Perse's mandarin voicing of Caribbean experience at a time when Perse was at the height of his career, and not merely as a critical afterthought in 1981, as might be supposed if one were looking only to *Caribbean Discourse*.

This revisionary poetic battle only becomes visible when Glissant's Paris writings are brought into relation with two of Perse's epic poems. *Vents* (*Winds*) was published in 1946, the year Glissant left Martinique for Paris, and was reprinted in 1953 in the first volume of Perse's collected poems, appearing just as Glissant was beginning to make his mark in the world of avant-garde poetry in Paris. Perse had first tried his hand at the epic in *Anabase* (1924); Glissant published a long poem responding to it called "Carthage," which was gathered in his 1960 collection *Le sel noir* (*The Black Salt*) but was originally published in 1956 the same year as *Les Indes*, in the pages of *Les lettres nouvelles*.[77]

Perse's *Anabase* is not directly interested in Xenophon's classical source but builds an entirely imaginary geography upon the mythemes of Orientalist travel writings (somewhat in the manner Italo Calvino uses in *Invisible Cities*), a feature that drew the attention and admiration of T. S. Eliot, who translated it in 1930. Glissant's "Carthage" extends the "prophetic view of the past" in *Les Indes* into the Mediterranean and Middle Eastern cultural imaginary that Perse appropriates in *Anabase*. With this Carthaginian perspective, Glissant's poem becomes a vessel for the echoing laments of peoples and cities whose names are synonymous with the defeated of the West, suturing the scars of the Punic Wars to the enslavement of the New World.

Readers of Perse's *Anabase* have noticed the prevalent use of *salt* in the poem's first canto. Perse's narrator calls himself *maître du sel* (master of salt) and the *trafic de sel* (the salt trade) is suggested as a metaphor for the "thirst" provoked in those seeking a higher spiritual knowledge.[78] John Drabinski notes that Glissant's "Carthage" repurposes its titular signifier "as a diasporic event, dislocated from linear time.... The salting of the earth in Carthage signifies its oceanic meaning, its proximity to the sea as history."[79] But in his poem, Glissant in fact answers "the master of salt" by taking up Perse's metafictional abstrusities and historicizing the tragic nature of a "traffic" that has cost the embodied flesh more than Perse's roving spiritual voyager could ever fathom:

> One forgets the
> first salt he tastes: behold him trafficking its essence. The world—and
> today one sees countless more plundered Carthages—feeds this fire
> within him to conquer, to kill. The docile sea is his accomplice.
> A people arrives; and is rationed its share of salt upon the labor of
> its wounds. At last free it laments upon the ashes. Salt is forever mixed
> with
> the victim's blood and with injured stones that were the toil of men.[80]

Glissant's black "salt of the earth" is not a commodity of abstract circulation; it is bitter seawater, at once forgotten and unforgettable because of its generality, because it repeats itself with ever "more plundered Carthages" heaped upon the ashes of history. Salt is the residual memory of the sea that unites distinct peoples whose wounds hurt in the same language—the memory of pain, the toil of men.

It is worth pausing to note the political implications and the ambition of Glissant's undertaking here, the scope of what is attempted between "Carthage," *Soleil de la conscience*, and *Les Indes*, these eruptions of a still-virtually-unknown black Martinican poet adrift in the cafés of Paris. Scholarship on Glissant and Perse has focused on filiation, but Glissant is not merely influenced by Perse's poetics. He deliberately and directly answers Perse—"Carthage" is a response to *Anabase*; *Les Indes*, a riposte to *Vents*.

It was during his US exile at the end of the war in 1945 that Perse began work on this second epic poem, which would address what he saw as a dark crossroads of history. The war, as he conceived it, represented humanity being buffeted by winds of change and fear, a storm that signaled the passing from one phase of civilization (a European legacy, now desiccated and withered from within) to a new pattern to be shaped by the United States of America, whose expansive landscapes would carry the torch onward, something like an updated version of Berkeley's "Verses On the Prospect of Planting Arts and Learning in America" (1752). In one of the few monographs in English devoted to the poet, René Galand calls *Winds* "an epic of mankind" that presents "the poet's summa, the conscious synthesis of his dominant motifs," and in which the titular winds challenge but also drive "explorers, conquerors, reformers, adventurers, dreamers," so that "the theme of geographical exploration is thus linked to the theme of historical becoming."[81]

One of the poem's leitmotifs is the cosmic tree of life, which struggles to persevere in the face of totalitarian barbarism and the threat of nuclear annihilation. The poem ends with a freestanding coda dated at the base of the text (highly unusual for Perse):

> Quand la violence eut renouvelé le lit des hommes sur la terre,
> Un très vieil arbre, à sec de feuilles, reprit le fil de ses maximes …
> Et un autre arbre de haut rang montait déjà des grandes Indes
>   souterraines,
> Avec sa feuille magnétique et son chargement de fruits nouveaux.
>   1945.[82]

In this final image, even as the "very old tree" of Europe that is now "barren of leaves" attempts to pick up its tired "thread of its maxims," "another tree of high rank is already rising from subterranean Indies, / With its magnetic leaf and burden of new fruits."[83]

This image would have immediately seized the attention of Glissant, whose later works feature the figures of the tree, the fruits of the New World, and "subterranean" or "submarine" relation. It cannot be a coincidence that "the Indies" from Perse's last page should reappear on the title page of Glissant's epic ten years later. Perse's *Winds* and Glissant's *Indies* both preoccupy themselves with the misadventure of human imagination impregnating the future of civilization with its visions; both share a grand theme of temporal disjuncture, the transition between two orders of power, one waning and the other on the cusp of being born, its submerged flanks like a chain of islands rising from the sea.

But Glissant goes further. He recenters the compass of Perse's prophetic vision of the future around his own "prophetic vision of the past," placing agency in the hands of the people produced by the colonization of the New World instead of an abstract Western man replenishing his stocks from its remaining untapped resources. What's more, Glissant's move can in no way be reduced to merely an aesthetic gesture.

Recall Glissant's odd inscription of his poem's date of composition, which I think O'Neill has mistranslated and misplaced. We can see now that this gesture echoes with a difference the fateful year of 1945 upon which Perse hinges the significance of his own epic. But why should Glissant's date matter—so much so that he included not simply the year but the three separate months, "Avril-mai-juin 1955," of composition as well? The answer is that these dates point to the Afro-Asian Conference held in Bandung, Indonesia, during the week of April 18–24, 1955, where the Non-Aligned Movement first took shape. This was an inflection point in anticolonial consciousness, an event that produced, as Vijay Prashad puts it, "a belief that two-thirds of the world's people had the right to return to their own burned cities, cherish them, and rebuild them in their own image."[84] Without romanticizing Bandung, it is still certain—beyond Prashad's affective rhetoric—that the conference held an epistemic significance for its attendees. It "summarized an alternative chronology of world events organized by intellectuals and activists of color who had been subjected to forms of racism, and class oppression."[85] Les Indes is Glissant's contribution to a conference he attended not in person but certainly in spirit.

Glissant's special emphasis on the spring months of 1955 informs us that the poem was composed not merely in the year of Bandung; it was begun the same month and completed in its immediate wake. By situating this time stamp where he does in the poem, Glissant is inserting it into its body, not placing it as a paraliterary mark for indexical or referential use, as O'Neill's placement of it on the title page of the 1992 translation suggests. The epic is a poetic genre that aims to include history within it. If Perse places 1945 at the conclusion of Vents, Glissant's "Avril-mai-juin 1955" incorporates the Bandung Conference into the body of Les Indes, as a fulcrum decisively shifting the direction of the winds of change.

With the alternative chronology of its form, the poem begins with a vision of the Indies in the European mind and, just before its end, gestures toward the collective imaginary of the so-called darker nations of the world, who at Bandung were determining the future—the rest of the relay to be run. Glissant's Blue Period writings, wrestling with Perse's West-centered version of postcoloniality, dwell in the penultimate moment before. To paraphrase Baldwin, the Indies, which began as a white man's dream, are transfigured as the dawning dream of the peoples they colonized—the dream of an end to white hegemony.

We Were the Indies

Because we cannot descry the human interests of the future *sub specie aeternitatis*, the fate of any single book can never be entirely known. It is never safe to reduce it to merely a set of sales figures or the number of its scholarly citations. The quantity of readers can mean less than who reads a work and how they read it. This is certainly the case with *Les Indes*, and I end my reflections on this poem by drawing attention to its impact on two of its most eminent Caribbean readers: the Guadeloupean novelist and essayist Maryse Condé and the Jamaican novelist, scholar, and theorist Sylvia Wynter.

Maryse Condé arrived in Paris in 1946, the same year as Glissant, not as a student but as a sixteen-year-old girl, the daughter of a privileged family obsessed with cultivating the good taste and lifestyle of the metropole away from their home life in Guadeloupe. Her island childhood is captured in her memoir, *Le cœur à rire et à pleurer* (1999; translated as *Tales from the Heart* in 2001), another portrait of the alienating formation of a black intellectual at the dawn of the era of decolonization. Born in 1937, Condé was too young to play a role in the Blue Period to which Glissant contributed with his early works. She came of age as that moment ended and revolutionary action once again became an immanent horizon of political possibility. Her formative years would pursue that trajectory, as she followed both her politics and her heart into the "African revolution," in Guinea and Nkrumah's Ghana.[86] But Condé's precocious intellectual awakening as a lonely, bookish, opinionated black girl in 1950s Paris was singularly marked by the works of black writers then just appearing.

In 2013, as part of a special issue dedicated to Glissant's life and work in the journal *Callaloo*, Condé chose to reflect not on the seminal *Le discours antillais* or on *La lézarde*, despite her interest in fiction. Instead, she remembers "reading that fabulous poem 'Les Indes' in 1955. I was twenty years old. I had hardly yet discovered Negritude, and there I was naively approaching this Édouard Glissant, like Aimé Césaire a Martinican writer, none of whose work I had read. I bought my collection of poems at the bookshop 'La Hune,' and sat down to read it on a bench by the church of Saint Germain des Prés."[87] Condé conveys something of the vertiginous effect of reading this grand poem as a black Antillean woman sitting on a bench in the heart of Paris: "These lines turned my ideas upside down, led me into unfamiliar and uncertain paths. *We* were The Indies."[88] As Glissant's poem unfolded it, "The world was not partitioned off, compartmentalized, as I had imagined, despite appearances to the contrary."[89]

Glissant's poem gave Condé a confidence and an imaginative range hitherto unimaginable from what she had believed to be her own marginal, provincialized position. The intellectual and creative fruits of this encounter are present very early in Condé's career. One can read it in her description of the Antilles as a "no man's land" stripped of any sovereignty claims (whether colonial or otherwise) in a caustic review of an anthology of Francophone Caribbean poetry from 1972.[90] And in the alienated, even cynical, voice of Veronica Mercier, the heroine of her first novel *Hérémakhonon* (1976), whose disillusioning experience of a postindependence West African state is also partly filtered through a bitterly ironic but also erotic relation to the black diaspora, as embodied for her by the handsome figure of a street sweeper on the rue de l'Université whom she remembers in the closing pages under the sign of a returning Parisian spring.[91] It would be an overstatement to say that one can read from this moment the birth of a writer—but it certainly helps reconstruct the importance of this text in its own time. It changes our image of 1950s Paris and the usual sketch of American black expatriates we are familiar with (e.g., Wright, Baldwin, Himes) to think of it also as the place where a young Maryse Condé read Édouard Glissant on a bench and saw herself and her future as a black writer open to the world in a new light.

We can also see echoes of the literary afterlife of *Les Indes* in the remarkable and overlooked role it plays in the thought of Sylvia Wynter, whose long career is only recently assuming its rightful place as one of the most important bodies of work in postcolonial and black studies. A distinctive aspect of Glissant's poem is its recuperation of Columbus's mistake—the projected fantasy of another India. The Indies are an error, but the errant voyage that follows produces a revolutionary knowledge of the world:

Et le marin dit qu'il croit même, enfants, qu'il est deux Indes,
    Deux levures d'or saignant!
Mais les Indes sont vérité.

And the sailor says that even he believes, children, that there
    are two Indies, two leavens of bleeding gold!
But the Indies are truth.[92]

Glissant accepts but subverts the European sailors' innocent, childlike dream of "two Indies." It is an ironic endorsement: the Indies of one man's fantasy are truth in a different sense, seen through the retrospective lens of a history available to the poet, who corrects the explorer from a point of view outside the sailor's epistemic frame.

This mistake, going against the theological teachings of the day, participates in what Wynter calls "the heresy in the discourse of Humanism" and, adopting Foucault's lexicon, "a counter-writing to the order of knowledge."[93] Wynter's scholarship—starting in the early 1970s at the University College of the West Indies, where she was particularly influenced by the historian Elsa Goveia, and continuing later at Stanford University—is preoccupied with the problem of reframing orders of knowledge. In Wynter's thought, what is required in contemporary critique is not a return to

European humanism but an analogous rift with the present order, comparable to that which the early moderns wrought upon the church's theological dogmas that held sway over the Middle Ages.

The Columbian contact with the New World is repeatedly invoked, to this end, as an ironic emblem for new horizons of knowledge. Her 1984 essay, "The Ceremony Must Be Found: After Humanism," even concludes by citing Francis Bacon's *Novum Organum*, comparing his own venture setting new foundations for knowledge to the explorer's: "just as Columbus did before that wonderful voyage of his across the Atlantic, when he gave the reasons for his conviction that new lands and continents might be discovered besides those which were known before; which reasons though rejected at first, were afterwards made good by experience, and were the causes and beginnings of great events."[94] For Wynter, as for Glissant, "The Indies" are the beginning of great events—events that have not yet come to pass because the revolutions that their "discovery" implied were themselves centuries in the making. The Bandung Glissant embeds through his time stamp, for example, is only one stop, though a decisive one, on the road toward the creolized future of a permanently interlinked global human society.

This rhetorical topos remains central to Wynter's 1989 essay "Beyond the Word of Man: Glissant and the New Discourse of the Antilles," which develops the same broad, transhistorical framework while responding directly to Glissant's *Caribbean Discourse*.[95] For Wynter, one of the key diagnostic features of Glissant's discourse is the "blocked/blockaded existential situation of the Antillean human subject as well as his or her empirical situation," one that she connects to the frustrated political ambitions of Thaël, the hero of *La lézarde*.[96] But she pushes further and urges "that we look at all the major themes of Glissant's works as themes which cross-link and cross-resonate with each other from one work, and one genre to another and as themes which constitute acts … performative acts of counter-meaning directed against the semantic character or behavior-regulating program, instituted by our present order of discourse."[97] This is what she herself performs in her reading, grafting Glissant's thought to her own preoccupations, which she rearticulates across his works, from the *Discourse* to the novels.

What Wynter's essay builds to, though, where it stakes its conclusion, is Glissant's early poetry and above all in *Les Indes*: "In his early epic poem *Les Indes*, Glissant had centered on Columbus's misconception within the context of the opposition, as Dash points out, between the reality and 'the illusion they sustain in people's minds.'"[98] Wynter then moves into an extended consideration of the implications of such paradigm-shattering encounters. While Wynter recognizes the need for a social maturation that can fertilize political emancipation, a project she finds in Glissant's novel *La lézarde*, her emphasis is on the underlying necessity of an imaginative and intellectual "Copernican shift" and a "cognitive autonomy" without which such politics cannot take hold. And it is this seismic shift from a Caribbean perspective that she connects back to the Glissant of *Les Indes*.

Wynter understands Glissant to perform that Copernican shift in *Les Indes*, making it the axis around which the centripetal force of *Caribbean Discourse* is generated. We might, mutatis mutandis, recognize *Les Indes* as the poem at the center of Wynter's ongoing project to formulate a reordering of discourse, the elevated "perspective of 1492" she goes on to elaborate in the 1990s. In her work from that period, Wynter seeks to account for "both the ecosystemic and sociosystemic 'interrelatedness' of our contemporary situation" by offering "a new world view of 1492 from the perspective of the species, and with *its* well-being, rather than from the partial perspectives, and with reference to the necessarily partial interests, of both celebrants and dissidents."[99]

We've seen the Columbian shift mark her conclusions before, but in the wake of her reading of Glissant, the sense and beauty of her thought is ramified, his insights contributing to the vision of a Caribbean matrix she sketches in the final lines of her essay: "the new frontiers of being and knowing that such a shift opens, that is to be, I believe, the gift of the New World to the Old, the gift specifically of that Other America, the Antilia of both Toscanelli's and Columbus's imaginary geography of some five centuries ago; today the Antilia of Glissant's dream for a fully realized archipelago, for the *avenir* of its small countries, for its collective freedom, as his oeuvre incites them to be, in their acts, in their desire. 'Mais les Indes sont vérité.'"[100] These closing lines, freighted with their own intonations of prophecy, look back to Glissant's poem of the midcentury while pulling those insights forward to 1989, that is, to the (putative) end of the Cold War.

By then, Édouard Glissant had spent nearly a decade working at UNESCO and would shortly move to the United States to teach. James Baldwin had died. Maryse Condé was beginning to publish novels that recovered archival voices from slavery and, in her 1986 novel *I, Tituba*, to creolize Salem and Nathaniel Hawthorne. Toni Morrison had published *Beloved*. Sylvia Wynter was still a relatively marginal theorist whose influence was mainly felt in the critical skirmishes over the direction and tenor of Caribbean literary criticism.[101] Some might have imagined that her quarrels would remain confined to the new precincts of area and ethnic studies and the small journals they served.

But today Wynter's theoretical writing is thriving at the heart of a discipline in which she for many years operated at the margins.[102] Ideas and the texts that bear them live according to variable calendars that are not always synchronous with the lives of those who write them. To put it another way, the temporality of reception is relative, elastic: what matters above all is perspective. One function of this study has been to recover and relay the connections that bind us to the flashes of the past so that we can see clearly how a midcentury moment in black writing came to be, why it mattered to those involved in making it, and how sometimes quietly or in unrecognized fashion the resonance of that moment has endured and may yet contain untapped potential for us now.

In 1957, Pierre Dumayet interviewed Édouard Glissant for French television on a cultural show called *Lectures pour tous*, with a focus on two books of poetry: *Soleil de la conscience* and *Les Indes*.[103] This archival record of Glissant might seem an apparently minor affair, but viewed through the prism of the intellectual and literary history I have traced, it rings with uncanny eloquence. Glissant begins by recounting a story about arriving in Paris in 1946 and encountering snow for the first time outside the Gare Saint-Lazare. He suggests that letters he wrote to friends back in Martinique trying to describe the snow that year were at the origin of the project that became *Soleil de la conscience*. In the interview, the two men discuss his Antillean background, and Glissant suggests, with a nod to the geopolitics of the Cold War, that in an era of "clashing" civilizations, he is reassured by the uniquely harmonious potential in the Antillean "synthesis."

With little time remaining, they pivot to a discussion of his latest publication, *Les Indes*. Dumayet wants to know what French readers should understand by this epic poem. Glissant seems to have anticipated the question; he knows the format requires a sound-bite response, and he has his answer ready: "S'il faillait résumer le poème d'une manière rapide, j'emploierais cette phrase: c'est Christophe Colomb qui est parti, et c'est moi qui suis revenue." "If I had to sum the poem up in one rapid phrase," Glissant says, "it would be thus: it was Christopher Columbus who left—it is I who have returned."

Vincent O. Carter's Exiles   [CHAPTER THREE]

I wipe my forehead with the back of my hand while he
studies me more closely. I don't look like a writer, he
thinks: I feel it. And then he thinks, How should a writer
look? His eyes grow narrow, as though he is on the verge
of asking me for my passport.

VINCENT O. CARTER, *The Bern Book*, 1953

What happens to black writers who take risks, who experiment formally but also, in a sense, biographically with their work and who, as a result, find themselves at the margins of an already-marginalized literary sphere? What needs to change in our grand narratives about the trajectory of black letters in the twentieth century in order that we recover these "outsiders"? One benefit of literary periodization is the impetus it provides to scholarship devoted to the recovery of missing or minor works. This principle applies to all literary studies, but within African American and Afro-diasporic studies, questions about archival loss and neglect are especially freighted.[1] Kinohi Nishikawa argues that the presumption that "the value of a recovered work rests primarily on its status as an *inherent* contribution to the African American literary canon" is an outdated fallacy that can obscure the significance of such "recoveries" by dwelling on an "ideology of textual presence" instead of making an "assessment of archival absence" that would ideally include "dwelling on the material conditions of a text's obscurity."[2]

The case of Vincent O. Carter's forgotten (and very nearly lost) writings from the 1950s and early 1960s provides an excellent example for precisely such a meditation. Two mutually reinforcing factors have converged to make Carter especially difficult to retrieve: his modernist sensibility and his self-imposed exile from the United States—further complicated by his hostility to literary community, including the expatriated network of black writers centered in Paris after World War II. The factor of exile can be blamed on Carter's eccentric temperament, an iconoclasm that he turned to literary profit but that made him socially invisible and practically unpublishable. The factor of style, however, is part of a pattern that has haunted literature that self-consciously presents itself as Afro-modernist, a descriptor that often overlaps with the category of the "experimental."

As Anthony Reed points out, "race and experimentation seem opposed" in most literary criticism, so that when they are invoked together two injurious assumptions get recycled.[3] On the one hand, critics continue to "tell the story as though white-identified techniques 'liberated' non-white writers from the limitations of race."[4] And on the other, "traditional genealogies of black writing tend to exclude this experimental subtradition" so that "experimental practices that fall outside of a handful of master tropes simply tend to be neglected."[5]

Although black experimental poetry and poetics have for some time seen a scholarly recovery, the black experimental novel has not fared as well.[6] William Melvin Kelley's novels, from *A Different Drummer* (1962) to *Dunfords Travels Everywheres* (1970); Albert Murray's trilogy *Train, Whistle, Guitar* (1974), *The Spyglass Tree* (1991), and *The Seven League Boots* (1997); Leon Forrest's *There Is a Tree More Ancient Than Eden* (1973) and *Divine Days* (1992): these books seldom generate sustained attention. Carter's work is far from being unique, but it presents an extreme case, in several respects.

In his work, several threads that characterize the specific quandaries of the Blue Period come together. Even the contingent fact that Carter came of age at a moment when black writers were identified with expatriation seems to have played an outsize role in his decisions about how and why to become a writer in the first place. His attempts to publish his work were equally afflicted by the swiftly changing feel of the times. But when he was ready, at last, to share his vision with the world, it was too late. The Blue Period had already ended, and a new affect, with a set of new cultural and literary politics, attended the reception of black writing.

This bad timing has long obscured a curious and little-known twist of literary history: James Baldwin was not the only African American writer visiting Switzerland in the mid-1950s. As it happens, in 1953, the same year Baldwin's "Stranger in the Village" appeared in *Harper's*, Vincent O. Carter was making his own voyage of expatriation, somewhat further north along the Alps to the city of Bern, where, for reasons that he would try to explain to himself and to a readership he imagined but never quite reached, he decided to stay for the following thirty years as one of the only black residents in that city.

The geographical coincidence of Switzerland and its symbolic resonance as a site of definitive "whiteness" at the heart of Europe is only one of the tantalizing similarities between Vincent Carter's autobiographical and essayistic meditations during this period and the essays of James Baldwin and Édouard Glissant examined in the preceding chapters. All three authors turned in this opening phase of their careers toward a defensive self-fashioning of literary authority, carved out through a process of agonistic isolation. By further isolating himself in a provincial rather than a cosmopolitan center, Carter lost the connections and access to cultural capital necessary for publication. His case raises important questions about how we should read such "outsider" texts that belong to a tradition yet have never been included in it, not only because of political and social marginalization but also because, even when they are reconsidered, they fail to appeal to the narratives we have retroactively applied to the period of their production.

To bring Carter and his work into view thus requires tracing the history of his (non)reception and filling in what little is known of his biography, a background essential to understanding the current place(less-ness) he holds. I follow this with readings of his two major works: *The Bern Book*, an essayistic memoir of Carter's arrival and first years in Switzerland, finished in 1957 and published in the United States in 1970, and *Such Sweet Thunder*, Carter's only published novel, a bildungsroman he started writing in the late 1950s and had mostly completed by 1963. The manuscript for the novel was rediscovered only in 2001 and published posthumously in 2003, twenty years after Carter's death in 1983.

Carter's writings show us that the Blue Period writer's aesthetic remove encourages a long view of one's place in literary history. They also show us that their formal commitments were not incompatible with a social and communal conscience. Black literature in this period could serve as a crucial tool for memorializing community, for retaining a record of specific patterns of black sociality, like those that Jim Crow segregation fostered. These qualities held little weight in the eyes of the political forces sweeping the postwar landscape. But Carter understood what those ideologies left out and what might become permanently lost unless the work of literature could keep black voices and memories alive for readers of a later day.

The Invisible Writer

Vincent Orieste Carter was born in Kansas City, Missouri, in 1924. The little we know about his early life has been mainly gleaned from the pages of *Such Sweet Thunder*, his luminous portrait of a black childhood in Jazz Age Kansas City and the early years of the Depression. The neighborhood he grew up in was a subsection of the historically black Eighteenth and Vine District. It was located at the northern end, east of the Paseo, and bounded to the north by Independence Avenue and what is now the Power and Light and Financial Districts to the West. The Kansas City Sanborn Insurance Maps (fig. 2) make it possible to visualize the neighborhood that Carter describes, a neighborhood that no longer exists, as it was replaced by the cloverleaf intersection of Interstates 29 and 70, completed between

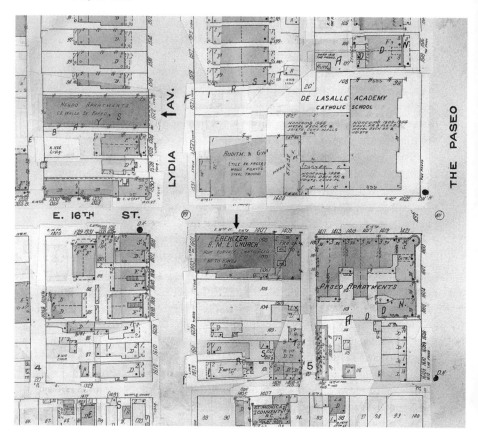

2 *Insurance Maps, Kansas City, Missouri, Volume 3, 1909–1957* (New York: Sanborn Map Co., 1957), 306 (detail). Note: "Negro Apartments" (upper left) and Ebenezer AME Church (center) are indicated by arrows. Copyright © 1957 by The Sanborn Map Company. Photograph: Missouri Valley Special Collections, Kansas City Public Library, Kansas City, Missouri.

1956 and 1958.[7] Carter's parents were both born in 1908, and Carter's extant correspondence suggests that his father died in 1968 or 1969, and his mother in 1972.[8] Joe and Eola Carter are the models for the characters Rutherford and Viola Jones, the parents of Amerigo Jones, the focalizing protagonist of *Such Sweet Thunder*. Like their fictional counterparts, they were teenage parents and working poor. Carter's father was a building maintenance man and later a bellhop in a hotel; his mother, like Viola in the novel, was a laundress.

Carter was drafted into the US Army in 1941, at the age of seventeen. He worked in a defense plant for a year before shipping out, and then participated in the Normandy landings in 1944 and the march toward the liberation of Paris. In 1945, while waiting to be demobilized, he appears to have gone to England to try to take classes at Oriel College, Oxford. But after failing exams, he returned to the United States, where he briefly worked as a cook on the Union Pacific Railroad before enrolling at Lincoln University in Pennsylvania, the country's oldest and one of its most prestigious historically black universities.[9]

Part of the Lincoln class of 1950, Carter quickly stood out as an aspiring literary talent. He majored in English, was president of the Philosophy Club and the Dramatic Club, and editor of the college paper, the *Lincolnian*, and he founded a group calling itself the New Literary Club, which professed to cater to "students interested in acquiring or improving their understanding and appreciation of the literary arts." He had a reputation on campus for being eccentric and introverted, an aloof persona given to wearing tweeds and smoking a pipe. These qualities are captured in his self-consciously effete yearbook captions: "not of this world ... ever in the world of becoming rather than the world of being ... I walk alone, barefooted in the spring ... uncanny ability for annoying the lecturer ... on to writing ... most abstract ... and still late for deadlines."[10] At Lincoln, he likely took courses with Roscoe Lee Browne, a graduate of the class of 1946 who had returned to teach English, French, and comparative literature as a charismatic, worldly postgraduate and talented athlete, before later embarking on his celebrated acting career in theater, film, and television.[11] After graduating, Carter moved to Detroit, where he spent eighteen months working in an automobile factory and taking classes at Wayne State University.

Shortly thereafter, with three thousand dollars in support from his parents and likely some savings, Carter left for Europe, following the vogue of the "rive noire." He arrived in Paris in the spring of 1953. A series of souring encounters there led him to move on further into Europe, first to Amsterdam, then to Munich, where he had American contacts from his time in the army, before pushing on into Switzerland. For the details of Carter's unusual trajectory, and most crucially, his decision to stay on in the Swiss capital (where over the following decade he would produce almost the entirety of his literary output), we are reliant upon his own account given in *The Bern Book: A Record of a Voyage of the Mind.*

Published by the John Day Company in New York City in 1970, *The Bern Book* was steered into a contract and got to press through the support of another American expatriate, Herbert R. Lottman (1927–2014), who became Carter's only conduit to the literary world. Lottman had attended New York University, studied abroad in Paris on a Fulbright in 1948, and returned in 1956 to try his own hand at writing a novel while working at the Paris offices of Farrar, Straus & Giroux and doing freelance journalism and criticism. Lottman would go on to become a successful biographer and cultural historian of nineteenth- and twentieth-century France, noted especially for his biographies of intellectuals and writers. But in the mid-1950s he was, not unlike Carter, a young man seeking to make a go of it as an American writer abroad.

Carter first contacted Lottman in 1957, reaching out to him by letter through a mutual acquaintance, Joe Kramer, an American medical student working in Bern. Kramer presumably put the two in touch under the assumption that Lottman's position as a white expatriate American in Paris with connections to the publishing world could be beneficial to an aspiring black expatriate writer in Switzerland. Carter seems to have imagined that a champion for his work acting on his behalf in cosmopolitan Paris would allow him to continue writing in provincial Bern. At first, this arrangement appeared to work. Carter sent Lottman updates and manuscript material, and Lottman returned words of encouragement and admiration.

Carter was working on a novel; in a letter from August 1958, he wrote, "I doubt if the new book will be finished before 1960—it is to be called *The Primary Colors*."[12] Carter's manuscript, which posthumously took on the title *Such Sweet Thunder*, was mostly completed by 1963. Lottman was impressed and showed the work to Ellen Wright, Richard Wright's widow, who was still living in Paris and who proved equally enthusiastic. With her support, the manuscript made its way to the offices of American publishers. According to Lottman, "between 1963 and 1968 *The Primary Colors* was read by eleven American publishers,"[13] but none was ultimately interested in taking it on.[14] Sometime in the 1970s, Carter gave up on trying to publish *The Primary Colors*. An unpublished, undated manuscript, likely from the late 1960s or early 1970s and carrying the working title "The Secret," concerns a writer's correspondence with a friend about his ongoing struggle to publish a book that keeps getting rejected.[15]

When their effort to get the novel published stalled, Lottman and Carter appear to have switched tacks and turned their attention to getting the autobiographical Bern material published instead. In 1970, Lottman published an article entitled "The Invisible Writer" in *Cultural Affairs*, the new quarterly journal of the Associated Councils of the Arts.[16] The title's allusive slant to Ralph Ellison's celebrated novel was not only alluring but also likely strategic. Ellison had joined the council's board in 1967, becoming its most prominent black representative and, as Arnold Rampersad notes in his biography, a vigorous defender of their activities.[17] In this elegiac article, which the John Day Company later redeployed to preface *The Bern Book*, Lottman laments the limited perspective of the publishing industry and evokes a spectral world of manuscripts, which he calls *la bibliothèque invisible*: unpublished books "circulating from hand to hand in the manner of the underground literature of contemporary Russia."[18] Lottman's Cold War analogy operates a surprising reversal, suggesting a kind of internal censorship in the capitalist West.

But of course, not all writers suffer invisibility equally, and one of the strange things about this introduction to Carter is the way it advocates for a neglected black author while simultaneously insisting that black writing is to blame for this invisibility, all the while speaking for the invisible black writer in question, in effect, producing a doubled elision. "Carter had been able to make me an admirer of black fiction," Lottman writes, "at a time I thought of it as simply a form of journalism (the best black writing of the time was protest and not fiction at all: *The Fire Next Time*, and Martin Luther King's *Letter from a Birmingham City Jail*)."[19] This framing suggests that black protest writing of the 1960s is why Carter failed to please white editors, who should nevertheless have known better and who allowed profit and political expediency to corrupt their taste. Lottman's praise for Carter's book includes a panoply of references to high modernism, including nods to James Joyce, Thomas Mann, William Faulkner, and Ernest Hemingway. In a bit of mannered phrasing, Lottman calls *The Bern Book* "this century's *Anatomy of Melancholy*." While this evokes some of the book's tone, there is not even a hint at the book's persistent theme of racial antagonism and the troubling effects of racial exoticism.

Lottman's eulogizing of Carter's writing was surely well intentioned, but this chance at a new reception was essentially a nonevent. The book did manage to get a reprint in 1973, and on that occasion, it even garnered a review by Nona Balakian in the *New York Times*.[20] Balakian's perceptive review, entitled "Black Odyssey, White World," captures the book's unsettling juxtapositions of poetic flight (she begins by evoking Rimbaud), mythic wandering, and racial alienation. But apart from this favorable review, there seems to have been no real critical interest in the book, and it quickly went out of print. Carter took up teaching English classes and began a relationship with one of his students, Liselotte Haas. He died in Bern in 1983.

The Bern Book and its author would not resurface until the turn of the millennium, when a series of chance encounters spurred a recovery. Darryl Pinkney formally reintroduced the existence of Vincent O. Carter to the world in his Alain LeRoy Locke lecture series at the Du Bois Institute at Harvard University in 2001. Entitled "Out There: Mavericks of Black Literature," these lectures were collected and printed the following year under the same title by Basic Books. Pinckney explains in his preface that he was given *The Bern Book* as a gift by Susan Sontag and Robert Boyers, who had come across it, apparently randomly, in a secondhand bookstore in upstate New York.[21] Pinckney's lecture provides an overview of the obscure fate of the author and his manuscripts, followed by a reading of *The Bern Book*, which veers from acknowledging its qualities as "a strange, disquieting, sometimes gorgeous account of what it was like for him to be the only black man living in Bern, Switzerland, between the years 1953 and 1957" to a moralizing indictment of Carter as "that familiar, defensive figure in the café, the man who refuses to be practical, the artist with impossibly high standards ... the black man who attacks the white friends who have just fed him or from whom he has just borrowed money."[22]

To be fair, Pinckney is a critic and novelist; his investments cannot be expected to be the same as those of a literary historian. But we find him nonetheless reiterating an unexamined commonplace about black expatriate writing, which endorses it only as a negative aberration: "The claim of *The Bern Book* now is not Carter's reputation—he was reviewed and filed away.... Carter's record of a voyage of the mind is also a record of trying, trying again, and failing. We can reject him, but we must accept his failure, because failure is also part of the history of the black American expatriate writer in Europe." This assessment recovers Carter only better to bury him with a normative disavowal, if not an outright dismissal. Pinckney asserts rather than argues for the "failure" of black American expatriate writing, recycling an inherited trope about black writing whose exclusionary effect may take place without our even having a chance to examine what it has left out. Carter's reputation is indeed not foremost in what's at stake anymore; but reading the recovered manuscripts ought to matter, because they indubitably exist and therefore must confirm, destabilize, or otherwise change how we understand the writing that emerged from this period.

This is especially true given that Carter's legacy no longer rests solely on the Bern memoir but also on his novel, *Such Sweet Thunder*, rescued at the last moment from oblivion. Chip Fleischer, a publisher from Kansas City and founder of the Vermont-based Steerforth Press, came across *The Bern Book* by way of a friend who noticed a copy, again, in a secondhand bookshop. Intrigued by Lottman's description of the manuscript for *The Primary Colors* in the preface, Fleischer decided to track it down. In the summer of 2001, he contacted Lottman, who informed him that Carter had died in 1983 and that his files on their correspondence had been lost while he was moving between apartments in Paris. Lottman recommended trying to find Carter's relatives in Kansas City, a search Fleischer undertook without success. Through several friends, however, Lottman was able to retrieve the name of Carter's Swiss girlfriend, Liselotte Haas, who it turned out was still living in Bern. She had the 805-page yellowing manuscript in a box under her bed. Haas sent it to Fleischer, and Steerforth published it in 2003 under the title *Such Sweet Thunder*, a tribute to its jazz-soaked pages and a fitting nod to Duke Ellington's tribute to Shakespeare, uniting two of Carter's artistic heroes.[23]

The novel was reviewed in the *New York Times* by Whitney Terrell, an up-and-coming novelist from Kansas City, a choice that strongly suggests the *Times*' editors assessment that the novel's publication represented a curiosity with some regional interest rather than a major literary event.[24] Terrell praises the novel's local color and recounts his sadness at discovering that "the novel's entire fictional world—its open porches, alleys and persimmon trees—had been replaced by the roaring throat of the Interstate."[25] He nevertheless goes on to disparage the novel's "demanding passages, occasional stream-of-consciousness riffs and unannounced flashbacks." He also reprises the standard political frame of reference for black writing, opining that Carter "is in essence a celebratory writer, not a voice of protest, and the thunder that sounds in his novel ... is meant to evoke the storm of sensation that illuminates American life."[26]

This negative press had substantive repercussions. The publisher, bowing to critical pressure, revised the manuscript, effectively redacting the author's opening. Carter's overtly Joycean experimentalism does make *Such Sweet Thunder* challenging by the standards of commercial fiction. But it is certainly less difficult than much of the Anglo-American modernist canon, including the likes of Beckett, Faulkner, and indeed Joyce; in fact, it is far less difficult in many respects than work by African American writers like William Melvin Kelley, Ishmael Reed, and Leon Forrest, whose *Divine Days* it arguably most closely resembles in ambition and style. All of this points to the rejection then and now of experimentation in literary form. But against that persistent negative appreciation, it also further confirms that a canon of black experimental fiction was already flourishing in the 1950s, one far richer than many suspect.

Heart of Whiteness

The flourishing canon of black experimental writing must include *The Bern Book*, given the indeterminacy of the text's genre and the eccentricity of its style. Both aspects are intertwined and reflect, in common with the other Blue Period authors in this study, the search for a method—a preoccupation with formal experimentation in the service of rendering black interiority, of prioritizing the "quiet" modes of resistance Kevin Quashie describes, modes that are personal, subtle, and psychological rather than public, explicit, and communal.[27]

Written entirely in the city of Bern between 1953 and 1957, Carter subtitled *The Bern Book*, "A Record of a Voyage of the Mind," a phrase that immediately highlights the text's ambiguous genre, situated somewhere at the intersection of travelogue, memoir, and personal essay. In his brief introduction, Carter makes clear he is not constructing a work of fiction: "I have no intention of making a book of this, of altering the facts and impressions which have cost me so much pain and effort to acquire," he writes.[28] He is concerned, rather, with recording a transformation within himself: "I merely intend to give utterance to certain strong feelings which have changed my life to such a great degree that I can say—neither in despair nor optimism, but with utter realism—that I shall never be the same."[29] This suggests a conversion narrative in which the transformation of racial consciousness takes the place of religious epiphany. It is a testimony: "the scene of my partial metamorphosis (which is still going on) is the city of Bern."[30]

The author's attitude toward this endeavor is one of ironic hauteur: "nor would I have thought that I intend these pages to represent a social scientific study of the city of Bern or of the Swiss nation." Like Baldwin and Glissant, Carter invokes the ethnographic, "social scientific" gaze only to disavow it; this pseudoethnographic discourse and its attendant tropes form a leitmotif in the text, which Carter calls "essentially a travel book, a *Reisebuch*."[31] Carter's use of German here is not incidental. He almost certainly has a material example in mind, namely the *Meyers Reisebücher*, the popular series of German-language guidebooks published between 1862 and 1936 by the Bibliographisches Institut, founded by the German industrialist and publisher Joseph Meyer (1796–1856). The Reisebücher series, which notably included a guide to Switzerland from 1897 and was reprinted several times, including in 1906 and 1910, was a handsome pocket-size book with colorful maps perfect for a curious bibliophilic visitor like Carter browsing secondhand bookstores in Bern in the 1950s.[32]

But there is a secondary significance to the choice of terms here as well. Meyers produced popular guidebooks, but the best-known product of the Bibliographisches Institut was its encyclopedia *Meyers Konversations-Lexikon*, a standard reference work published in successive editions from 1839 to 1984.[33] This may explain why Carter doesn't compare his work to the more familiar Baedeker, which is never referred to as a "Reisebücher" but as a "Reiseführer," more literally "travel guide." It seems likely that Carter wanted the term *Reisebücher* to convey a project whose extended connotations are not leisure but knowledge.

In an article that revisits the little-known history of blackface minstrelsy in Germany and its lingering afterlives, Jonathan Wipplinger observes that the theoretical definition of the comic, or "der Komisch," in the 1896 *Meyers Konversations-Lexikon* was divided into three separate categories: objective, subjective, and naive. The reference book illustrates the lowest form of comedy—the objective—by offering three examples: "of someone who had first appeared to be quite secure in his gait; of the laughter of children and the uneducated in experiencing things beyond their comprehension; and finally of the experience of *seeing a black person for the first time*. As we are told, the objectively comic exists 'für den der zum erstenmal einen Neger sieht.'"[34] The ambivalent comic valence of "seeing a black person for the first time" is the central conceit around which Carter organizes his own *Reisebuch*. Indeed, the text is organized as a digressive set of reflections prompted by the aporia, the rhetorical impasse, which marks the underlying disbelief surrounding the narrator's site of enunciation: how can a black man be a writer—and what is that black writer doing in the city of Bern?

The Bern Book begins with the narrator recounting his habitual strategies of evasion whenever (inevitably on a regular basis) he is called upon to explain his profession and, by extension, his presence in the Swiss capital:

> "Are you a musician?"
> "No," I reply—coldly.
> "Student?" he persists, noticing now my ancient briefcase.
> "No, I'm not a student," I reply, a little irritated but not altogether unsympathetic.[35]

The narrator maintains a reserve of ironic sympathy for the confounded inhabitants who seemingly cannot help themselves in their interrogations. But when he finally avows that he is a fiction writer, the fact settles in hard:

> He has never or seldom met or heard of, though he suspects there probably must be, Negroes who write.... I can literally see him straining his imagination to accommodate the new idea of me with which I have confronted him. I can feel him lifting me out of the frame of his previous conception of the universe and fitting me first this way and that, like a piece of a puzzle, into the picture of the writer his mind is conjuring up. He is struggling with Goethe and Rilke and Gotthelf and Harriet Beecher Stowe and me.[36]

The inclusion of Jeremias Gotthelf, the pen name of Albert Bitzius (1797–1854), on this list is a subtle but pointed way to convey how the purported outsider reappropriates authority (in this case, the literary authority of an imputed canonical awareness) and shows exactly what he knows better than his interlocutor. There seems to be a kind of literary-insider joke here, too: Gotthelf's best-known work, *The Black Spider*, is a horror story (with a self-evidently suggestive title to the eyes of a black author) constructed around the small-minded fears and repressed desires unleashed by the inhabitants of a Swiss village upon the arrival of a stranger in their midst.

Despite the narrator's assurances that he is in fact a writer and that he came voluntarily to Switzerland, his interlocutor cannot be satisfied: "'But *why* did you come to Bern anyhow?' What he really meant was: Why did you come to Bern? That is to say: Why didn't you stay in America? And that meant: I know why you didn't stay in America you poor devil! Aren't you glad to be in Bern where the people are not mean to you?"[37] Once again, Carter effectively reverses the authority of the Bern native, dissecting his intentions with a one-sided tracking that reinterprets and reassembles the other's mind. The language game is just that—a game the narrator has learned to play by force of its constant iterations. The questions of the Bernese are predictable, the scripts unvarying, and the narrator has perfected the art of toying with his pursuers. He tells us that he always waits for the conversation to reach this crucial and inevitable turn before leveling the answer he knows will disturb them the most: "'Oh, I've come to study the decadence of European culture. Look at that!' I exclaimed exultantly, pointing discretely to a puny young man sitting on the opposite end of the bar. 'Have you ever seen anything like that? A grown man drinking beer with a straw!… I've heard that Switzerland is one of the most primitive countries in Europe, where the cultural level of the people is the lowest possible and unthinkably decadent.' I smiled inwardly as he writhed in his seat."[38] The subversive inversion of relations between provincial and cosmopolitan, primitive and civilized, racial blackness and cultural whiteness, is grist for the textual mill.

Although there are indications of pain and melancholy in Carter's relations to his adopted surroundings, his narrative suggests a process of sublimation through humor. Like Baldwin in "Stranger in the Village," Carter is initially horrified by the fact that children run after him in the street shouting "Neger! Neger!" unaware of how that word echoes for a black American. But Carter is also tickled when the townsfolk of Bern take to addressing him "on the street as '*Der Negus*!'" in the months after Haile Selassie's visit to Bern in 1954.[39] Again, reversal and racial irony are twined, the complicit discourses of colonial authority and white supremacy challenged by the voice of a black subject who wields his knowledge of their workings against them. The Blue Period aesthetic of ironic ethnographic reversal that we saw Baldwin deploy in a tragic mode and Glissant in an epic one emerges in Carter as high comedy.[40]

This is reflected in *The Bern Book*'s parodic relation to the stylistics of classical European travel writing. The text is replete with mock-Victorian chapter headings; sardonic observational asides suggestive of Sterne's *Sentimental Journey*; the casual dispensation of digressive generalizations on national character; and habits typically associated with the literature of the grand tour, a literary pilgrimage trope that Lisa Colletta reminds us "is not just adventure nor merely leisure" but "rooted in Western culture's ideas of taste, sophistication, knowledge, and class."[41] Consider a sampling of chapter headings:

"Why I Did Not Go to Paris"

"A Chapter Which Is Intended to Convey to the Reader the Writer's Fair-Mindedness"

"EVERYBODY, Men, Women, Children, Dogs, Cats, and Other Animals, Wild and Domestic, Looked at Me—ALL the Time!"

"Some General Changes in My Attitude As a Result of My Preliminary Experiences with the Bernese People"

"A Little Sham History of Switzerland, Which Is Very Much to the Point, and Which the Incredulous or the Pedantic May Verify by Reading a Formal History of Switzerland, Which I Have Certainly Never Done, and Will Probably Never Do"

Mikhail Bakhtin defines "double-voicing" as a discourse that "has a twofold direction—it is directed both toward the referential object of speech, as in ordinary discourse, and toward *another's discourse*, toward *someone else's speech*."[42] Carter's narration precisely employs such a double-voiced stance. He grapples with the phenomenological experience of intense racialization in a "white" space while simultaneously and playfully interlaying that experience within a discourse that is usually deployed either against or in ignorance of persons like himself—those who are passively assumed not to possess the requisite "taste, sophistication, knowledge, and class" or to have opinions worth considering.

And yet *The Bern Book* trades precisely on these very indexical markers of cultural authority and power, which is what makes its premise so humorous. Carter jests when he says that he is in Switzerland to study a "primitive" culture, but his ethnographic readings of the inhabitants of Bern inevitably do end up constituting something like a study of their "whiteness." Among the book's many digressions, he considers the suitability of trams as a method of public transit, the precarious social status of girls who work in tearooms, the tendency of the Bernese to overdress, aspects of Swiss politics both domestic and international, and the many difficulties in trying to secure lodgings in Bern as a black man. He is particularly concerned by the Swiss tendency to stifle any creative impulse, such that artists are forced eventually to leave and go into exile—a none-too-subtle rapprochement of a Swiss and American cultural "whiteness" obsessed with order, regulation, and commerce, inimical to artistic experimentation and creativity.

This ethnographic study of "whiteness" comes to a kind of climax with

Carter's relativizing "discovery"—an epiphany he subsequently attempts to share with his Bernese coffee shop companions—that the Swiss have an inferiority complex vis-à-vis the Germans, that "they, the Germans, are to the Swiss what white Americans are to black Americans!"[43] It is not only that Switzerland is provincial; it is also that the Swiss themselves are analogically "black" with respect to the Germans. By relativizing and destabilizing the presumed authority and centrality of "whiteness," Carter exposes it as a socially sanctioned discourse operating on ignorance and parochialism, one that deflates under scrutiny and individual example.

A Stillness as Intense as a Roar

Carter's critique of white European norms and assumptions can be said to constitute the core argument of *The Bern Book*, its site of engagement with racial politics. But the project of unveiling racial bias and prejudice cannot account for what Claudia Tate might call *The Bern Book*'s "surplus desire," the "unconscious discourse … those longings that are inscribed in the novel's most deeply encoded rhetorical elements," features that exceed the conceivable and legible political aims set forth therein.[44] These excesses, like Carter's loving descriptions of the city of Bern, of his solitary wandering through its streets and of the views from its bridges, all suggest that emblematic figure of modernity we now recognize in a familiar line from Walter Benjamin back to Baudelaire: the flâneur.

Is the category of the flâneur available to the black subject?[45] Put another way: What is the function of loitering in an overwhelmingly white space? What does it do to black thinking and black writing? What changes when one loiters in what has predominantly and historically constituted itself as a racially exclusionary genre? Tate's framework allows us to see that the unconscious desire of Carter's text, the surplus that keeps propelling its narrative forward, is precisely the fantasy that the status or the category of the flâneur will become available to the black writer. The urban passageways of Bern effectively become the test sites for a desire that the narrative repeatedly reenacts as a series of disappointments and disruptions, each characterized by the reassertion of racialization.

For example, after Carter takes up a job writing for Radio Bern, he comes to believe that he has finally been accepted by his colleagues and friends because they begin to call him "Herr Carter" and not simply "Der Neger." But this accomplishment in relative assimilation only emboldens one of them to ask Carter to take a role as a street vendor in a play, where he is "supposed to cry out, 'Oysters! Oysters!' melodiously and smile ingeniously, happily, childishly, as Negroes are supposed to do."[46] Carter balks at the stereotype, clearly a cheap imitation of DuBose Heyward, but

ends up "accepting it because I needed the money."[47] He fears being rid-
iculed and ashamed on stage, but to his surprise, the audience is respect-
ful and the "good taste" of the director allows him to leave the playhouse
feeling "triumphant." But in its wake, this triumph is immediately undercut; it was really just a triumph of repression, of having trained himself to
ignore and elide slights, not their disappearance:

> I even learned to enter the Mövenpick without flickering an eyelid.... A
> friend walked up to me one day, as I was ordering a beer, and ordered one,
> too, exclaiming that it had been a long time since he had seen me, con-
> cluding with the observation: "Wince, [sic] you're the only nigger in Bern,
> are you not? I was just thinking of it today." And I, without spilling a drop
> of beer from my glass or choking upon a hidden desire to throw it into my
> friend's face, replied: "Why, yes—yes—I ... believe I am," placing the glass
> quietly upon the counter. I had never felt better in my whole life.[48]

This sublimation of internalized racism is the passive cost the black flâneur
must bear. The emotional valence of the last line in the passage is far from
clear; the hesitant diction and the adverbial modification to the ensuing
gesture both color the assertion with a powerfully tense and ambivalent
irony. The desire for assimilation—although it's not even clear that's entirely what it is—is belied by a textual unconscious brought to the brink of
violence, left simmering with an unspeakable surplus of feeling and of remembrance that must be actively suppressed.

   If the flâneur is the figure of literary modernity, then the literature of the
Blue Period records the attempt of black writers like Carter, ideologically
homeless and possessed of a melancholic disposition, to make flâneurism
their own. The "blue" perspective is in part the view produced by the isolated black consciousness in the white crowd; the style of thought it produces is pointedly evasive and digressive. But it is also a doubled negation
maneuvering against the disciplinary power of capital and the power exerted by the expectations of racial constructs. As Susan Buck-Morss has
said: "The fantasies which populate the reverie of the flaneur are also a
form of resistance. Like the worker's daydreaming at the machine, they
are a survival of that 'heroic laziness' which Marx feared was threatened
by industrialism."[49]

   Carter's peripatetic reveries are a form of resistance to the laws of productivity in this sense, yet they must also simultaneously, and paradoxically, resist the stereotype of the "lazy black," illustrating the differential
precarity of this role for the black subject. There is, in effect, an uneven
access to reverie in a world where a cosmopolitan modern black writer is
still expected to play the role of the minstrel, a world where no matter their

own desires, the black writer must first overcome a far greater socially and historically sanctioned set of desires that others have for them. Part of the melancholy comedy of Carter's account is precisely that, despite his apparently sincere affection for his adopted European milieu and his valiant attempts to embody the café-loitering writer's "heroic laziness," he must still undertake yet another heroic struggle: to endure the ceaseless and blatant racialization of his person.

With its brocaded meditations on the city's architecture and social life, Carter's text could be said to conform to the precepts of the vogue for psychogeography among the situationist vanguard at the time. Instead, tellingly, it reveals certain assumptions underpinning situationist psychogeography in the first place, such as the receptivity of urban space to the presence of loafing white writers. How ironic that a black vanguardist writing at the same time (and unbeknownst to them) was performing a critique of psychogeography avant la lettre, as it were. Indeed, *The Bern Book* is arguably more radical than Guy Debord's *dérives* and *détournements*, and arguably more "heroic" in its dedication to art and literature than, say, Ernest Hemingway's 1964 *A Moveable Feast*, a classic memoir of American flânerie in Europe. After all, Debord's critiques of spectacular capitalism, while highly prescient, had little to say concretely about the politics of race and decolonization, and Hemingway, who famously tells us he was poor but happy during his time in Paris, was never called a nigger at his favorite bar.[50]

Debord and the situationists, frustrated with the Old Left and its ideological dogmas, were obsessed with "strategy." For Debord this meant using aesthetics to disrupt the normal functions of spectacular capitalism and open breaches for political action and thought. In the Blue Period, black writers like Carter were thinking along the same lines but with a critical difference: the quotidian occurrence of racialization was foundational to the production of subjectivity for them, unlike for the situationists and other Western Marxists, who treated race as secondary, symptomatic, and ancillary to the dialectic of class struggle. This explains the insistent turn in Blue Period writings to the grounds of everyday experience and the interiority of black subjectivity—this was the black psychogeography that remained uncharted, unprofitable, and often unpalatable to the political common sense of the day.

The politics of loitering are complex. In the writings of the Blue Period, they embody an affective relation toward an oppressive organization of society while also supplying prospectively the ideal of a society that does not yet exist but that could or would under other circumstances. As Buck-Morss puts it: "The gesture of loitering points in two directions. It is a condemnation of capitalism to which exploitative labor and unemployment are intrinsic. But it is also the hellish, negative image within existing society of that which could become positive within a radically different one."[51] For Carter, a loitering black writer adrift in a white world that has not yet caught up to the possibility he is trying to incarnate, the city of Bern becomes that "hellish, negative image," full of a promise that could be enjoyed only within the paradigm of a future world "radically different" from the one he can see from the vantage point of the midcentury.

This negative landscape—or landscape in negative—presented by the high-contrast figure of his own blackness against the enduring whiteness of an overidealized Europe, forced the writer into a retreat into the self. In a passage set off toward the end of the book he writes: "In the city of Bern I have encountered a stillness which is as intense as the roar of the traffic of New York. There I could not hear for the noise; and here in Bern I could not hear for the silence."[52] *The Bern Book* is saturated with passages like this, reflecting its characteristically Blue Period melancholy and sense of monastic retreat. This turn of mind foreshadows the Buddhist philosophy that Carter would eventually adopt in the 1970s and that would grow ever more important to him in his final years, as he gave up hope in the publication of his novel and eventually stopped writing altogether. In a sense, for Carter the Blue Period never ended. As the new militancy of the late 1960s and 1970s changed the terms of black writing and discourse, he remained in Bern, refusing to return or to engage with the new times.

The end of *The Bern Book* returns this problem of temporality to the framework of the Cold War. The narrator pens an eerie and surreal dream letter addressed to General Henri Guisan, a military hero famed for mobilizing Swiss resistance against the possibility of a Nazi invasion. The letter hints, with a sly campy verve, at Cold War paranoia ("I have *not* been spying"), and there is a Swiftian mischievousness to its last pages.[53] Carter suggests that he has knowledge of the Swiss military's acquisition of uranium, and he recommends they use it to defend themselves and keep it secret: "you must not let the Russians and Americans know it."[54] He recommends the plans for national defense (to which he has somehow gained access) that call for the Swiss to "flood the valleys, plug up the holes and run underground until all this nonsense is over."[55] He describes a dream vision of the city of Bern as it would appear re-created in "submarine" form, hidden away from a world presumably blasted away in a Cold War–triggered nuclear disaster. This apocalyptic vision of the world above and the recommendation of a stay in the world below the surface do not fail to echo Ellison's *Invisible Man*.

Blue Period writers tend toward configurations that echo the idea of

Ellison's strategic "hibernation." Like Baldwin's higher view of history in the Swiss village of Loèche and Glissant's island consciousness of history's reversal seeded in the depths of a Parisian winter, Carter's errant perch in the Swiss capital transforms the hypervisibility of blackness and its attendant alienation into a new perspective imbued with newly conceived literary and intellectual authority. In Carter's imagination, the entire capital of one of the "whitest" countries on Earth can be transfigured from a provincial administrative capital to an imaginary spiritual retreat for a black artist willing to risk terrible isolation to live beyond the forces of political history, beyond the reach of the Cold War rivalries that would obliterate him. For Carter, there is little hope for the independent black artist in the present and only a dim sense of a utopian postapocalyptic world. His *Reisebuch* records a voyage of a mind that cannot escape this aporia and must instead think through the condition of being "black and blue" as a willed and chosen form of exile.

The Bern Book is, in this respect, somewhat like the diary of a pioneer frontiersman who has "gone native"—except that the irony of a black perspective on that inversion can never be fully sublimated. The melancholic comedy of this predicament, always at the edge of a cool fury, is the book's subject: if it were fictional, this rhetorical performance would yield an allegorical "thought experiment," a speculative racial allegory. But the authenticating documentary quality of this "life experiment" (supplied, for instance, by the author photographs taken in Bern) gives the text a testimonial pathos that makes it altogether harder to pin down. By the time one reaches its culminating apocalyptic ruminations and philosophical consolations, there is a parallax effect: the dead end of the narrative meets our knowledge that the writer's life—although it did later end there in Bern—did not end then with the publication of this strange, estranged text in 1970.

It very nearly did, though. Vincent Carter's legacy might have been summed up entirely by *The Bern Book*. Indeed, for several decades after his death in the early 1980s, it was all that was known of his work. It turns out, however, that this picture of Switzerland was only half the story; the other half would prove a sharp contrast. In his fiction, Carter would bend and stretch novelistic form to reconstruct the phenomenological, social, and experiential qualities of the world he had left behind, the memory, the sounds, music, and violent sensations, of the black American community that made him. It is a great irony that Carter, arguably the most isolated and alienated writer of the Blue Period, produced one of the most intensely lyrical, Proustian, and vibrant novels ever written about an African American community.

Archive of "The Village"

In an undated letter from 1973, Vincent Carter wrote to Herbert Lottman in Paris about his return to the United States the year before to attend his mother's funeral. This letter is important for several reasons. First, it is written in a fluid style very different from his other more colloquial correspondence, suggesting its personal importance to the author, who clearly used the occasion to compose his thoughts. Second, in a key passage, Carter connects the major themes that animate his manuscript, which then had the working title *The Primary Colors:* family, jazz, and the urban fabric of Kansas City. Mourning his family members is linked to mourning the passing of a community and the world they made, which has been physically erased by the major Cold War urban-planning project of the 1950s: the rise of the highway system and its attendant development of suburbs, the interlinked social transformations that precipitated what Thomas J. Sugrue calls the "postwar urban crisis" and has popularly come to be called "white flight."[56]

Because so little documentation on Carter is extant, it is worth quoting at length from this letter, which (unless new material surfaces) appears to be the most significant document we have for contextualizing his view of his only completed fictional work:

> My father died like that, unobtrusively, about five years ago. My mother didn't want me to know about his illness because she didn't want me to worry, so he died before I could get there. She would have gone the same way had friends not sent word. She died last year, facing south, naked as a baby, with her eyes wide open, as though she were gazing upon some distant horizon. And I think she was. We had spent seven weeks together, forty-nine days and nights. We had talked a lot and laughed a lot (there were no tears) and prepared ourselves for the journey. "It's not far, just close by, through an open door …" Joe Thomas played it on his horn at the funeral. Quiet and easy he played it, like a fine jazz-man, without sentimentality, and in perfect taste. And I was happy about the whole thing because I knew that that was the way she wanted to go.
>
> She told me what to do with her things. I did it, and walked out of the empty apartment in which I came to live from the alley down on Independence Avenue when I finished grade school when I was twelve, and where she and my dad had lived for over 35 years.
>
> It had all changed, Herb, it was all different now; the people were gone and the houses were gone; in their place was a super highway—only the light was the same: sunlight at seven in the morning, at noon, at five o'clock

in the evening when dad used to come home from the hotel. Perhaps it was when I boarded the plane for New York that I realized that nothing had been lost. I had written it all down—that fabulous world of childhood, the world of mom and dad young, laughing and in tears. It was all in *The Primary Colors*, my way, and what I couldn't say, because one can never say it all, is written in my heart.[57]

This letter makes clear that Carter's writing was motivated by the urge to preserve a community whose way of life and material traces had been obliterated by the postwar transformation of Kansas City's urban fabric, a transformation that took place precisely during the years of his Swiss exile. The novel he wrote was organized, accordingly, with two forms in mind: the autobiographical *Künstlerroman* narrative of a young black boy's journey from Jim Crow soil into literary and artistic consciousness, and the social realist documentary, a work of historical reconstruction whose bricks-and-mortar realism is intended to memorialize a community.

These two commitments brought conflicting formal pressures to bear upon the text. For the *Künstlerroman*, Carter followed Joyce's example in *Portrait of the Artist as a Young Man*, opting for an organic narration with a syntax mimetically evolving as the subjective awareness and intelligence of his protagonist expands. The archival component, however, required an empirical accuracy, a grounding objectivity to counterbalance the introversion of the artist with the collective experience of a community. Carter's solution was to turn to the black press, to use the robust print culture of the prewar African American newspaper as a choric vehicle. It is no coincidence that Carter turned to the black newspaper as a literary device; it is consistent with that medium's archival potential, especially during the years leading up to the Cold War. The polyphonic capaciousness of its claims to racial representation made it vital, which in turn makes it an excellent vantage point from which to analyze the novel.

The black city life that flourished in the interwar period despite, and in some ways because of, Jim Crow grew out of the Great Migration of black Americans out of the South. This massive transformation, as Isabel Wilkerson notes, left its "imprint everywhere in urban life," affecting "the social geography of black and white neighborhoods, the spread of housing projects as well as the rise of a well-scrubbed black middle class, along with alternating waves of white flight and suburbanization."[58] Carter's parents were early migrants to Kansas City, and he grew up with a mixed generation that included older settlers (some of them Exodusters) and an ongoing influx of new arrivals from the South, all crowding into the Eighteenth and Vine "colored" section of town. By taking as his subject matter the lives of ordinary people seeking to establish themselves in a new metropolis, *Such Sweet Thunder* is recognizably part of what Farah Jasmine Griffin calls "the migration narrative," which involves departure from the South but also "confrontation with the urban landscape [of the North] usually experienced as a change in time, space, and technology as well as a different concept of race relations."[59]

In her influential 1981 essay "City Limits, Village Values," Toni Morrison (circling back to, inter alia, Baldwin and Chartres) argues that black writers and therefore the black literary tradition has always maintained an attitude toward the city distinct from what she calls the "responses of mainstream American writers to post-industrial decay."[60] There is, she suggests, a distinct sense of belonging *within* urban space that reflects communal or what she calls "village values," with their own sensibility, loyalties, and mores. As Morrison writes, "the affection of Black writers (whenever displayed) for the city seems to be for the village within it: the neighborhoods and the population of those neighborhoods."[61] For this reason, black writers can imagine, and by implication black readers might seek out, "a hero who prefers the village and its tribal values to heroic loneliness and alienation."[62] Carter was attracted to both. In *The Bern Book*, he adopted the pose of the alienated heroic expatriate to acquire (while also subverting) the trappings of the literary field dominant in the early postwar years. But when it came time to write his novel, he turned back to embrace the "village" he grew up in, his home patch of Kansas City.

In *Signs and Cities: Black Literary Postmodernism*, Madhu Dubey is skeptical of Morrison's views (in "City Limits, Village Values" and the 1984 essay "Rootedness: The Ancestor as Foundation") on the relation of blackness, writing, and cities. For Dubey, the "dramatic transformations of US urban order since the 1970s have rendered the idea of community increasingly abstract and experientially unknowable, feeding into the crises of representation associated with postmodern culture."[63] Dubey suggests that instead of advancing nostalgic arguments invested in "the notions of community and national identity that might be represented through print culture," the better and "properly postmodernist" thing to do was "to welcome the impending technological and political obsolescence of print culture, having exposed its imagined community to be a false totality."[64] Dubey's argument—and what it elides—ought to provoke a reconsideration of what counts when we interrogate the archive of print literature and its relationship to racial representation, community, or, in Morrison's terms, "the village."

Dubey contends that Morrison's argument is oxymoronic: "the novel is political to the extent that it can address an audience—'you'—that is equivalent to the village or the community. But by the logic of Morrison's own argument, the emergence of the novel is contingent on the disappearance of exactly this sort of community."[65] It seems entirely plausible, however, that works can speak to audiences and be "about" them whether or not that community continues to exist (the case of Holocaust literature and literature of the Jewish diaspora comes to mind). And Morrison's theory of the black novel relies not upon the disappearance of a community but upon the disappearance of certain material forms that did, in fact, historically bind that community. This includes the pieces of the urban fabric with both economic and social functions (e.g., mom-and-pop stores, black-owned banks, social-club meeting houses, storefront churches), as well as their organized advocacy and expression in the public sphere via local newspapers that were owned by, employed, and explicitly directed at community members. It is no coincidence that the decline of these self-determining aspects of the black urban community was coterminous with the gutting of the inner city by highways and the precipitous decline of tax revenue and property value precipitated by white flight, transformations that began in the 1950s and created the very conditions that Dubey attends to in her analysis of the black novel post-1970.[66]

Dubey's periodizing project aims to historicize the response of post-1970s (mostly post–civil rights) writers to a fractured audience comprising a black community divided by class between a population that was able to take advantage of the changes wrought by the civil rights agenda (through affirmative action, for example) in order to move away (often to previously unavailable suburbs) and those left behind in deteriorating urban cores with high rates of joblessness, defunded public assistance and public housing, and a flood of foreign drugs from the destabilizing late–Cold War conflicts in Central America.

But for Dubey's periodization to make sense, we need a discrete periodization of the early Cold War years that led up to it, one that contends with the drastic material transformations that interrupted the promise the Great Migration generations sought to fulfill in the urban North. Redlining and housing segregation is a part of that story. Less discussed, however, is the role of the interstate highway, a Cold War project that fundamentally altered the structure and space of American life along racial and class lines as Tom Lewis makes clear in his history of the implementation and consequences of the Federal-Aid Highway Act.[67] The case of Kansas City's black neighborhoods is both an exemplary and a devastating casualty of this phenomenon. To understand what is at stake in Carter's *Such Sweet Thunder*, one must reckon not only with what he set down for the record but also with what the loss of the "village" he describes means in the context of American history, and African American history in particular.

The pressure of Dubey's claims for the rejection of "the village" as a concept lies in what she calls "the extreme difficulty of sustaining folk claims to racial representation in the medium of print literature."[68] Because she is heavily invested in the trope of the book and its afterlife in a historical period in which she is correct to assert its weakness relative to newer technologies of mediation, she fails to appreciate the wealth of at least one medium of print literature that sustained during its heyday a robust claim to racial representation: the black newspaper. A robust consideration of that medium would have to include the allegedly subliterary genres of pulp fiction that circulated widely in black communities in the interwar and postwar periods, and indeed continue to enjoy a vast (though often unrecognized or disparaged) circulation to this day.[69] Indeed, much of this fiction circulated in serialized form in the major African American newspapers like the *Defender*, the *Baltimore Afro-American*, and the *Pittsburgh Courier*.[70] And as in the case of Kansas City, we ought also to include the paraliterature produced by amateurs with only local means and typically designed to reach only a local audience.

One example is *Kansas City: Mecca of the New Negro*, a coffee-table-size book assembled and self-published (presumably at the author's cost) by Sonny Gibson, an amateur historian and collector from Kansas City (his biographical notice indicates he was also "Vice-Chairman of the Charlie Parker Memorial Foundation").[71] The volume chronicles the development of black Kansas City from the 1870s to 1951, exclusively through photocopies of articles, advertisements, notices, and editorials excised from the city's black newspapers. This is a scrapbook of Kansas City viewed through the eyes and ears of its black community, from its founding to the midcentury, when the record abruptly stops. On the last page of the volume, Gibbs writes: "Many of our people, in 1997, are left with only fragmentary reminiscences of early years. It is my hope that this illustrated work will provide you with a retrospective glimpse of the Negro Life in Kansas City." Here the audience, "you," and the author are mediating a story to be recovered from within and about "the village." At stake in that recollection is a keen sense of temporality, of "our people, in 1997"—well into the postmodern moment. There's something political at stake, it is implied, in acquiring knowledge of a community that built itself up against the odds before a process of disintegration set in sometime after the 1950s.

Another example of this paraliterature is a booklet entitled *Your Kansas City and Mine*, published in Kansas City in 1950 by William H. Young and Nathan B. Young Jr., brothers and the sons of Nathan Benjamin Young (1862–1933), the prominent educator who eventually became president of Missouri's Lincoln University, the historically black public land-grant institution.[72] *Your Kansas City and Mine* celebrates the centenary of the incorporation of Kansas City in 1850, as well as pride in the reelection of fellow Missourian President Harry S. Truman for a second term in 1948.

But the Youngs also compiled stories on anything and everything related to black life in Kansas City, creating an encyclopedic snapshot of the city at midcentury: the local newspaper the *Call* has its own entry, as do the Kansas City Monarchs, champions of the Negro League; there are various notices on notable figures, including Mrs. Alphia Smith Minor, a "mulatto woman" said to have opened "the first dressmaking shop carrying Ladies Ready-To-Wear in Kansas City," and her grandson Julius Jones, operator of a barbershop and pool hall on Eighteenth Street; there are pages for the Cheerio Boys and Beau Brummel social clubs, the women of the Junior League, and a profile of Mrs. Henrietta Patterson, age 102, born a slave near Warrensburg, Missouri; and there are several pages of studio photos of ordinary children from black families around the city.

The volume has solidly middle-class ethics and aesthetics; it could be said to illustrate the advanced stages of the "politics of respectability," primed for the postwar photo documentary.[73] Its authors hope their volume can help push for racial progress, building on the achievements amassed over the previous century of struggle out of slavery. In their foreword they write:

> While America's heterogeneity and the State of Liberty's democratic welcome is the essential strength of our great country, its residuary of segregation out of the slavery regime has kept the dual pattern in contact. Kansas City has been one of the border victims of this crypto-American pattern. Thus Your Kansas City & Mine must too have its duality—its double meaning.... Kansas City, located in the heart of the Nation in the next quarter century (1950–'75) can take a lead in demonstrating the ultimate American way of life. To that single purpose this duplex edition of Your Kansas City & Mine has been dedicated ... To the Kansas Citians of the future—especially of the Year 1975 (children pictured herein shall be the grown-ups then) the publishers and the sponsors do offer this mid-century edition of Your Kansas City & Mine as a milestone of progressive hope—hope for a strong and just City of the Future.[74]

There is something indelibly tragic about these words when one considers them from our current vantage point, with full knowledge of what is to come. This pathos also emerges in the felt need to portray "the village" (the racial double sense of which the authors highlight in the possessive implication of "Your Kansas City and Mine") in the best light possible, to demonstrate a community's worthiness of civil equality.

But the real village was never this monolithic in its civic uprightness or in its politics. It is this variety, tumult, class conflict, the high and the lowlife, the gamblers, prostitutes, and jazz musicians, but also the laundresses, doctors, preachers, teachers, and crawdaddy criers, who Vincent Carter assembles in the musical phrasing of his novel. The instinct of Sonny Gibbs and the Young brothers to create an archive out of, and with, the black press and use it to tell a story is also Carter's: countless churches, theaters, shops, and nightclubs that have vanished under postwar freeways and urban blight appear in *Such Sweet Thunder* and are cross-referenced, as it were, in *Kansas City: Mecca of the New Negro* and *Your Kansas City and Mine*. In *Such Sweet Thunder*, Carter weaves these polyphonic discourses together in the key of black life, in the vernacular, and it was his genius to see that the black newspaper could provide the formal solution for representing this communal cacophony forged in adversity but brimming with hope.

Thinking Aloud with the *Voice*

Such Sweet Thunder tells the story of its hero, Amerigo Jones, as he comes of age and of his parents, Rutherford and Viola Jones, members of a black working-class family trying to get by and dealing with their son's boyhood and adolescence in Jazz Age and Depression-era Kansas City. This was a period of spectacular corruption and violence in the city, but also one of cultural ferment as the nightlife scene, and especially its jazz clubs, flourished under political boss Tom Pendergast, who helped make Kansas City the "Paris of the Plains."[75] The novel is written in an experimental stream-of-consciousness clearly modeled on Joyce, with some hints of the influence of postwar magical realism, particularly that of Günter Grass's *The Tin Drum* (1959).[76] Lyrical, impressionistic, and dominated by black vernacular dialogue, *Such Sweet Thunder*'s episodic structure emphasizes atmosphere and voice over narrative development. The plot itself is conventional if threadbare. Amerigo undergoes various traumas and adventures as he roams ever further from the alleyway house in the black ghetto where he grew up. He falls in love with Cosima Thornton, a middle-class, light-skinned girl whose father disapproves; the novel closes on the eve of Amerigo's departure to join the army in 1940, with the suspense of whether he and Cosima will go together to their high school prom.

　　Such Sweet Thunder is told from Amerigo's point of view as one extended flashback, framed for us at the opening by a vignette. On a cold night, on the battlefields of Europe, soldier Amerigo Jones seeks out kindling to build a fire when he comes across a scrap of newspaper:

> The floor was spotted and stained with filth. At the toe of his boot he spied a piece of soiled paper just behind the can. He stooped to pick it up. The match went out. He lit another, and bent over to inspect it more carefully.

The *Voice*! Damnit! Anxiously now he lit another match and saw that he held a part of the society page in his hand. His eyes fell upon the face of a young woman in the center of the sheet, stained by a muddy boot print and torn in such a way that little more than eyes, nose, and a corner of her mouth, which seemed to be smiling, were visible.[77]

The image is of Cosima, and the caption informs Amerigo she is to be married. This is rather contrived; Fleischer and the editors at Steerforth in fact cut this opening in their paperback version of the novel. This is a shame because, however flawed as a narrative device, its symbolism underscores the importance of black Kansas City's newspaper—the key that unlocks the lost world of the novel. The newspaper fragment is, in effect, Amerigo's madeleine, the Proustian catalyst for his remembrance of things past. It inaugurates the dialectical relation I wish to examine between Carter's novel and the fictional local newspaper that animates it.

The *Voice* is easily identifiable as Carter's stand-in for the historic *Kansas City Call*, which, after the *Chicago Defender*, is one of the oldest black newspapers extant, and still published today from the same offices on Eighteenth Street in the heart of Kansas City. To this day, it has always operated as a weekly, appearing on Fridays.[78] Founded in 1919, the *Call* was the brainchild of Chester Arthur Franklin, who was born to Exodusters in Texas in 1880.[79] His father, George, was himself in the newspaper business and founded the *Omaha Enterprise* in Nebraska, which had an important run in the 1890s. The Franklins were typical of that professional class of African Americans identified by Darlene Clark Hine, which laid the groundwork for the civil rights movement by developing "parallel organizations" that exploited "the Achilles' heel of white supremacy" and took up the "imperative to develop a range of distinct institutions that they controlled."[80] The Franklins had no choice but to turn adversity into advantage. The first edition of the *Kansas City Call*, published on May 6, 1919, was only a four-page sheet printed at two thousand copies; it sold for a nickel. When Franklin was able to invest in a Linotype machine, it sat idle for almost a year because the all-white printer's union in Kansas City wouldn't let any of their members train him or his staff to use it.[81]

Clara Franklin, his mother, worked side by side with him in the office and went door to door in the neighborhoods to sell subscriptions. Franklin understood early on that cultivating a relationship with the community was good civics and good for his bottom line, and he took steps to ensure his paper would cover and respond directly to that community. As early as 1924 he was urging readers "to help us by calling the office and telling us what is going to happen as well as what has happened," and he made a point of insisting on the paper's role in promoting and soliciting society affairs: "Send an invitation to every party, wedding, dinner, etc. to the social editor of the *Call*. That gives us news of what to be ready to publish." A section titled "The Editor's Mail Box" provided a forum for correspondence and dialogue.

With the Great Migration underway, Kansas City's black population was growing, with a continued influx of migration from the South. The 1920 census reported 101,177 people living in the Kansas City metro area, 14 percent of them African American.[82] The *Call* grew steadily apace with this population growth, expanding from a circulation of 2,000 in 1919 to 16,737 in 1927. In 1928, Franklin purchased a thirty-two-page Goss Straight Line printing press that could print and fold twenty-four thousand papers a day. Clara Franklin devised a collection method that allowed the *Call* to become the first black newspaper to have its circulation certified by the Audit Bureau of Circulation. In the postwar years, the paper grew even more rapidly, with its readership peaking in 1950 at just over forty thousand subscribers.[83]

Carter's novel grants us insight into the material and social conditions of this circulation, moving us beyond facts and figures and into the practices of everyday life. Early in the novel, a young Amerigo tries to make out the significance of the objects in his family's tiny living room: "He looked questioningly at the magazine rack between the lamp and the chair, but it remained merely a dumb shadowy form engulfed in a faint, almost misty aura of blue, cluttered with detective-story magazines, last week's copy of the *Voice* and yesterday's copies of the *Times* and the *Star*."[84] The place of the *Voice*, stand-in for the *Call*, on the rack along a spectrum of popular and informative print culture confirms the statistics of the *Call's* impressive growth; its readership, though likely dominated by middle-class blacks, clearly penetrated the poorer alleyway tenements of the working classes, too. The presence of the *Times* and the *Star*, the white morning and afternoon dailies, respectively, suggests the double lens or double consciousness through which the black community quite literally reads itself. The *Voice* is identified explicitly at various points as a black paper, for example, early on when the local pastor invites a speaker from the National Association for the Advancement of Colored People to talk to his congregation and exhorts them to follow the political news in the *Voice*. But interestingly, Carter never explicitly tells us that the *Star* (the more significant of the two dailies) is white. Instead, he wraps it in contextual clues. Some are subtle, like the way Rutherford systematically turns to the *Star* when he's looking for news on foreign affairs; others less so, as in a late scene in which an adolescent Amerigo hoping to ask for a job enters the downtown hotel where his father works as an elevator operator: "He floated into the rich leather-upholstered atmosphere of the lobby, reverberating with subtle sniggers and discretely amused noses and the distracted glances of eyes resting upon the saw-toothed edges of the *Star*."[85]

The real *Kansas City Star* had a long history of conspicuous silence on race issues, systematically refusing to report, for instance, on the regular bombings of black homes throughout the 1920s as middle-class blacks attempted to move into white neighborhoods with better housing. Indeed, between 1921 and 1928 this wave of bombings (up to seven in one year) was denounced only in the black press, with the *Call* partnering with the NAACP to launch independent investigations when the police failed to act.[86] In a bitterly sardonic 1926 editorial in the *Call* entitled "America's Adventure in Brotherhood," Chester Franklin wrote: "The other morning as I lay in bed, I heard an explosion, the second in six weeks' time—Kansas City was at work on its housing problem."[87] By contrast, the *Star* refused even to print any photograph of a black figure well into the late 1920s, a tradition broken only when Tom Lee, a black boatman from Memphis, rescued a group of white engineers from a sinking riverboat.[88]

In Carter's novel, newspapers not only reflect Jim Crow practices and attitudes; they are also vessels that transmit a kind of pedagogy for living with Jim Crow. Education is the great theme of the novel, its promise of uplift and escape, and its enlistment into the ways of the world, a dramatization of the fall from innocence that occurs when black children learn what they must face and what their place in the world must mean. Carter renders this dramatically by turning once again to the body of the black press. Here, Amerigo is at his aunt's house:

> "That's just fine," she said. "Here I'll tell you what." She reached for an old copy of the *Voice*. "Put your paper on the top and copy out the letters that show through." He started copying the letters. Meanwhile she put her coffeepot on the stove and settled down in the rocking chair, her glasses resting on the tip of her nose, the way Unc wore his. She picked up a dress from the table and started to mend it. He worked intently, oblivious to everything except the black letters that shone through. He spelled the letters out as he wrote:
>
> "D ..... E A T ... H! ... C O M EEEE—S TO FAT HER OF FIVE. F-I-V-E spells five! BOY OF SIX-TEENDIES IN H O S P I T A L F R O M P O I C E B R U T A L I T Y N A A C P D R I V E G E T S U N D E R W A Y.
>
> "Look!" He held up the lettered sheet of paper with pride.
>
> "Unh-huh, that's good ..." she said in a distracted tone, intent on her sewing. "One of these days you'll be readin' an writin' as good as me!"
>
> He began to trace the picture in the center of the page. There was a

tree in the middle of the picture. A black man was hanging from one of its branches. His eyes were popping out.

"Don' he look funny!" he cried, holding up the paper. Aunt Lily looked at it, and then she looked at him, and then her eyes darkened.

"Naw, honey, he don' look a bit funny to me. What if it was your daddy?"

He studied the picture carefully. He looked curiously at the white people standing around the hanging man. He felt Aunt Lily's eyes on him. It does look funny! he thought, and at the same time he was stung by a feeling of shame.[89]

Apart from this lesson in the ABC's of race in America (plus a few beatings and chasings by police officers), there is virtually no direct representation of serious racial violence in the novel. Carter mostly represents it as a constant yet intangible threat, everywhere and nowhere: a white noise. When Amerigo gets home and shows his mother the picture of the lynching he's traced over in that week's copy of the *Voice*, she scolds him mildly and orders him to bed.

News of racial violence is not a shocking event in the lives of Aunt Lily and Viola Jones, just a weekly revenant, a specter that Carter suggests people have come to assume as a permanent and regular background to their daily concerns. This sequence underscores Jacqueline Goldsby's notion that lynching was (and is) first and foremost a "cultural logic," a form of spectacular violence whose pedagogic function—to inculcate into black populations their fixed station in an otherwise rapidly changing and modernizing society—is undergirded by the state's tacit acceptance of black people's vulnerability to lethal retaliation. Goldsby's argument that "literature is particularly responsive to historical developments we cannot bear to admit" finds in Carter's novel an additional vindication.[90]

In *Such Sweet Thunder*, the violence in the poor and working-class section of Kansas City's ghetto is often intramural in nature. Crime and despair are a source of social friction. A dramatic shooting takes place in the alleyway one evening and draws the attention of the *Voice*'s strident editorials. This penchant for covering crime in the black community in graphic and sensationalizing terms was a well-known characteristic of Chester Franklin's *Kansas City Call* and a source of tension within the black community. Franklin's editorial line for the paper appears to have mixed his conservative convictions and sense of civic duty (he was a lifelong Republican and "race man") with his instincts for good business. But he had an overriding preoccupation with intraracial violence. Starting in 1924, he ran a front-page box, complete with an illustration of a gallows, called "Murder-a-Week," which tallied homicides, often alongside eye-catching headlines. These generated a good deal of backlash from the community, with letters regularly running in the paper chastising Franklin for exaggerated depictions of violence.

In 1923, perhaps sensing he needed fresh perspectives, Franklin hired a promising twenty-two-year-old editor from Minnesota by the name of Roy Wilkins, whom we know for the work he would go on to do a decade later as the famed editor of the *Crisis* in New York (taking over its editorship from W. E. B. Du Bois) from 1934 to 1949, and his subsequent leadership as executive director of the NAACP at the height of the civil rights movement from 1955 to 1977. Wilkins and Franklin's new wife, the highly educated and talented Ada Crogman, daughter of a prominent professor at Clark Atlanta University, both attempted to mitigate the tabloid tendency of the paper.[91] Wilkins began writing a column called "Talking It Over," which covered race and politics at the local and national level but also evinced the more conciliatory and dialogic tone he was striving for in the paper. *Such Sweet Thunder* takes up precisely this call-and-response dynamic between the paper and its public in a key scene. When a gambling argument turns deadly on Amerigo's alley, we get an account of street gossip from the voices of neighbors talking to one another and then back-to-back versions of the event viewed from both the *Star* and the *Voice:*

> That night at supper Rutherford read the article about it in the *Star*: "Wilbur Rhodes, thirty-one, Negro, five feet seven inches tall and weighing one hundred and eighty-six pounds, was shot to death last night in an alley between Independence Avenue and Admiral Boulevard at approximately two-twenty A.M. by John Waters, forty-seven, Negro, six feet three inches tall, has a dark brown complexion and an oval knife scar on his chin. When last seen—"
> The following Friday evening after supper, Rutherford unfolded the pages of the *Voice* and read:
> "GAMBLER SLAIN IN DEATH VALLEY!" Ain' that a damn shame! He looked over the paper at Viola.
> "Let me see," she said.
> "Here, look."
> "That's awful!"
> "Why," said Rutherford, "why in the hell do they have to exaggerate like that? A man reads this paper an' gits *fightin' mad!*"[92]

The white paper's neutral journalese goes down better with Rutherford than the *Voice*'s all-caps hysterics, although Carter signals, in the emphasis on physical attributes reported in the *Star*, its echoes of the Wanted poster, suggesting their neutrality is more apparent than real.

What happens next is even more telling. A resident in the alley, Mrs. Nancy Cunningham, writes a letter to the *Voice* demanding an apology and suggesting they send someone down to take stock of the high character of the real inhabitants of the alley, among them a very talented and bright young boy named Amerigo Jones. And the paper responds. A few days later a good-looking young man calls on the Jones's family: "Oh I'm sorry, Mister Jones, I should have—Robert Jordan, editor of the *Voice*. You see, I was asked to visit you by one of our readers, and eh I decided to take eh-to take her advice. Ehhem. But let me explain, last week a man was killed here in this al-street, and we-we eh we-reported it. A little too strongly for Miss Nancy Cunningham I'm afraid."[93] Is this visitor making the rounds on behalf of the paper modeled on Roy Wilkins? It's impossible that Carter didn't know who Wilkins was, given that the period of the novel's composition in the early 1960s coincided with the apex of Wilkins's profile in the national limelight. I haven't found any direct evidence that Wilkins made house calls in this manner, but it is in line with all the circumstantial evidence that he or another representative of the paper did indeed go door to door to solicit or follow up on letters to the editor. In any case, insofar as Carter uses the character of Robert Jordan as a mouthpiece for the paper's ideals and uneasy class relationship with its readers, he hews to ideals that Franklin espoused but that Wilkins more passionately believed in. It is unquestionably significant that it is "Robert Jordan," not the paper's owner, who delivers a defense and apologia for the *Voice*. For the Jones family and young Amerigo, this visit from an ambassador of middle-class respectability and the community's chief organ is a source of immense pride. When the apology appears the following Friday in the *Voice* with an account of Mr. Jordan's visit, Rutherford cuts it out and sticks it in the family album, and we learn that "everybody who visited the house had to read it and listen to his account of it."[94]

Before leaving the family home that day, Robert Jordan asks Amerigo what he wants to be when he grows up. The little boy replies that he hopes to be "the president of Amer'ka!": "Rutherford, Viola, and Mr. Jordan exchanged embarrassed glances. Then Mr. Jordan's face took on a dreamy, slightly sad expression, the same expression as when he had spoken of how he had sold newspaper as a boy. He placed his hand thoughtfully upon Amerigo's shoulder and said: 'Why not? Yes! Why not! A man's no bigger than his dreams …'"[95] It's another pathetic moment, one that relies on the ironic construction provided by the child's point of view to convey to us the straitjacketing of human aspiration by Jim Crow. After Robert Jordan leaves, Viola wonders whether the newspaper man meant what he said about her son's possibilities. Rutherford is skeptical, but appreciative of the paper's role in binding the community to itself: "He prob'ly means it—in a way. I mean deep down inside. But you know, it's kinda like business, you have to be nice to the customers.... Just the same, it does make you feel better when you speak out an' the *Voice* answers back."[96] The segregated world viewed from within is complicated; it is both more transparent and ebullient to itself and more fatalistic about the boundaries that encompass it. For the characters in this novel, the black press offers a rare and tangible promise of real social ascension—but one that can take you only so far.

A remarkable passage toward the end of the novel poetically fuses these interrelations of the paper, the community it served, the imagination of a boy, and the novelist who animated him. It opens with Amerigo poring over the society pages of the *Voice*, filled with glittering social clubs. Roy Wilkins recalled some of them in his autobiography: for men, the top of the ladder was the Ivanhoe Club and its Christmas ball at the Paseo; for the black women of Kansas City, there was the "Merry-We Social, The Matinee Matrons, the Forget-Me-Not-Girls, the Mysterious Few Whist Club—brave little outposts of middle-class normalcy in a hostile white world. Corinne Wilson, the *Call*'s society editor presided over this gay, chatty empire."[97] As Amerigo turns the pages, the colors, tones, and their associations blend into a continuum:

> The black, white, and grayish personages who filled the squares and rectangles on the pages of the *Voice* came to the forefront of his mind in a procession of colors: smiling ladies and gentlemen bursting with crimson distinction, deep tragic purples and criminal greens, mellow beauty-queen browns, snooty beiges and off-whites, serious fudge-browns, scholastic gray-blacks, and everywhere the gold-rimmed black-blackness of the One and Only Living God.
>
> Eighteenth Street spread out before him like a huge page of the *Voice*. All the buildings appeared as photographs and the flickering signs as headlines. He stood on the corner and watched the motley-colored procession of figures walking up and down the street, talking, laughing. He breathed in and out the picturesque smells of barbershop and pool hall, drugstore and tavern, the Sunday-afternoon heat, the slightly wilted after-church freshness of Sunday suits and dresses reflected upon the polished surfaces of parked and moving automobiles, agitated by nervous lights upon the marquees of theaters, the honking horns of taxis and the voluble mellifluence of friendly greetings: "Hey Joe!" cried one tall dark man to another tall dark man on the opposite side of the street. Just then the streetcar rushed between them, casting the greeter's reflection on its windows like a chain of photographs whisked through the air.[98]

This expressive panorama, melding a dream of mediation through print capitalism with a subtly crafted scene of urban interpellation, encapsulates the concept of imagined community.[99] In Amerigo's vision, text and sign, heads and headlines, interanimate one another. The scene of everyday life is seen representatively, reiterated through its circulation in the printed "voice" of people who recognize themselves in what they read. In this bygone world of organic unity, even the "One and Only Living God" shows up as regular feature, in the sense of appearing in every "issue" and as a general, suffused presence whose "gold-rimmed" blackness is almost a stylistic attribute or a way of being in the world. The cumulative and synesthetic collage of the "picturesque" here contributes to the collective shimmer of these vignettes, whereas the oneiric and nostalgic language betrays the consciousness of the exile in a way that threatens to outstrip the plausibility of the young boy's vision without, I think, quite doing so.

The subject of this dream is "Eighteenth Street," the beating heart of prewar black Kansas City. It is also, of course, the consciousness at the center of the novel, Amerigo, whom we are watching come into an awareness of the means of production and the hermeneutic meanings made possible when the world reflects your agency back to you. Hence, the figural importance of this scene of intraracial interpellation, one that incidentally gives black flâneurism a sociality and a notion of collective, or at least plural, participation that revises the version we inherit from Baudelaire and Benjamin—and that Carter effectively satirizes in *The Bern Book*—that privileges the spectatorship of the anonymous man in the crowd "who goes botanizing on the asphalt."[100] For Baudelaire, the flâneur enjoys a subversive Machiavellian sovereignty of perspective, he is "a *prince* who is everywhere in possession of his incognito," precisely the attribute that Carter cuttingly understands to be intrinsically unavailable to him in the Swiss capital.[101] Benjamin, concerned with historicizing the same figure in the history of capitalism, says that "in the flâneur, the intelligentsia sets foot in the marketplace."[102] But neither Amerigo Jones nor the passing "Joe" of this scene are members of the intelligentsia; and it is their mutual instantiation of recognition, not their social anonymity, that makes strolling through the urban space of Kansas City a source of sovereignty, one that is subversive insofar as it reproduces Morrison's black "village" within the dominion of a city controlled by power structures intent on securing white interests at the expense of black ones.

In his novel, Carter folds those Benjaminian touchstones of modernity, the photograph, the newspaper, the interiorization of public space emblematic of the Parisian arcades, into a Morrisonian configuration. For Carter, the arcades of black Kansas City (a city once known as the Paris of the Plains) are the pool hall, the streetcar, and the barbershop, and they provide him with a model that expresses the very opposite of its European counterpart, which he experienced (under the sign of his exclusion) in Bern, where, we must keep in mind, he was writing from. Notice how one black voice calling to another is interrupted in such a way that the face of the caller is reflected back for the narrator as a "chain of photographs" that is, per the logic of the extended metaphor, more like a newsreel, while the streetcar becomes an animated version of the city's black organ of representation that reflects social desire back upon the subject. It is as though even the vehicles emblematic of Kansas City's urban modernity know and speak the language of the black people who holler back and forth across its tracks.

Even this streetcar, a vehicle a young boy like Amerigo would plausibly be enthralled by, is chosen here for specific associations. Kansas City's system was notable for having never segregated its streetcar service, from its inception in the 1880s until its closure in 1957.[103] In this light, the streetcar and its "chain of photographs" reads as a counterimage to that landmark of American midcentury photography, Robert Frank's "Trolley, New Orleans (1955)" from *The Americans*, which was published in France in 1958, right around the time Vincent Carter was beginning work on *Such Sweet Thunder*. Frank's photograph, with its rigidly enframed trolley riders caught in a sequence of tableaus evocative of US racial hierarchy—"stately as a frieze on a Greek temple entablature," as one critic puts it—is an iconic representation of US segregation, an image said to haunt the American psyche.[104] By contrast, Carter is haunted by the vernacular black modernity that was thriving in the city he grew up in and that, in the space of a few years, was suddenly erased—though not entirely, as the printed newspaper, the *Voice* that is the *Call*, lives on as an archive for the novel to reanimate as a village.

The *Voice* speaks, or rather sings, the city into an animated color strip. Its printed matter is not arrayed in rigid columns; it extends and radiates outward, a site of improvised social reciprocity and affection, like a jazz solo. "The grain," Roland Barthes famously said, "is the materiality of the voice singing its mother tongue."[105] That grain is the stuff that Vincent Carter built his novel out of, channeling it like Bennie Moten's orchestra into one great river of sound. The novel is a repository for that sound, a recording device specially attuned to the jazz of the city but most of all to the grain of Kansas City's chorus of black voices.

The brimming pages of *Such Sweet Thunder* show us that the Blue Period need not be thought of as a library of works imbued with alienated consciousness, political evasion, and inward reflection. The era's affects and politics could engender just the opposite as a style. Still, the melancholic exile of Vincent Carter in the white Alps and the vivid reconstruction of black sociality in Kansas City are not unrelated. The extremity of the former and the intensity of the latter bespeak the drastic and perhaps necessary homelessness of a black writer's consciousness. Fortunately, the novel was not lost, and the full breadth of Carter's experiments with genre, medium, and style has come into view. To see it in its entirety, however, requires restoring his work to its place among the constellation of those expressive writings of black postwar sensibility.

Gwendolyn Brooks's and Paule Marshall's Elusions

CHAPTER FOUR

What she wanted to dream, and dreamed, was her affair.

GWENDOLYN BROOKS, *Maud Martha*, 1953

Reviewing Gwendolyn Brooks's autobiography, *Report from Part One*, for the *New York Times* in 1973, Toni Cade Bambara confirmed for readers a dividing line between the poet's career pre- and post-1967 that has held sway in assessments ever since.[1] Brooks herself repeatedly insists in the autobiography that 1967 was a watershed moment, most directly through a 1971 interview with Ida Lewis for *Essence* magazine reprinted in the text. The conversation opens with Lewis asking Brooks, "How did you, a Pulitzer prizewinner, get turned on to the black revolution?"[2] It's a leading question, and a loaded one at that. It implies that the prize itself is antithetical to political engagement and perhaps even counterrevolutionary in nature.

It also implies the existence of an earlier, depoliticized Brooks, clipped by her coveting the recognition of (white) cultural authority, and one who has now (surprisingly enough) been converted to the cause of racial solidarity. Brooks answers:

> The real turning point came in 1967, when I went to the Second Black Writer's Conference at Fisk University ... there I found what has stimulated my life these last three years: young people, full of a new spirit. They seemed stronger and taller, really ready to take on the challenges ... I was still saying "Negro," for instance. [LeRoi Jones] came in while I was giving my reading, and I said, "Ah, there's LeRoi Jones," and everybody just went mad. The audience wasn't quite aware yet that he was the new messiah, but he was very much admired.[3]

Brooks's characteristic use of sardonic understatement cannot conceal the underlying gender politics of this momentous changing of the guards between these two major figures of black poetry in twentieth-century America. There's no question that Brooks admires LeRoi Jones (then soon to be Amiri Baraka). But his casual interruption of her reading and his usurpation of the audience's attention and affection are legible forms of what Erica Edwards has diagnosed as the "charismatic leadership scenario" in black political discourse.[4] Brooks is all too aware that Jones is admired not merely as a poet but as a "new messiah."

Elsewhere, Brooks writes of this moment with mock-solemn self-deprecation while slyly suggesting the masculinist shift of the new radicalism. She describes arriving at Fisk having come "from white white white South Dakota State College," where she had been rapturously received: "I had been 'loved' at South Dakota State College. Here I was coldly Re-spected [*sic*]. Here the heroes included the novelist-director, John Killens, editors David Llorens and Hoyt Fuller, playwright Ron Milner, historians John Henrik Clarke and Lerone Bennett.... Imamu Amiri Baraka, then 'LeRoi Jones,' was expected."[5] This entirely male roll call, representing the major exponents of the burgeoning Black Arts Movement, is framed in apposition to female poets (including herself) who are suddenly terribly out of place, women like "Margaret Danner Cunningham—another Old Girl, another coldly Respected old Has-been—and an almost hysterical Gwendolyn B. walking about in amazement, listening, looking, learning."[6] Brooks hams up this third-person account with tropes of gendered undesirability, which belie both women's considerable achievements (Brooks was the first black American to win a Pulitzer Prize, and in 1956, Danner became the first black editor of *Poetry* magazine).

Brooks goes on to describe her "hysterical" visage as bearing the "dotty expression in the eyes of a cartoon-woman."[7] But in her description, it is the charismatic men who come off as hysterical with their cartoonish theatrics: "Up against the wall, white man! was the substance of the Baraka shout, at the evening reading he shared with fierce Ron Milner among intoxicating drumbeats, heady incense and organic underhumming. Up against the wall! And a pensive (until that moment) white man of thirty or thirty-three abruptly shot himself into the heavy air screaming 'Yeah! Yeah! Up against the wall, Brother! KILL 'EM ALL! KILL 'EM ALL!' I thought that was interesting."[8] "Interesting" is a superb example of what our contemporary locution calls "throwing shade."[9] Far from being a full-throated endorsement, this is a tart and shrewd assessment of the over-heated self-indulgences of Baraka's rhetorical style, to say nothing of such rhetoric's political promise. What emerges from a careful reading of these passages is how cunning Brooks is in her navigation through the changing political winds. She embraces this revolutionary moment while simultaneously calling out the gender performance of power relations that undergird it, about which she is respectfully agnostic but clearly skeptical.

Readers of *Report from Part One* have not always sufficiently appreciated the instability of its claims—its many competing currents of enthusiasm, irony, and sarcasm. An unorthodox, fragmentary, and experimental
text built of an assortment of interviews, scrapbook keepings, family photographs, old letters, and news clippings, *Report* is elusive and playful, like
a cubist collage of found materials that affirms Brooks's sincere affection
for the qualities of ordinary life and ordinary people. In this way, it is typical of the canny strategies of both savantish self-fashioning and literary
gamesmanship that Brooks deploys in her poetry as well as in her prose.

The very title, *Report from Part One*, foregrounds but does not resolve
the question of whether the poet's life and work hinges on a temporal
frame. It implies a future *Report from Part Two*, which was indeed published by Third World Press in 1996—although, curiously, the second volume begins by recycling material from *Part One* and consists mostly of
short observations about fellow poets encountered during Brooks's travels and conferences in the 1980s. More importantly, these temporally
weighted titles and Brooks's recursion to 1967 as a key pivot suggest that
a new horizon of political possibility bore upon the expression of artistic
sensibility.

But how should her poetry on either side of that dividing line be read
and understood? Contemporaneous reception of the *Report from Part One*
was puzzled on this question. Some readers, seeking to confirm preconceived narratives—especially those favorable to the emergent discourse
of black nationalism—tended to read Brooks in stark terms or offer contradictory assessments. Don L. Lee (then soon to be Haki Madhubuti) depicts Brooks's poetics in his preface to *Report from Part One* as having undergone nothing less than a racial schism. He puts his case in brute terms:
"*Annie Allen* (1949), important? Yes. Read by blacks? No. *Annie Allen* more
so than *A Street in Bronzeville* seems to have been written for whites. For
instance, 'The Anniad' requires unusual concentrated study ... this poem
is probably earth-shaking to some, but leaves me completely dry."[10] For
Lee, the first half of Brooks's career holds merely incidental interest as an
impressive display of ability, designed to appeal to white readers and their
sensibilities. This view, consonant with Lee's politics at the time, combines a dubious empirical claim with an assertion of personal preference,
both steeped in an unflattering racial essentialism.

In fact, Brooks's many early poems published in the *Chicago Defender*
(which circulated well beyond Chicago) had reached a wide black audience. On September 18, 1949, Brooks was featured on Richard Durham's
Destination Freedom radio show on WMAQ Chicago, a popular and pioneering local program with a leftist leaning, sponsored by the Urban

League and staffed with local artists like Oscar Brown Jr. and writers from the *Defender*.[11] In his 1949 review of the book, J. Saunders Redding suggested only "another Negro" could "get the intimate feeling, the racially particular acceptance and rejection, and the oblique bitterness" of the verse.[12] Langston Hughes, in his 1950 review of *Annie Allen*, declared that "the people and poems in Gwendolyn Brooks's book are alive, reaching, and very much of today."[13] And while there is no accounting for preference, Hughes considered Brooks's output in those early years to be the fine standard against which all other poetry he read was to be measured.[14]

Toni Cade Bambara, despite sharing much of Lee's political outlook, takes a far more nuanced view in her *Times* review of the autobiography, arguing that terms like *change* and *shift*, with respect to the apparent turning point in Brooks's career, "may be too heavy-handed, somewhat misleading, for in rereading the bulk of her work, which 'Report' does prompt one to do, we see a continuum."[15] The same is true of Joyce Ann Joyce, another "Afrocentric" critic who nevertheless perceives continuity rather than disjuncture across the 1967 dividing line.[16] The difference between the drastic schism laid out by Lee/Madhubuti and Bambara's and Joyce's sense of a continuum points to the difficulty of finding a framework for Brooks's poetry that does justice to its aesthetics and its politics, on either side of the 1967 Fisk writers' conference.

In this chapter, I argue that Brooks's pre-1967 work is both symptomatic and responsive to a period-specific articulation of cultural politics that dominated the early Cold War years. Brooks was mounting a critique that engaged debates around the politics of black representation in the literary field; the contemporaneous fervor surrounding the sociological study of the "Negro Problem"; and the pressures of a rising black middle class that was asserting an assimilationist ideology, one that had force and specific implications for the normative inscription of black womanhood at the time. These debates were emerging in the print and media culture industries of Chicago, which were in the process of "selling the race," notably through the vehicle of the Johnson Publishing media empire, as Adam Green has chronicled.[17]

To understand Brooks's approach to these questions, it is necessary to understand the poet in the context of her elected milieu, what Leela Gandhi calls the "affective communities" that shaped her thinking and dialogically informed the innovations Brooks introduced into black poetry and prose. This requires that we reconsider Brooks's relationship to *Negro Story* magazine, the black literary journal that nurtured her and served as the hub of her literary and social network during the crucial period of her literary formation: the years from 1940 to 1945, when she was assembling the material that would go into her first poetry collection *A Street in Bronzeville* (1945) and her novel *Maud Martha* (1953).

I proceed to reevaluate *Maud Martha* as an experiment in prose that breaks in important ways with the tradition of the Popular Front aesthetics that had dominated the previous decade but is no less political for doing so. Brooks's specific commitments to depicting black (and female) interiority cannot be reconciled with Mary Helen Washington's contention that the novel belongs to the school of fiction Michael Denning dubbed "the ghetto pastoral." Instead, *Maud Martha* refashions political dissent as a force located within the alienated individual, sparked by her experience of divestment from dominant cultural norms and the ironic failures of her integration into US liberal capitalism.

The novel constitutes a critique of what Alan Wald has called "Cold War modernity," and what I prefer to call, from the local vantage point of segregated black Chicago, the domestic, middle-class, assimilationist values of "kitchenette modernity."[18] But it does so not through satire or protest, but through the repurposing of high-modernist description, which accords freedom in the very act of attending to the inner life of a young black woman, but especially to linger there because it is the part of her that forever eludes the trappings of normativity, whether those be the forces of race, class, gender, or any other involuntary ascription. *Maude Martha*'s location of a counterforce in its heroine's fierce interiority finds echoes in Paule Marshall's novel *Brown Girl, Brownstones* (1959), which picks up Brooks's innovations and connects them to a diasporic impulse that redirects political hope outward, a foreshadowing of the more overtly transnational political projects of the post-1965 Black Power era. They share the same impulse and sensibility turned into literary strategy: the portrait of the artist as a young woman whose elusion of the forces around her depends on the sovereignty of her imagination, a quality and power of inwardly held conviction the novels must therefore convince us of.

Resituating and discretely periodizing Brooks ultimately helps us more clearly see the political and intellectual work that her poetics proposed, even if that work was not always fully grasped at the time. It vindicates, but also explains, her transition to the explicit Black Power political aesthetic that would come to the fore after the Fisk conference. Placing her within the Blue Period makes legible the culverted continuity of her radical politics (and their independent and affective commitment to black liberation, beyond the Left or the Right as such). We come to understand that Brooks's formal transition to the post-1967 work was an inevitable response to a new historical framework for black political and aesthetic discourse, one that her previous work, properly understood, both anticipates and effectively prophesizes.

The Chicago Renaissance

In April 1934, a seventeen-year-old Gwendolyn Brooks, then a junior at Englewood High School on the South Side of Chicago, revised her already previously drafted "New Year Resolutions," setting out the goals she intended to achieve before graduation. The first two resolutions pertained to publication: "1.) Have at least ten stories accepted and paid for by January 1st, 1935. 2.) Have at least twenty-five poems (new poems) published by January 1st, 1935." The next two resolutions suggest her self-conscious awareness of the importance of respectability to her social advancement, and the racist tropes her dark skin would confront: "3.) Become softer mannered. 4.) Become pleasanter." But perhaps the most remarkable resolution concerns the founding of a periodical, for which she made extensive and highly detailed plans: "5.) Found, "The Pioneer Star," monthly. To include 4, original, typewritten stories, 4, original, typed poems, 4 original drawings. Nine issues by January 1st, 1935."[19] This aperçu into the precocious mind of a young gifted and black literary talent tells us a little about Brooks's extraordinary ambitions.

It also illuminates her specific and savvy understanding of the role of the small publication in establishing literary bona fides. Brooks grasped the importance of control over the means of production when it came to the reception politics of "the field" of black cultural production and the positions it took in relation to the field of (white) power.[20] It may have been utopian for Brooks to imagine assembling and publishing her own version of Harriet Monroe's *Poetry* magazine at seventeen, but it was not as naive as it may seem. As the center of gravity of the black cultural and literary world shifted from Harlem to Chicago in the early 1930s, social and institutional opportunities for black artists began to flourish there.[21] Reading circles, salons, study groups, and small publications, many of them either directly or indirectly supported by the Communist Party or leftist organizations, gave young black writers a new sense of careerist possibility, even as it created bonds of intimacy and bohemian rebellion among fellow travelers. These institutions are also notable for having been organized, directed, and led by black women.

Our understanding of the Chicago Renaissance has greatly improved over the past two decades. Building on Bill Mullen's foundational work in 1999, scholars like Stacy Morgan (2004), Adam Green (2007), Robert Bone and Richard A. Courage (2011), Ayesha Hardison (2014), Mary Helen Washington (2014), and Jacqueline Goldsby (2014) have added depth and texture to the networks, material cultures, and populist politics that made Chicago the dominant hub for African American artists of the Popular Front era.[22] The presence there of the most influential black newspaper in the country, the *Defender*, would be supplemented through the late 1930s and during the war years with a vibrant print culture that went a long way toward establishing a black public sphere. In 1937, Dorothy West launched *New Challenge*, her reboot of Harlem's *Challenge*; this placed a black woman at the head of a pioneering black Marxist publication, and when Marian Minus joined the masthead (after a dustup over Richard Wright's negative review of Zora Neale Hurston's *Their Eyes Were Watching God*), a queer one as well.[23] John H. Johnson's *Negro Digest* appeared in 1942 and paved the way for his mass-market, middlebrow black magazines *Ebony*, founded in 1945, and *Jet*, in 1951.

The war years saw an explosion of (often briefly lived) experimental and literary small magazines like *New Vistas*, *Expression*, and *Negro Youth Photo Script*, which revolved around a small coterie of aspiring black writers and poets, including Richard Wright, Margaret Walker, William Couch, Grace Tomkins, William Attaway, Margaret Taylor-Burroughs, the Bland brothers (Edward and Aldon), Frank Marshall Davis, Earl Conrad, Margaret Danner, Fern Gayden, Theodore Ward, and, of course, Gwendolyn Brooks and her husband, Henry Blakely, also a poet. These writers intermingled in the various reading circles and study groups of Bronzeville, including the South Side Writers Group, the Allied Arts Guild, and Inez Cunningham Stark's poetry seminar—a self-consciously leftist and integrated atmosphere epitomized by the 1944 Interracial South Side Cultural Conference.[24]

The most important small magazine to emerge from this ferment was *Negro Story*, a quarterly that saw a two-year run of nine issues from May–June 1944 to April–May 1946.[25] Founded and edited by Alice C. Browning, and coedited for the first three issues by Fern Gayden, the magazine consciously sought to meld the Popular Front aesthetics and wartime antifascist politics of the Chicago renaissance (as well as the vanguard posture of the Harlem Renaissance) with the credentializing and vetting functions of Whit Burnett's *Story* magazine, then at the height of its influence.[26] These complementary facets can be said to represent the respective backgrounds of the founding editors. Gayden was a social worker, teacher, poet, and activist who had helped to found the South Side Writers Group and later presided over the South Side Community Art Center. Browning was from an upwardly mobile family and pursued a "talented tenth" path, taking a degree from the University of Chicago and, in 1941, an MA from Columbia, where she studied the African American novel under Vernon Loggins. Browning produced *Negro Story* out of her home at 4019 Vincennes Avenue, only a few blocks away from Gwendolyn Brooks's home in those years, the Tyson on Forty-Third Street.

While short lived, *Negro Story* proved a clearinghouse for the leading postwar male writers, Richard Wright, Ralph Ellison, and Chester Himes, who all published in its pages and served as editors at-large.[27] In the pivotal last years of the war, *Negro Story* was also a meeting ground and a haven for women determined to challenge expectations of what it meant to do literary work and how that work might intersect with one's personal life—as a way to critique socioeconomic conditions and gendered scripts, but also through experiments in the representation of black female interiority. Together, these women were engaged in what we could call, following Ayesha Hardison, the project of "writing through Jane Crow."[28]

The postcolonial scholar Leela Gandhi, in her book *Affective Communities*, proposes that we break free of "the unsatisfactory theoretical choice between the oppositional but repetitive forms of cultural nationalism on the one hand and the subversive but quietist discourse of hybridity or contrapuntality on the other" in colonial and anticolonial relationships.[29] She argues that we ought to attend instead to those interstitial spaces that summon "countercultural revolutionary practices" and escape the hegemonic ideologies of the day by binding like-minded subcultures through a "politics of friendship" in an "existentially urgent and ethically inventive enterprise."[30] While the politics and affections of Gandhi's subjects arise against the backdrop of the English Raj and mine against that of wartime Jim Crow Chicago, they share a need for tertiary spaces of relation and an expression of dissidence that, though broadly leftist and socialist in its attitudes, is more oriented toward the personal. These spaces are more concerned with the pleasures (and perils) of social intimacy than the proletarian categories of "the crowd," "the march," or "the factory strike" favored by classical Marxist analysis. This makes Gandhi's "politics of friendship" a better descriptor for the world of the black literary arts circles in Bronzeville, given their political commitments, the importance of affect to their constitution, and the forging of their aesthetic inclinations.

The potential to create and dissolve elective communities depends on sustaining the projective imagination of their projects; they are always, in this minimal sense, adventures in desire as well as in intellection or politics. The South Side Writers Group, for instance, came apart allegedly over disputes that were originally interpersonal in nature. Frank Marshall Davis claims in his memoirs that "it broke up after rumors that some of the girl members were lesbians and had gotten into a dispute over still another chick."[31] He goes on to quote from a letter he received from Alain Locke on this subject, which compares the group's infighting to "the Russians of the early Nihilist movement" and bemoans the Negro circles for their emotiveness, in his view an excessive cocktail of "suspicion, jealousy, and libidinous envy."[32] Davis's and Locke's patronizing and paternalistic attitudes aside, the presence of alternative erotic, affectionate currents (empowering to some, transgressive to others) is not insignificant to the aesthetic forms adopted by the *Negro Story* circle of writers, sometimes in the journal itself.

Brooks and the *Negro Story* Circle

One of the defining characteristics of *Negro Story*'s editorial voice is its self-conscious cultivation of a rhetorical intimacy and playfulness, its expression of imagined community as literary coterie. This approach to cultivating its readership is consonant, but also often in tension, with the Popular Front politics that Bill Mullen argues infused the project from its inception. The editorial of the magazine's inaugural May–June 1944 issue, entitled "A Letter to Our Readers" and cosigned by Gayden and Browning, declares, "We, the editors, as Negro women, not only welcome the opportunity to participate in the creation of a better world, but feel that we have an obligation to work and to struggle for it."[33] It goes on to declare, in a classic formulation of talented-tenth snobbery, "We also believe that Negroes have a great opportunity to achieve integration with the best elements of our society."[34]

Browning and Gayden employ this high-minded and orotund style only in the inaugural editorial, however; the following issues adopt that chatty, intimate voice that is the trademark of a publication reliant on a close-knit local community, and on correspondence, particularly with black soldiers serving in the military (among them members of the South Side group like William Couch and Edward Bland). An editorial postscript underscores this note: "We want very much to please all of you, and for that reason we want you to write us."[35] Anne Meis Knupfer has described *Negro Story* as a "writer's workshop" for black fiction writers at midcentury, and Maureen Convery is equally astute in noting the publication's role in "the development of an ecology of writing."[36] In the back of the issue, where Browning and Gayden gathered responses from their readers, one Dorothy Rappe wrote: "If your magazine should become a sort of official organ for the group, success could but be assured."[37]

The question of what that success should look like in terms of literary aesthetics greatly preoccupied the *Negro Story* circle writers. Black writers' "technique," "maturity," and ability to combine "racial themes" with "universal" appeal are recurrent and typical concerns of both the magazine's leadership and their readers, including elder statesmen like Fenton Johnson and Alain Locke, who approved specifically of the magazine's avoidance of propaganda. Yet the table of contents for the inaugural issue of *Negro Story* also reflects the dominance of Popular Front aesthetics and so-called protest fiction in its prose selections. Richard Wright's story "Almos' a Man" (collected in the posthumously published *Eight Men*) centers on the thwarted masculinity of its hero, Dave Sanders, in the rural South; Nick Aaron Ford, the pioneering academic and critic then teaching at Morgan State College, contributed a story entitled "With Malice toward None," described as "A Long Short Story about a Negro Who Was Almost Lynched"; and Aldon Bland's story "Let's Go Visiting," subtitled "She Did Not Trust White People," navigates tense interracial conversations in a middle-class parlor setting. Virtually all the contributions center on relations between black and white characters.[38] A majority of these stories also wear their antifascist politics on their sleeves: Himes's first *Negro Story* publication, "He Seen It In the Stars," playfully recounts the dream of a black theatergoer who falls asleep at the movies and wakes to find himself in Nazi Germany; the heroine of Bessie Scott's story "Into the Wild Blue Yonder" subtly bridges an antifascist arc from 1935 to 1945, when she learns that her husband has been killed by Mussolini's troops in the Ethiopia campaign. Many stories concern mistreatment, segregation, and hypocrisy in the American armed forces.[39]

A notable exception to this pattern is "Chicago Portraits: A Series of Sketches of Chicago Life," by Gwendolyn Brooks. This is the first prose publication by Brooks, but even more important (and surprisingly overlooked) is the fact that it is—with very minor alterations—the prose vignette that eventually became the chapter entitled "Kitchenette Folks" in *Maud Martha* almost ten years later.[40] In these sketch portraits of Bronzeville folk, there are no white characters and no interest in white racial attitudes and discrimination, either. They could be said to enact the "plotless realism" that Alice Browning calls for in one of her *Negro Story* editorials—but they stand out and apart from the other impressionistic short fiction in the magazine in ways that go beyond questions of plot or "protest."

The first sketch purports to tell us about a man with the unlikely name Oberto (a compound of Othello and Roberto?) who is pleased with his wife, Marie, despite her elaborately recounted "domestic sins." Her lackluster care for the household is contrasted, by way of the grapevine, with her neighbor's: "Nathalia, the wife of John the laundryman, kept her house smelling of Lysol and Gold Dust at all times." But Nathalia fails in her body care; she has "no acquaintance with the deodorant qualities of Mum, Hush, or Quiet," while Marie wears "My Sin perfume" from Lanvin and "clothes out of *Vogue* and *Harper's Bazaar*."[41] The tone of Brooks's narration is highly ambiguous. At times, it suggests the clichés of advertising: "Oberto thanked his lucky stars that he had had sense enough to marry his dainty little Marie." At others, it evokes the nosy gossip of cramped neighborhoods where people are always involving themselves in somebody's business and where women's behavior can be socially policed and judged in very specific ways: "Some folks did not count Marie among his blessings.... It was rumored, too, but not confirmed, that now and then she was obliged to make quiet calls of business on a certain Madame Lomiss, of Thirty-fourth and Calumet."[42] The characters neither develop nor appear to have anything other than a rhetorical reality: they are cutouts, a collage of voices collected by the narrator and presented in medias res.

There is no obvious referent in the text to racial oppression or to a larger scene of symbolic social struggle, such as the war against fascism, or discrimination in the classroom, the workplace, or social settings. Instead, Brooks's text operates entirely discursively, developing a wry, ironic deconstruction of popular attitudes as informed by the products of 1940s commercial and media culture. Ayesha Hardison makes the innovative argument that the scenes of reading (and being "racially" read) in *Maud Martha* reflect a concern with the scripts of the emerging middle-class consumer and their impact on how black female bodies are read—and require reading.[43] The presence of this prototext in the pages of *Negro Story* tells us that although Brooks's affective politics of friendship in her "circle" were unquestionably those of the Popular Front Left, she was already in 1944 thinking about how to advance a poetics that attended to "discursive dilemmas underlying black women's relationship to hegemonic culture."[44] That Brooks's prose sketches appear in *Negro Story* confirms her immersion in the populist politics of the day, as well as her social and affective connection to community (including the writers at the publication). Yet "Chicago Portraits" is a piece of experimental writing, in a way that Richard Wright's "Almos' a Man" is not. It shifts the kinds of questions that could be raised by a black writer. It intimated that a new black aesthetics might be forged not through the ideological projection of leftist content, symbolic revolt as a plot point, or epiphanies of racial or class consciousness, but through the repurposing of modernist form by a populist sensibility.

We can see the same aesthetic departure operating in Brooks's poem "Revision of the Invocation," which *Negro Story* published as its prize-winning poem in the May–June 1945 issue. The prize was funded by the Chicago District Congress of Industrial Organizations United Electrical Radio and Machine Workers and announced in the March–April 1945 issue. The labor union's support for the prize poem is cited by both Bill Mullen and Mary Helen Washington as evidence of *Negro Story*'s (and, by association, Gwendolyn Brooks's) connection to organized leftist politics. This is indisputable, and as I've suggested, a necessary context for understanding Brooks's incipient literary career in the Blue Period. But the poem itself suggests a compromise between the direction Brooks wanted to take in her poetic experiments and the external pressure to adopt a style of Popular Front address, one that she was never entirely comfortable with.

The subtitle of "Revision of the Invocation," which is "(The Negro: His pleas against intolerance)," announces it as a public apostrophe in the rhetorical tradition of the abolitionist tract. The speaker of the poem is, per the subtitle, the abstracted American "Negro," who has come to reject respectability as a condition for equality:

> Men of careful turns, haters of forks in the
>   road,
> The strain at the eye, that puzzlement, that
>   awe—
> Not as a craver of tolerance do I come,
> Begging that you bear me, that you endure
> Me, that you shrug, squeeze out the scanty
>   smile.
> Nor do I now ask alms, in shame gone hollow,
> Nor cringe outside the loud and sumptuous
>   gate.
> Admit me to our mutual estate.
> ....
> There are no magics or elves,
> Or timely godmothers to guide us. We are
>   lost, must
> Wizard a track through our own screaming
>   weed.[45]

If we read this as the voice of the pleading Negro, then the stilted formality of the speaker's voice appears at cross-purposes with its stated intent. The indifferent posture that the Negro asserts is his right to inhabit is belied by the strict composure that the claim rhetorically rests on. It feels rather like the occasion of the poem has overwhelmed its ability to express honestly. Things become more doubtful and stranger still when we reach the lines toward the end of the poem that invoke childhood, play, and fantasy. One can only wonder what the union members must have made of it, not because they would lack the cultural sophistication to appreciate it, but because the whole poem seems slightly askew—in a word, odd.

But there is a good reason this poem does not seem appropriate to the occasion for which it has been contrived. In reality, it is only one piece of a greater poem, whose subject is not "the Negro," but a very particular, carefully constructed, working-class, dark-skinned black girl with a fervid imagination. The poem that won the *Negro Story* poetry contest is more commonly known to us as the conclusion of Brooks's epic poem of black girlhood, *Annie Allen*, published in 1949 (and winner of the Pulitzer Prize in 1950); it appears as section 15 of the "Womanhood" sequence. This makes sense of the otherwise-inscrutable title of the poem as it appears in *Negro Story*; the invocation referenced is that of the opening of *Annie Allen*, Brooks's adaptation of the classical trope of the invocation of the muse in epic poetry.

This is remarkable for several reasons. It tells us that *Annie Allen* (for which Brooks went through an involved editing process with *Harper's* in 1948–1949) was already conceived as early as 1944 and also that substantial portions of it, including a conception of its ending as a "revision" of its opening, had already been composed by the spring of 1944. The poem that Brooks submitted for the *Negro Story* prize was part of an experimental project to fashion an innovative poetics that aimed, as Evie Shockley has shown, to "tell a poor, black woman's story by using two highly traditional, highly ceremonial (masculinist) formal structures: the epic genre and the rhyme royal-like stanza."[46] Shockley has argued persuasively that *Annie Allen* is not in fact a mock epic, as is sometimes claimed; rather, Brooks deliberately reinvents the epic as a quest for the validation and freedom of black interiority, as Shockley puts it, a "search first *within herself* for the nurturance and the resources she needs to create a satisfying life in the face of the challenges she faces as an African American woman."[47]

While the broad political commitments of such a project were consonant with the expectations of *Negro Story* and a prize funded by labor unions, the editors (or Brooks herself) recognized that it had to be repackaged as a Popular Front broadside. Hence the subtitle, which attempts to dress up the apostrophe to make it legible as a "protest" poem similar to, say, "Open Letter," Owen Dodson's contribution to the same issue, an antifascist and anti-racist solidarity poem whose last stanza apostrophizes in the familiar language of "the brotherhood of man":

> Brothers, let us enter that portal for good
> When peace surrounds us like a credible universe.
> Bury the agony, bury this hate, take our black
>   hands in yours.[48]

Brooks's lines are only obliquely aimed at the audience Dodson directly addresses. The development of consciousness in *Annie Allen* is not aimed at racial reconciliation or the solution of mass Popular Front politics; it is the growth of authority and independence, the announcement of a young, black, female poet staking her claim, on her own terms, within a tradition she is well-aware has always actively excluded her. As Lesley Wheeler writes, "Brooks as a poet, only barely still in the persona of Annie Allen, knocks on the door of the Anglo-American tradition, demanding to be admitted to its 'high' company."[49] In Brooks's fully formed poem, the men who are "haters of forks in the road" are the Robert Frost of "The Road Not Taken" and the band of brothers then dominating the American poetry scene, including T. S. Eliot and Wallace Stevens. When *Annie Allen* won the Pulitzer in 1950, the leading contenders it beat out were Robert Frost and William Carlos Williams.[50]

In her editorial announcement for Brooks's first prize for part of this poem, Alice Browning affirms Brooks's intimacy with the *Negro Story* circle, referring to her as "Gwen" and framing her win as a proxy victory for the group itself. After giving readers an overview of Brooks's career to that date, she writes: "We forgot to mention Gwen's equally charming husband—we mustn't neglect these men because they deserve credit for encouraging their talented wives.... Oh yes, one thing more—do you remember the clever little prose sketch by Gwen in our first issue?" Browning's framing does not exceptionalize Brooks but rather presents her to readers through the politics of friendship, the affective community that these women are forging together, with a nod to the men who support them and the elusive aesthetics of Brooks's first contribution, an experiment that was, in retrospect, a sign of things to come—the astonishing sequence of *A Street in Bronzeville* (1945), *Annie Allen* (1949), and *Maud Martha* (1953). The seeds for these projects were planted in *Negro Story*. They emerged out of the rich soil of Chicago's Popular Front, but they also broke new ground formally, pointing Brooks toward a future conjuncture that would require an aesthetic adapted for a harsher, more repressive, and more isolating cultural landscape.

MAUD MARTHA'S "KAITCHENETTE" CONVERSIONS

The word *kitchenette* is a twentieth-century Americanism, a diminutive derivation coined by the writers of *Variety* magazine, where it first appeared in print in 1910.[51] Founded in New York City in 1905, *Variety* first established itself as a trade journal catering to the flourishing show-business industry of vaudeville, Broadway, and Tin Pan Alley; its writers also quickly acquired a reputation for catchy neologisms. *Kitchenette* really caught on in the early 1920s, at the height of the Jazz Age, when it came to connote an ideal of modern urban domesticity even as it continued to enjoy a close connection to the world of entertainment. In 1921, Irving Berlin penned the song "In a Cozy Kitchenette Apartment" for the first installment of his *Music Box Revue*.[52] The song lyrics convey the promise of marital intimacy wedded to the spatial concessions of city living: "Oh, what bliss / When it's time to kiss / In a cozy kitchenette apartment for two!"[53] In Jazz Age Chicago, "kitchenette" apartment construction was especially popular in the neighborhood of Uptown, attracting investors, wealthy residents, and upscale commerce and leisure.[54] As Berlin's lyrics and Uptown's fortunes suggest, white Americans were enthusiastic about urban life and imagined a future shaped by city living.

The kitchenette of this rising urbanite class abruptly lost its sheen in the wake of the Great Depression. The same Uptown apartments were "converted" by landlords seeking to squeeze out profits in a depressed market by renting them to poorer ethnic migrants willing to share the same space in higher numbers. On the North Side of Chicago, Uptown's kitchenette housing stock took in poor, white, ethnic arrivals.[55] On the South Side, where Chicago's black population was legally segregated into a compressed, neatly demarcated ghetto bounded by rail tracks, the term *kitchenette* likewise came to be associated with dilapidated slum housing.[56]

A 1932 report produced by the Committee on Negro Housing, whose members included Nannie H. Burroughs, the educator and civic leader, and Charles S. Johnson, the prominent University of Chicago sociologist and director of the National Urban League, devoted a chapter to these apartments, "The Kitchenette." The report remarks upon the rapid expansion of this type of dwelling "in the last two years," and notes the markedly worse conditions of such units—"devoid of adequate sanitary conditions, light and air"—available to black residents even though "Negroes in kitchenette apartments pay more than do whites for even better apartments." The report contends that the kitchenette "lowers the moral tone" of its inhabitants and argues for a connection to a rise in "sex delinquency cases among Negro girls."[57]

By the Depression years, the term *kitchenette* had thus undergone a reversal from an ideal of urban living to a symbol of urban blight. And by the end of World War II, especially in the context of the city of Chicago, the term would evoke the living conditions of Horace R. Cayton and St. Clair Drake's *Black Metropolis* (1945) and endure in what historian Arnold Hirsch calls "The Second Ghetto," cemented in place by the planning and policy failures after the war. This doubling down on a formal system of segregation, this time with support from the federal government, took place even as the black population of the city swelled during the wartime years as migrants (who for the most part could not enlist in a segregated army) flocked north to take up defense jobs. Hirsch notes that the Chicago Community Inventory estimated that at least eighty thousand kitchenette conversions were carried out between 1940 and 1950, a period during which Chicago's nonwhite population increased by more than 80 percent.[58] Prone to destruction by fire, infested with rats, and with little or no access to heat and water, the all-American kitchenette by midcentury epitomized a shift in American attitudes toward urban living, from a vision of white domestic bliss to a nightmare of black urban despair. Kitchenette life was left to ethnic whites and poor blacks, while those with means (primarily middle-class whites) fled to the suburbs.

Gwendolyn Brooks introduced the kitchenette as the defining enclosure of the emergent postwar condition of poor and working-class African Americans. In the poem "kitchenette building" (her lowercase) from *A Street in Bronzeville*, she presents it as the site of a set of social conditions but also one that binds its inhabitants to—and separates them from—certain discursive possibilities:

> We are things of dry hours and the involuntary plan,
> Grayed in, and gray. "Dream" makes a giddy sound, not strong
> Like "rent," "feeding a wife," "satisfying a man."

The poem does not begin with a description of poor plumbing, lack of heating, or crumbling walls. It could have. Frank London Brown's novel *Trumbull Park* (1959) opens with his protagonist Buggy Martin listing the degradation of the same South Side interiors: "the Gardener building was real old, like Mr. Gardener, and rotten. Rotten from the inside out. Rotten toilets. Rotten windowsills. Rotten lamp cords. Rotten porches."[59] Instead, Brooks's "kitchenette building" listens for and enumerates the consequences of an "involuntary plan" for the speaker's socially constructed subjectivity, especially those aspects that regiment the duties and expectations defined by gender roles.

The declaration "we are things" places the speaker and the reader at the crossroads of what Fred Moten calls "the scene of objection."[60] Brooks evokes a long history of black commodification and failure of individuation, as when we learn in the fourth stanza that the speaker's ruminations are taking place while in the hallway waiting for "Number Five" to use a shared bathroom. "The history of blackness," Moten has said, nevertheless "is testament to the fact that objects can and sometimes do resist."[61] The appalling conditions of substandard housing and racist redlining did fuel a massive resistance movement, which eventually took on the shape of the civil rights movement, which grew during the 1950s and became the central, defining, and explosive political crisis of the 1960s. A literature that spoke directly to, and about, the effects of that resistance also emerged in Brown's *Trumbull Park*; Lorraine Hansberry's 1959 play, *A Raisin in the Sun*; and Julian Mayfield's 1961 novel, *The Grand Parade*.[62]

Brooks is attuned to a different form of resistance, however. She is interested in the resistance that takes place in ordinary, everyday life—that which is prior to formalized political action and encounter, the remainder that James C. Scott calls "the infra-political," a hidden transcript of working-class and underclass practices, and that Robin D. G. Kelley has argued forms a vital source of resistance in black working-class culture.[63] These kinds of everyday resistance are versions of what Michel de Certeau calls "tactics" and "ways of operating"; his theory is particularly relevant to Brooks for the way he reads these in relation to built space. "The weak must continually turn to their own ends forces alien to them," De Certeau says, adding that "many everyday practices (talking, reading, moving about, shopping, cooking, etc.) are tactical in character."[64]

The experiment in prose that Brooks began during the war years and that became the text of *Maud Martha* in 1953 tests the possibilities of these tactical maneuvers. At its center lies the force of a black working-class woman's will, exerted within the constraints of the South Side housing projects that define her everyday existence. The exercise of this will articulates a degree of freedom at once constituted by, and defiant toward, this hostile territory. Brooks recognized early on that the autonomous assertion of her own interiority would constitute a riposte to the racist constructions perpetually attempting to regulate it. She could see how representing a black infrapolitical working-class perspective using the techniques of literary modernism was already inherently subversive. Hortense Spillers, in her reading of the novel, makes this the focal point of her argument for its specifically feminine and racial character. "The demonstration, I believe, of woman-freedom is the text itself that has no force, no sticking point other than the imaginative nuances of the subject's consciousness," she writes. "Maud Martha's drama remains internal, and that interiority engenders the crucial aesthetic address of the work."[65]

Like other signal texts of the Blue Period, *Maud Martha* functions as an "aesthetic address" that records a resistant autonomy, what we might call a tactical dwelling in black interiority. Maud Martha's domain is, to use Kevin Quashie's excellent formulation, "the sovereignty of quiet."[66] Many scholars have noticed the importance and intensity of interiority in Brooks's novel, like the black feminist scholar Barbara Christian, who notes how "[Maud's] sense of her own integrity is rooted mostly in her own imagination—in her internal language."[67] Mary Helen Washington, in an influential reading, argues that the silence and reticence, the "constant self-analysis and self-consciousness," of Brooks's heroine are the effect of a rage that cannot find an outlet, one that went unrecognized by black and white critics steeped in the sexist and patriarchal assumptions of the Eisenhower 1950s.[68]

Quashie presses for a more expansive and a more persuasive case that the representation of Maud Martha's mind, her idiosyncratic and unaccountable way of thinking, are the novel's subject—the irreducible free-dom of the inner life, from rage to joy and everything in between: "This is what is so unusual about *Maud Martha*, that it privileges the inner life so unerringly and never falls prey to the tendency to order or organize that life in relationship to the social world, especially discourses of race, gen-der, or class. These are moments, impressions, and they are significant in the moment but not necessarily beyond it—certainly not conclusively. This is a way the inner life works."[69]

It is strange that one of the most famous novels about the "way the inner life works," Virginia Woolf's *Mrs. Dalloway* (1925) is seldom read in conjunc-tion with *Maud Martha*. This is all the more surprising given that Woolf's concern about the gendered representation of subjectivity is of special im-portance to her and Brooks alike. In her essay "Women and Fiction" (1929), Woolf puts her finger on the evanescent and private character to which women's lives are relegated under a patriarchal order: "Often nothing tan-gible remains of a woman's day. The food that has been cooked is eaten; the children that have been nursed have gone out into the world. Where does the accent fall? What is the salient point for the novelist to seize upon? It is difficult to say. Her life has an anonymous character which is baffling and puzzling in the extreme. For the first time, this dark country is beginning to be explored in fiction."[70] Woolf's use of an Africanist trope, "this dark country," to describe regions heretofore unexplored by fiction should, of course, give us pause. It reminds us that interiority and subjectivity are not in fact divisible from the forces that act from without upon the bodies that house them. Belonging to an imperial state involved in a colonial project tends to influence one's thinking, even when addressing apparently un-related topics like literary criticism—a point, incidentally, made vivid by the permeable, flickering unconscious with which Woolf endows Clarissa Dalloway and Septimus Smith. Woolf might not have known or been able to grasp it, but the question of "where the accent falls" was also Brooks's.

This question can be thought of, in part, as a problem of description. For the writers we most closely associate with modernism, Dora Zhang has ar-gued, description is primarily a private epistemological problem that car-ries over into stylistic practice and formal experimentation. They seek to incorporate, Zhang suggests, new ways of describing objects, scenes, and, above all, people that might elude description's traditionally referential or indexical function. Echoing Michael Levenson's observations about de-scriptive functions in Henry James's dialogues, Zhang proposes that mod-ernist description attempts to reach past reciprocity of understanding to discover expressions that "impart no theoretical or figural knowledge."[71]

In the familiar critical view, the modernists seek to incorporate a delib-erate fuzziness, reflecting a subject bewildered by rapidly evolving technological, industrial, and social changes that are outstripping the mores of the Victorian order. The modernists' sentences and perspectives are designed to reproduce the sensation of stumbling through this maze of overstimulation, of struggling to find or recover a correspondence between language and experience, thought and empirical observation, fluid and involuntary impulses of memory—all this with the constraints of an ordered sequence on the page that must necessarily make choices about where to begin, what to include, and when to stop.

For black writers like Brooks, however, the inherited tropes of late nineteenth-century literary traditions pose another distinct set of problems. For them, description is preeminently a social problem and a political liability; in private life (indivisible from social life in the slave narrative, the originary genre for black writing about the self), it is almost always a weapon of harm or for shame—one that can prove fatal. When James Joyce's Stephen Dedalus speaks of wanting "to create the uncreated conscience of his race," the Hibernians he has in mind are, of course, historically colonized and despised by England. But he is nevertheless articulating a social problem in personal terms, and crucially, in terms that he envisions as falling under the purview of the agency, power, and dignity of his own subjectivity. Ralph Ellison's "invisible" man responds allusively by seeking "to create the uncreated features of my face," a face whose mistaken identification is the source of a violent altercation that opens that novel.[72]

Indeed, the notorious problem of black suspects "fitting a description" is the social reality that the black writer, the black narrator, of modern fiction, must confront. She must seek to counterpose, perhaps even (I use the word advisedly) to *integrate*, the modernists' innovative thinking about the possibilities of description with a black writers' need to outrun, subvert, or otherwise preemptively disallow description from serving the hegemonic scripts and plots of racial dominance—including, of course, those constructed by white writers. Just as James Baldwin reverses Jamesian negation, Édouard Glissant reappropriates the epic, and Vincent O. Carter repurposes flâneurism, Gwendolyn Brooks refashions modernist description as way to navigate the political and aesthetic impasses of what she experienced as the Cold War's kitchenette modernity.

In the Blue Period, writers like these are the inheritors of both modernist experimentation and the ongoing search by black artists for ways to repurpose the master narratives that had long encoded black subjectivity within predefined stereotypes. These artists are, for the first time, poised to negotiate these competing concerns by forging new molds capable of harboring free thought, unbeholden to communal, social, or ideological imperatives—whether those cherished or explicitly demanded by the Left or those tendered forth by anticommunist Cold War American liberals on the Right.

That Land of Blue

Brooks's novel presents an excellent example of a writer adapting modernist descriptive modes in this manner. *Maud Martha* tarries, feigns, holds narrative time at bay—but crucially without allowing description to double as ascription. Hence the importance of the heroine's qualitative discernments that stand as ends in themselves, the "lyrical surplus" of thoughts that remain extraneous to plot development, that refuse to fold neatly into established racial allegories.[73] These descriptive strategies, new approaches to representing black thought and affect, explain the prevalence of formally eccentric texts like Brooks's *Maud Martha* in this period—fugitives, so to speak, from the plantation of proletarian social realism and from the complacent (or even jubilant) narrative of ethnic assimilation into US liberalism.

Recall, for a moment, the famous opening of Saul Bellow's contemporaneous novel *The Adventures of Augie March* (1953): "I am an American, Chicago born—Chicago, that somber city—and go at things as I have taught myself, free-style, and will make the record in my own way: first to knock, first admitted; sometimes an innocent knock, sometimes a not so innocent. But a man's character is his fate, says Heraclitus, and in the end there isn't any way to disguise the nature of the knocks by acoustical work on the door or gloving the knuckles."[74] The pugilistic swagger of this assertion of national belonging and priority—"first to knock, first admitted"—begs the question of who was first to knock and what happened to them. Maud Martha is, of course, also "an American, Chicago born," and she, too, "will make the record in her own way." But Augie's affective relation to the nation-state, with its sweepingly Whitmanian implications, is the opposite of Maud Martha's diremption and inward-looking lyricism. Making the record in her own way entails, as Mary Helen Washington observed, an unwelcome claim of literary authority that labors under the foreknowledge of its own dismissal and illegibility.

By comparison, consider the opening of Brooks's first chapter, "description of Maud Martha," which enumerates the heroine's delights in a single highly ramified sentence: "What she liked was candy buttons, and books, and painted music (deep blue, or delicate silver) and the west sky, so altering, viewed from the steps of the back porch; and dandelions."[75] The complexity of this opening is generated in part by Brooks's use of a deliberately stilted syntax, in particular the subordinated subjunctive "so altering" that shifts the grammatical subject midsentence, suggesting even as it enacts an almost kaleidoscopic, "altering" point of view. The use of free indirect discourse not only gives us a set of complicated images in its "painted music"; it also lists them in such a way as to convey a cadence of thought. The semicolon before the last fragment, "and dandelions," is a poetic device; it sets that last item off rhythmically, a move reminiscent of the poetic prose compounds of William Carlos Williams.

Brooks, very much a poet by vocation, uses style to help us overhear how Maud Martha thinks, the particularities of her perception. We get a portrait of young Maud Martha as a thinker, a dreamer, and, we might guess by her love of books and metaphor, a budding poet. What we emphatically do not get is what the title of this chapter promises, a "description of Maud Martha," at least in the conventional realist sense, where a character is described externally for the reader at the outset. In fact, nowhere in the opening chapter do we get a hint of what Maud Martha actually *looks* like. Tellingly, it is only in the last paragraph that we get an indirect account through a comparison to her light-skinned sister Helen. By the end of the first chapter, then, we have a rich sense of Maud Martha's interior life and her own judgment that the most relevant, or perhaps only relevant, detail about her physical appearance is her dark black skin.

Woolf opens *Mrs. Dalloway* with a sentence famous for its solid declarative simplicity: "Mrs. Dalloway said she would buy the flowers herself."[76] Like Maud Martha, Mrs. Dalloway likes flowers, but the ones she proposes to purchase herself, rather than using her maidservant Lucy's labor, are expensive ("delphiniums, sweet peas, bunches of lilac; and carnations"), cut and prepared in a store as attractive commodities to be purchased by the bourgeois women of London to furnish their homes.[77] In that world, flowers are to entertain guests, to accompany male proposals, or to signify attitudes of taste (as with Sally Seton's method of cutting off the heads and placing them in bowls of water); they function as a way to illustrate womanhood going with or against the grain of conformity.

Maud Martha's dandelions, by contrast, suggest the beauty of an abundantly prevalent weed and the leisure of childhood (dandelions being a favorite for blowing their seedlings off the stem).[78] For Maud Martha, flowers are not a decision to make or a symbolic token of one's relations to things and people. They are first and foremost an occasion for indirect reflection, a mirror to her inmost sense of her place in the world—lowly, plain, but brightening nonetheless: "She liked their demure prettiness second to their everydayness; for in that latter quality she thought she saw a picture of herself, and it was comforting to find that what was common could also be a flower."[79] This is psychological self-portraiture of a precociously mature kind, done by way of a careful, orderly, almost taxonomical self-regard that checks, sorts, and comments upon the daydreamy list that precedes it. The use of the indicative mood, "for in that latter quality she thought she saw," coupled with subordinate clauses that render the kernel of thought ever more elusive, carries a tonality more Jamesian than Woolfish.

Why does Brooks accentuate this vestibular analysis in lieu of a description of a more straightforward sort? One reason could be her awareness of the pressures of the racist tropes through which the figure of the young, dark-skinned, black woman has entered American literature. The self-possession of Maud Martha's self-description, viewed through the prism of a historical lineage, reads like a deliberate counterwriting of the infamous scene introducing Topsy in *Uncle Tom's Cabin* (1852). The passage when St. Clare presents his new purchase to Ophelia must be quoted at some length to give the full measure of its violent reification:

> She was one of the blackest of her race; and her round shining eyes, glittering as glass beads, moved with quick and restless glances over everything in the room. Her mouth, half open with astonishment at the wonders of the new Mas'r's parlor, displayed a white and brilliant set of teeth. Her woolly hair was braided in sundry little tails, which stuck out in every direction ... Altogether, there was something odd and goblin-like about her appearance,—something, as Miss Ophelia afterwards said, "so heathenish," as to inspire that good lady with utter dismay; and turning to St. Clare, she said, "Augustine, what in the world have you brought that thing here for?"[80]

Here is one ambivalent source, the literary genesis, for Brooks's "we are things" in "kitchenette building," and indeed, this source surfaces explicitly in her novel. Maud Martha has taken note of her neighbor Maryginia Washington, a light-skinned elder lady, who is said to have "loathed the darker members of her race but did rather enjoy playing the *grande dame* ... while they played, at least in her imagination, Topsys."[81] Maryginia's colorism and deployment of the pickaninny type are presented as casually symptomatic of Bronzeville's kitchenette small talk. Maud Martha passes no explicit judgment on Maryginia for these attitudes. But this passing reference to the American racist archetype inescapably informs our view of the effort at self-determination entailed in Maud Martha's decision to judge herself by her own standards.

The difference between the depictions of Mrs. Dalloway's determined agency to get her own flowers and the drift of Maud Martha's interior life—like dandelion seedpods floated on a puff of air, then contemplated—is not reducible to their class identity, to Clarissa's conscious belonging to a world of bourgeois solidity and mastery versus Maud Martha's dreamy detachment from a world of racism and poverty. Woolf's struggle is to convince her readers of the merit of attending to an ordinary woman's quotidian preoccupations and to persuade them that her fragmentary stream of consciousness compellingly captures it in flight. Brooks must do all this under the considerable pressure of a literary history that has relied on, and constructed itself against, the racial stereotyping of black women as over- or underemotional, unintelligent, excluded from modernism's otherwise keen interest in the inner life of the mind.

Searching for modernist precursors, D. H. Melhem compared Maud Martha to Gertrude Stein's mixed-race character Melanctha Herbert from the middle story in Stein's *Three Lives* (1909), while noting that the racialist stereotypes that the narrator of Stein's story employs "mar" and dim its representational capacities.[82] The comparison nonetheless usefully contrasts the struggle over interiority when racial blackness is factored into the equation. Lisa Ruddick, who reads "Melanctha" as a text struggling with the psychological theories of Stein's college mentor William James, has argued that the heroine's "wandering attention" and "experiential promiscuity" are allegorical of a Jamesian psychological type that is doomed in Darwinian terms because of its "unselective perception" and incapacity to act and think selfishly.[83] In other words, for Stein, Melanctha's blackness is concomitant with a symbolic lack; her interiority is of interest insofar as it is defective and theoretically illustrative of a dispersive psychic weakness that Stein might have feared was also her own. Melanctha cannot and does not survive; we learn that she dies of consumption in abject poverty. Brooks, by contrast, sees the very same ingredients of wandering and promiscuous attention as a source of vitality and a bulwark of autonomy that elude the racialist snares that surround her. Maud Martha not only survives; at the end of her narrative, she is also gravid and in phase with the natural world around her. The famously paratactic and declarative repetitions of Stein's mechanically taxonomical narrator are the antithesis of the magpie, pointillist specificity of the free indirect discourse through which we perceive the "painted music" of Maud Martha's mind.

Brooks makes an elective appropriation of her modernist predecessors, but, like her heroine, she takes the limited space of the kitchenette and adds her own subversive conversions to its master plans. Where black interiority has been scorned or simply elided, she reinscribes its presence as irrepressibly *there*, thinking for itself, marking its florescence in the "blue" spaces of its own invention. This way of describing and ascribing features to one's character might seem ordinary enough, but Maud Martha's musings are pointedly ordinary.[84] They are meaningfully so, insofar as they represent a hard-won reprieve from a history of literary misrepresentation, instrumentalization, and slander. And they are strategically so, inso-far as Brooks had to cannily forge a descriptive language that her readers would find plausible for a character whose social, familial, and racial be-longing a priori overdetermined so much of what they were willing to be-lieve she could be.

This tension is especially evident when it comes to Maud Martha's thwarted desires and furtive attempts to cultivate her mind, to her intel-lectual vehemence. Brooks uses a romantic intrigue to emphasize this pre-dicament. Maud grows infatuated with David McKemster, a young black student trying to integrate himself into the white literary culture of the University of Chicago; she is stymied when David dismisses her out of hand on account of her dark complexion. She ends up marrying Paul Phil-lips, a vain and socially ambitious grocery clerk who settles for her despite her dark skin but never ceases to entertain his attraction to lighter-skinned women, with whom Maud Martha must compete for his attentions.

In these cramped circumstances, good books matter. In an acidly comic scene, Brooks contrasts Paul's and Maud Martha's understand-ings of aspirational middle-class mobility through the politics of reading. In bed together as a newly married couple, he picks up a paperback copy of *Sex in the Married Life*, a book he bought for her instruction: "I want you to read this book … but at the right times, one chapter each night be-fore retiring."[85] Maud Martha pretends to accept this injunction but in-stead, through subterfuge, reads the novel *Of Human Bondage* by Somer-set Maugham, which relates the fate of Philip Carey, a medical student and sometime aspiring artist whose attachment to Mildred, a faithless woman, nearly ruins his life.

If this seems like an odd choice for Maud Martha, that's because it is. It was not Brooks's first preference. As Mary Helen Washington observes, "Brooks had originally chosen a book by Henry James, one of Brooks's favorite models for writing fiction but Lawrence [her editor at Harper's] called that selection 'improbable,' so Brooks changed it to the more pop-ular and less highbrow *Of Human Bondage*."[86] Washington assumes this represents an effort on the part of the editors at Harper's to move Brooks toward more "universal" content, that is, by liberal-minded writers who appeal especially to white readers. But Henry James was the paragon of that liberal-mindedness, the writer most championed by Lionel Trilling, among others, so this reasoning must be, at best, incomplete. It's more likely that the editors found it implausible to imagine a black woman hav-ing the capacity to read the protomodernist prose of Henry James. This, of course, flies in the face of Brooks's own late-modernist appropriations of James (among others), but the editorial assumption would be that the readerly life of Maud cannot be as complex or subtle as the writerly life of her creator. This redaction, tamping down the ardor and ambition of Maud's intellectual life, is a blow that strikes at the very heart of Brooks's creation.

We can't know for sure which Henry James novel Brooks had in mind, but by far the most logical choice is *The Portrait of a Lady*, his most popular novel—but more importantly, the story of a woman whose desire for independence of mind and spirit are ultimately crushed by her entrapment in a loveless marriage. This choice rhymes thematically with the plot and themes of *Maud Martha* in a way that *Of Human Bondage* clearly does not. The fact that Brooks's editor at Harper's could not imagine what Brooks could is itself a commentary on the challenge that any assertion of black interiority and its attendant politics of reading provokes. That challenge extended at the time to the good sense of someone tasked with reviewing a bold new manuscript by a Pulitzer Prize–winning writer. In that case, the editor had the upper hand; Maud Martha's imagination was clipped to suit the editor's sense of what was appropriate for a black woman to read.

The politics of reading and being read—the act of reading itself as a figure for interior life—is a central concern of the novel. Beyond the fact that liking books is one of the first things we learn about Maud, stealing away time to read, learning about new books, and reading the world around her are some of her most preoccupying activities. Maud is an especially fine reader of the social and cultural scripts being foisted upon black women. The emergence of a black print mass media (especially John H. Johnson's Chicago-based publishing empire, with its flagships *Ebony* and *Jet*), presented a highly prescriptive attitude toward gender roles, aggressive colorism, and normative sexuality. Adam Green has argued that in the mid-century, "Johnson Publishing offered a grammar for postmigration black experience, one matching new realities of urban societal complexity, and material change.... Far from selling out African Americans, Johnson Publishing in its early years sold the race new identities, a process that encouraged imagination of a black national community and made new notions of collective interest—and politics—plausible."[87] This production of imagined community is one of the critical backgrounds that informs Maud's melancholic dissatisfactions, producing a white noise that constantly infiltrates and interrupts her consciousness, notably her time for imaginative novelistic reading.[88]

As Ayesha Hardison has shown, *Maud Martha* in this way mounts a searing critique of these new identities circulating in Johnson's periodical empire, in particular their impact on black women. From her earliest prose sketches that prefigure *Maud Martha*, Brooks consistently showed an interest in teaching her readers, especially her women readers, how to use irony, parodic imitation, and surreal juxtaposition as strategic "tactics" to counter and creatively reappropriate the power of these media images. For Hardison, the novel is "a metafiction that purposefully excogitates how black women read, internalize, and embody hegemonic and nonhegemonic discourses," and thus it "intrinsically considers how black women are read—that is, negated—by white society and commodified by black publications."[89] Reconstructing the imagination of black womanhood beyond the boundaries imposed by Jane Crow and Johnson's ladies' magazines included, for Brooks, the possibility that an ordinary black woman might choose to read Henry James, might apply as tactical an intelligence to assessing Isabel Archer as she would to deconstructing pinup girls and home economics.

In a reading life, the mind is elsewhere. It inhabits spaces that can't be controlled or dominated from without. Nor are those spaces easily categorized. Brooks is adamant that what is most lively about Maud Martha is her mind, and nothing suggests that her states of mind reflect an undivided subjectivity. On the contrary, her very name alludes to Alfred, Lord Tennyson's "Maud" (1855), a poem that is quintessentially, as Allison Pease points out, "a narrative of self-division" whose motley metrical compositions (which unsettled and baffled contemporaneous readers) "create unsustainable moments of imaginative achievement that fail to fulfill expectation in the context of the surrounding narrative."[90] Brooks never renounced her affection for Tennyson or for the other poets she read and imitated in her youth, as evidenced in her enigmatic unpublished juvenilia.[91] Brooks's allusion was recognized early on by D. H. Melhem, who posits that it "recalls Tennyson's Maud grappling with passion and duty."[92] This seems right, although it leaves open the interpretive question of whether Brooks seeks to impute to her heroine the neurasthenic twitchiness of Tennyson's speaker or the titular otherworldly muse of his obsessive affections, whose "venturous climbings and tumbles / and childish escapes" present an ideal of unattainable innocence and uncorrupted maidenhood that the world of men (and their violent martial ambitions) cannot ever fully master.[93]

Both possibilities seem pertinent to the novel's dramatization of its heroine's consciousness. Maud Martha is keenly aware of those affects within her that remain unintegrated and, Brooks suggests, unassuageable: "She could neither resolve nor dismiss. There were those scraps of baffled hate in her, hate with no eyes, no smile and—this she especially regretted, called her hungriest lack—not much voice."[94] This "baffled hate" is not without voice entirely; the whole novel, close as it is to her point of view, is testament to Maud Martha's capacity to find words for what is singular about her experience. But the lessons her life has taught her produce an incommensurability of knowledge that issues a division between that which is voiced and the rest, much more by implication, that remains beyond articulation.

The morbid tone of Tennyson's "Maud," it has been argued, is a reflection of the poet's incapacity to summon confidence in the power of elegy to adequately memorialize grief, as he had done in his celebrated "In Memoriam."[95] The shadow of "Maud" in Brooks's novel is most salient in its explicit irresolution about the capacity of language to capture the internalized "scraps," the remainders, the scars that are inevitable for a racialized subjectivity. For Maud Martha, racism is not an overbearing systemic force. It is a thousand cuts that divide her mind and spirit, that exist for her as a fragmented interiority of felt experience. This is why conflict in *Maud Martha* is primarily waged in and through a mental battlefield where the protagonist's fierce concentration of mind is often the pertinent factor.

Some of that moxie is unaccountable and some of it strategic. As a young mother with few resources, and largely dependent on her husband, she can ill afford the costs of open confrontation. Thus, in an apparently unremarkable scene of domestic married life, martial figures unfold within her internal dialogue: "Do you want to get into the war? Maud Martha 'thought at' Paul, as, over their wine, she watched his eye-light take leave of her."[96] The irregular prepositional use is meant to give *thought* the force of action, direction—an almost electrical shock of concentration that, if voiced aloud, would strike Paul like a blow across the face. This scene is typical rather than exceptional to the novel, and a great many of Maud Martha's interactions can be said to involve various ways of attacking others or protecting herself from them by "thinking at" them rather than acting out physical resistance.

Another instance of this is when Maud Martha is waiting at her friend Sonia Johnson's beauty parlor. When an apparently well-off and friendly white woman comes in to make a sales pitch for a new beauty product, Johnson is particularly ingratiating in agreeing to her offer. As she's leaving, the white sales lady casually remarks: "I work like a nigger to make a few pennies. A few lousy pennies." Maud Martha is convinced Johnson wouldn't let this woman use that language in her own store without making some remark and so begins to doubt whether she has really heard correctly. But after the white woman has left, Johnson comes over and deliberately explains to Maud Martha that she thinks "our people is [*sic*] got to stop feeling so sensitive about these words like 'nigger' and such," and she suggests that there's no point to resisting all the time: "Why make enemies? Why go getting all hot and bothered."

Brooks gives her heroine the last word, but that word is not spoken. Instead, it is made self-evident through repetition: "Maud Martha stared steadily into Sonia Johnson's irises. She said nothing. She kept on staring into Sonia Johnson's irises."[97] This insinuation of self-doubt and un-spoken intensity into apparently banal quotidian situations makes this passage eerily prophetic of the microaggression prose poems that Clau-dia Rankine will come to write much later in her own book-length prose-poem *Citizen*.[98] Indeed, as another poetically driven narrative of a woman struggling to navigate raced expectations in a blithely unaware and often violently ignorant society, *Maud Martha* can be seen as the closest precur-sor to Rankine's work.

Maud Martha's last major action is one of self-gathering, restraint, heroic composure. It is staged as a war of impulses within her own mind as she commits herself to shielding her daughter Paulette from the full knowledge that the shopping center Santa Claus refused to shake her hand because she was black: "Feeling her mother's peep, Paulette turned her face upward. Maud Martha wanted to cry. Keep her that land of blue!"[99] The use of repetition as an index of the cogitative is not restricted to sit-uations of racialization. In a manner strikingly akin to Woolf, Brooks em-ploys deictic sentences to do the work of existential synecdoche, pointing through descriptions of the surrounding environment to the elusive skein that binds together the full span of impressions available to a conscious-ness aware of being alive. From *Maud Martha*:

> She did not have to tip back the shade of her little window to know that out-side it was bright, because the sunshine had broken through the dark green of that shade and was glorifying every bit of her room. And the air crawl-ing in at the half-inch crack was like a feather, and it tickled her throat, it teased her lashes, it made her sit up in bed and stretch, and zip the dark green shade up to the very top of the window—and made her whisper, What, *what* am I to do with all of this life?"
> And exactly what was one to do with it all?[100]

From *Mrs. Dalloway*:

> For she was a child, throwing bread to the ducks, between her parents, and at the same time a grown woman coming to her parents who stood by the lake, holding her life in her arms which, as she neared them, grew larger and larger in her arms, until it became a whole life, a complete life, which she put down by them and said, "This is what I have made of it! This!" And what had she made of it? What indeed? sitting there sewing this morning with Peter.[101]

Clarissa Dalloway's magnifying, telescopic view into her past is Proustian and retrospective, where Maud Martha's smooth paratactic connection to the life force in her sunlit opening is attached to the present and looks ahead to the prospective life still to come. But both insist on the largeness of their heroines' view of life. Maud Martha may have only a "little window" in her kitchenette to look out of, and Clarissa may be sewing with Peter; the domestic is inextricable from the quality of their lives as women. But they are not restricted to a domesticated view of those lives—the emphasis is on what exceeds that frame, even if it cannot be named.

It's worth remembering, too, that the kitchenette was as serious a symbol for the Cold War as the hydrogen bomb or a battlefield in Korea. The Khrushchev-Nixon Kitchen Debate of 1959 is sometimes thought of as an amusing, if symptomatic, occasion for the clash between Soviet and American schemes for the utopian future. But behind it lies an important truth: the domestic sphere was enlisted in the ideological struggle, and in many ways, it could even be said paradoxically to represent the front lines of that battle. For Mary Helen Washington, "If the culture of the Cold War was designed to produce smooth surfaces for US consumption—images of domestic family tranquility with the woman's place in home and family, good wars, and the harmony of racial integration, interracial cooperation, and black docility—Maud Martha disrupts on every front."[102] Yet crucially, Maud Martha's disruptions cannot be answered by either of the Cold Warrior's tendered projects. When Mrs. Dalloway declares, "This is what I have made of it!" her subsequent two questions, "And what had she made of it? What indeed?," register a subtle shift of thought from the habitually rhetorical to the genuinely existential. Similarly, when Maud Martha asks, "What, *what* am I to do with all of this life?" the interrogation is clearly unanswerable in political, ideological, or even strictly materialist terms. Mrs. Dalloway speaks nonetheless in possessive and agential terms; however one looks at it, her life is something she has *made*. Maud Martha's life is yet to come, and her struggle is with the sense of her unfulfilled futurity, what she will do given that the world is not yet ready to recognize the fullness of her personhood. For both women, the entire implication is that there is an abundance of feeling, desire, and imaginative thrust that remains unrecognizable to the forces that have shaped their circumstances. Whether it is simply a choice about what one is reading, the refusal to dismiss one's dreams ("what she wanted to dream, and dreamed, was her affair"), or the self-satisfaction of quiet observation, *Maud Martha* challenges us, as Elizabeth Alexander argues all of Brooks's poetic writings do, "to see what's underneath and inside the façades we have willingly and unwillingly worn."[103]

Maud Martha's darting imagination produces what amounts to a kind of poetic counterstudy to St. Clair Drake and Horace Cayton's *Black Metropolis* (1945). It is designed to recoup everything that must necessarily slip through the sociologist's sieve. Her mode of curiosity allows for a receptivity to the exorbitant vivacity of black vernacular—passing rumor, racy gossip, casual anecdote, and stray parable—without the need to explain or justify its function. These supplemental details and interjected clippings flicker into earshot like stray radio waves whose lower frequencies are indeterminate with respect to formal political categories. Summing them up cannot give comfort to liberal or conservative arguments about black poverty. They cannot dispel or confirm the host of racist myths that saturate American popular culture. They could equally give credence to a Moynihan Report or a Kerner Commission. To Brooks, *black liveliness* matters, and her poetics are a testament to her determination to press language into any syntax that will convey that quality, independent and indifferent to any horizon of expectation.

How should we read her experiment from the point of view of literary form? One line of criticism has attempted to classify *Maud Martha* as a category of proletarian fiction that Michael Denning calls the "ghetto pastoral." For Denning, this denotes novels that, with or without a strict fidelity to naturalism, imbue working-class characters with heroic or allegorical values, producing a kind of pastoralism—a notion Denning borrows from William Empson's well-known study of the pastoral.[104] While Denning's category is compelling in many respects, it is also incredibly diffuse, embracing writers as diverse as Tillie Olsen, Gertrude Stein, and Michael Gold; it is not always entirely clear what won't count as a ghetto pastoral in his eyes.[105]

Denning's epigraph to his chapter on the ghetto pastoral is from Michael Gold, the Marxist novelist and critic for the *New Masses* who famously excoriated Gertrude Stein for her bourgeois values and described her as a "literary idiot."[106] Gold declared of his own fiction, "When I think it is the tenement thinking. When I hope it is the tenement hoping. I am not an individual. I am all that the tenement poured into me during those early years of my spiritual travail."[107] The statement "I am not an individual" could not run more directly counter to the spirit of *Maud Martha*, whose intensely explored individuality is not only deeply prized by Brooks but also, as I have argued, an important end in itself precisely for the ways it fails to perform the type of social synecdoche Gold sought to achieve.

In a telling bit of annotation that Mary Helen Washington has thankfully unearthed in Brooks's papers, there is a bit of marginalia in a review by Eleanor Ross Taylor of Sylvia Plath's *Ariel* (1967). Brooks circled the line: "one chief pleasure of poetry, the feeling of having come upon a silence, a privacy, upon intellect existing unselfconsciously somewhere out of reach of camera." Washington says that she is including this tidbit "as a caution to anyone attempting to pin down Brooks's political or personal views" and that "she meant to create a poetic persona that could not easily be apprehended."[108] Clearly the power of reading and writing to allow one to exist "somewhere out of reach" is at the heart of Brooks's understanding of literary power. This is a way of thinking about power that can't be reconciled with the ghetto pastoral.[109]

Barbara Foley has argued that for proletarian literature, "the key issue to be addressed was not the knowledge or theory of class struggle, but practice: would the reader take sides and get out into the streets?"[110] Can *Maud Martha* be said to operate in that manner? The answer is clearly no. Yet to thereby divest it of a political consciousness seems equally false if one accepts, as we ought to, that the political can exist beyond its material instantiations and, indeed, sometimes must. The truth is that Gwendolyn Brooks's *Maud Martha* resembles Tillie Olsen's *Yonnondio* about as much as it resembles Virginia Woolf's *Mrs. Dalloway*, which is to say that it cannot comfortably be located squarely in either camp. It requires a fresh category that articulates its aesthetics and politics under a new configuration, one that is best understood as a "blue" response to a period when the orientation of the writer and the direction of world politics cannot fuse in good conscience.

Brown Girls and Blue Books

Elusion exacts a cost, and not all attempts at it are successful. But a failure to escape is not equivalent to giving up on a desire for subterfuge. What remains is not perforce neutral. It is striking that two of the great black novels of the 1950s, Gwendolyn Brooks's *Maud Martha* (1953) and Paule Marshall's *Brown Girl, Brownstones* (1959), are portraits of black women who explore the possibilities of eluding the normative scripts of their respective upbringings. They acquiesce neither to black submission nor to any prescriptive notion of black resistance. They do not join revolutionary movements; they do not become leaders of their communities; they are not martyrs to state violence; they do not murder their symbolic or real oppressors. These Blue Period books are preludes to possible action down the line, but they remain interested chiefly in what goes on in the mind of women whose decisions lead them along a path of alienation and dissidence toward a self-determined autonomy.

Marshall's 1959 debut, having fallen out of favor during the high tide of the Black Arts Movement, was rehabilitated by the work of the feminist critics Barbara Christian, Valerie Smith, and Mary Helen Washington in the early 1980s. During this same period, even as she continued to publish works of fiction, Marshall also produced autobiographical, critical, and essayistic writings that have helped solidify our understanding of the contexts and trajectory of her writing, in particular its indebtedness to Brooks's *Maud Martha* and Ellison's *Invisible Man*. In her autobiographical essay "From the Poets in the Kitchen," Marshall writes: "My mother and her friends were after all the female counterpart of Ralph Ellison's *Invisible Man*. Indeed, you might say they suffered a triple invisibility, being black, female and foreigners. They really didn't count in American society except as a source of cheap labor. But given the kind of women they were, they couldn't tolerate the fact of their invisibility, their powerlessness. And they fought back, using the only weapon at their command: the spoken word."[111] And Marshall told Washington that until she read *Maud Martha*, she felt that "it was rare to see a black woman in literature, with a conscious, interior life."[112] Like Maud Martha creating a poetic world out of her kitchenette, Paule Marshall learned the craft of writing in "of all places the ground floor kitchen of a brownstone house in Brooklyn."[113] The women who sat around the table in that kitchen made poetry out of everyday practices, imposed their own way of operating, "fought back" against a condition of powerlessness. The gift of that social instruction (and induction), the "rich legacy of language and culture they so freely passed on to me in the wordshop of the kitchen," in Marshall's evocative phrase, articulates a common link to Brooks and Ellison. I would describe this as a Blue Period novelistic aesthetic: the resistant potential of the alienated but lucid individual, and the conversion of despairing circumstances into occasions for radical transformations of the self. The echoing of these strategies between these texts is striking. Reading them in dialogue gives us a sense of their importance as key texts of the Blue Period during which they emerged.

Brown Girl, Brownstones is largely set in the 1940s and recounts the early life trajectory of a young black woman, in this instance not on the South Side of Chicago but as the daughter of Bajan immigrants to Brooklyn. Where Brooks focuses on early marriage and motherhood, Marshall's plot is centered on her heroine Selina Boyce's resistance to, and eventual sublimation of, her parents' divergent reactions to their newly adopted country. Selina's father, Deighton, dreams of a return to the native land; her mother, Silla, is hitched to the ideal of assimilation and, understanding that the path to that position in US society passes through property ownership, determined to become the owner of a brownstone.

Both Maud Martha and Selina belong to an intermedial social class. Maud Martha is not a factory worker or a laundress, but neither is she a successful member of the rising black middle class; Selina's mother gets work in a defense factory when the war starts, and her father works with other Bajan men from the neighborhood in a mattress factory until a work accident disables him. Her immigrant community is resolutely upwardly mobile, however, so both characters are poised between the rungs of a lower working class, but one with strong aspirations.

Maud Martha is immersed in a world of advertised commodities, home comforts—the glamour of lifestyles projected through Hollywood or glossy New York fashion magazines like *Vogue* and *Bazaar*—but lacks the means to attain them. These symbolic fruits of paradise are perpetually held out of reach, their distribution sharply bounded at every turn by class and racial hierarchies, spatial restriction, verbal hostility, and intraracial color prejudice. Selina is a reluctant and skeptical beneficiary of the limited access to the fruits that her parents moved to America to secure for her, a major source of friction with her mother. Selina longs, above all, for a relational and social warmth that money can't buy, one that she associates with her father and his nostalgia for the home island. In neither of the two novels are these mismatches and dislocations of positionality resolved. To borrow from the contemporaneous title of Langston Hughes, they are the "montage of a dream deferred."[114]

The central difference between Maud Martha's early life and Selina Boyce's growth from girlhood to the threshold of womanhood is the institution of marriage. Among the kitchenette folks in Bronzeville, there seems to be little avoiding it or the children that follow. Maud Martha is not opposed to marriage and regards it as pragmatic for beings needful of others. She muses: "People have to choose something decently constant to depend on … The marriage shell, not the romance, or love, it might contain. A marriage, the plainer, the more plateaulike, the better. A marriage made up of Sunday papers and shoeless feet, baking powder biscuits, baby baths, and matinees and laundrymen, and potato plants in the kitchen window."[115] Maud Martha does not, and cannot, conceive of a revolt that would fundamentally destroy what she regards as pleasant and useful conventions for living. Her quest is to carve out a space within that social fabric that will still somehow answer to her inmost aspirations for herself while also securing the safety and flourishing of her children in a world saturated by antiblackness.

Selina seeks to make a far more decisive break. She cannot buy into the American way of life, especially as it is pursued by her community of Afro-Caribbean immigrants who are, at least theoretically, trying to incarnate the ideals of the "model minority." As Mary Helen Washington notes, "not one person in this novel is unemployed," although, to be fair, some—like Suggie and Clive—are not exactly respectable either; these latter two represent an internally dissenting class of Barbadians that Selina will align herself with.[116] Marshall's novel is plotted around its protagonist's youthful rebellion against bourgeois restriction and immigrant assimilation. Selina systematically rejects the classic pillars of Louis Althusser's "ideological state apparatus": she disdains the church, specifically her father's enthrallment with Father Peace, a very thinly disguised Father Divine of Harlem; she is alienated from her schooling ("everything that happened at school had the unreality of a play viewed from a high balcony"); and she eschews marriage by taking up an unmarried sexual relationship with the bohemian artist Clive.[117]

As we've seen, compared to Selina Boyce's disappointments, Maud Martha's are harsher, more bitter for being so hard-won. She doesn't get to go to college. She can only envy the facility with which the young "beau" David has already learned to master the habitus of the academic, "the educated smile, the slight bow, the faint impervious nod," the way he complains to her that he's at a disadvantage because his parents never discussed Parrington's *Main Currents in American Thought* at the dinner table.[118] She doesn't enjoy sexy getaways to her lover's sofa as Selina does with Clive. She endures a passionless marriage to Paul and the austere exigencies of raising a child. And while there are distinctions within the Bajan community (Suggie's loose ways ostracize her, for example), Selina is not assailed by the implacable colorism that haunts every aspect of Maud Martha's life.

This is perhaps the difference that allows Selina to find the courage to betray the assimilationist cause of her community, including their attempts at organized political action and internal self-policing. "The Association" in *Brown Girl, Brownstones*, not unlike "The Brotherhood" in *Invisible Man*, seeks to enlist Selina's talents. It is hardly surprising that when Selina finally breaks with the association, the fracture is of existential proportions. Stepping off the speaker's platform after she has theatrically and very publicly declared that her "dedication was false" is tantamount to going into exile: "The loud rustle of her gown, the staccato tap of her heels in the stiff silence bespoke her final alienation. And as the familiar faces fell away behind her, she was aware of the loneliness coiled fast around her freedom."[119] There is, of course, a "loneliness coiled fast around freedom" in Maud Martha's life, too, or rather, in her evasions from that life, and her struggle to retain her hopes and dreams.

The hero of black consciousness in the Blue Period has lost faith in ideological affiliation, whether it's the right downtown social club like the Foxy Cats Club in *Maud Martha* (liberal assimilation or integration), the Barbadian Block Association in *Brown Girl, Brownstones* (nationalist communitarian uplift), or the Brotherhood in *Invisible Man* (communism). These figures are driven instead by epiphanies that point to imaginative evasion, hibernation, fugitivity in diaspora—strategies of alienation that establish a holding pattern as one hopes for a better day to come. Each of these novels, in its own way, allegorizes the formation of racial consciousness as a form of resistance while remaining agnostic, pessimistic, or openly hostile toward organized politics and ideological structures that others think they should take comfort in, place their hopes in, or in some other way commit themselves to.

At issue here is not just the freedom of their own poetic imagination and self-determination but the structure of epiphany itself. One over-looked aspect of *Brown Girl, Brownstones* is the way Marshall connects Se-lina's rejection of the social constructs around her to a sexual awakening that is channeled through her newfound idiosyncratic assertiveness and confident self-pleasuring, traits that she associates with specifically Afri-can American (as opposed to Barbadian) culture. When Selina first learns in a lunchroom huddle about a girl in her school who has gone "all the way" with a boy, Marshall uses direct speech to cue the reader to the un-named girl's American blackness to differentiate her from the other West Indian girls in the conversation: "Girl, I was so embarrassed I almost fell out." The exchange with Selina is brief, but the distinctively idiomatic use of *girl* as an emotive interjection that shades into a cognitive one estab-lishes and demarcates a complicity of feeling that sets them apart from the other girls who are frightened and judgmental of these revelations. In fact, Selina recognizes that "she was envious. For the girl seemed sud-denly awakened into life ... She had thumbed her nose at them, at her nag-ging aunt, at everyone ... Could she, Selina, if given the chance be that bold?"[120] Selina, of course, will be that bold, choosing to sleep with Clive and refusing to accept the scholarship award that her community wants to bestow upon her.

But before she can reach that stage of assertion, she passes through a phase during her first year of college which can be described only as that of a *flâneuse* out on the town. In a long, digressive frieze full of noirish al-lure, Marshall describes Selina refusing to socialize with her college class-mates and instead "every afternoon" taking "long reckless walks" alone into Midtown Manhattan.[121] Her poise and desire are aligned with the ur-ban space itself, a sexualized, self-fashioning spectacle of excess that can-not be controlled or domesticated. "Evenings always found her striding, head up, tam askew, through Times Square, that bejeweled navel in the city's long sinuous form.... She walked with a swagger here, gazing boldly into those faces, always hoping to happen upon some violence, or to be in-volved in some spectacular brawl."[122] Selina uses her time alone to culti-vate a way of moving through the world that allows her to cast off the striv-ing respectability politics and bourgeois ethics of her immigrant mother. Indeed, as we discover by the framing of the vignette, Selina's flânerie is psychologically transitional; she is replacing her mother with a surro-gate in Miss Thompson, the African American hairdresser who provides

Selina with a cathexis to a broader conception of her own blackness, one conceived as a commonality of feeling and sensibility rather than as class or political affiliation. The expression of that blackness has a form—the sound of the Blue Period—the experimental bebop and jazz of the midcentury. Marshall uses it as the emotional canvas upon which to paint Selina's alienated but enlivened interiority:

> For hours she stood outside the Metropole, listening to the jazz that poured through the open doors in a thick guttural flow that churned the air into a pulsating mass; sometimes the music was thin and reedy, sometimes brassy and jarring, yet often soulful, and always expressing the chaos in the street. She would shift amid the crowd for a glimpse of the sailors strung along the bar, the brilliant streak of a woman's blond hair in the dimness and smoke, a gleam of silver on the drums, the pomaded head of a Negro musician. Standing there with her books stacked on the ground between her legs, her fists plunged in her pockets and her lean body absorbing each note, she would feel sucked into the roaring center, the lights exploding inside her, and she would be free of the numbness.[123]

There is an unmistakable autoeroticism to this passage. With its whiff of polymorphous perversity and suggestions of an alternative curriculum where Selina's reading life, "stacked on the ground between her legs," is at once a source of phallic authority she has mastered and what Eve Kosofsky Sedgwick would call "the revelatory power of the Muse of Masturbation," which calls her toward a rising, vectorless, climax whose very rhythms and aural seductions merge with the sound, and above all its erotic sociality, one that the "Negro musician" sends radiating out from inside the jazz club and into the street.[124] The free indirect specification of *Negro* is once again not incidental. It resurfaces in the following chapter when Claremont Sealy, who is accused of being a communist by the other members, urges the community to use *Negro* instead of *Barbadian* in the association's slogans. Selina will seal her division from her fellow Bajans by picking up on this same internal quarrel as justification for her contempt: "Clannish. Narrow-minded. Selfish.... Prejudiced. Pitiful—because who out there in that white world you're so feverishly courting gives one damn whether you change the word *Barbadian* to *Negro*? Provincial! That's your Association." The field of formal politics holds no appeal to Selina and represents everything she detests; it is the very opposite in form and spirit of the flowing, self-authorizing, and self-fashioning black sensibility that she identifies with, even as an outsider to it, a young woman still finding out who she is, peering in from the sidewalk, feeling—through the music—the warmth of something she can understand wanting to be a part of. Those qualities that Sedgwick so shrewdly identifies with Marianne Dashwood in Austen's *Sense and Sensibility*, "a certain autoerotic closure, absentation, self-sufficiency," are in Selina's case not punished by illness, but they nevertheless result in a foregone movement toward self-ostracization, an exilic subjectivity, the typical denouement for a Blue Period novel.[125]

Like Gwendolyn Brooks, Paule Marshall does not equate individual alienation with a dissolution of affective community, even when that alienation seems to require actively dissenting from formal, institutional, or inherited communal bonds. What these novels insist upon is that the conditions for freedom, whether collective or individual, must first be located in and emerge from within a self-discovered personhood. When Selina is forced to confront "with a sharp and shattering clarity—the full meaning of her black skin," that intensely private experience nevertheless takes on a much broader, and indeed social aspect.[126] Through that diremption, she comes to feel for herself how it is that her own life is bound to that of American blacks, how she is "one with Miss Thompson ... one with the whores, the flashy men, and the blues," and even one with her chief antagonist, "the mother," and through her, all Bajan women.[127]

The work of these novels, the role of the innovative poetics that they marshal, is to express and give rhetorical shape to the possibilities of an affective politics that carves out a space for the individual. Selina's epiphany is the first of many footsteps that Paule Marshall's fictional heroines will take in future novels as they do the work of gathering all that has come down the roads of the triangular diaspora.[128] But in *Brown Girl, Brownstones*, the thrust of the implication is projective; we leave Selina (not unlike Isabel Archer) in midflight toward a destiny we cannot know. Ellison's narrator decides to wait things out underground. Maud Martha's last (but perhaps best) hope lies in a future generation, in the child she is carrying and that the universe seems to shine on in the last line of the novel: "the weather was bidding her bon voyage."[129] A hibernation, a generation, diasporic evasion—these are the lines of flight, or rather, of sight.

Selina's last vision of Brooklyn is an indictment of a postwar order that under all its shining commercial trinkets is cannibalizing itself. The middle-class blocks where she grew up have become "ravaged ... a vast waste—an area where blocks of brownstones had been blasted to make way for a city project."[130] Like a scene from a wartime newsreel, she sees how "a solitary wall stood perversely amid the rubble ... a carved oak staircase led only to the night sky."[131] She is looking in upon the rise of the postwar housing projects, then still under construction, the funereal air of their "monolithic shapes" hulking over "this giant cairn of stone and silence."[132] The rise of this "kitchenette modernity" across America, from the black ghettos of Chicago's South Side to the blasted brownstones of

Brooklyn, leaves black writers of this moment with no obvious weapon. The great social and labor movements can no longer operate in the hysterical atmosphere of the Red Scare. The language of oppression and resistance, how they are experienced, distributed, and mediated—all of this is changing. Against the onslaught, the gift of the artist can seem, as Selina's last gesture suggests, "a frail sound in that utter silence."[133]

Yet resistance in these texts, if read the right way, can be just the opposite of frail: it can be shockingly explosive, radical precisely for the ways it goes beyond the ideological frameworks of the period. I want to close this chapter on Brooks by examining a remarkable but little-commented-upon scene in *Maud Martha* that serves as a bridge to my consideration of Richard Wright's *The Outsider*. The scene takes place near the end of the novel, when Maud Martha, who needs to save money for her coming child, goes to work as a cook for the Burns-Coopers, a wealthy couple who live in the ritzy Chicago area known as the Gold Coast. After enduring Mrs. Burns-Cooper's endless account of the fine things in her life that will forever be out of her reach, Maud Martha is reprimanded by the husband, Mr. Burns-Cooper, for not peeling potatoes with sufficient finesse. Maud decides then and there to quit. She reflects on the fact that her employers will never understand her reasons: "One walked out from that perfect wall, spitting at the firing squad. What difference did it make whether the firing squad understood or did not understand the manner of one's retaliation or why one had to retaliate? Why, one was a human being. One wore clean nightgowns. One loved one's baby. One drank cocoa by the fire—or the gas range—come the evening, in the wintertime."[134] This startling image of violence, resistance, and fierce pride is shockingly close to the stark existentialist posture of Damon Cross in Richard Wright's *The Outsider*, the novel that I turn to in the next chapter. The icy fury contained by Maud Martha's composure turns the incident at the Burns-Cooper household into a summary execution. The act of being scolded and degraded as "the help" is met with fearless contempt. Retaliation is declared not as optional, but in some sense as already accomplished, hovering as a suspended sentence over the unsuspecting, wealthy, white couple. The jarring juxtaposition of such violence to domestic tranquility—of the "firing squad" to "cocoa by the fire"—only underscores the enormous tension coiled up, ready at any moment to be set loose "come the evening." The seemingly incidental qualification, "or the gas range," creates a sense of pending explosion, the pilot light ready.

One cannot help think, too, of the narrator of *Invisible Man*, who reminds his readers that despite having denounced the Brotherhood and its formal platform of revolutionary politics, he has not renounced action itself, only delayed it: "a hibernation is a covert preparation for a more overt action."[135] This image of the black outsider who has abandoned the terrain of formal party politics, of the revolutionary masses, but lurks, waiting out the winter of our discontent—this incendiary image, which is also Selina Boyce's and Maud Martha's, is the cool blue flame of a revolt to come, one that, as we will see, can achieve violent ends that remain, even now, difficult to contemplate directly.

CHAPTER FIVE

Richard Wright's Negations

A human being lives not only his personal life as an individual, but also, consciously or subconsciously, the lives of his epoch and contemporaries; and although he may regard the general and impersonal foundations of his existence as unequivocal givens and take them for granted, having as little intention of subjecting them to critique as our good Hans Castorp had, it is nevertheless quite possible that he senses his own moral well-being to be somehow impaired by the lack of critique.[1]

THOMAS MANN, *The Magic Mountain*, 1924

In 2015, the Indian novelist and essayist Pankaj Mishra published a column in the *New York Times* entitled "Whatever Happened to the Novel of Ideas?" In it, Mishra proposes that, at least in America, "in the postwar period, serious intellectual life retreated from the public sphere to the university. The "'campus novel' came to represent the 'novel of ideas.'"[2] To bolster his claim, Mishra cites approvingly essays by Philip Rahv in 1940 and by David Foster Wallace in 1997, each respectively alleging the mediocrity of American fiction relative to the European ideal set by writers like Robert Musil and Thomas Mann. Mishra, for his part, opines that "even Saul Bellow's *Herzog*, the most bracing American novel of ideas, seems narrowly focused on private experience when compared with *The Magic Mountain*."[3]

Setting aside a somewhat facile assessment of achievement in the European novel, it is striking how blinkered these claims are by the assumption that the novel of ideas is necessarily a novel by a white author that invokes ideas of Anglo-European heritage. Mishra concedes the example of James Baldwin, the only nonwhite author he mentions, who cannot "be accused of thematic shallowness or moral poverty," but this is only to better sideline him rhetorically from the very category in question.[4] This occlusion is all the more surprising (and dismaying) coming from the pen of a contemporary postcolonial thinker.

Philip Rahv had the excuse of living in a very different intellectual and historical climate; one suspects he needed to make bold claims to bolster his bona fides at *Partisan Review*, the magazine he founded in 1934. In his essay "The Cult of Experience in American Writing," Rahv argued that, seduced by their relative prosperity, American writers had come to believe that American society was "in its very nature immune to tragic social conflicts and collisions." It is remarkable to see even a committed leftist intellectual describing the Jim Crow United States as "immune to tragic social conflicts." It is also telling that Mishra, who claims this American illusion was broken only by the terrorist attacks of 9/11 and the ensuing War on Terror, can go all the way back to Rahv's 1940 essay, yet fail to mention Richard Wright's *Native Son*, one of the most famous American novels of the twentieth century and published the same year. Mishra does not quote the lines from Rahv's essay that immediately precede his selected excerpt, lines that make it clear Rahv does not (unlike perhaps Mishra) believe the novel of ideas requires a hero who belongs to the creative or managerial class: "The intellectual is the only character missing in the American novel. He may appear in it in his professional capacity—as artist, teacher, or scientist—but rarely as a person who thinks with his entire being, that is to say, as a person who transforms ideas into actual dramatic motives.... Everything is contained in the American novel except ideas."[5]

Ironically, this is perhaps the most accurate description one can make of Bigger Thomas, a character who "thinks with his entire being" and whose ideas about how to act upon them drive the arc of his tragic plot. In the pool room scene from book 1, for example, Wright employs an extended paragraph that uses the billiard balls scattering off one another as an objective correlative for Bigger's internal deliberations over whether to confront Gus about his plan to carry out a robbery: "[Bigger] rose and sent the balls whirling with a sweep of his hand, then looked straight at Gus as the gleaming balls kissed and rebounded from the rubber cushions, zig-zagging across the table's green cloth.... Gus stood without speaking and Bigger felt a curious sensation—half-sensual, half-thoughtful. He was divided and pulled against himself."[6] What follows is another half page devoted to tracking these internal divisions in real time, Bigger's calculations—the scattering matrix—that this confrontation requires. These are the thoughts of a desperate man with a violent temperament; but it *is* thinking, and it is quite explicitly (some would say crudely) the transformation of ideas into dramatic motive, the results of which will become evident when Bigger decides to return to the pool hall after going to the movies. The billiards evoke the deterministic naturalism that Wright is espousing. In the manner of Dreiser, or Zola, or Dostoyevsky—all powerful influences on Wright—they are there to illustrate the novel's theoretical machinery, which is to say its investment in using fiction to demonstrate powerful ideas, including ideas about determinism, historical materialism, and literary naturalism itself.

In case this wasn't clear enough, Wright provided an entire intellectual scaffolding for the reader in the form of his prefatory essay "How 'Bigger' Was Born," in which he emphasizes how deeply his novel is informed by his theory of modernity, by the rise of ideological politics and mass psychology, by the specters of fascism and communism, and by the implications of all these for subaltern subjects:

> From far away Nazi Germany and Old Russia had come to me items of knowledge that told me that certain modern experiences were creating types of personalities whose existence ignored racial and national lines of demarcation, that these personalities carried with them a more universal drama-element than anything I'd ever encountered before; that these personalities were mainly imposed upon men and women living in a world whose fundamental assumptions could no longer be taken for granted: a world ridden with national and class strife; a world whose metaphysical meanings had vanished; a world in which God no longer existed as a daily focal point of men's lives.[7]

If this does not announce a novel of ideas, then it's hard to imagine which American novel could possibly count as one. Yet in three critical assessments by left-leaning intellectuals (one of them nonwhite) seventy-five years apart, one can find no recognition that Wright, or indeed that *any* black writer, has contributed to the tradition of the novel of ideas. Nor is this attitude confined to the blindness of one or two critics—it is received wisdom. In a cultural history of the Depression published in 2009, the literary scholar and historian Morris Dickstein makes exactly the same assertion as Mishra, right down to citing Rahv's essay and praising Bellow as the sole exception: "Ideas and those who live by them have rarely figured in American fiction. (Saul Bellow's work, which began appearing soon after Rahv's essay, was a notable exception.) Perhaps because later American thinkers hardly ever exercised real power or influence, the drama of ideas rarely fired the imagination of American writers."[8] There is much one could say about the formation of this intellectual commonplace, but I want to focus on Mishra's postwar periodization, where only Bellow seems to register.[9] One can reasonably debate the extent to which *Native Son* ought to count as a novel of ideas. I am tempted to describe it as a crime novel steeped in American naturalism that erupts into a novel of ideas when Boris A. Max, Bigger's communist lawyer, takes the stand to defend his client as the victim of American oppression—for most readers and critics, with fairly disastrous results.[10] But even if we momentarily bracket *Native Son*, the postwar and early Cold War years, the Blue Period of this study, are surely the very moment at which black writers are most emphatically making this type of novel their own.

The first and most obvious (*pace* Mishra and others) example is Ralph Ellison's *Invisible Man* (1952), a novel powered (almost exclusively) by "the drama of ideas" Mishra pines for and celebrated for that very fact.[11] The other example, in so many ways its dark obverse, is Richard Wright's *The Outsider* (1953), published almost simultaneously, a book that was immediately attacked and remains a relatively marginalized novel in the context of Wright's oeuvre. Arna Bontemps's caustic quip is often recycled: "He has had a roll in the hay with the existentialism of Sartre, and apparently he liked it."[12] Ironically enough, the homophobic undertones of this jab imply a recognition (and telling anxiety) that this novel is precisely what Mishra and others say doesn't exist—an American novel that is too European, too full of *ideas*, terms that Bontemps sutures to a queer liability designed to undermine both the ideas themselves and the man behind them.

But while lay readers and critics have always found reasons to condemn *The Outsider*, the novel has received kinder attention from one corner in particular: black intellectuals.[13] Recent studies by Lawrence Jackson and Vaughn Rasberry give the novel renewed scrutiny and praise. Tommie Shelby has written a sweeping essay on Wright's place in the canon of African American political thought.[14] Paul Gilroy argued for *The Outsider*'s merit as an articulation of Wright's "radical view of modernity" and of his expansion of the category of blackness as a site of enunciation beyond "the narrow definitions of racialized cultural expression": "the Negro is no longer just America's metaphor but rather a central symbol in the psychological, cultural, and political systems of the West as a whole."[15] Cedric Robinson also proffered this view in *Black Marxism* in 1983.[16] Robinson was, in turn, drawing on Harold Cruse's positive assessment of *The Outsider*, although Cruse bristled at the fact that Wright strayed from his nationalist impulses under the noxious influence, in his view, of white Marxists.[17] These readers have all been drawn to the novel for the way it dramatizes ideas about race, modernity, identity, and the nature of politics, often with a special reference to the thought of Hegel, Kierkegaard, and Sartre—all figures in the broader tradition of so-called Continental philosophy—who are repeatedly alluded to throughout its pages.

In what follows, I argue that *The Outsider* is, indeed, a novel of ideas, but not merely for the purposes of laying claim to the genre or pointing out what many others have already pondered, namely the impact of Wright's philosophical readings on his late fiction. Instead, by reframing this book as a Blue Period novel, it becomes possible to understand the formal choices and the thematic ones in relation to each other, and to read these as symptomatic of the peculiar affect of the alienated black writer and thinker in the early Cold War. I do this by first excavating the tension between commitment and alienation in Wright, a tension already present in his Depression-era manifesto "Blueprint for Negro Writing" (1937). I trace its development up to the Blue Period and consider it in relation to the early

writings of Frantz Fanon, whose own efforts at what he called disalienation represent strikingly similar conclusions arrived at in the same historical moment. Finally, I end with a reading of *The Outsider* that shows how
its narrative structures and affective logics dramatize Wright's rejection of
social realism and his embrace of a form of nonaligned black thought that
he hoped could be conveyed or preserved through literature. Retracing
this trajectory is necessary to make sense of where Wright ended up; but I
also emphasize the radical dissension of that end point.[18] As Adam Shatz
succinctly puts it, in the last phase of his tragically brief career, Wright
"thundered against black churches and concert halls for ostracizing Paul
Robeson, who had been blacklisted and stripped of his passport. As much
as he despised Robeson's Communism, he hated Robeson's racist enemies far more: the blacklisting of black intellectuals he said, had led him
to change 'my position towards those who are fighting Communism.'"[19]

Mad at everyone, unmoved by reflexive racial solidarity, scornful of organized leftism, but virulently and passionately anti-racist and furious at
the forces of anticommunism and political reaction, Wright was writing
fiction for a world he fundamentally believed was shaped by the exhaus-
tion of all Western philosophical and moral authority. He didn't have a
positive vision to fill in its place. His attempts to fashion a new literary form
that would adequately express his despair involved a plinth of stark misogyny that he indelibly built into his own foundations; it, too, necessitates a
thorough accounting. For all these reasons, *The Outsider* stands apart like
a monolith: austere, brutal, but also clarifying. It is a novel that has often
resisted understanding and explanation. When we allow the periodizing
framework to illuminate its logic of negation and nonalignment, the formal and ideological pressures of Wright's work are returned to their rightful proportions, and we can see with a clear view in equal measure the
achievement and severe limitations of what is there.

From Blueprint to Blue Period

Richard Wright's "Blueprint for Negro Writing" has long assumed canonical status as a landmark work of African American literary criticism.[20] Ever
since its appearance in the inaugural (and only) issue of Dorothy West's
little magazine *New Challenge* in the fall of 1937, it has remained, alongside
"The Ethics of Living Jim Crow," one of Wright's most widely cited essays.
Interpretations of "Blueprint" have typically understood its aims as twofold. First, it is a sharp repudiation of the generation of the Harlem Renaissance, dismissed acidly in the essay's opening sentence as "prim and
decorous ambassadors who went a-begging to white America."[21] Second,
it is a manifesto calling for the infusion of a nationalist spirit into black

writing, a rallying cry for black literary artists to "accept the nationalist implications of their lives" and produce a writing "carrying the highest possible pitch of social consciousness … a nationalism that knows its origins … that knows its ultimate aims are unrealizable within the framework of capitalist America."[22] This is to be carried out through a shift in the consciousness of the individual writer, who will merge a study of Marxism (a necessary but insufficient stage) with traditional black folklore to forge a perspective that will speak to the "Negro masses" and bring them into shared consciousness. Wright's plan for black literature entails a psychological weapon in the service of collective emancipation: "when a people being to realize a *meaning* in their suffering," he intones in a celebrated passage, "the civilization that engenders that suffering is doomed."[23]

The thrust of these polemical maneuvers isn't only theoretical; it also reflects changing social formations and cultural fortunes, a changing of the vanguards at the time. As Gene A. Jarrett has put it, "*New Challenge* did for Wright in 1937 what *The Survey Graphic Number* did for [Alain] Locke in 1925: it led contemporaries and later scholars to appoint Wright as dean of a black cultural renaissance and to identify the renaissance with the city of Chicago."[24] Indeed, "Blueprint," though signed only by Wright, is really the product of collective study, the defining statement of Chicago's South Side Writers Group, which Wright founded to further organize black artists and intellectuals at the margins of the National Negro Congress of 1936.[25] This sometimes overlooked aspect of the text's composition suggests that the dialectical tension between the individual writer and "the masses," which lies at the center of the manifesto's intellectual position, is replicated at the level of the social production of the text itself. In other words, "Blueprint" is a deeply conflicted enunciation, a piece of rhetoric trapped between its desire for action, thought, and socialization as a group project, on the one hand, and on the other, an opposing desire for singular authorship, for individual recognition, for triumph in a competitive cultural field, and for the autonomy required to forge the instruments of consciousness.

Wright in fact explicitly acknowledged these wavering, unresolved, internal contradictions in "Blueprint." For the Negro writer, he admits, "nationalism is a bewildering and vexing question, the full ramifications of which cannot be dealt with here."[26] Jarrett argues that this evasion reflects Wright's inability to achieve his desired "New Negro radicalism," which was riven from within because it "required both Marxism and racial nationalism in theory, but they could not coexist in practice."[27] This irresolution is further evidenced (one might even say telegraphed) in the headings of the last two of its ten sections: "Autonomy of Craft" and "The Necessity for Collective Work." These concluding sections, concerned with the "professional" prerogatives of writers in general, and of the "isolation of the Negro writer" in particular, remain underexamined. Attention has invariably gravitated instead to the clash between Marxism and black nationalism within the manifesto, and its impact on *Uncle Tom's Children* (1938) and *Native Son* (1940), the signal texts that putatively execute its literary agenda.[28]

The manuscript drafts for the "Blueprint," however, contain passages, ultimately not included in the version published in *New Challenge*, that suggest a suppressed but fascinating subtext: the coterie dynamics of the South Side Writers Group and the ill-fated convolutions that went into the making of *New Challenge* itself. Excavating these buried and marginal elements draws "Blueprint" into a new light. The manifesto is only partly about how one makes literature instrumental to class and racial consciousness. At its heart lies an abiding fear of emotional loneliness that Wright's politics of affective solidarity—not with the masses but among the vanguard—hopes to overcome. It aspires to be a blueprint for revolutionary proletarian texts, but it captures the blue note of the severance of black intellectuals, who by virtue of their very aspirations find themselves alienated from the cultural sources that ostensibly animate their projects.

This dissonant affective valence aligns "Blueprint" not with *Uncle Tom's Children* and *Native Son*, the proletarian realist texts that catapulted Wright to fame, but as Brannon Costello has argued, with the modernist alienation of the rejected novel Wright continuously worked on during the same period and that was published posthumously in 1963 as *Lawd Today!*[29] This novel, with its bleak working title, "Cesspool," is modeled on Joyce's stream of consciousness, Dos Passos's "camera eye," and T. S. Eliot's allusive fragmentation, and it is obsessed with anomie.[30] As Costello remarks, "Clearly *Lawd Today!* does not end with the revolutionary élan that Mike Gold advocated for the proletarian novel."[31]

The seemingly contradictory need to reconcile revolutionary élan with depressive atomization is what this novel and "Blueprint" have in common. They both point to a negative affect that remained a fixation throughout Wright's career and paradoxically nourished his evolution as a writer. Cheryl Higashida's assertion that "Blueprint crystallizes the structure of feeling that was African American literary radicalism in the thirties," is thus even richer than she perhaps intended—not because of its advocacy of black "cultural front" aesthetics theorized by scholars like Barbara Foley, Michael Denning, and Brian Dolinar, but for the structure of feeling underlying those overt expressions of popular militancy.[32] Negative affect is the key, I believe, to Wright's pronouncements.[33] As we will see, the immediate conditions that led Wright to publish "Blueprint" in *New Challenge* are rife with the ambivalent tensions that made their way into the very structure of the text.

Dorothy West and the Making of New Challenge

As Verner Mitchell and Cynthia Davis's indispensable study of Dorothy West and her literary circle makes clear, the little magazine projects that West founded and edited, first *Challenge* (1934–1936) and then *New Challenge* (1937), were attempts to renew and extend the spirit of camaraderie, sexual freedom, and artistic autonomy that had characterized the Renaissance of the 1920s.[34] Against a headwind of belatedness, these magazines intended to provide a haven for a black vanguard tinged with nostalgia in a moment when the orientation of the Depression years was championing a populist, mass-oriented press with its eye on the revolutionary future. Clashing perspectives were inevitable, given the gulf between West's upbringing as an educated daughter of Boston's rarefied black bourgeoisie, well connected to the talented tenth (her cousin was the poet Helene Johnson), and Richard Wright's boyhood in Natchez, Mississippi. Wright longed for fraternal intellectual struggle, which he'd first encountered in Chicago's John Reed Club. West's ideal of literary community was inspired by the bluestocking whites she saw as her peers, like Elisabeth Marbury (Zora Neale Huston's literary agent) and her partner Elsie de Wolfe: "wealthy, socially-conscious, unmarried women" who patronized the world of culture and letters.[35]

Although West had money, as a twenty-five-year-old woman, she was also sensitive to gender dynamics and was determined, like Pauline Hopkins a generation before her at *Colored American Magazine,* to be a woman clearly at the helm.[36] Sexual and artistic liberty was also important to West, who was close with Wallace Thurman and hoped *Challenge* would take up the mantle of queer modernist experimentation that marked the latter's editorship of *Fire!!*[37] *Challenge* was built around relationships of women, friends, and comrades who shared both aspirations and apartments.[38] Marian Minus, a graduate of Fisk and a precocious, leftist intellectual, met West in the early 1930s; the two quickly became friends, then became professional collaborators, and "probably became lovers."[39]

Minus's influence set the stage for a reboot of *Challenge* under a new editorial stance, one more in line with the Popular Front politics of 1936 that the South Side Writers Group was espousing. Minus moved West to the left, but she was also intellectually mentoring Wright, who became romantically infatuated with her, apparently misreading both her sexuality and the nature of her relationship with West.[40] The relaunched *New*

Challenge thus represented an ideological course correction, but it was one made under the pressure of an internal critique, one that was never disinterested and was typically leveled in highly gendered terms. Even Wallace Thurman had accused *Challenge* of being "too pink tea and la de da—too high schoolish."[41] West's invitation to Minus and Wright to sign on as associate editors to *New Challenge* injected tensions that the new magazine wouldn't survive.

In 1937, Wright was leaving Chicago for New York, where he would take up a position as a reporter at the Harlem bureau of the *Daily Worker*, a mouthpiece for the Community Party of the United States of America (CPUSA).[42] In addition to his romantic interest in Minus, Wright was motivated by his own ambitions. *New Challenge* could secure an outlet for his short stories (eventually gathered and published in 1938 as *Uncle Tom's Children*). It also presented the chance to emulate magazines like *Partisan Review* and *New Masses*, which he had contributed to and considered more intellectually and politically sophisticated. This meant giving the magazine the hard edge of ideas, a direction that Wright understood in unequivocally masculinist terms, telling Langston Hughes in a letter that he intended to give it "balls, à la *New Masses*."[43] To do so in 1937 was to align the magazine with the CPUSA. Wright did so unilaterally, effectively usurping West's editorial authority by using his friendship with Ben Davis, editor of the *Daily Worker*, to publicize *New Challenge*'s release, yoking it by association to the party's orbit. West correctly perceived the attempt as a hostile takeover, and rather than cede control, she shut it down.[44] It didn't help matters that Wright had meanwhile discovered, apparently to his shock, that the magazine had less money than he thought and that Marian Minus was not interested in men.[45]

In effect, then, Dorothy West's *New Challenge* inadvertently set up a clash between generations, ideologies, and gender politics. Her friendship with Minus and their involvement in the South Side Writers Group had to contend with the patronizing attitude of the men around her, even though the sophistication that West and Minus were trying to bring to the magazine was as au courant as anyone could be in 1937. In their minds, it was to be a literary outlet for the Popular Front aesthetics that the South Side Writers Group was then cultivating; their outlook was resolutely antifascist, vanguardist, and internationalist. Hughes, for instance, submitted poems by the Afro-Cuban poet Nicolás Guillén that he was translating in Madrid in the thick of the Spanish Civil War. He wrote to West on letterhead from the Alianza de Intelectuales Antifascistas, recommending she forward issues of *New Challenge* to Guillén's editor in Havana and to the Alianza in Madrid and signing off with his typical ebullience: "Madrid is pretty wonderful! You all ought to be here."[46] The truth is that Wright seems to have been especially fixated (one suspects out of insecurity) that a masculinist authority should predominate in this women-led periodical.

Wright's maneuvers give an early glimpse into a defining fault line that runs through his writing, namely the fearful, fundamental schism in his mind between women and ideas, between female authority and intellectual life. This is not simply to restate the charge that Wright was a misogynist whose attitudes bled into his work. Cheryl Higashida has argued persuasively, for instance, that Wright's stories from this period are informed by the shift to a populist tack by the CPUSA that resulted from the Scottsboro trials' increasing emphasis on the role of women and mothers as proletarian heroes. She argues that the character of Aunt Sue in the story "Bright and Morning Star" "refutes the masculinist logic of proletarian struggle that demonizes white women's desire and renders black women invisible."[47] Higashida's revisionist reading aims not to rehabilitate Wright entirely, but rather to make the point that feminist critics "miss the mark by assuming that Wright's portraits of women are distorted because of his identity as a black man and, even worse, a black male Communist."[48] But while any crudely identity-based critique of Wright is indeed shortsighted, what remains true about Sue (a transparently shallow and sentimental creation) and, with few exceptions, the other female characters in Wright is that they are not sources of serious thought; their ideas, and possibly even their access to ideation, are obscure at best. Why is this pattern is so pervasive in Wright's work?

There is no question that for Wright, there is a masculinist tilt to the plane of ideas. Yet it is jarring to learn that material that specifically endowed women with a conscious role was included in an early draft of "Blueprint" but cut from the published version: "'Negro women who carry the triple burden of their sex, of their race, and of their class,'... 'the baffled thoughts of that Negro woman social worker who works in the slum areas of her race,'... 'that ... Negro girl reading the True Story magazine' [are all part of] 'a landscape teeming with questions and meaning' [for the black writer]."[49] It seems unlikely that Dorothy West or Marian Minus called for these lines to be cut from the essay, which leaves us to ponder why Wright thought to include the inner and intersectional life of women, only to leave it out. (Perhaps he worried the line about the social worker might seem to point to Fern Gayden, who had helped him and his family when they arrived in Chicago.) Yet even these excised lines suggest a female subjectivity that is primarily passive or in disarray, an object for study in the world by an active (male) observer, rather than the subjecthood of an equal woman who will contribute writing to the Black Nationalist project envisioned in "Blueprint."

Let us not forget that the essay's opening attack on the Renaissance writers of the 1920s (whom West had celebrated in the first *Challenge*) is phrased in gendered terms, alleging that they were "curtsying to show that the Negro was not inferior." Perhaps this is why Wright thought better of making his case for the Negro woman. Perhaps he reasoned that his text could not afford any "softness," anything that would detract from its being the kind of "serious criticism" Wright accuses black writers of having never faced up to. Perhaps it was a response to the awkward personal history of the manifesto's composition, Wright's baffled response to Marion Minus's sexual fluidity, a source of jealousy and infighting that would contribute to the dissolution of the South Side Writers Group and *New Challenge* itself.[50] Whatever the case may be, the crux of the matter is that Wright's intervention in "Blueprint" and the immediate context of its publication involved the deliberate and self-conscious projection of a critical persona he hoped would be perceived as intellectual, radical, and explicitly masculine.

Blue Notes in the Blueprint

"Blueprint for Negro Writing" was not only collectively forged before it was individually signed; it was also only one of several competing statements that issued from the Dorothy West circle. Indeed, Marian Minus issued a manifesto of her own, which appeared in the final issue of *Challenge*, published in the spring of 1937 just before Wright's appeared in *New Challenge* in the fall.[51] Entitled "Present Trends in Negro Literature," the manifesto lays out an argument very similar to Wright's. With declamatory rhetoric, she, too, emphasizes alienation and the need to turn to the past: "The Negro writer has the right and must claim the heritage which has been many times denied him in a land where he has been an eccentric alien."[52] She, too, blames black writers in generational terms, though without using Wright's gendered pejoratives.[53]

Within the pages of *New Challenge*, "Blueprint" also competed with statements such as Eugene C. Holmes's "Problems Facing the Negro Writer Today," which emphasized partisan antifascist engagement, and "A Note on Negro Nationalism," by Allyn Keith, a pseudonym for a contributor from the South Side Writers Group, probably Edward Bland.[54] These clamoring, sometimes anonymous voices betray the fissile interpersonal dynamics that would be *New Challenge*'s undoing. Ironically, Wright's rallying cry for solidarity among black writers considerably undermined it.

"Blueprint" is an insider's address to this fractured world of young black writers. The melancholic "isolation" and parochialism that Wright identifies would have resonated with its intended audience. *New Challenge*'s collectively voiced inaugural editorial echoed the theme in its first paragraph: "Through [the magazine] we hope to break down much of the isolation which exists between Negro writers themselves, and between the Negro writer and the rest of the writing world."[55] Ralph Ellison reiterated this in personal correspondence from 1939: "We have overcome the cultural and intellectual isolation of Negro writers," he told Joe Lazenberry, an old friend from Tuskegee days.[56] Margaret Walker, half a century on, reprised the theme using the same terms.[57]

More than nationalism, it is the problem of isolation that stuck. As Michel Fabre has astutely noted, the 1937 "Blueprint" reprised Wright's earlier intervention at the American Writers Congress of 1935, where he described "The Isolation of the Negro Writer" as a distinctively affective burden: "You may not understand it, I don't think you can *unless you feel it*. You can understand the causes, and oppose them, but the human results are tragic in peculiar ways."[58] Wright narrativized this visit to the congress in *American Hunger*, highlighting the humiliation of facing racist segregation, unlike his white peers, and the paradox of his lonely protest against the party's dissolution of the John Reed Clubs.[59] Standing against the party, Wright increasingly saw himself as a renegade intellectual without a home, a figure akin to André Malraux's hero Kyo Gisors, who gives a speech in *Man's Fate* that sounds much like "Blueprint" itself: "A civilization becomes transformed, you see, when its most oppressed element— the humiliation of the slave, the work of the modern worker—suddenly becomes a *value*, when the oppressed ceases to attempt to escape this humiliation and seeks in it his reason for being."[60]

When Wright alludes in "Blueprint" to "a Spanish writer [who] recently spoke of living in the heights of one's time," he is referring to the heterodox Spanish thinker José Ortega y Gasset, who wrote *The Revolt of the Masses*, published in Spanish in 1930 and translated into English in 1932.[61] In material ultimately deleted from the published version, Wright doubles down on that allusion in the concluding paragraphs: "Negro writers must live on the heights of their time and weave their subject matter into artistic patterns with their will to live."[62] It's unsurprising that Wright toned down and deleted references to Ortega y Gasset, a thinker suspicious of the will of the masses. But Wright's never entirely suppressed attraction to him cuts against any reading that "Blueprint" confirms the Negro writer at one with the people. Quietly, Wright was invoking a model of the intellectual as isolated from, and perhaps necessarily opposed to, the masses.

Where and with whom did Wright want to stand? In its published version, "Blueprint" concludes by calling on black writers to set aside "malice and jealousy," which is followed by a note of ascent: "Every first-rate novel, poem, or play lifts the level of consciousness higher."[63] The unpublished draft doesn't stop there, however; it continues with a metaphor emphasizing not the verticality of a racial mountain but the rhizomatic sol-idarity of racial roots: "Every contribution fertilizes the soil out of which we as writers grow. We need each other."[64] How different the tone of this final, isolated, eventually mooted sentence is: "We need each other." The conclusion of this hidden blueprint is supplicatory, vulnerable—one might even say stereotypically feminine.[65] How far this end seems from the words of the austere expatriate Wright twenty years later: "I declare un-abashedly that I like and even cherish the state of abandonment, of alone-ness; it does not bother me; indeed, to me it seems the natural, inevitable condition of man."[66]

In the draft materials for "Blueprint," there is also a telling correction on the first page. Wright's draft asks: "How can the gap between Negro workers and writers be closed?"[67] In edits, he replaced *closed* with *bridged*, which made it to publication. It's a suggestive edit, reminding us of the closing words of *Black Boy*—"I wanted to build a bridge of words between me and that world outside"—and of Cross Damon's dying words in *The Outsider:* "I wish I had some way to give the meaning of my life to oth-ers.... To make a bridge from man to man."[68] Wright clearly believed that the act of writing itself was that bridge. The ambivalence of "Blueprint" suggests, however, that the socially conscious writer, no matter how gifted or committed, is still left standing on one bank or the other, looking out across the open divide.

The central question in "Blueprint" is how to make literature instru-mental to class and racial consciousness without the writer becoming an instrument of political demands. I would argue that Wright's expressive mediation of this question produced a negative affective turn, the blue-ness of the blueprint, as it were. As we've seen, the exclusion of women from this discourse suggests that this turn was homosocial as well, a be-lief that friendship between leftist men of ideas could alone sunder the profound sense of alienation inherent to the black (male) writer's pre-dicament. This is, of course, deeply ironic given the history of Wright's combative interpersonal relations with other famous black male writers throughout his life.

A careful reading of the "Blueprint for Negro Writing" shows that Wright's manifesto is not merely the ideological declaration of the black writers' duty to adhere to the project of social realism; it is also a confes-sion of affective dissonance. It purports to advocate for and celebrate a collective movement, but it, in fact, is steeped in the conditions of nega-tivity that will likely ensure the failure of that very project. The author of this sweeping manifesto, which is supposed to function as a passport for black writers to claim a home inside the Communist Party, cannot quite bring himself to believe in the promise he is setting forth. The ambivalence built into this blueprint, and one it cannot dispel, is an early sign of the trajectory Wright's thinking would pursue—from a "blue" reservoir of feeling concealed beneath his party affiliation to a new conjuncture in the postwar period, when Wright allows that affect to come to light and, in effect, embraces it as the central conceptual framework that connects his writing to his lived experience.

The seeds of Wright's defection from the Communist Party are already latent in this work. Wright's public break with the Communist Party would come with his essay "I Tried to Be a Communist," his contribution to Richard Crossman's anticommunist anthology *The God That Failed*, published in 1949. One of the concepts from that classic formulation of anticommunist thought and rhetoric is the "Kronstadt moment," named after the anti-Bolshevik rebellion of sailors in 1921, which Louis Fischer, in his own contribution to Crossman's anthology, describes as an epiphany of defection, a moment of sudden revulsion and conversion away from the communist cause.[69] Part of the interest in excavating Wright's deep ambiguities concerning the allegiance of the black writer to party doctrine is that it shows that his break was not a Kronstadt moment, a sudden or strategic break with communism, but a long-held dissonance with party politics that evolved into a public divorce from the party itself.

Studies of Wright's correspondence with his close friends, Horace Cayton, Ralph Ellison, and Chester Himes, have shown that Wright's position privately began to shift rapidly in the early 1940s, deepened during the war years, and became increasingly strident between 1945 and 1947, as the terrors of a post-Holocaust and nuclear-armed Cold War dynamic became entrenched in the public imaginary.[70] Michel Fabre has cited Wright's letter of August 21, 1955, to Edward Aswell, his editor at Harper's, as the best evidence for dating Wright's official (but nonpublic) severance from the CPUSA. In his letter (written retrospectively, at the height of Red Scare McCarthyism), Wright tells Aswell: "As you know I broke with the Communist Party in 1942; I left under my own steam. I had intuitively realized much of what is now in the daily press about the Communist Party, including its infiltration by the FBI agents, etc."[71] The self-serving and self-exonerating work Wright is performing in this letter must be considered carefully given the timing of its composition; Congress passed the bipartisan Communist Control Act in 1954. Indeed, as William J. Maxwell's readings of American intelligence files gathered on black writers have shown, Wright was deeply aware that his words to Aswell were very likely to be scooped up by J. Edgar Hoover's ghost readers at the Federal Bureau of Investigation and informants for the Central Intelligence Agency, who were, Wright firmly believed, tracking him closely abroad.[72]

It's interesting, then, that Wright's disavowal exceeds itself in this letter with the inclusion of a kind of existentialist affirmation that harkens back to the self-fashioning autobiographical humanism of *Black Boy*: "I felt a kind of grim exhilaration in facing a world in which nothing could be taken for granted," he tells Aswell, "a world in which one had to create and forge one's meaning for one's own self."[73] Wright had been given a framework, a world of ideas, and now that scaffolding had been ripped away: "I was a Communist because I was Negro. Indeed, the Communist Party had been the only road out of the Black Belt for me. Hence Communism had not been for me simply a fad, a hobby; it had a deep functional meaning for my life."[74]

This last phrase relating the "deep functional meaning" of ideology to a way of life raises another specter haunting Wright: his relationship to fascism, or as Vaughn Rasberry rightly insists, illiberal modernity.[75] Mark Christian Thompson has argued that fascism exerted a special attraction on black writers in the interwar period and that this attraction eventually finds its most overt expression and realization in the figure of Cross Damon in *The Outsider*. Thompson posits that "Wright's fear and dread expressed in *The Outsider* is not only that there is a possibility that African America will take on the characteristics of a totalitarian state (if the black nation were to achieve statehood), but also that the human condition as totalitarian is 'essentially' that of the African American."[76] For Wright, he says, "in the twentieth century totalitarianism marks the existential condition of the human."[77] Like Thompson, Rasberry finds that the postwar exilic writings (both the nonfiction travel writing and *The Outsider*) point to "what Wright perceived as the condition of 'terror in freedom' afflicting the postcolony."[78] His analysis, not unlike that of Abdul JanMohamed, also limns Wright's autobiographical writings as quasi-philosophical narratives that demonstrate the totalitarian terror and the Agambenian "state of exception" that underpin the amoral condition Wright famously calls the "ethics of living Jim Crow."[79]

All these studies converge in different ways upon how Wright's texts are unusually laden with analogies and allegories that seek to dramatize the discursive traffic of ideas that dominated intellectual life from the mid-1930s through the early Cold War. Wright seems to have entertained, at least momentarily, a fascination with the illiberal modernity proposed by fascism; in the postwar years, existentialist thought, totalitarian critique, and a vigorous defense of secular modernization in the postcolony had begun to overlap. What these readings leave out, though, is the question of literary form itself. In other words, why are these ideas couched in literary texts (lyrical autobiography, travel writing, and fiction) rather than in philosophical treatises or essays? What is it about these forms that remained important to Wright?

Although Wright was certainly attempting to understand, and in some sense reveal, the implications of the ideologies of his day, among them fascism, the writing he produced is what I would call, adapting Rasberry's phrase, an antitotalitarian literary aesthetic. This was writing that Wright understood to be in opposition to the literary doctrines of social realism that he had earlier embraced. Between 1937 and 1947, Wright's engagé commitment to the nationally framed, Leninist vanguardism of "Blueprint" evaporated along with the collective aesthetics it put forth. But its affective remainder—its negative affect and gendered spirit of isolation—would come to the fore as sublimated in the global, nonaligned alienation of his "Blue Period."

Voyage Inward: The Retreat from Social Realism

One of the most tantalizing texts in Richard Wright's corpus is the unfinished manuscript for his novel *Black Hope*. Wright announced the genesis of this project in his prefatory essay to *Native Son*, "How Bigger Was Born," published in 1940. "I am launching out upon another novel, this time about the status of women in modern American society," he declared. Writing with his characteristic speed and titanic vigor, Wright had a 961-page draft ready for his editor Paul Reynolds by early February 1940.[80] This would have been his first and only fiction to take a black female character as protagonist. Wright promoted the work in the *New York Herald Tribune* in 1941 as "a sort of feminine counterpart of *Native Son*."[81] Despite Wright's lightning progress and the initial enthusiasm for the project that he shared with his editors, a final draft was perpetually delayed, and the project was eventually abandoned.

The tragic hero of *Black Hope* is Maud Hampton, a twenty-seven-year-old, light-skinned mulatto and a graduate of the University of Chicago. She comes up to New York and falls in love with Freddie Rogers, "a tall, brown-skinned, slender young man who has turned down a lucrative job at the post office in order to write."[82] Freddie is an idealistic thinker and reader, as Hazel Rowley's biography suggests, "an idealized Richard Wright." It is impossible not to be struck by the resemblance of this initial plot setup to the dalliance sketched out by Gwendolyn Brooks between Maud Martha and David McKemster. It is not merely the coincidence of the name Maud, but also the erotic exploration of the life of the mind as an unstable waver in the color line, that makes this similarity so compelling.

Unlike Brooks, however, Wright envisioned a melodramatic archetypical tragic mulatto plot that ends in tragedy. Maud is ambitious and unsatisfied with her life as a social worker, and she becomes frustrated with Freddie's lack of aspirations to upward mobility. In a plan to improve her lot, she starts taking arsenic wafers that, though they make her violently ill, progressively lighten her skin until she can pass as white. In her new skin, she becomes the housekeeper for an old bedridden white millionaire who leaves her a fortune upon his death. With her new money, she finally has the life she thought she wanted, but she cannot reconcile her new social position with her guilt and her still-ardent love of Freddie. Maud ends up committing suicide but leaves her fortune to her black maid Ollie and bequeaths her mansion to the black Domestic Workers' Union.

Wright scholarship has considered this text for the ways it complicates our understanding of his gender politics and literary ambitions. Ayesha Hardison's *Writing through Jane Crow* devotes a chapter to *Black Hope* arguing for its importance in recasting prevailing views about Wright's misogyny.[83] Hardison persuasively unpacks many of the remarkable facets of this manuscript, not least the way it "endorses political alliances between black and white women as well as between working-class and middle-class women."[84] She also acutely points out Wright's insistence upon a solidarity-based politics as fundamental to psychological and social well-being: "Maud exacerbates her social death when she passes for white, but she hastens her literal death when she impedes black worker's struggle for political subjectivity. She protects herself rather than champion the disinherited, and her guilt over this duplicity pressures her to self-destruct … yet in order to atone for her transgressions, she wills her house to the domestic worker's union for its headquarters and thus facilitates collective 'black hope.'"[85] Everything about this plotline fulfills the political and aesthetic charter of the leftist Popular Front, and if *Black Hope* had seen the light of day, there is no doubt it would have been understood to belong to the category of proletarian fiction. But it is not only the plotline that fits the bill.

Wright approached *Black Hope* in much the way he had *Native Son*, with an attention to documentary realism. As Rowley recounts, "Wright collected newspaper cuttings, and talked to social workers"; he brought a stenographer with him to conduct interviews at the Domestic Workers' Union in Brooklyn; and he made a point of investigating an article about the Bronx "slave market," the popular term for "street corners where black women would stand waiting for white housewives to approach, single them out from the group, and employ them for an hour or two for anything between fifteen and thirty cents an hour."[86] As Rowley puts it, Wright "took the dry facts and added imagination and poetry."[87]

Wright was simultaneously working on another project, *12 Million Black Voices*, which was published by Viking in 1941, and for which he took Works Progress Administration staff photographers Ed Rosskam and Russell Lee all over the South Side of Chicago to document black living conditions, joining the ranks of a genre established by the iconic Farm Security Administration images by photographers like Dorothea Lange and Walker Evans. Wright also had the opportunity during this time to dip into the charts and statistics compiled by his friend Horace Cayton that would eventually go into *Black Metropolis*.[88] Both of Wright's projects at the time proceeded along Popular Front assumptions and methodologies; both were attuned to the beliefs that literature could have a direct, instrumental impact on the consciousness of workers and that the job of cultural workers was to document these "conditions" and tap into the revolutionary potential seething there.

Barbara Foley has argued convincingly that *Black Hope* had all the ingredients to become a major novel that would have placed the "hope" of popular resistance to fascism in the hands of working-class black women. In doing so, Wright could have captured the portrait of an entire generation of working and middle-class female activists, many but not all of them communists, like Vicki Garvin, Marvel Cooke, Claudia Jones, and Thelma Dale, whose work in social, cultural, and labor movements has been chronicled by Dayo F. Gore.[89] One of the most vivid artistic representations of this generation of women's resistance is Alice Childress's 1955 play *Trouble in Mind* and its central character Wiletta Mayer, a middle-aged actress who stands up to the racist scripts being forced on her at the cost of her job.[90] Wright's Maud Hampton, in addition to being his most substantive female character, would have been in good company and certainly would have been received as a contribution to this burgeoning field of literary production and social activism.[91]

Ayesha Hardison argues that Wright repeatedly displaced and set aside *Black Hope* in favor of an obsessive turn to masculinist texts like *The Man Who Lived Underground* (published in excerpts in 1942 and 1944, and in full in 2021), *Black Boy* (1945), and *The Outsider* (1953). This succession, she argues, "suggests a compulsory engagement with black masculinity that permanently stymied the progression of his female-centered text."[92] There is no doubt that Wright's failure to realize his one female-centered text speaks to a deep struggle with issues of gender and representation. But true as that may be, it is also clear that another major reason for Wright's incompletion of *Black Hope* is that his literary sensibilities had changed profoundly.

The Popular Front aesthetics that animated Wright's work through the 1930s, culminating with *12 Million Black Voices* (1941), ceased to be compelling to him. Going forward, interiority would take the place of social realism, and psychology (and psychoanalysis) would take the place of Marxism in Wright's outlook. We can see traces of this shift even earlier in the era of "Blueprint," as I have suggested, and in Wright's aggressively negative review of Zora Neale Hurston's *Their Eyes Were Watching God* (1937). The unfortunate correlative is that Wright was incapable of seriously conceiving the realm of ideas and the affective relation to them from the subjective point of view of women. In other words, the turn to an inward, psychological novel of ideas necessarily brought with it his misogynistic reflexes. And this turn was catalyzed by a shift in Wright's politics and aesthetics.

The year 1941 was pivotal for Wright. On the global stage, the attack on Pearl Harbor brought the United States into the war and drastically changed the domestic political landscape. The evidence of political turbulence with respect to the Communist Party started to spill over. Wright, already hurt by the party's cool reception of *Native Son*, was deeply disappointed by the communists' uncritical pledge of allegiance to the war effort.[93] In fact, one of the key breaking points for Wright was the official adoption of this position. Wright took a strong stand for black non-cooperation with the war effort in an article entitled "Not My People's War," printed in *New Masses* on June 17, 1941. He articulated what would essentially become the Double Victory, or Double V, campaign (launched in the pages of the *Pittsburgh Courier* in 1942) but from a position of negative reservation: "If this is a war for democracy and freedom, then we fight in it, for democracy, for freedom. We shall fight as determinedly against those who deny freedom at home as we shall fight against those who deny it to others abroad."[94]

A week later, on June 22, Hitler invaded the Soviet Union. *New Masses* blazoned its July 8 special issue "Why This Is Our War," and writers reacted to news of the invasion. As Michel Fabre notes, Wright had been set to receive the Spingarn Medal and had prepared a speech that mirrored his sentiments in "Not My People's War." The CPUSA demanded he make changes to tone it down, to assure the audience that black Americans would support the war effort and defend democracy. Wright's response was to tone up the black nationalism of his speech, making clear he was accepting the award "in the name of the stalwart, enduring millions of Negroes whose fate and destiny I have sought to depict in terms of scene and narrative in imaginative fiction. It cannot be otherwise for they are my people, and my writing—which is my life and which carries my convictions—attempts to mirror their struggle for freedom during these troubled days."[95] Although there was no single Kronstadt moment for Wright, the party's attempt to dictate his words and pressure him into placing its own aims above those he felt were incarnated by the Spingarn award certainly caused a significant deterioration of relations.

For the world, and for all intellectuals, 1941 was a momentous and ominous year. But for Richard Wright as a writer, 1941 was also pivotal because he came across a story in the magazine *True Detective* about a white man who had decided to live underground, coming to the surface to steal and then disappearing again into the world of the sewers. Wright immediately sensed something important, the germ for a new novel, and began work on *The Man Who Lived Underground*, a novel published in its entirety for the first time only in 2021. "I have never written anything in my life that stemmed from more sheer inspiration," he declared.[96] Deeply infused with the spirit of Kafka and Dostoyevsky, it marked a sharp turn away from documentary realism and toward a deeper investment in exploring interiority and alienated consciousness.

Fred Daniels, Wright's protagonist, begins the novel as a respectable churchgoing man who is unjustly arrested by white police officers searching for a black suspect. They take him to a holding cell where they proceed to torture him in order to extract a confession (this aspect of the novel, appallingly and ironically enough is arguably its most realistic feature).[97] But even before this violence in detention begins, what Fred sees when he looks out the window of the police car hauling him away tells us that this cannot be a social novel and that he cannot be its proletarian hero: "Without looking he knew that the sidewalks were filled with black people, people like himself, but he did not want to think of them; at some time during the recent past they had become alien to him."[98]

During a reprieve in the police cell, Fred manages to give his torturers the slip and secures his escape by taking advantage of an open manhole that allows him passage into the "watery blackness of the underground."[99] This deliquescent escape through a murky, narrow passage with strong invaginating overtones secures the novel's generic transition into a surreal and symbolic ideational space. In his essay "Living On," Derrida defines *invagination* as "the inward refolding of *la gaine* [sheath, girdle], the inverted reapplication of the outer edge to the inside of a form where the outside then opens a pocket."[100] In *The Man Who Lived Underground*, the (tellingly contrived) plot device of the manhole allows the novel to fold back on itself, to pull the outer and exterior signs and significations of blackness and redeploy them inwardly in a new pocketed space within but below the social novel of public and overt racial oppression and its resistance. Fred Daniels leaves behind the police for a subterranean space where his blackness can't be policed. Elaborating upon the concept of invagination, Derrida notes that "it is precisely a principle of contamination, a law of impurity, an economy of the *parasite*. In the code of set theory, if I may use it at least figuratively, I would speak of a sort of *participation without belonging*—a taking part in without being part of, without having membership in a set. With the inevitable dividing of the trait that marks membership, the boundary of the set comes to form, by invagination, an internal pocket larger than the whole; and the outcome of this division and of this abounding remains as singular as it is limitless."[101] In going underground, Wright creates a space that is parasitic upon the structure of the proletarian novel or perhaps, in Nathaniel Mackey's terms, a "paracritical hinge" opening it to a "disparate mode of articulation."[102] Shifted into this vestibular modality, Fred Daniels, is a character who can participate in blackness without belonging to it, whose focalization of consciousness will simultaneously fold what is singular (but also "impure") about the materiality of black life away and redeploy it as a limitless and unbounded interiority that is related to the communal whole but no longer contained by it.

This voyage of extractive rebirth is allegorized in a scene where underground Fred (who was a regular member of a Baptist church) comes across "a colored folks' church down in one of them sunken basements." His reaction is not to join them or ask for help: "he wanted to observe the church service without being seen, without being a part of it."[103] His desire to spectate is not voyeuristic, though; it is the expression of a break in the sociality of his being (one that was occurring even before his torture at the hands of white officers): "His life had somehow snapped in two. But how? When he had sung and prayed with his brothers and sisters in church, he had always felt what they felt; but here in the underground, distantly sundered from them, he saw a defenseless nakedness in their lives that made him disown them. A physical distance had come between them and had conferred upon him a terrifying knowledge."[104] Fred's "knowledge" is never quite specified, and that's because the entire structure of the narrative is effectively standing in for it. Eventually he is recaptured, and the crisis of his division from the black community of believers is doubled with a fundamental crisis of communication—an inability to be *believed* by anyone, most immediately his white captors. The novel's structural and metaphorical oppositions—between community and alienation, faith and knowledge, the borderless "womanly" terror of the recessive darkness and the power of words to banish the pall of isolation and ignorance—these all have a deeply autobiographical resonance when considered in tandem with Wright's essay "Memories of My Grandmother," which sensibly accompanies the Library of America edition:

> My grandmother was an enemy of all books save those based upon or derived from the Bible. Whenever I neared home with any books other than those sanctioned by the Seventh-Day Adventist Church school to which I was made to go, I'd push them under my coat and steal to my room and secrete them under the pillow on my bed. Hours later I'd go to look for my books and they would be gone. But I'd never confront my grandmother and ask her where they were; long experience had taught me where they were.

I'd go to our wood-burning stove in the kitchen and lift up the lid, and sure enough, there in the black ashes would be what was left of my books.[105]

Without committing to a crude biographical fallacy, one cannot help but be struck by the potency of this as a primal scene not of sexual but of textual violation—where the intimate fear of loss and "lifting up the lid" upon a consummation in fire and ashes has left a bitter severance in Wright that violently divorces (in his mind) the matrilineal female religious hand from the secular spirit of the book as a passport to the autonomy and security of access to the world of ideas. Such a purely psychoanalytic interpretation may not account for every aspect of the novel. But surely it must be privileged, not least because Wright himself was actively using his growing interest in psychoanalysis to reorient his idea of the novel away from its social realist conventions and toward the novel of ideas.

Wright's intense interest in psychology and psychoanalysis has more recently received fresh attention. Jay Garcia has reassessed the complex working relationship between Wright and the psychiatrist Fredric Wertham. Scholars have long been aware of the influence on Wright of Wertham's book *Dark Legend: A Study in Murder* (1941), a clinical investigation of matricide. But fewer have considered Wertham's psychiatric readings of *Black Boy* or Wright's collaboration with Wertham in setting up the Lafargue Clinic he opened in Harlem in 1946, which Wright described in his essay "Psychiatry Comes to Harlem" (as did Ralph Ellison in his essay "Harlem is Nowhere").[106] In 1943, Horace Cayton invited Wright to address the Institute of Psychoanalysis in Chicago, and afterward, Cayton accompanied Wright on a trip down to Fisk University, where Wright was to give a talk. As Rowley relates, the two men bonded, and the sociologist opened up to the novelist about his anxieties and his desire to try psychoanalysis. The talk inspired Wright to delve deeper into his own past as part of his remarks to be given at Fisk. The reception to this exploration of selfhood was so electric that it inspired him to begin *Black Boy* (1945), arguably Wright's most lyrical and moving work.

If the 1940–1941 manuscript of *Black Hope* shows both a missed opportunity and the potential apex of a tradition Wright was in the process of discarding, it's also worth mentioning the nonexistent but projected manuscript he hoped to write in 1945. This is a text outlined in his journal, after an evening out during which he had confided in his friend and editor George Davis about it (it is interesting to note how often editors are Wright's closest confidants):

I explained to him that I wanted to write before I die a series of novels, something like Proust's *Remembrance of Things Past*. I do not want to do it in Proust's style, but in some manner native to America and the Negro. After all, Proust was a Jew living in Paris, rich and in touch with all the latest developments in art and science; he found that associational thinking and memory, which he borrowed from psychoanalysis, could form the scaffolding of his massive work; and so he took it for his own and used it. I must find something likewise to hang my theme of Negro life upon…. I do not want to do this in terms of a family for my aim is not to depict moral customs and traditions and social changes, so much as the subjective voyage spanning centuries. It is a spiritual journey that I wish to depict, not a material one…. The more I think of the word VOYAGE, the more I like it. The title should have that word in it.[107]

Wright's all-caps title "VOYAGE" for this vast imagined project—which would encompass a "subjective voyage," "a spiritual journey"—echoes the title of Baldwin's prospective essay on James's *The Ambassadors*, "The Self as Journey," and the full title of Vincent O. Carter's memoir: *The Bern Book: A Record of a Voyage of the Mind*. All three are drawn to this term to mark a formal experiment informed by a new attachment to interiority.

It is by no means revelatory that Wright was a great admirer of Proust, whom he mentions reading in Chicago in the 1930s in *Black Boy*. What has gone insufficiently appreciated is Proust's enormous importance to Wright as key to finding a new way to write, one fundamentally different from that which Wright had cultivated to that point. In this passage from Wright's diary, Proust (who stands for something like "literary form") is combined with the possibilities of psychoanalysis to allow the novelist to go beyond the traditional turf of realism (i.e., moral customs, traditions, social changes).

This was a transgressive pursuit on three counts. One, because in 1945, the thought of a black writer even comparing himself and his ambitions to Proust would be considered outlandish (we have seen with the editing of *Maud Martha* evidence of this attitude vis-à-vis Henry James). Two, because black interiority was still a novelty in literary representation. Lastly, invoking Proust and the novel of "subjective" life in his private life and diary, Wright confesses his wish to emulate a writer considered the epitome of bourgeois decadence. This was heretical to the social realism that "Blueprint" and the writing of the 1930s was supposed to espouse.

Clearly, the projected novel that Wright describes is not the one that he ended up producing in 1953 in *The Outsider*. One question is, then, Why does that novel differ so much from the ideal put forward here? Another is: What, if anything, of this project is in one way or another still animating it? To speculate about the distance across which the two echo each other, one needs to come to terms with what Wright did decide to fill his novel with:

interiority, violence, alienation, terror, and pathology. The locus classicus for understanding the entanglement of these forces in black subjectivity is the work of Frantz Fanon. It is therefore to Fanon we must turn to begin to make sense of Wright's most powerful Blue Period novel.

Toward a Theory of Revolutionary Alienation

The missed connection between Richard Wright and Frantz Fanon is undoubtedly one of the great losses of black intellectual history. Both attended the First Congress of Black Writers and Artists organized by Alioune Diop and *Présence africaine*, which was held at the Sorbonne in Paris from September 19 to 22, 1956.[108] Wright was part of the American delegation and spoke on the first day; his talk, "Tradition and Industrialization," was out of step with the emphasis on *négritude* favored by most of the panelists. Fanon was part of the Martinican delegation that included Louis T. Achille, Édouard Glissant, and Aimé Césaire, all of whom Fanon knew from either Paris or Fort-de-France. Fanon was the last speaker of the morning session on September 20. His speech, entitled "Racism and Culture," was likewise uninterested in *négritude* and made pointed but (given his surveillance by the French intelligence agencies) discreet references to the situation in Algeria.[109]

Although both were present for at least most of the congress, there is no evidence that Wright and Fanon actually spoke with or formally recognized each other. Fanon may have felt disinclined to approach Wright because the American had never responded to what was effectively a fan letter he had sent him in 1953. In any case, this would be their last possible chance to meet in person. For Fanon, the congress was his last public speech in France. He, too, received a muted reception, then quickly departed and was back in Algeria by September 30, where the National Liberation Front campaign that would come to be known as the Battle of Algiers was just beginning, a sequence of events that would consume the rest of his brief life.[110] Under other circumstances, perhaps George Lamming—who also presented a talk at the conference, "The Negro Writer and His World," and who did speak with Fanon—could have been the bridge connecting them, but Wright had distanced himself from Lamming for personal reasons at that moment.[111]

The only other point of possible contact had come three years earlier, when Fanon posted that letter to Wright from Saint-Alban, the provincial psychiatric hospital known for its pioneering therapeutic treatment of alienation, where Fanon had sought out a position after completing his medical studies at Lyon.[112] The date of the letter, January 6, 1953, is important; it was sent just months after the publication of Fanon's first book,

Black Skin, White Masks, in the summer of 1952. Indeed, in his letter, Fanon introduces himself as the author of the "essay *Black Skin, White Masks* published by Seuil in which I tried to show the systematic misunderstanding between whites and blacks."[113] He tells Wright that he has read all of his books, naming *Native Son, Black Boy, 12 Million Black Voices*, and *Uncle Tom's Children*, and says that he is planning to write a study of his works. He adds: "Eager to circumscribe in the most complete way the breadth of your message I'd greatly appreciate your letting me know the title of those works I might be ignorant of."[114] Wright never replied, and it seems Fanon never pursued the essay project dedicated to Wright's writings.[115]

Today we are better placed to reconstruct this missed dialogue between Wright and Fanon's texts, the interrupted or phantom correspondence they bear. Previously unavailable Fanon documents gathered by Jean Khalfa and Robert Young include articles Fanon published in *El Moudjahid*, the wartime newspaper and news bulletin of the National Liberation Front for which Fanon was a regular contributor from 1954 to 1961. A number of these were gathered in *Toward the African Revolution*, published in 1967, but others have languished in the archive until recently. Among them is a review of Richard Wright's *White Man Listen!* (1957) from August 3, 1959.[116] Though unsigned, the review is unmistakably Fanon's, to say nothing of what would have been his obvious interest in the topic given the situation in Algeria at the time.

The review strikes a tone of frustration and disappointment. Fanon opens by chastising the "sterile" posture of any oppressed person addressing himself to the heart of his oppressor ("'au coeur' de ses oppresseurs"). He attacks Wright's description of psychological attitudes between the races for being overly abstract, lacking direct contact with concrete realities ("sans relation directe au concret"). He accuses Wright of addressing only the "elites" and not the people, and of offering no real proposals for the type of action to take to end the oppression of the people. Wright, Fanon says, has an "unjustified and irrational" confidence in the West. The article ends with what feels like a rather acerbic quip: "Has Richard Wright learned anything from recent history? One doubts it."[117] Fanon clearly felt wounded by Wright's silence and what he perceived as Wright's failure to follow through on the call to resistance, to do as Fanon himself did: to join the revolution in the Third World and not merely comment on it from afar.

Parsing the review also reveals some strategic differences between Fanon and Wright, despite the affinities they shared in their worldview. Wright had dedicated *White Man Listen!* to Eric Williams, the historian and future prime minister of Trinidad and Tobago, and to "the westernized and tragic elite of Asia, Africa, and the West Indies—the lonely *outsiders* who exist precariously on the cliff-like margins of many cultures—

men who are distrusted, maligned, criticized by left and right, Christian and pagan—men who carry on their frail but indefatigable shoulders the best of two worlds—and who, amidst confusion and stagnation, seek desperately for a home for their hearts: a home which, if found, could be a home for the hearts of all men."[118] One cannot help but notice the allusion to the title of his 1953 novel and, despite its conventional usage, the emphatically masculinist tilt in this passage. Wright clearly conceived the role of the black intellectual as one of tutelage to the Bandung generation, the emerging counterelites of the Third World who he hoped would steer a black humanistic course out of the totalitarian nightmares wrought by the racist West and the Stalinist Soviet Union.

From Fanon's point of view, this is a strategic mistake, and more concretely, a political one. From his perspective, Wright hasn't gone far enough in his alienation from the cultural influence of the West and hasn't grasped that his disalienation can come about only if he entrusts the revolution not to an enlightened leadership class but to the *Lumpenproletariat*. These disinherited "wretched of the earth" are the only ones, in Fanon's estimation, who could be trusted not to betray the newly won independence movements to neocolonial interests.[119] This is, of course, one of the central theses of *Les damnés de la terre*, published in 1961. Reading between the lines, one can hear Fanon accusing Wright of having allowed himself to become what he considered the worst fate: the alienated bourgeois intellectual. Whether this is a fair assessment is debatable.[120] More significant is the question of alienation itself—or rather, the dialectical evolution of alienation and what Fanon called *disalienation*, a bind that seems to define the central problem for black writers in this period and one that, per Fanon, can resolve itself only in revolutionary commitment and action.[121]

One irony of this debate is that, in the early, prerevolutionary phase of his career, Fanon was himself the classic, brooding, alienated intellectual. Jean Khalfa includes a fascinating portrait of a young Fanon in 1948 as described by Raymond Péju, the owner of a prominent bookstore in Lyon who befriended him. Fanon apparently spent many afternoons browsing this secondhand bookstore and discussing not only literature (especially poetry by Césaire, Char, Aragon, Breton, Éluard, Damas, Senghor) but also his experiences of racist incidents around town.[122] Aside from poetry, Fanon's primary intellectual preoccupations and influences at this time were theater, psychology (including Lacan), and philosophy, primarily the phenomenology of Maurice Merleau-Ponty and the existentialism of Jean-Paul Sartre. Coincidentally, these were the very same interests animating Wright in his exile years in Paris. Fanon read literature, especially black literature, as though he were reading case studies; Wright was increasingly drawn to the idea of using the novel as a case study, as a thought experiment, a mental laboratory where he would unleash pathological characters.[123]

One of the appendixes to Khalfa's compiled Fanon documents is an annotated catalog of Frantz Fanon's library, which was donated to the Algerian National Archives.[124] The editors have singled out for special attention any passages from the books that appear underlined or otherwise marked with marginalia. With this, we can see the textual trace, as it were, of the importance of Wright for the young Dr. Fanon. His copy of *Black Boy* is heavily marked in at least nine separate places, including notably the famous passages on "the bleakness of black life" and Wright's mention of Kafka's *The Castle*.[125] Of great interest, as well, are the many passages heavily marked in Fanon's copy of Sartre's *Situations*, specifically those where Sartre is reading and analyzing Richard Wright.

At the end of "The Lived Experience of the Black Man," the fifth chapter of *Black Skin, White Masks* (1952), Fanon famously interpolates Bigger Thomas as a figure for the modern black identity that has yet to emerge, to discover its place on the world stage: "It is Bigger Thomas—he is afraid, terribly afraid. He is afraid, but of what is he afraid? Of himself. No one knows yet who he is, but he knows that fear will fill the world when the world finds out." Out of this dread, Fanon foresees action, and he quotes approvingly from Wright's preface, "How Bigger Was Born": "In the end Bigger Thomas acts. To put an end to his tension, he acts, he responds to the world's anticipation."[126] Less noticed is also Fanon's nod to *12 Million Black Voices* in a strange passage on the situation in black America: "*The twelve million black voices* have screamed against the curtain of the sky. And the curtain, torn from end to end, gashed by the teeth biting its belly of prohibitions, has fallen like burst *balafon*. On the battlefield, marked out by the scores of Negroes hanged by their testicles, a monument is slowly rising that promises to be grandiose. And at the top of this monument I can already see a white man and a black man *hand in hand*."[127] Fanon invokes this prophetic image with something like revolutionary envy. This is a far cry from the kind of language the National Association for the Advancement of Colored People and Martin Luther King Jr. would have in mind for rallying a vision of whites and blacks, hand in hand "at the table of brotherhood." Like a gothic version of Césaire, it is typical of Fanon that the language of his anguish and alienation should seem itself to be so symptomatically neurotic.

But it also seems far from coincidental that Wright is interpolated within a brooding passage that is obsessed with wounded manhood, with monumental castration. As is the case for Wright's novels, the trials and terrors of black masculinity are a central feature of Fanon's phenomenology. *Black Skin, White Masks* often examines interracial sexual desires and taboos, as expressed in contemporary literature, popular narratives, and anecdotes; tellingly, discussion of intraracial desire and relations is absent. The black man is at his worst (most passive) state of alienation for Fanon in the West Indian: "The Martinican is a crucified man. The environment which has shaped him (but which he has not shaped) has torn him apart, and he nurtures this cultural milieu with his blood and his humors. The blood of a black man, however, is a fertilizer much appreciated by the experts."[128] The figurative construction is loosely Nietzschean, but it is hard not to see in this Antillean "type" the dissociated and eventually bled-out Cross Damon who would appear in *The Outsider*.

Fanon and Wright seem to converge on the same metaphors, one might even say the same literary style. Fanon, having immersed himself in the scientific literature of the West, turns that discourse against itself, seeking a way to disalienate himself from it. Hence the jarring instability of register in *Black Skin, White Masks*, where the language of lab reports and academic journals is infiltrated and interrupted by lyrical outbursts, surrealist montage, and the hyperbole of revolutionary slogans and manifestos. Wright's writing is less jittery than Fanon's, but it is not without assumed neuroses, especially a recurrent reference to "industrialization."[129] They share a faith in both the diagnostic possibilities of form and the therapeutic value of symbolic, sexual, and political expressions of violence, as channeled through a phenomenology of blackness, the *Erlebnis* of the black man.

What they diagnose is the wasteland produced by white supremacy. "The West" is the patient etherized upon the table. Racism, as Lewis Gordon would later say, is the "bad faith" of the white world.[130] The dissociation of sensibility, the proliferation of sexual neuroses, the entrenchment of dehumanizing pathological behavior, the mechanization and exploitation of labor—these must be cured, Fanon says, wherever necessary by violence. But the purpose of all this is a world more humane, more fully realized: "May man never be instrumentalized. May the subjugation of man by man—that is to say, of me by another—cease. May I be allowed to discover and desire man wherever he may be."[131] This is why Gordon is surely right when he describes Fanon as "fundamentally a radical, critical, revolutionary, existential humanist."[132] Wright certainly seemed on his way to embracing the same values.

Yet the literary creations that Wright and Fanon proposed as vehicles for this revaluation of values, this commitment to a more ethical world, turned out to be some of the most discomforting, even chilling writing in the canon of black letters. Even the plays that Fanon wrote while he was a medical student in Lyon are dense with hermetic surrealism and a claustrophobic strain of fear and loathing.[133] Part of what is so difficult about

Black Skin, White Masks is that it wears so many textual masks; it slips in and out of genres, personae, and styles; it is stark, experimental, uninterested in accommodating an audience. "Why am I writing this book?" Fanon writes. "Nobody asked me to. Especially not those for whom it is intended."[134] One hears the same defiant disregard in a letter Wright wrote to Ellison as he was wrapping up *The Outsider*: "I've waded right out into the question of the Negro's relation to the Western world.... I have not the slightest notion what the critics will say about it. I know the Negroes will not like it, not one bit."[135] Wright and Fanon's writings from the late 1940s and early 1950s combine the desire for a mass audience with a total refusal to give that audience what it wants.

Their commitments are deeply determined by the Blue Period in which they are writing. The specter of racial warfare and its totalitarian grip on human consciousness presented to both men a clear and present danger of postwar reality. Both writers hovered at the edge of the social sciences without pledging themselves wholeheartedly to any of its disciplinary formations. They were impressed by Western philosophical discourses but not intimidated by them. Both demonstrated something like racial pride while treating black vernacular culture with a (sometimes disquieting) analytical detachment and, in the case of *négritude*, with suspicion and even outright hostility. They share an almost obsessive concern with the objective determinants of subjective experience; they want to disorient and submerge the reader in a traumatic affective dislocation, yet still persuade that reader to take a political side.[136]

These are the coordinates of what we could call, following Jonathan Flatley, "the affective mapping" in aesthetic and intellectual terms of the response from the perspective of black thinkers to the problem of meaningful freedom and the pursuit of human dignity in the context of the West's imposition of totalitarianism (whether of the Left or Right) as the telos of postwar modernity.[137] Although it isn't new to suggest that Wright's *The Outsider* is an existentialist novel, it's useful to take the measure of its broad consonance with Fanon's articulation of the problems and opportunities particular to racialized subjects in the postwar world. The two disagreed on the political implementation of such a project. Wright favored a top-down approach that would endow a vanguard elite with the power to accelerate preindustrial, nonwhite societies into an industrialized future that would let them make a self-determined exit from Western modernity. Fanon believed in a revolution of the Third (World) Estate from below, a revolution against the West that would be permanently secured by a redistribution of power to the agrarian nonwhite proletariats of the globe. In sensibility, they nevertheless converged upon a disalienation from the pathologies of racialization as the foundation for a new humanism, what Fanon would famously call, in the last line of *The Wretched of the Earth*, the project of setting afoot "a new man."[138]

Fanon and Wright envisioned a role for black literature and black writers in this grand project that would no longer be legible in terms of protest or universalism, or even the mobilizing promises of social realism. They wanted a deeper shock therapy, a writing that would delve into the interiority of alienated black consciousness and produce a wholesale transformation of default conceptualizations of the modern world. This implies the combat of ideas, steeped in rhetorical and symbolic violence. This is the crucible that produced *The Outsider*, a novel of ideas in which Wright emplots nothing less than the confrontation between the logics of modernity and its pathologies, and, facing them down, a black hero of Fanonian violence struggling to find his way from alienation to disalienation. In it, we find Wright's most passionate, and desperate, attempt to think outside what he considered the totalitarian ideological parameters set forth by the opposing Soviet and US empires. The novel stages a conflict whose dramatis personae would be the *esprit de système* of the Cold War ideologues and the antitotalitarian consciousness of a tortured and isolated black spirit—one with nothing to lose and nothing to gain by pledging allegiance to either side, a blue hero for a black novel of ideas.

Going Inside: *The Outsider* and Literary Form

Who is Cross Damon? The first name Wright bestows upon his antihero textually indexes him as both an allegorical Christ figure and as the algebraic random value, the unknown quantity (X). This symbolic name for the unknown would come to be associated in the postwar period with American racial blackness through Malcolm (né) Little who replaced his "slave name" with the letter X while in Charlestown State Prison two years before Wright completed his novel.[139] This social anonymity is self-asserted as the root of Damon's intellectual personality: "[He] had no party, no myths, no tradition, no race, no soil, no culture, and no ideas—except perhaps the idea that ideas in themselves were, at best, dubious."[140] His surname adds to this the connotation of the demonic, suggesting both a fallen angel and a figure severed from grace.

This negative and cynical characterization places Damon recognizably in the tradition of the hero of the European novel of ideas, as emblematized, for example, by Ulrich in Robert Musil's *The Man without Qualities*, who hovers with ironic hauteur over the decadence of Vienna at the turn of the century.[141] But despite his claim to have "no race," a piece of bad faith we examine at greater length below, Cross Damon is a *black* man without qualities. Unlike Ulrich, who lives in a time and place enshrined in cultural criticism as a preeminently generative site of modern intellectual life, Damon must bear the additional burden of what Lindon Barrett calls the "discontinuity of western modernity" interposed by "racial blackness."[142]

Where Musil could assume a vantage point for his character on native ground, so to speak, Wright's relation to even that tradition is of an endemic outsider. Damon's spectral position is necessarily constructed in part out of the notion reiterated by Hegel, Kant, Hume, and Thomas Jefferson, among others, that black peoples have no history, no intelligence, no inventions, no interiority, no native—or natal—claims to intellectual existence.[143] Nahum Chandler elegantly posits the problem of *The Outsider* as "the problem of the Negro as a problem for thought."[144] It is therefore, inherently, also a problem for literary form.

In his first novel since *Native Son*, published a decade before, Wright conducts a literary experiment that inscribes his own fugitive trajectory out of social realism, out of the Communist Party, and beyond the borders of the US state. These shifts are highly conditioned by the discourses and operative forces (legal, political, ideological) of the Cold War. Joseph Keith uses the terms *epistemologies of unbelonging* and *alienage* to describe the compromised citizenship and state-sponsored anticommunist repression efforts, like the Smith Act, the Internal Security Act, and the McCarran-Walter Act, which severely blunted the momentum of the cultural Left in the early Cold War.[145] As Keith points out, these were the years when "the term 'alien' gained a general meaning in the national language as a 'foreign subversive.'"[146]

This atmosphere of tension, surveillance, and exile is distilled to a dark concentrate in *The Outsider*. Wright is constantly punning on, or alluding to, the "alien." Indeed, the novel's title can be read as a pun on the Latin etymology of the word *alius*, or "other," that which is of or from the outside. The epigraph to "Dread" and the title of the first chapter come from Kierkegaard: "Dread is an alien power which lays hold of an individual, and yet one cannot tear oneself away, nor has a will to do so; for one fears what one desires."[147] And Wright dedicates the novel to Rachel, "my daughter born on alien soil" (fig. 3).

We first meet Cross Damon in the depths of a Chicago winter. He is introverted, educated, and bookish (we learn he majored in philosophy at the University of Chicago), but he is working at the central post office on the South Side. The fact that this is a plausible position of employment for a college-educated black man is itself a quiet comment on the racial ceiling for social advancement. Significantly, we are introduced to Damon through a scene in which he is alienated from a gathering of black men that includes his fellow postal workers. On his way home at the end of a shift, he overhears a "crowd of Negroes" being talked at by a man

A new novel by

RICHARD
WRIGHT

The
Outsider

By the author of "BLACK BOY" and "NATIVE SON"

3 Richard Wright, *The Outsider* (New York: Harper and Brothers, 1953) (first edition, front cover). Author's photograph.

convinced he knows the real truth behind "flying saucers" (UFOs being, of course, a quintessential feature of the Cold War imaginary). Wright uses the scene to set up a joke with multiple resonances. The man declares that the men from Mars are black: "That's why they hushed up the story. They didn't want the rest of the world to know that the rest of the universe is colored!"[148]

With signifying finesse, this is a joke on one level about segregation and on another about the political consciousness produced by the Bandung moment. But Wright also uses the occasion to make a point Kierkegaard would sanction. The man explains to the crowd that whites see UFOs everywhere because they are fearful, and they are fearful because they are guilty. The crowd in the café enjoys the conceit, and even Cross Damon finds himself unable to resist laughing. But behind this outward appearance of sociability, Wright indicates Damon's more profound alienation: "His heart went out to these rejected men whose rebel laughter banished self-murder from his thoughts. If only he could lose himself in that kind of living!"[149] Damon turns out to be the alien in a situation meant to bind him to others by racial affiliation.

This scene exemplifies how the novel operates through ideas—namely, through vernacular translations of philosophical concepts. In a flashback to Damon's courtship of his wife, Gladys, they exchange remarks at a downtown party where the rest of the crowd is white:

"They think they're *something* and we're *nothing*," she snapped.

"It's up to us to make ourselves something," he argued. "A man creates himself…"

"You are a *man*," she said simply.

He understood now; it was the helplessness of dependence that made her fret so. Men made themselves and women were only made through men.[150]

Here Wright uses italics as signposts to key up one-liner reductions of the philosophical systems of his friends, Jean-Paul Sartre and, with the rejoinder, Simone de Beauvoir. Existentialism's bad faith and Kierkegaard's spheres of existence make similar appearances. The quasi-pedagogical function of these vernacular glosses points to Wright's view of the novel as a vehicle for making ideas accessible and disseminating them to his audience, reaffirming his tutelary approach to intellectual engagement.

But this emphasis on vernacular philosophizing should not be confused with Wright's attitude toward black vernacular culture. On this point, Wright breaks decisively with Ellison (as he had in 1937 with Hurston), and he uses the opening of the novel in another way to signify on *Invis-*

ible Man. Damon's fellow coworkers tease him for his bookishness but also show concern and affection for him as they see him turning increasingly to the bottle:

> "I wish I had a dollar for every book you got," Joe sighed.
> "Now, honest, Crossy, how come you don't read no more?"
> "I've put away childish things," Cross said.
> "Aw, be yourself, man," Booker said.
> "I am what I am," Cross said.[151]

Ellison had used the biblical phrase as a key epiphany for his narrator, a moment of Derridean play merging the tropes of black experience with those of an existentialist assertion: "This is all very wild and childish, I thought, but to hell with being ashamed of what you liked. No more of that for me. I am what I am! I wolfed down the yam and ran back to the man.... 'They're my birthmark,' I said. 'I yam what I am.'"[152] For Ellison the "birthmark," the always-present mark of black *différance*, is the source of an ecstatic self-authorization and critique. His lesson is that the vernacular is already good enough; whatever supplementary meaning a subject requires can be found there. Wright divorces his hero from the laughter, camaraderie, and signifying play that bind the black men he works with. Even the friend (not coincidentally named Booker), who seems to know Damon best, cannot reach him.

Per the list of attributes that Cross Damon does not have, there is a generalized sense that we are to understand Wright's protagonist through a *via negativa* of all the things that do not allow us to know him. This produces stylistic consequences as well, as in the opacity produced by Wright's use of deliberately allusive language, like Damon's quotation of both Exodus 3:14 and Corinthians 13:11, via Ellison's *Invisible Man*, in the preceding dialogue. Wright employs what Adorno evocatively calls "language without soil," an irreticent index of his deracinated consciousness, although the quality of that language shifts over the course of the novel.[153]

In the earlier Chicago chapters there is an obsession, perhaps a reckoning, with confessional psychoanalysis and the female body. Often the invocation is so flagrant that the free indirect discourse appears to speak for Damon. "He yearned to talk to someone, he felt his mere telling his story would have helped. But to whom could he talk? To his mother?... There was not a single man to whom he cared to confess the nightmare that was his life."[154] The desire for talk therapy nearly overwhelms the narrative thrust of the novel. The figure of the mother looms so immediately, so large, and Damon's articulation of his neuroses are so meticulous, that it sometimes sounds as though he were performing self-analysis: "He was conscious of himself as a frail object which had to protect itself against a pending threat of annihilation. This frigid world was suggestively like the one which his mother, without her having known it, had created for him to live in when he had been a child."[155]

Abdul JanMohamed argues that "Wright's misogyny is a product of a deep disidentification with women in general and with black women in particular," and that it is also connected to "a deep, abiding, and untransgressable identification with his mother ... and by extension with the slave mother, whose child is torn away from her arms by the master."[156] From the outset, this crippling matrix is present as a kind of hysteria that Cross Damon is already fleeing, even before the narrative is really set in motion. The first several chapters deal with Damon's panic over what to do about Dot, an underage girl whom he has impregnated and who is refusing his entreaties for her to get an abortion and insisting on marriage instead. When his mother mildly chastises him over his sexual behavior, he flies into a rage and accuses her of "confusedly seeking his masculine sympathy for her sexually blighted life."[157]

Damon's hysteria (I use the term advisedly) seems a projective reflection of the dichotomy in Wright's gendered imagination of the type of the intellectual. To be fair, there is some satirical bite to this. And if it were merely a character trait and not a feature of the novel, it might even be welcome. But the structure of *The Outsider*, in fact, doubles down repeatedly on a blatant and stereotypical bifurcation, wherein anything associated with the mind must occur in a homosocial relation between ideationally equal males, and anything involving the body is feminized, devalued, and regarded as a threat to his autonomy and capacity for social integration.

Early on, Damon wonders whether he could reach "rebels with whom he could feel at home, men who were outsiders not because they had been born black and poor, but because they had thought their way through the many veils of illusion? But where were they? How could one find them?"[158] This transracial brotherhood is impossible and inaccessible in the presence of women. Damon, in a conflicted way, even suggests that women threaten to displace intellectual activity by causing him to pursue them in like manner—that is, into oblivion or depravity: "Ideas had been his only sustained passion, but he knew that his love of them had that same sensual basis that drew him achingly to the sight of a girl's body swinging in a tight skirt along a sunny street."[159]

We learn that Damon's first action after the birth of his first child with Gladys was to go on a bender and, in his haze, sleep with a stranger whom he brings home. The underage and pregnant Dot is described as "a tall yellow girl" and "a passionate child achingly hungry for emotional experience."[160] It's hinted that she has a conniving side, a mark of intelligence

that Damon accordingly prizes, but only because she is still easily intellectually dominated. When she teams up with her friend to try to pressure him, his ability to see through them (almost literally) is, in the logic
of the novel, a confirmation of their inferiority: "He could almost see the
little wheels turning in the brains of both girls as they planned their next
move. Men had to consult together for concerted action; women simply
gravitated together spontaneously, motivated by their situation in life as
women."[161] The chess game played by men is happening elsewhere, and
Cross Damon will have to leave Chicago to find it. The petty trappings of
adultery with poor, uneducated girls on the South Side are too slender a
plot for the scale of his ambitions and his philosophical preoccupations
with the nature of the modern world.

His wife, Gladys, however, puts up more resistance; she is older and
smarter than Dot. Damon's response is to try to torture her, beating her at
random moments and then gaslighting her, pretending to have no memory of his actions. He calls this a "complicated psychological attack," and
these episodes (which recall some of the anecdotes Fanon describes in his
field hospital notes) appear to allude partially to the popular Cold War fear
of "brainwashing" and indoctrination stoked by prisoner-of-war accounts
from the front lines of the Korean War.[162] The fact remains that Gladys's
will has to be broken by physical force. When the torture plan fails, Damon
submits to her retaliatory conditions (confiscation of his pay and separa-
tion without divorce); only the plot twist of a train wreck saves him from
having to carry these through.

The "L" train accident is a fortuitous deux ex machina, but one detail in
particular makes it highly revealing of the novel's overall schema. To free
himself from the chaos and darkness of the train's twisted steel, Damon
must walk through a female corpse: "He stepped upon the body, feeling
his shoes sinking into the lifeless flesh and seeing blood bubbling from the
woman's mouth as his weight bore down on her bosom."[163] The condition
for Damon's liberation, his transition to the state of freedom where he can
live the life of the mind, and from which the novel of ideas can take flight,
is predicated on literally traversing the female body, which here is no longer a body at all, but, explicitly as Hortense Spillers distinguishes it, the
"zero degree" of "flesh."[164] Cross Damon is confronted less by the death
of a subject or a person (notice the absence of a face and, interestingly, of a
race) than by what Luce Irigaray calls "awoman," a fungible substance that
"mixes with bodies of a like state," in this case amalgamated as merely a
gothic detail for a crash scene.[165]

Paula Rabinowitz has shown how thoroughly indebted the imaginary
of *The Outsider* is to film noir and what she calls pulp modernism.[166] This
helps make sense of some of the gendered violence we encounter in the

novel, not to mention the hardboiled dialogue: "'Darling, I'll never do that to you,' Dot said sweetly, too sweetly."[167] But one must be careful not to read this violence too stylistically and the ideas behind it unseriously. One major function of the nod to pulp and its lowbrow associations is Wright's effort to orchestrate a genre transition—or rather a genre purification, in the sense of Mary Douglas's conception of the relation of pollution to the sacred. Cross Damon's fear of women is a fear of contagion and capture. "Dirt," Douglas famously says, "offends against order."[168] And if what Damon really wants is an order of ideas, then what Wright wants is a novel of that order. But creator and hero are trapped, or fear they will become trapped, in the dirty novel of social realism, in the kitchenette, in the South Side ghetto pastoral. Pulp is the style, the natural grammar of that world—but it is part of what Wright is seeking to leave behind for higher ground. Its presence is a symptomatic trace of this effort.

Just after Damon murders Joe, an old friend who could have identified him and blown his plan for escape, there is a remarkable passage in which the prose suddenly shifts to a deep focus. Seized by fatigue, Damon is resting in an alleyway when a man comes out of a building and tosses out the contents of a garbage can. Wright catalogs the refuse:

> The steaming pile was crowned with a mound of wet, black coffee grounds that gleamed in the light of the street lamp; some of the grounds spilled over a bloodstained Kotex which still retained the curving shape of having fitted tightly and recently against the lips of some vagina; there was a flattened grapefruit hull whose inner pulpy fibres held a gob of viscous phlegm; there was part of a fried sausage with grease congealed white in the porous grains of meat; there was the crumpled cellophane wrapping from a pack of cigarettes glittering with tiny beads of moisture.... His blood felt chilled. He had to shake off this dead weight and move on.[169]

In this quite literally ad nauseam list, Wright compresses into Cross Damon's consciousness a torrential, alluvial disgust, a primal revulsion with domestic kitchenette life and metonymically the female body (here discarded as a soiled sanitary pad), whose primary, seemingly sole function is the social reproduction of that life. The near-hallucinatory, fish-eye-lens precision of the passage suggests an excess of meaning unhinged from its objects. The scene recalls the grand and grotesque visions of Roquentin in Sartre's *Nausea* (1938), a novel of ideas with a solipsistic young man as its hero, and undoubtedly a key model for Wright.

The use of anaphora ("there was") marks the almost liturgical tone of Damon's spiritual revulsion with ghetto life and Wright's decisive rejection of the "kitchen-sink realism," to use a term borrowed from British postwar film, which also infamously featured alienated and adrift "angry young men." For Damon and for Wright, the bricks and mortar of the South Side must be thrown out; they are "dead weight," bits of female-impressed matter holding spirit back. Wright contrived a plot to hang his novel of ideas upon—and his pursuit of Cross Damon, or Cross Damon's pursuit of a philosophy upon which to make some sense of his existence, becomes from this point onward the motor of the plot, which moves dialectically to a resolution in death.

The train, a vehicle that Farah Jasmine Griffin has shown is key to the imaginary of migration literature, is where *The Outsider* first gets free, picking up the steam of its aspiration—the freedom to be the kind of novel it wants to be.[170] It is no coincidence that it is in motion on the train to New York that we get one of the novel's most quoted passages, which comes through the voice of Damon's eventual antagonist, the hunchbacked district attorney Ely Houston: "Negroes, as they enter our culture, are going to inherit the problems we have, but with a difference. They are outsiders and they are going to know that they have these problems. They are going to be self-conscious; they are going to be gifted with a double vision, for, being Negroes, they are going to be both *inside* and *outside* our culture at the same time ... they will become psychological men, like the Jews.... They will not only be Americans or Negroes; they will be centers of *knowing*."[171] Wright deliberately gives these lines to a figure who stands in as a composite for the arm of the white law, the white establishment, and the state intelligence apparatus—suggesting that if these elements have a certain sympathy for the position of the Negro, it is ultimately paternalistic. Houston's language suggests a "study" of Du Bois, a passive, monitoring analysis. He recognizes Damon's intelligence, however, and the function of the scene is to show the hero leveling up to the chessboard of ideas, where the real power held by white men lies.

Negroes may become centers of knowing, but the point is to enter the circle of those who know, who have foresight through study and mastery. For Wright, to know the present, to transcend "the veil," requires not Du Bois's racial double consciousness but the unmasking of ideology. When Cross Damon arrives in New York, he will acquire a new identity, encounter the Communist Party, and meet the only woman he will ever love, Eva, a white painter of abstract expressionism. Each of these plot developments furthers the pursuit of ideological unveiling that is at the heart of the novel's conception of itself as a black novel of ideas. The relentless fugitivity that characterizes Cross Damon's feverish (and violent) path of flight is supposed to evade the snares of race and ideology. But what his increasing abjection and irrecuperable alienation show is that it is precisely his blackness that residually becomes more unavoidable as the factor that makes him different, that renders him symbolic of an entire population that is intractable, unusable, ungovernable, and therefore also expendable.

Upon his arrival in New York, Cross Damon will try on different new aliases (Charles Webb, Addison Jordan), but the name he settles on and that sticks with him is Lionel Lane. The choice of this name has not been much remarked upon in criticism of *The Outsider*, but it's a highly illuminating choice, intended to signify upon two Lionels. The first is the preeminent literary critic of the period, Lionel Trilling. Although this may seem an unlikely connection, we know Wright appreciated Trilling, especially for his assessment of *Black Boy*, which Trilling reviewed for the *Nation*.[172] But more important to Cross Damon's predicaments is Trilling's first and only novel, *The Middle of the Journey*.

Published in 1947, *The Middle of the Journey* is often read as a roman à clef (Trilling would later admit basing the character Maxim Gifford on Whittaker Chambers). It is also a novel of midcentury Cold War politics that explores one generation's attraction to radicalism, conservatism, or a "middle"-course liberalism that tried to stave off the extremes of passion and corruption on either end. At the time of composition, Trilling was a professor at Columbia University and the first Jew to gain tenure in the English department of an Ivy League school.[173] One of the controversial aspects of his novel is that none of the characters, all of them upper-middle-class intellectuals, is Jewish. We can assume Wright was reading the novel in 1949 (despite its having been widely panned by critics) because it appears on his library-lending card at Shakespeare & Company marked "Dec 13," immediately above a borrowing of an unnamed book by Heidegger.[174] Wright's interest in it makes sense. It is a novel that seeks to transcend (some would argue suppress) its ethnic ties while explaining the lure and the dangers of ideology. Cross Damon (a.k.a. Lionel Lane) is no liberal, but he is, like Trilling's protagonist John Laskell, a character attempting to evade the extremities of ideological commitment.

The other Lionel who comes into view, more intimately, is Cyril Lionel Robert James, a close friend of Wright's during the years of his second marriage to Constance Webb (whose last name and initials match the first pseudonym Cross Damon adopts). C. L. R. James ("Nello" among friends) met Wright in 1944, and together with Ralph Ellison, Horace Cayton, and St. Clair Drake, they planned to work on a book proposal together about the race problem. They hoped to form an intellectual circle, a "Thinking Coterie."[175] These men represented for Wright the "politics of friendship"; even through their disagreements (James was a Trotskyist), they formed an affective intellectual community.[176] According to James, when he visited the Wrights in the Canadian countryside in August 1945, Wright showed him a shelf full of books and said: "Look here, Nello, you see those books there? They are by Kierkegaard. I am not concerned about his popularity. I want you to know something. Everything that he writes in those books, I knew before I had them." James goes on to say, "What he [Wright] was telling me was that he was a black man in the United States and that gave him an insight into what today is the universal opinion and attitude of the modern personality."

Conversations on the major issues of the day were one of the great attractions between the two men. In a November 1945 letter, James told Constance Webb that he "wanted to talk to him [Wright] more than to anyone else in America (political and literary)."[177] James also made introductions for the Wrights to George and Dorothy Padmore, who would become close friends and intellectual mentors with respect to the Pan-African movement.[178] The last night in New York before the Wrights left for Paris in 1946, James Baldwin depicts a solemn Wright who "talked a great deal about a friend of his who was in trouble with the US immigration authorities, and was about to be, or already been, deported."[179] That was C. L. R. James who, after being trailed and harassed by the Federal Bureau of Investigation, was eventually arrested in 1952 for being a "subversive" under the then-newly-passed McCarran-Walter Act.

While Wright was writing *The Outsider* in London, James was interned at Ellis Island, where he wrote another major text of the Blue Period, *Mariners, Renegades, and Castaways* (1953). As Joseph Keith has argued, C. L. R. James's study of Melville not only sought to rearticulate the meaning of America from the subaltern (and incarcerated) margins but also challenged the form of the novel itself through "an effort to decenter the realist novel as the privileged form of postcolonial representation."[180] With the rapprochement that Keith makes between *The Outsider* and *Mariners*, I would go further to say that both texts pose formal questions about what it means to face a world system that wants to use you, kill you, or lock you up. Keith is right that the minor character Bob Hunter in Wright's novel, a Trinidadian who works for the Communist Party but gets denounced when he begins putting black interests ahead of the party and is eventually deported, is meant to represent James's plight. But "Lionel Lane," the voice of the black intellectual who emerges out of Cross Damon in New York City in the second half of the novel, pays homage from afar to Wright's friendship with James, too, the gift of words cast in the isolated darkness from one "center of knowing" to another.

For Lionel Lane, the affection of ideas finds its object in his love interest, the white "nonobjective" painter Eva with "an undeniable childishness about her," who is initially involved with the Communist Party leader Gil.[181] In a scene that seems cribbed from a script produced by or for the Congress for Cultural Freedom, Lionel falls in love with Eva over a shared understanding of abstract expressionism.[182] "There is really no nonobjective painting without either a strong assumption of atheism or an active expression of it, whether the nonobjective painter realizes it or not," he tells her when they're alone. Their dialogue continues:

> "I'd not have thought that a colored person would like nonobjective art. Your people are so realistic and drenched in life, the world … Colored people are so robustly healthy."
>
> "*Some* of us," he said.
>
> "And you're not? How did that happen?"
>
> "It's a long story," he said. "Some people are pushed deeper into their environment and some are pushed completely out of it"
>
> "Do you feel that much aloneness?" she asked in surprise.
>
> "Yes; and you?"
>
> "Yes," she said simply and was silent.[183]

Wright is not often associated with the visual arts. Painters and visual artists rarely appear in his works and even among his wide swath of high-culture acquaintances.

He may have had in mind his affair with Joyce Gourfain back in the days of the South Side Writers Group in Chicago.[184] Gourfain was a white woman married to a wealthy communist and living in Hyde Park. An aspiring writer and painter, she "often complained to Wright that Party duties took time away from the writing and painting she was trying to do," exactly as Eva does of Gil. Gourfain introduced Wright to Henry James's *The Art of the Novel*, one of his favorite works of literary criticism and one he would recommend to Ellison.[185] It's possible that Wright wanted to ground his New York scene with a specific, au courant reference: few cultural products are more powerfully associated with New York in the late 1940s and early 1950s than abstract expressionism. It's also possible that Wright was making a bid for a black appropriation of that style, as Jacqueline Goldsby has suggested Norman Lewis, Romare Bearden, and others did.[186]

But the scene clearly also functions analogically as a metacommentary on the form—on the art of the novel, if you will. Like her diary entries, which Lionel will furtively read, Eva's artwork endows her with the currency that the novel trades on: interiority. This love scene (such as it is) is premised on the theory of the racial opacity of inner feeling; her discovery, to her surprise that, despite being black, Lionel, too, has a hidden psychic wound creates a bond between them that breaks the bind of realism as representation. Lionel's passionate reading of her work as he gazes over the surfaces of paintings in her studio serves as a primer, and possibly even an apologia, for the harsh aesthetic of the novel itself:

In her work she seemed to be straining to say something that possessed and gripped her life; she spoke tersely, almost cruelly through her forms. Her painting at bottom was the work of a poet trying to make color and form sing in an absolute and total manner. There was a blatant brutality about her volumes, some of which were smashed, cracked and presented a tactile surface carrying an illusion of such roughness that one felt that the skin of the hand would be torn by touching it.... He wondered what life experiences made her paint such images of latent danger ...?[187]

Eva puts some sensuality back into the world of ideas, for a moment reconnecting mind and body—in this case, a soulful if childish mind and a white female body. But her overall impact is relatively negligible.

The real bravura passages that the novel is building up to are Lionel's grand disquisitions on the nature of modernity, which he delivers under a Dostoyevskian cross-examination by Blimin, a party hack who is trying to get him to reveal his identity and make his allegiances clear. Lionel delivers what we know from Wright's exilic writings to be essentially his own modernization theory, his own secularization thesis, his own convictions of the looming totalitarian future and of the ruse of ideology as a mask for raw, perfectly cynical industrial power and for further technological development. Marxism's "bristling economic theories" are "vastly clever fishing nets which they dragged skillfully through muddy social waters to snare the attention of shivering and hungry men."[188] Lionel elides the role of American racism, but he savages the tenets of American exceptionalism: "America, under the ideological banner of free enterprise, fought a bloody civil war and defeated its agrarian provinces and launched itself, with no pre-history and practically no traditions to check it, upon a program of industrialization the equal of which, in terms of speed and magnitude, the world has never seen. From my point of view, this industrial program justified their dazzling progress by claiming that an organic relationship obtained between their ideas and industrialization. But really, there was none."[189] Lionel relegates liberals (like Lionel Trilling) to a pathetic historical footnote as well intentioned but ultimately useless: "They did an impossible job with great skill, those liberals. Future history will regard the liberals as the last great defenders of that which really could not be defended, as the last spokesmen of historical man as we've known him for the past two thousand years."[190]

There is certainly something more compelling about the imaginative resources that Ellison commands in *Invisible Man*—the way he fashions a black novel of ideas that feels organic to the cultures and contexts of its creation. But it is also fair to say that with Wright's *The Outsider*, there has never been before or since a black novel of ideas that so relentlessly, so deliberately and ruthlessly, lays out a vision of utter despair, a vision of a broken world beyond repair and with black personhood condemned at its founding—of what we, in intellectual circles today, call Afro-pessimism. Here is Lionel on modernity and its futures:

> There is no escaping what the future holds. We are going back, back to something earlier, maybe better, maybe worse, maybe something more terrifyingly human! These few hundred years of freedom, empire building, voting, liberty, democracy—these will be regarded as the *romantic* centuries in human history. There will be in that future no trial by jury, no writs of habeus corpus, no freedom of speech, of religion—all of this is being buried and not by Communists or Fascists alone, but by their opponents as well. All hands are shoveling clay on to the body of freedom before it even dies, while it lies breathing its last.[191]

At the end of *The Outsider*, Cross Damon a.k.a. Lionel Lane is dying. At his side is Ely Houston, the investigator who has been trying to track his crimes but who now serves as his confessor: "I wish I had some way to give the meaning of my life to others.... To make a bridge from man to man.... Men hate themselves and it makes them hate others.... We're strangers to ourselves."[192]

Because Wright failed to answer his letter inquiring about more of his works, *The Outsider* would remain one of the few Wright titles never to enter Frantz Fanon's library. But had he gotten the novel, we know he would certainly have agreed with Cross's words: "Man is returning to the earth ... for a long time he has been sleeping ... he is awakening now ... and finding himself in a waking nightmare ... the myth-men are going ... the real men, the last men are coming.... Somebody must prepare the way for them."[193] For Fanon, of course, the way is already prepared by the people; the intellectuals simply have to join them, as he did in Algeria. Fanon's anticolonial poetics share affinities with Wright's but also differences; together they cover a spectrum, a swath of the black midcentury affect vibrating through the Blue Period.

But they do not cover it all. Gwendolyn Brooks's celebration of resistance through ordinary acts, and by ordinary people, is yet another version. And so is the work of Wright's putative nemesis, Zora Neale Hurston, who, after years of being sidelined and prevented from making enough money from writing to sustain her career, ends her 1942 *Dust Tracks on a Road* likewise in a retreat to private alienation, but one that sounds far more agreeable, full of the pleasures of rest, coffee, liquor, reading Spinoza, and "writing for myself, if for nobody else."[194] There were always many paths through modernism for the black writer, although perhaps none ever equaled Hurston's ability to operate "at the crossroads of the modern and the folk."[195] Wright's decision to bear an infernal Cross is only one way—the "cosmic Zora" is another.

The bridge from man to man that Damon wishes for cannot be built without first repairing the bond between men and women. As necessary as it is to deprovincialize blackness, it cannot come at the cost of destroying the sentience of another sex. The problem isn't that *The Outsider* is a violent novel; the problem is that the violence it believes it requires stands in the way of Damon's ability to know the world in other ways. His blinkered pursuit of freedom negates alternative "centers of knowing," the kind of supplemental knowledge he might have gained, for example, if he could have heard in Gladys not someone trapping him but someone trapped *by* him, and by the raced and gendered power that gives him the latitude to assuage his rage and confusion, while it affords her no protection other than her endurance and bare wits.

The Outsider is a brilliant, deeply pessimistic novel of ideas. One of those ideas—going back to the game of wits played out by Babo, "that hive of subtlety" of which Captain Delano is dimly aware in Melville's *Benito Cereno*—is that the most dangerous thing imaginable is a black person with too many ideas. But some of the ideas that might have powerfully served Wright, specifically with respect to the dread of his mother that he repeatedly expressed, and that he at times treated therapeutically in his writing, would come from thinkers he would never meet: "The black American male embodies the only American community of males which has had the specific occasion to learn who the female is within itself, the infant child who bears the life against the could-be fateful gamble, against the odds of pulverization and murder, including her own. It is the heritage of the mother that the African American male must regain as an aspect of his own personhood—the power of 'yes' to the 'female' within."[196] These famous lines from Hortense Spillers are part of an answer that criticism of Wright must continue to grapple with. We are not done excavating the tortuous self-harm of his inability to regain the fullest aspects of his own personhood.[197] That means, however, that there is also much more "within" his work that we have the power to say yes to, if we give it the chance to speak.

Cross Damon's "bridge of words" speaks, as all words got down in books do, across time and space. They find their most direct echo in the words that close Wright's memoir *Black Boy*, a scene that is probably one of the finest things he ever wrote. It is May Day, and the communists are marching outside. Wright sits alone in his room listening to the parade but turning inward, definitively, to find the answers he needs within himself: "My problem was here, here with me, here in this room, and I would solve it here alone or not at all."[198] The dramatic tension becomes centered on the act of writing itself—or rather, on its inevitable inadequacy: "I picked up a pencil and held it over a sheet of white paper, but my feelings stood in the way of my words. Well, I would wait, day and night, until I knew what to say. Humbly now, with no vaulting dream of achieving a vast unity, I wanted to try and build a bridge of words between me and that world outside, that world which was so distant and elusive that it seemed unreal."[199] "A bridge of words," Cross Damon's "bridge from man to man": these are, again, expressions of Wright's dream for what literature, taken at its highest potential, can be. What Theodor Adorno says of the poetry of Stefan George, could be said with great justice of those writers, like Wright, who were navigating the impasses of the Blue Period: "The expression of his poetry may have been condensed into an individual expression which his lyrics saturate with substance and with the experience of its own solitude; but this very lyric speech becomes the voice of human beings between whom the barriers have fallen."[200]

The idea that one can find recourse in, and even carve out resistance from, a place of isolation, alienation, and near despair—something like this posture is common to Maud Martha in Chicago, to Cross Damon in New York, to Selina Boyce in Brooklyn, to Ellison's underground man in Harlem. We sense it when we imagine James Baldwin in the Swiss mountains, Édouard Glissant in Paris, Vincent O. Carter in Bern, Frantz Fanon in Lyon, and Richard Wright in his "narrow room" at the end of *Black Boy*. They all seem cut from the same cloth, working out a similar tune: call it a Miles Davis *Kind of Blue*. It is as though the blues of an earlier era were stretched across an abstract expressionist canvas, drawn back to their source as an idea, or rather a kind of feeling hibernating in the mind—a sense that it is worth holding out a little longer, waiting for a future day when the bridges will go up, and the walls will come down.

Writing for a Future World   [CONCLUSION]

But if history now is to become televised theatre, where are the
intellectuals to stand? In the audience? On the stage? Or in the
prompter's cramped and dusty pit?

WILLIAM DEMBY, *The Catacombs*, 1965

This book has treated an age-old question that attends to the making of
literature and its critical reception: what difference does its place in time
make? Underneath the vault of that question are many others that are especially salient to black writers working in the early postwar period. What
does it mean to write for a future world? What kind of writing does one
produce in a time when the momentum for action does not yet seem available, yet the need for it is all the more intensely coiled up, held inwardly,
carried through the world? How does frustrated expression tinker, seek
new languages, new articulations, new ways of grasping and trying to convey a reality that is only still emergent, on the cusp? What does it mean to
believe that the kind of writing one is producing in the present may end up
being only retrospectively appreciated by a future public? What aesthetics attend to the audacity of unknowable orders of social, political, and
personal relations—not a politics of utopia but a sober clear-eyed assessment of deferred yet inevitable political futures? What is it to *feel* a future
deferred?

The structure of feeling that impressed itself upon black writing in the
Blue Period left a distinctive and coherent trace. The sensibility of that literature was not always readily appreciated and more often dismissed or
misconstrued. In these pages I have offered some examples of how reading these works—some well-known, others less so—enhances our understanding of the aesthetic and contextual interest they bear. Nonetheless,
this study cannot pretend to have been exhaustive with respect to the field
of black literary production even in that restricted frame. There are perforce numerous other salient examples of texts that warrant being read
through the model I have proposed.

One such example is George Lamming's lyrical novel *In the Castle of
My Skin*, with its memory of boyhood life fringed with the taste of mortal-

ity, the nostalgia of the *paradis perdus* that Proust's narrator describes as the necessary tonic for any memory that has been resurrected through the force of poetry—whose plausibility lies precisely in its awareness of being irreparably lost to the present of its narrated recollection.[1] Lamming wrote about his home village of Carrington in Saint Philip Parish, Barbados, from a boarding room in London. In *The Pleasures of Exile*, Lamming writes: "We are made to feel a sense of exile by our inadequacy and our irrelevance of function in a society whose past we can't alter, and whose future is always beyond us.... sooner or later, in silence or with rhetoric, we sign a contract whose epitaph reads: To be an exile is to be alive."[2] This hiatus, produced by the sense of an unalterable past, an unusable present, and an elusive future, dominates the novel's affective tone. In the melancholy diary entry that gives the novel its title, the narrator, G, makes clear that the self that is leaving the island remains unknown to those he is leaving behind: "The likenesses will meet and make merry, but they won't know you, the you that's hidden somewhere in the castle of your skin."[3] Lamming understood that to be black in the Blue Period is to be an exile biding for a future time.

In *The Narrows*, Ann Petry gave herself the space and time to linger over the inner lives of the denizens of her fictional small town of Monmouth, Connecticut, in ways that the proletarian realism of her first and most successful novel, *The Street* (1946), did not. These included characters like her protective heroine Abbie Crunch and the earthy, warm blueswoman Mamie Powther, as feminist readings of the novel like those of Mary Helen Washington, Hazel Arnett Ervin, and Farah Jasmine Griffin, who has called it Petry's "masterwork," have always insisted.[4] These aesthetic strategies did not win Petry favorable reviews at the time, however. Wright Morris, then near the height of his critical reputation (ever since in severe decline), panned the novel in the pages of the *New York Times Book Review*. In a backhanded compliment, he dismissively called Petry's Mamie Powther "a café-au-lait Molly Bloom."[5] Petry's ethical concerns don't seem to have registered for him. Yet she painstakingly and elegantly conveys the cruel, banal circumspection that attends to keeping a young black man alive in a world where his strong and handsome features are likely to be more of a liability to his longevity than an asset.[6]

And Abbie Crunch's valid fears for the young black man she has adopted and raised—a counterpoint to Mamie's freewheeling insouciance—were endemic to middle-class black communities caged in by Jim Crow attitudes toward interracial sex. It speaks volumes that Emmett Till's murder in 1955 is hauntingly presaged in the novel's opening sentence, which describes Abbie's aversion to looking at the river Wye, where her Link Williams liked to swim as a boy and where his corpse will end up being dumped as the catastrophic denouement of the novel takes its course. Petry's unhurried narrative pace, attuned and attentive to the many shades of black life, and desirous of giving quiet dignity to the inner life of her characters, demands to be taken on its own terms. In its defiant and keen interest in interiority—in the quiet, quotidian anxieties of black life—*The Narrows*, too, is recognizably a Blue Period novel, one that predictably could find contemporary support neither in the activist Left nor in the liberal establishment.

The horizons of my study have hewed to the United States and the Caribbean, but the affective coloring of the Blue Period touched black writing across the diaspora. And while African literature from the continent skews the time frame slightly, there are nevertheless several highly suggestive candidates that fit well within the patterns that I have established. Among them I would count the Ivorian writer and diplomat Bernard Binlin Dadié, who produced a trilogy of autobiographical dispatches about his travels to the metropolitan centers of the West. *Un nègre à Paris* (1959; *An African in Paris*), *Patron de New York* (1965; *One Way: Bernard Dadié Observes America*), and *La ville où nul ne meurt* (1969; *The City Where No One Dies*) offer scathing and satirical observations on the trials of traveling abroad as a black man and the tribulations of interpreting and dissecting the social and cultural mores of Paris, New York, and Rome. The Sudanese novelist Tayeb Salih's *Mawsim al-Hijrah ilâ al-Shamâl* (1966; *Season of Migration to the North*) is a classic account of postcolonial alienation as embodied by the intellectual Mustafa Sa'eed's tortured and paranoid relations with white women in England, and also by his friend, the narrator, being stuck in an ambivalent aporia, torn between the *sittlichkeit* of his Sudanese village and the Western modernization that is promising to transform the postindependence state. In a similar vein, there is the divided conscience of Mugo, the antihero of Ngũgĩ wa Thiong'o's *A Grain of Wheat* (1967), whose alienation from "the Movement" of revolutionary resistance (his stand-in for the Mau Mau uprising) echoes that of Ellison's invisible narrator and his disaffiliation from "the Brotherhood" and Selina Boyce's rejection of "the Association" in Paule Marshall's *Brown Girl, Brownstones*.

Surveyed from a decent height, the literary landscape of the Blue Period is crowded enough, if also, fittingly, lonely. It's true that many of these writers lived in various states of exile; but there is also the fact that we have tended to keep them apart in our reading, and *that*, at least, is something we can change. This book has offered one possible model for how to undo this tendency—to illuminate and explore the constellation that was there all along.

In this conclusion, I examine in succession two apparently contradictory signs of the Blue Period, one foretelling an opening and the other announcing a closing. The first attends to the ironies surrounding one of the signal literary events at the very center of this period, the First Congress of Black Writers and Artists, held in Paris in 1956. This momentous gathering, historic in nature, at which many (though not all) of the writers in this study crossed paths, is a fitting metaphor for one paradox of the Blue Period: its combination of a synchronous affective pull and an alienating—and ultimately isolating—dispersal of literary production. It was arguably the most ambitious attempt ever to convene the totality of the literary and intellectual black world. Yet as Nadia Ellis has shown in her penetrating account of the mutual misprisions between African American and Caribbean writers at the congress, it was also an occasion for "fraternal agony" and, above all, a reminder that diasporas are "forged out of contest rather than agreement."[7] What gives the congress its remarkable and enduring appeal, however, is not any illusory consensus around identity, culture, or politics. Rather, it is the event's historicity itself—the sense that it was unveiling a decisive temporal precipice—a viewpoint whose world-historic singularity and significance its participants were fully aware of. In the pages that remain I return to that moment, to give a sense of its significance and simultaneous evanescence, qualities analogous to the conditions for black literary culture of that historic place in time.

Finally, if every period has a beginning, it must also have an end: How did the Blue Period close? I answer this question by considering work by two major poets and two lesser-known novelists whose trajectories from the mid-1960s onward all convey that sense of an ending. Each in their own way questions the viability of Ellisonian hibernation. They demonstrate their awareness of a cultural and political shift toward a militant consciousness that would eventually supplant and even eclipse the writings that came before it, sometimes including their own. For some, like Amiri Baraka, it spelled the explosive emergence of a career embracing the ideological and political imperatives and grabbing the cultural spotlight. Others, like William Demby, couldn't cross over, their work illegible and out of phase with the new sensibilities. The vicissitudes of their contemporary reception and the challenges of the marketplace are the trial by fire that any writing must endure. The literary historian at sufficient remove cannot restore or bestow laurels. But clarity is still necessary. I have argued for the usefulness and explanatory power of my periodizing argument. In the end, though, I hope also to have made the case for the inherent vitality, density, and variegation of black letters in these early postwar years, to have given the reader a sheer sense of how much is there.

Back to the Future

On a bright September day in Paris in 2006, exactly half a century after the original convening the First Congress of Black Writers and Artists, a crowd of delegates from across the diaspora once again filed into the Amphitheatre Descartes of the Sorbonne. Recording his impressions of the proceedings for posterity, as James Baldwin had in 1956, was the Nigerian poet and literary critic Niyi Osundare.[8] The event was intended to pay homage to the past and serve as a spur to deeper mutual engagement in the future. The credo of the conference was "that we may not forget."[9] Remarkably enough, there were still many living links to celebrate. Representing Alioune Diop, the founder of *Présence africaine* who had organized the congress of 1956, was Christiane Yandé Diop, who had been at his side then.[10] Christiane took over the helm of *Présence africaine* after his death in 1980, sustaining the journal and publishing arm through difficult years, and in the process becoming the first black woman to head a French publishing house.[11] Original attendees Édouard Glissant and the Haitian poet René Depestre returned to Paris to celebrate the anniversary. Aimé Césaire, then ninety-two years old, sent a videotaped message of greetings from Fort-de-France, Martinique.

Naturally, the conference was attended by many of the towering figures of letters and intellectual life from across Africa and the diaspora. Wole Soyinka used the opportunity to draw attention to the genocidal killings in Darfur, southern Sudan. Henry Louis Gates Jr. the director of the W. E. B. Du Bois Institute at Harvard University spoke about Richard Wright and his place in the memory of the first congress and presented *Encarta Africana*, his in-progress project to digitize the massive encyclopedia *Africana*, coedited with Kwame Anthony Appiah. Sharing the dais for the session on globalization were Abiola Irele, Molefi Asante, and the sociologist Thomas L. Blair, who spoke of the rise of a "Black Europe." The poet Daniel Maximin from Guadeloupe gave a reading. The poet and activist Nancy Morejón of Cuba gave the talk "Women in the Dynamics of Contemporary Development." As Osundare put it, "For five good days, writers … traded ideas with intellectuals; ambassadors and civil servants joined issues with politicians and former liberation fighters."[12] The Jazz Planet All Stars from the University of Pittsburgh gave the closing performance in the grand UNESCO hall.

Yet despite the impressive array of speakers and interventions, and the celebratory and moving linkages of past and present, Osundare worried aloud that the celebrations of 2006 would turn out to be merely a footnote to the landmark occasion half a century before:

Throughout the week, I couldn't help asking: where are the likes of W.E.B. Du Bois, Richard Wright, James Baldwin, Aimé Césaire, Frantz Fanon, Léopold Sédar Senghor, Alioune Diop, Ben Enwonwu—those titanic figures who roared from the podium in 1956, or who, prevented from doing so, sent their powerful words across the oceans? Is our generation short of such epochal figures? Many of the presentations I heard were thought-provoking, but I did not see in them the seminal fire, inaugurative élan, regenerative anger, fearless intelligence, and nationalistic passion that propelled the 1956 group into such permanent relevance in our consciousness and our discourse on the Black condition.[13]

It is too soon to judge the accuracy of this assessment, but it seems intuitively and, to some extent, empirically self-evident. This does not mean that the generation of 1956 was inherently more accomplished or more endowed with native genius. Rather, it points to the particularly vital and generative conditions of the first congress, a historical conjunction that was in many ways exceptional. It was also fleeting. In his own chronicle of the congress, "Princes and Powers," Baldwin inserts a brief window of speculation that captures this sense of momentous but also uncertain change: "Nothing is more undeniable than the fact that cultures vanish, undergo crises; are, in any case, in a perpetual state of change and fermentation, being perpetually driven, God knows where, by forces within and without.... I wondered just what effect the concept of art expressed by Senghor would have on that renaissance he had predicted and just what transformations this concept itself would undergo as it encountered the complexities of the century into which it was moving with such speed."[14] Baldwin covered the congress as an observer for *Encounter* magazine, a Cold War cultural front for the Central Intelligence Agency, as he would later note.[15] This revelation of the specter of US intelligence and, indeed, the tonal shift in Baldwin's own writing by the time of his revised appraisal in *No Name in the Street* (1972) are testament to the "speed" with which a new, more violent, cynical, and tragic era had taken hold. In between, Baldwin had witnessed the political assassinations of Medgar Evers, Malcolm X, the Kennedys, and Martin Luther King Jr.; the racism of the South where he felt compelled by the surging civil rights movement to do his part; the brutality of repression against the budding black militant movements like the Panthers, the Revolutionary Action Movement, and others; the carpet bombing of Vietnam; the bloody war for independence in Algeria (where Frantz Fanon was already buried); the terrorism of the Secret Armed Organization in France; and the many bloody wars for independence inflamed by Cold War proxy brinksmanship raging across the African continent.

Richard Wright, with whom Baldwin had sparred in the pages of *Zero* and in the cafés of Paris, whom he had listened to disapprovingly at the first congress, the friend and rival who had been his champion for his first major literary fellowship, and who had tried in vain to form a community of black writers abroad—by many accounts, the pilot light of African American writing in the midcentury—had died suddenly in Paris in 1960. In "Alas, Poor Richard," Baldwin seems nearly overwhelmed by the shocking pace and ephemerality of so much that had transpired: "the world which produced Richard Wright has vanished and will never be seen again. Now, it seems almost in the twinkling of an eye, nearly twenty years have passed since Richard and I sat nervously over bourbon in his Brooklyn living room. These years have seen nearly all of the props of the Western reality knocked out from under it, all of the world's capitals have changed, the Deep South has changed, and Africa has changed."[16] Wright would not live to see the revolutionary rage and counterrevolutionary zeal that rose like a thundering crescendo throughout the 1960s.

Part of what made the moment of 1956 so special, then, was the transient viewpoint it offered—a view from the mountaintop and across the oceans, drawing together a diaspora of ideas and feelings that the writers at the congress intuitively understood would be profoundly consequential, but whose definitive shape still lay in the future. Édouard Glissant quarreled with Aimé Césaire and the Haitian poet René Depestre over definitions they assumed would shape the destiny of black poetry and the peoples of the Francophone diaspora. In his essay, "Note sur une 'Poésie Nationale' chez les peuples noirs," published in *Les lettres nouvelles* in March 1956, Glissant spoke of nothing less than the poetic birth of a new kind of culture ("l'expression poétique d'un nouveau genre de culture"). And he declared that "a black 'national poetry' will therefore, above all, be a poetry of 'intention,' not de facto national, expressing aspirations rather than a fixed situation, it will evolve at the same time as the future of black francophones peoples is decided" (*exprimant des aspirations plus qu'une situation arrêtée: elle évoluera en même temps que se décidera l'avenir des peuples nègres de langue française*).[17] In the pages of *Présence africaine* Aimé Césaire, ever uncompromising, ever transcending categorizations, defended the dignity of a race-conscious blackness without prior authorizations from the warring "isms" of his time: "To be conscious of one's blackness when one lives in a world infected by racism; thinking that this consciousness imposes upon oneself certain obligations—first among them a duty of solidarity with the most insulted people of History—does not deserve the pomp of any word ending in 'ism.' This is only a case of human decency—and an elementary one at that." For both it was emphatically clear this was already a revolutionary moment, pregnant with an explosive future that would play itself out in a turbulent context and with highly unpredictable outcomes. Césaire said then: "We are grand enough to run at our own risk and perils the great adventure of liberty; we obtain our poetry at this price: our right to initiative as much as our right to err. I am for poetry. And for the Revolution too."[18]

For all their disagreements, interpersonal quarrels, drifts into and out of alienation, all these writers shared this sense of extraordinary perspective, a sense of futurity, a shift so important that older ways of writing could no longer capture the affective particulars and imaginative élan that it entailed.

Baldwin thought Wright's speech at the congress was patronizing and out of touch in its propositions. But in his last paragraph on the meeting, he effectively gave Wright the last word, paraphrasing statements that directly echo his own words from "Stranger in the Village": "Richard Wright spoke briefly, saying that this conference marked a turning point in the history of Euro-African relations: it marked, in fact, the beginning of the end of the European domination."[19] This rather melodramatic statement hovers over the text's ending, a bit of literary irony that the editors of *Encounter* may or may not have fully grasped. Baldwin depicts the black writers, poets, and intellectuals pouring out into the streets of Paris as night falls: "Boys and girls, old men and women, bicycles, terraces, all were there, and the people were queuing up before the bakeries for bread."[20] Old Europe, Baldwin slyly implies, dysfunctional and self-absorbed, does not even notice the "new-world-a-coming," the contours of which are already being hotly debated within the Descartes amphitheater on their very doorstep. The black writers walk down these same streets full of the knowledge that they stand on the precipice of a new age, one in which they will play a crucial role as witnesses, as the leaders of new states, as revolutionary martyrs, as philosophers of a civilizational order yet untried—a Copernican shift in the balance of power.

If Baldwin's essays were merely journalistic, as the occasion for this one was, they would no longer have anything to say to us. But of course, Baldwin was never interested in simply reporting and recording the congress. He was trying to comprehend and to capture the spirit of the moment and its significance for the ages. The diffusion of twilight in the closing cadences of Baldwin's essay is there because Baldwin is steeped in an awareness of the long view and the struggles still to come that it portends. It is a metaphorical coloration, like W. E. B. Du Bois's "Dusk of Dawn," a symbolic haze of intoxicating hope that it is too soon to enjoy, whose full promise is destined for a future world that will no longer be denied.

Poetic Revolutions

In his last major poetic effort, *Ask Your Mama: 12 Moods for Jazz* (1961) Langston Hughes produced a stunning high-modernist collage reprising mimetic line breaks and jagged juxtapositions and rhythms designed to evoke midcentury jazz and bebop, a suite of poetic strategies that he had adopted a decade earlier in his breakthrough collection *Montage of a Dream Deferred* (1951). Both collections fall within the Blue Period, and their experimental formalism and preoccupation with interiority bear its aesthetic signatures, making this phase of his career distinct from both earlier and later works.[21] *Ask Your Mama* forsakes the agitprop populism of the 1930s for an aggressively avant-garde freedom on the page, a literary analogue to something like Ornette Coleman's revolution in "free jazz" as it burst upon the scene in his debut record *Something Else!!!!* (1958). Hughes sends black vernacular signals into orbit over the lawnmower suburbs of Eisenhower America, in a black-Sputnik-bop-noise-opera of internationalism and Pan-Africanist freedom dreaming. Its defiant, rhapsodic allusiveness is highly reminiscent of Melvin B. Tolson's experiments in *Libretto for the State of Liberia* (1953) and the suite of poems gathered in *Harlem Gallery* (1965), and it rightly belongs, along with Gwendolyn Brooks's *A Street in Bronzeville* (1945), *Annie Allen* (1949), and *In the Mecca* (1968) to the high watershed moment of midcentury Afro-modernist poetics.

Although there is no reason to doubt that it shares in Hughes's underlying leftist convictions, it sounds and reads nothing like *Scottsboro Limited* (1932) or, for that matter, most of the popular verse taught in schoolrooms around the world that Hughes is principally known for. The particular celebrity of his poem "Harlem" with its famous interrogation—"What happens to a dream deferred?"—that is typically read as a mantic foreshadowing of the riots and rebellions of the 1960s, occludes the extent to which the discovery of the rest of Blue Period Hughes is unhappily deferred for lack of a political motive or movement that can be easily assigned to it. If this study can do something in this regard, it is to show how the poem's politics are no less evident but that the difficulty of its aesthetics has blunted its reception, a challenge that can be overcome when we restore its historical sensibility and proximate literary contexts.

If my periodization schema is valid, we ought to equally see a shift in Hughes's work after 1965. This is, in fact, precisely what occurs. The title for his posthumously published collection, *Panther and the Lash: Poems of Our Times* (1967), "almost certainly came from the founding in Oakland, California that year, 1966, by Huey Newton and Bobby Seale, of the most militant black organization to date—the Black Panther Party," Arnold Rampersad notes in his biography.[22] Although the collection recycled old poems, some of them going back as far as the 1920s, it was deliberately "updated" with new, politically current ones, like Hughes's poem for Patrice Lumumba and his poem "Black Panther," a figure who "in his desperate boldness / Wears no disguise, / Motivated by the truest / Of the oldest / Lies." Commenting on this radical signaling, Rampersad cites an unpublished note that was to accompany the volume that describes its contents as "not purely imaginary or contrived poems for the sake of form or word music." Rampersad concludes of Hughes that it was "impossible for him to be 'above the struggle.'"[23]

Yet despite its activist leanings, Hughes's *Panther* mostly failed to connect with a political discourse being driven by the fiery Stokely Carmichael and an ars poetica defined along the virulent lines laid down by Amiri Baraka's "Black Art" (1965). Even a towering and respected figure like Langston Hughes, whose late style flowered magnificently during the Blue Period, could not contend with the intensity of emotional and expressive reaction by younger black Americans to the assassination of Malcolm X in 1965.

There are undoubtedly other events and factors that would have brought the Blue Period to an end, but nothing so dramatically and decisively changed everything as the immediate collective conviction that Malcolm's death represented a martyrdom. For Baraka, the event was both the dramatic apex and the hinge upon which he constructed his autobiography. It touched every level of his life: his social performance, his most intimate personal relationships, the meaning of his creative work, and perhaps deepest of all, his sense of authenticity, masculinity, and guilt. His trajectory offers more evidence for that year as the dividing line closing the Blue Period.

Baraka (at the time still LeRoi Jones) had been part of a bohemian "downtown" crowd in New York's Greenwich Village and the Lower East Side. This was the evolving social scene Baldwin had integrated in the late 1940s and to which Anatole Broyard had played cultural ambassador of hipness from 1946 through the 1950s. This was a place and time where interracial dating was fashionable, when "literary criticism was enjoying a vogue," and when "Kafka was all the rage."[24] By the time Baraka arrived on the scene in 1954, there was a flourishing vanguardist poetry scene, nourished by the Black Mountain and the New York school poets. Baraka socialized with the young black poets, including Ishmael Reed, Lorenzo Thomas, David Henderson, and Askia Muhammad Touré, who had come together on the Lower East Side to form a workshop, reading series, and eventually also a magazine under the same name *Umbra*.[25]

The *Umbra* social-literary formation perfectly captures the combination of radical politics and experimental aesthetics that define the Blue

Period. On the one hand, these writers were absorbing and refashioning modernism, especially Charles Olson's projective verse and Frank O'Hara's casual vernacular. On the other, they were adamantly politically radical and determined to foreground racial experience in their poetics. As the poet Eugene Redmond said, "Once one read Umbra ... there was no question of the journal's involvement in the struggle—or of the need for a purely literary black magazine to serve as a forum and laboratory for new aesthetic experiments and analyses."[26] Organizers in the South who were active in the civil rights movement, such as Charlayne Hunter-Gault, Andrew Young, and James Meredith, came down to the Umbra workshops when they were in New York City.[27]

The poetry Baraka produced during this period reflects this vanguardism. His first two collections, *Preface to a Twenty Volume Suicide Note* (1961) and *The Dead Lecturer* (1964), the latter dedicated to the Black Mountain poet Ed Dorn, relentlessly foreground alienation, anomie, and venomous jealousy: the poems are raw dissections of an interiority at war with itself. The social scene was equally fissile, riven with factionalism and personal grievance. In his autobiography, Baraka gives a firsthand account of how the appearance of revolutionary forces began to tear the downtown scene apart.[28] Baraka eventually aligned himself with Umbra's more militant wing, gravitating into the orbit of Larry Neal and Maxwell Curtis Stanford Jr., who had founded the Revolutionary Action Movement in Philadelphia and was in favor of pursuing armed insurrection.[29] The tipping point would come on February 21, 1965, recounted in a now-mythologized vignette of the advent of 1960s radicalism. Baraka sets the scene around which his life would turn a corner, and with it, a major chapter in black US literary culture:

> February 21, 1965, a Sunday. Nellie and I and the two girls were at the Eighth Street Bookstore, at a book party. I had a cap, hunting jacket, and round dark glasses, the dress of our little core. I was being personable and knowledgeable. Both Vashti and Shammy and some others were in the bookstore, discreetly separate from my party. Suddenly, Leroy McLucas came in. He was weeping. "Malcolm is dead! Malcolm is dead! Malcolm's been killed!" He wept, repeating it over and over. I was stunned. I felt stupid, ugly, useless. Downtown in my mix-matched family and my maximum leader/teacher shot dead while we bullshitted and pretended. The black core of us huddled there, my wife and family outside that circle. We were feverish and stupefied. McLucas wept uncontrollably. I called a couple fellows in the corner over, but they were dazed and couldn't hear immediately. Joel Oppenheimer said, "That's the trouble with the black revolution. Roi's giving directions and nobody listens!" But who and what

was I to give anything, or he to make such a statement? "It's all bullshit!" went through me. "All!"[30]

In her own recounting of the events in her memoir, Hettie Cohen, Baraka's first wife (whom he calls Nellie in his autobiography) is more succinct, but the emphasis on abrupt rupture is the same: "As soon as Roi heard of the killing he said 'Here,' handing me his half-full champagne glass, and the next minute, with his entourage, he was gone."[31] The dream had exploded.

The time of blue alienation was at an end, a rupture that would cut through to the very core of the writers and poets experiencing it and usher in a new wave of aesthetic possibilities, rhetorical strategies, relationship to community, and battles over representation, authenticity, militancy, feminism, and Afrocentrism. For Baraka, most immediately and most intimately, it meant leaving his wife, and their children, because she was white. His personal circumstances had been swallowed by the march of history, a tectonic shift from which none could hide: "What was the correlative or parallel scene being played all over the world which meant the same thing in all the different sectors and levels of human experience? That open call for that splitting up. As if the tragic world around our 'free zone' had finally swept in and frozen us to the spot."[32] This is, of course, self-dramatizing, but in terms of the impact on black literary and artistic culture, it would prove accurate. There would be no turning back.[33] Baraka was determined to be out in front of it, leading the way: "In a few days I had gotten my stuff out and gone uptown. We had seen a brownstone on West 130th Street and this was to be the home of the Black Arts Repertory Theater/School. My little girl, the older one, Kellie, picked up instinctively a sense of my departure. She said to me, 'You can't go anywhere. You're one of the funny things.' But in a minute or so, I was gone. A bunch of us, really, had gone, up to Harlem. Seeking revolution!"[34]

Artists Turned Partisans

The hope of an independent Congo, Patrice Lumumba, was slain in 1961; Malcolm X, the hope of radical black America, assassinated in 1965. That same year, Watts was a battle zone and Algiers the capital of a successful anticolonial revolution.[35] Amílcar Cabral was leading the African Party for the Independence of Guinea and Cape Verde, just one of several wars being waged that would ultimately bring an end to five hundred years of Portuguese colonial presence in Africa.[36] Régis Debray brought the concepts of revolutionary guerrilla *foco* theory into the vocabulary of restless students in the imperial metropoles.[37] This was the heyday of Cuba's Organization of Solidarity with the Peoples of Africa, Asia, and Latin America, first assembled at Havana for the Tricontinental Conference of 1966, where Che Guevara ominously promised "two, three ... many Vietnams."[38] It was the advent of Third Worldism, when Marxist-Leninism effectively made its last stand; a time when violent insurrections and even more spectacular and effective repressions seemed to constitute what amounted to an undeclared third world war.[39]

This dramatic rise in action and explicit violence shattering a previous lull of contained but simmering tension is dramatized in two lesser-known late novels of the Blue Period, William Gardner Smith's *The Stone Face* (1963) and William Demby's *The Catacombs* (1965). Both are informed by the experience of expatriation, but what is of interest to me is their common sense of an inflection point, one that signaled the end of an era in which expatriation meant something that it can no longer sustain. Both novels are explicitly about leaving America for hideaways in Europe and then returning to America to be part of a revolutionary movement at home.

William Gardner Smith began his writing career in 1943 as a reporter for the *Pittsburgh Courier*.[40] He was drafted into the US Army in 1946 and completed an eight-month tour, stationed as an occupation soldier in Germany, an experience that formed the basis for his first novel, *Last of the Conquerors* (1948). Smith seized on the allegorical force of the figure of being a black soldier abroad and leveraged that irony at the very moment when Truman, under pressure from A. Philip Randolph, was moving to desegregate the US Armed Forces.[41] Hayes Dawkins, Smith's black soldier is stationed in a unit staffed with racist Southern officers. He discovers racial tolerance in the Germans who are the purported vanquished enemy and has a love affair with a young German woman named Ilse. The relative freedom and richness of culture she exposes him to create a profound disillusionment in him about his country.

Like Wright, Smith found American culture barren and crudely materialistic. "America's is a superficial civilization," he wrote in "The Negro Writer: Pitfalls and Compensations," his contribution to a 1950 special issue of *Phylon*: "It is soda-pop land, a civilization of television sets and silk stockings and murder mysteries, and contempt for art and poetry."[42]

Smith returned to France in 1951 and, thanks to his language skills, eventually secured a job with Agence France-Presse, a job that gave him excellent opportunities to measure the simmering tensions that would soon explode in the Algerian War of Independence. These tensions drive the plot of *The Stone Face*, a novel of ideas in which the basic dualistic racial allegory of *Conquerors* is stretched across a Fanonian canvas of struggle in the hour of global decolonization. That Smith would end up writing such a novel is not surprising; even before his departure for Europe, his contribution to *Phylon* outlined a stance uniquely available for black writers precisely because of their alienation from the Cold War's binary ideological camps. White writers, Smith contended, would turn in disgust from America to communism only to "become disillusioned with the Soviet dictatorship" and go running "back to Capitalism," scurrying "back to the very decaying system which lately he had left, a system he now calls 'Democracy,' 'Freedom' and 'Western Culture.'"[43] For Smith, the special "advantage of the Negro writer" who has been "denied many freedoms, robbed of many rights," is that he "rejects those aspects of both American Capitalism and Russian Communism which trample on freedoms and rights. Repelled now by both contending systems, the Negro writer of strength and courage stands firmly as a champion of the basic human issues—dignity, relative security, freedom and the end of savagery between one human being and another. And in this stand he is supported by the mass of human beings the world over."[44] The experience of blackness at the dawn of the Cold War era, Smith believed, would eventually result in literary productions that alone could see beyond the ideological straitjacket of the conflict and reach a wide-lensed conception of ethnic and ethical solidarity. As we have seen, he was not alone among black writers to make this assessment. Wright had announced his nonalignment in the pages of *Franc-Tireur* in 1948; Aimé Césaire came to similar conclusions in his letter to Maurice Thorez of 1953. Under cover of pseudonym in the pages of the Trotskyite review *Fourth International*, C. L. R. James, in a joint review of Smith's *Last of the Conquerors* and Norman Mailer's *The Naked and the Dead* (1948), echoes the same line:

> We live in an intensely political age and theory and historical experience show us that the condition of any artistic development is an uncompromising hostility to the values of Stalinism and to those of American bourgeois society. Whoever capitulates to either of them is lost…. Each side poses an "either-or" and seeks to encompass the whole field. Perhaps it is in the systematic, and truly philosophical opposition to the decay and perversions of these two barbarisms that young writers, fortunate enough to begin where Mailer and Smith begin, can find their way to those deeper levels which will nourish and not desiccate their talents.[45]

The fact that Mailer, despite posing as the radical gadfly, would go on to devote thousands of pages to *Harlot's Ghost* (1991), a novel consummately devoted to reconstructing the heroic early years of the Central Intelligence Agency in its battle against Soviet communism, neatly exemplifies Smith's point about white writers returning to the fold. Despite Mailer's lustily pursued fame and Smith's considerable obscurity, the quality of that same novel also suggests it was Smith who went deeper and Mailer whose talents grew increasingly desiccated. Smith did feel the pull of the committed trajectory to the Left strongly, and in *The Stone Face*, he dramatized the black artist-intellectual's eventual acceptance of the need to prioritize a revolutionary consciousness.

Since the 1990s, scholars have been engaged in recovering and rehabilitating this neglected novel.[46] Tyler Stovall and Kristin Ross have pointed out its importance as a firsthand witnessing—and one of the very few contemporary accounts in English or French—of the terrible police-led massacre of Algerians that occurred in Paris on October 17, 1961.[47] This brutal episode was internally censored and effectively blocked out of France's official and public memory until the mid-1990s, when a wave of revisionary historiography of the Algerian War thrust the so-called *événements* of October 1961, and the role of the chief of police Maurice Papon in instigating them, back into view to great controversy.[48]

In *Against Race*, Paul Gilroy commends Smith's novel for its transnational reframings of oppression even as he faults Smith for falling back in the novel's narrative conclusion on an unfortunate "capitulation" to "a narrow version of cultural kinship" that retreats from the novel's cosmopolitan ideals because of the protagonist Simeon Brown's choice to return to the United States.[49] Rather than criticizing the political correctness of Smith's plot in *The Stone Face*, my periodization allows us to see the historical determination of that plot. The novel, yes, is partly about Gilroy's politics of racial cosmopolitanism, but it is also about the end of a period of productive alienation for black writers and intellectuals. For them, disalienation comes with the recognition that revolutionary action requires a new formal relationship to one's artistic practice.

Simeon Brown is a classic instantiation of the Blue Period type, the alienated black intellectual. Simeon is a black painter in his midthirties who wears an eye-patch covering the result of an act of brutality at the hands of racist white police officers in Philadelphia. He has left the United States for Paris, where he is living in a small studio by the Café Tournon (the favored hangout of the black expatriate crowd), profiting from the relative peace and lack of racial hostility, and pursuing what is described as an abstract, allegorical painting of human hate: "the face of un-man, the face of discord, the face of destruction."[50]

As in his earlier novels, Smith is less concerned with depicting character than with using subjective positionality to implicate his characters in systems of power and complicate their representation within those systems. By befriending Ahmed, an Algerian working with the National Liberation Front, Simeon comes to see the truth of the Algerians' experience at the hands of the French, that they are, as he tells his black compatriot Babe, who doesn't want to get involved, "the niggers of France." Through his Jewish girlfriend, Maria, who has survived the death camps, he comes to appreciate the threat of the fascists and their manner of thinking about undesirables. When Patrice Lumumba is assassinated in the Congo by Mobutu Sese Seko and Moïse Tshombe's henchmen, he realizes that blackness of skin cannot guarantee that one is on the right side of history.[51] Similar complications arise when he brings Ahmed and his radical National Liberation Front friends to a café with Maria, where her Jewishness brings out their anti-Semitic bigotry. His knowledge of the conditions facing the Algerians eventually forces Simeon to choose sides. He can no longer live a bohemian existence untroubled by the fate of those around him. Smith's novel methodically aligns its theory of solidarity along the line of bodies placed in the "state of exception," a coalition of those who in Giorgio Agamben's terms exist only as "bare life."[52] In this novel, American police beat and torture blacks; Nazi storm troopers beat and torture Jews; French riot officers of the Compagnie Républicaine de Sécurité beat and torture Algerians. The marking of certain bodies for unpunishable violence, meted out in unspeakable ways, is underlined with a scene devoted specifically to disclosing the French military's use of torture in its "war on terror." Smith describes in graphic detail the torture of National Liberation Front women, describing the methods and mechanics of waterboarding, beatings, and the electrocution and mutilation of their genitals.[53] The body is the site upon which politics is finally inscribed in violence and, following Levinas, where the ethics of the face is extinguished.[54] This argument culminates dramatically with Smith's reportage style (he was a practicing journalist) account of the "events" of October 1961.[55] Simeon is clubbed and arrested in the confusion but released once the French identify him as an American. Witnessing the massacre, and getting caught up in it, breaks any residual thought of alienation, and Simeon completes his Fanonian transition to a disalienated and committed subjectivity. There is no longer room for ambiguity or retreat. Those who can recognize the face of the Other and see in it their own are arrayed on one side; opposed are those who wield the baton against the oppressed.[56] The closing pages of the novel are a roll call of what the historian John Munro describes as the postwar "anticolonial front," a suite of interlinked freedom struggles, each making up "components of a wider offensive against the citadels and far corners of the imperial structure of racial capitalism."[57] If Frantz Fanon had lived to write a novel, it might have resembled what William Gardner Smith created in *The Stone Face*.[58]

In an important sense, though, *The Stone Face* was a novel that could be written only *then*. Its vision is not naive enough to think that the revolution will solve everything; but it is also just naive enough to believe that a sweeping revolution was imminent and that it would be largely successful. What matters to the plot is that for Simeon the die is cast.[59] The last lines of the novel are explicitly devoted to showing that the aesthetic form Simeon has worked in up to this point—the abstract painting in his Paris studio—can no longer hold.[60] The old forms no longer make sense; new realities have penetrated, and the artist can no longer hide from the revolution outside.

Like Simeon, William Gardner Smith would do his part by placing his professional talents in service of the revolution. He traveled to Kwame Nkrumah's Ghana for Agence France-Presse but was forced to leave when Nkrumah was deposed in 1966. Smith returned to the United States in 1967 and 1968 to provide what we would call today "embedded reporting" on Black Nationalist movements, assessing "the transformations which underlay the black revolt."[61] The resulting chronicle, *Return to Black America* (1970), is an intimate account of the high tide of organized black militancy that deliberately blurs the lines between reportage, advocacy, literary autobiography, and journalistic profile. For Smith, the division, to the extent that it had once existed between partisanship and literary creation, was no longer desirable or realistic. Like his hero Simeon, he had put down the paintbrush of the Blue Period. The pen in his hand was a sword.

History from Below

Our appreciation of William Gardner Smith's revolutionary commitment can no longer be dissociated from the bitter truth of the largely unfulfilled promises and terrible human costs that were to come. Another way of saying this, by way of Hayden White and David Scott, is that *The Stone Face* is emplotted as a "romantic narrative" of anticolonial discourse. Coincidentally, it was published in 1963, the same year as the revised edition of C. L. R. James's *The Black Jacobins* that Scott reads so brilliantly in *Conscripts of Modernity*. We might observe that it, too, falls under the description Scott applies more generally to our tragic relationship to that romantic narratology: "The horizon that made that erstwhile story so compelling as a dynamo for intellectual and political work has collapsed. It is now a superseded future, one of our futures past."[62]

If part of what characterized the Blue Period is that it was a time when black writers grappled with the problem of writing for a future world, then we ought to take seriously the need to reckon with Scott's postcolonial futures past, the obligation to remember them as a condition of our own freedom. One of the last masterpieces of the Blue Period, a metafictional, high-modernist novel by William Demby, anticipates this question, posing it from the perspective of an alienated black intellectual ensconced in the heart of Old Europe. The novel takes place in Rome, haunted by the architecture that Freud famously analogized with the deep interior of the unconscious mind of Western civilization itself. Demby called it *The Catacombs.*[63]

During the war, Demby served in the army in Italy and North Africa, and after heading home to the United States to study at Fisk on the GI Bill, he returned in 1947 to Rome, where he quickly became a fixture in both American expatriate and Italian postwar artistic circles.[64] Notably, he was closely associated with the vanguard of the Italian film world, working as an assistant to Roberto Rossellini on his film *Europe '51.*[65] *The Catacombs* emerges directly from that experience. Asked about its conception, Demby said: "I decided to write a novel where I could do what I was doing in the movies: have a theme, a *soggetto*, follow the day's news, accept the daily torture of writing not just to produce, but for the metaphysics of what I was doing."[66]

The translation of this metaphysics into novelistic form is a poetics of fragmentation and metanarrative. *The Catacombs* collates the notes and observations of one "Bill Demby," a scriptwriter working in Rome, as he struggles with his project to write a novel about a young black actress named Doris. Apparently "one of Elizabeth Taylor's handmaidens in Twentieth Century-Fox's Cleopatra colossal now being filmed," Doris is having an affair with a mutual Italian friend, Raffaele, referred to throughout the text as "the Count."[67] As the novel progresses, it becomes clear that Bill is falling in love with Doris himself. Doris is persistently more interested in the prospect of improving her future career opportunities than in the men who are courting her; she becomes pregnant but refuses to reveal who the father might be and disappears before either Bill or the Count can find out.

This love-triangle plot serves mostly as an allegorical motor. Doris is literally an extra in the otherwise-all-white Twentieth Century (the studio name punning on the historian's bracket) production of historical memory; the Count, who "dresses like a junior executive in a Manhattan advertising agency" is "a traditional figure in Italian folklore; a young man who has fine manners, always sitting at some café."[68] Demby describes their relationship as figuratively embodying what Sharon Holland calls "the erotic life of racism."[69] For the Count, Doris is the stereotype of "the black goddess, or the black woman who is easily available, the woman who comes from colonialism," a role she chafes at and finally determines she is unwilling to play.[70]

The novel's true interest lies in a desperate (and ultimately failed) attempt to awaken from the nightmare of history—to read through the palimpsest of pasts making insurgent claims on the present. The Eternal City of Rome, and its underworld, Sara Marzioli argues, "enacts a spatialization of the past yielding to the irruption of history in the present" and functions "as a topographical and architectural metaphor for the entangled narrative, whose open end sees Doris disappear in its maze."[71] The city's ruins are an allegorical figure for the history of Western imperialism, just as Cinecittà (where Cleopatra is being filmed) is the factory of its aspirational fantasies, and just as the hive of gossip swirling through the cafés of Rome reflects the present day's involvement in the myriad Cold War conflicts raging across the globe, foremost among them the Algerian War.[72] The Rome that the novel inhabits is therefore both deeply historical and, following Italian modernist painter Giorgio de Chirico's conception of his paintings, a "metaphysical" symbol of the contradictions of European modernity in the totalitarian century.[73]

As Marzioli points out, through its overt conflation of historiographical fiction with the archaeological metaphor of knowledge and its relationship to power, *The Catacombs* actually anticipates the "linguistic turn" of subsequent decades, especially Hayden White's emplotted historiography, Jean-François Lyotard's metanarratives, and Foucault's archaeology of knowledge.[74] Demby's novel is, indeed, cross-cut with intertextual news reports that Bill reads each day in the newspapers and that are beamed around the world by Telstar, the new satellite—prophetic of the advent of the twenty-four-hour news cycle. The simultaneity of television and mediatized events "tear" the continuity of history to pieces, reminiscent of the technique of *décollage* practiced by Mimmo Rotella, who we learn is Bill's favorite Italian artist.[75] Demby places the alienated black intellectual in the cockpit of a Cold War capital, where he observes and critiques a modern world whose technologies of self-representation are converting all aspects of culture, politics, and art into a perpetually alienated simulacrum, the advent of what Guy Debord would describe in 1967 as "the society of the spectacle."[76]

Through these cutting techniques, *The Catacombs* becomes, among other things, a counterhistory of the Cold War, described from a black outsider's perspective. James Hall makes this point by reading *The Catacombs* alongside Paule Marshall's *The Chosen Place, the Timeless People* (1969) as novels proposing what he calls an "antimodern voice," not in the sense of antimodernist but, on the contrary, interested in modernist literary form as a means to articulate postures that remain ecstatic, apart from, and outside the modernity being forged by the ideological warfare of the Cold War. These fictions rethink and rewrite their historical present by attending to the lag that "racial time" creates with respect to its interests and imperatives.[77] As Hall nicely puts it, both novels are "invested with a significant and thoughtful 'indirection,'" one that is "suggestive of grounds for action, even responsibility, as existing in the space somewhere *between* their literary dystopias and the hegemonic ideology of progress."[78] *The Catacombs* powerfully captures the fear and paranoia of its historical moment, even as it seeks out this betweenness, its edges, its margins, its uncaptured axes of fugitivity.

As Bill sits in Rome reading from Walt Whitman's Civil War diaries, he makes subterranean connections across history that the Count, and even his white American friend Alex, cannot: "I put down the book. The room becomes so quiet, so still, that I seem to float, backward and forward in time. The American Civil War, the Algerian War. Plastic bombs!… The renegade officers of the European Secret Army who call their bargain-basement terrorism, their cowardly bargain-basement heroics, 'revolutionary warfare.'"[79] When the news from America worsens, and the sense that a civil war might break out becomes more urgent, Bill decides he must return, to get involved, to confront "the underground tremor of violence that was threatening the neoclassical structure of Jeffersonian America."[80]

The novel's culminating set piece involves his return to the United States, which is bookended by two major historical events: the March on Washington for Jobs and Freedom and the assassination of John F. Kennedy. In both cases, the gravitas of the occasion is undercut by a cynicism and skepticism with respect to the co-optation of events:

> Now I was shoulder to shoulder with the marchers, thousands and thousands of smiling brown and white faces, moving slowly like a sluggish river of humanity toward the white marble isolation of the Lincoln Monument. Abraham Lincoln was dead. But his statue there at the monument was at least twenty times the height of the flesh-and-blood freedmen marching to be free. We are clean, well-groomed, self-consciously well-behaved. Slouching policemen watch us as we sing: "We shall overcome someday…"… Little by little, though, the initial feeling of triumph and exhilaration begins to fade. I become an intellectual again, my critical faculties become alert, and I can no longer join in the holding of hands and the singing. Suddenly an insidious cynical voice begins whispering in my ear that what I am witnessing, participating in, is only a summer pageant of brotherhood, some strange new hybrid form of political manifestation, a kind of animated advertising slogan, a "revolution" only in name.[81]

Demby sounds a "blue note" in this transitional text, feeling out the new revolutionary politics on offer. The iconic March on Washington, so central to our mythologies of racial advancement, is, for him, evacuated of its assumed authenticity.

Bill relies on an inside voice that tells him not to trust the spectacle he is supposed to identify with. This negative affect prompts him not only to dissent but also to interrogate his own position, his own complicity as a black intellectual: "Obviously history was being made that hot day in August in Washington, D.C. But who was making it?... if history now is to become televised theatre, where are we the intellectuals to stand? In the audience? On the stage? Or in the prompter's cramped and dusty pit?"[82] Underneath the grand narrative of a political movement toward hope, Demby's narrator senses something very much like a bad joke: "And suddenly it doesn't seem real ... I haven't the slightest idea what we're doing here, where we are going. *To a tomb?*"[83]

David Scott has proposed that tragedy is the genre that best describes the postcolonial freedom struggle. Demby takes a discomforting alternative view: that the genre of this struggle, carried out historically just as a mediated "society of the spectacle" began to colonize the totality of public discourse, is the tragicomic. "Theatrically, historically, the assassination of John Fitzgerald Kennedy was a terrible mistake," Bill observes. America is sick in ways that repeatedly lead to farce, to bad television. The mid-century Cold War actors who thought they were guiding statecraft prudentially to secure the hegemony of their values in fact lost the thread of the narrative—they dropped the script. The assassination of Kennedy (and, the novel proleptically intimates, those of Martin Luther King Jr. and Malcolm X) should not have happened. And yet they did. Their loss, so often estimated to be political—the loss of a hopeful resolution to racial Reconstruction in America—dealt a blow to the very coherence of the wider project of Enlightenment, with Old Europe as bound up in its fortunes as those of the New World. Under such conditions, the future may indeed be a grotesque comedy, a farce in which pantomimes and simulacra desperately try to patch the gaping holes—constantly restaging what Daniel Boorstin in 1962 was already calling *pseudo-events* in a futile effort to retrieve the memory of real ones.[84]

It is a troubling vision—certainly, not one that could have been popular in 1965 or in the decade that followed, when the romantic narrative that Scott seeks to revise held a powerful hold, especially on black revolutionary imaginaries. Yet there would subsequently emerge an entire body of theory that articulated the concerns of just such an impasse. Although parts of those very efforts now seem historically bounded, it is by no means evident that they have been superseded by a clearer vision of what we have become or what lies ahead. Doris at the end of *The Catacombs* melts into the darkness of the underworld maze, where the enigma of what she wants and where her future lies is neither revealed nor foreclosed—it is simply invisible.

The Roman catacombs are vast and deep. The narrative of history and the black riposte to it ring out again and again through its chambers. Seemingly distant yet interlinked voices bump into each other in the dark. In the troubling years I have been at work on this book, the notion that the Western Enlightenment may culminate in a tragicomic farce swallowed up by the frenzied society of the spectacle it has spun out is not nearly as satirical as it once seemed. One effect of stepping back and attending closely to the Blue Period is that it gives us the opportunity to retrieve and repurpose those writings that appeared in the years right before the storms hit—the catastrophes that continue to rage into the present.

The uneasy, introspective, and dissonant qualities of that span of years in the past century resound for us like weird echoes coming through on the lower frequencies. They send word from a time just before one world-historical order fell apart and another struggled—continues to struggle—to be born. Their sense of time is not ours. Yet sooner or later, most of us will confront a sense of dissonance with the signposted direction of history or find ourselves alienated from every ideology on offer. Who knows then but that one of these "blue" books will speak to you?

Acknowledgments

This book is the product of a long journey that started at Princeton University, where I first began to ask the questions that became the focus of my graduate studies. I wish to thank first and foremost the members of my dissertation committee, Daphne A. Brooks, Kinohi Nishikawa, and Joshua B. Guild, to whom I owe an enormous debt for their patience, rigor, and above all teaching—by example, by instruction, and through their intellectual generosity and collegiality. I wish to thank the members of the Department of African American Studies at Princeton, especially Imani Perry, Eddie Glaude Jr., Ruha Benjamin, Tera Hunter, Wallace Best, and Valerie E. Smith, as well as F. Nick Nesbitt in the Department of Comparative Literature, who kindly read drafts of my chapter on Édouard Glissant. I am no less indebted to my present home, the Departments of English and of African and African American Studies at Harvard University, which have provided the resources—both intellectual and material—for this book's completion. I would like to thank Glenda Carpio, Louis Menand, and Ross Posnock of Columbia University for their extensive comments and queries during our manuscript workshop, as well as the Department of English for funding it—a crucial event that allowed me to substantially revise the book and that they generously committed to despite the limitations imposed by a global pandemic. At Harvard, my teaching, research, and study have benefited from the scholars and writers I have been so fortunate to be in community with. I wish to thank especially Henry Louis Gates Jr., Tommie Shelby, Robert Reid-Pharr, Sarah Lewis, Tracy K. Smith, Brandon Terry, Robin Bernstein, Jamaica Kincaid, Emily Greenwood, Homi Bhabha, Beth Blum, Jean-Christophe Cloutier, Teju Cole, Tara K. Menon, and Neel Mukherjee, among many others. This book owes a very special debt to the close friendship and intellectual companionship of Joshua Bennett, Ernest Julius Mitchell, Jarvis R. Givens, Roshad Meeks, Timothy

Pantoja, and Justin D. Mitchell, who have shaped my thinking and writing throughout these years. I would like to thank Brent H. Edwards and Fred Moten, who provided advice and encouragement at crucial junctures, and Brooks E. Hefner and Paul Devlin, for sharing their expert knowledge of the archives of black periodicals, oral histories, and interviews. I might never have become a literary scholar if it weren't for the mentorship and guidance of certain faculty members at Amherst College, most especially Marisa Parham, John Drabinski, Andrea B. Rushing, Jeffrey B. Ferguson, and William H. Pritchard. I also wish to acknowledge those editors (and comrades), Jon Baskin, John Palatella, David Marcus, Jennifer Szalai, Sophia Nguyen, and Natasha Lewis, who gave me the opportunity to publish and influenced my approach to writing for a general audience during the years when I was also working on this manuscript. Some of the research for this book simply would not have been possible without the prior heroic labors and commitments of Chip Fleischer, Liselotte Haas, and Oliver St. Clair Franklin, who have kept Vincent O. Carter's name from disappearing and who generously gave of their time and, even more importantly, provided direct access to materials and manuscripts that could not otherwise be obtained. I also wish to acknowledge the archivists of the Schomburg Center for Research in Black Culture, Princeton University's Firestone Library Special Collections, the staff of Columbia University's Butler Library Periodicals and Microforms Reading Room, and Christina Davis and Mary Walker Graham of the Woodberry Poetry Room at Lamont Library at Harvard. Finally, this book would not exist were it not for the deep love of my entire family and many dear friends who have been at my side, near or far, along the way. Most of all, I give thanks to Namwali Serpell, for her intellectual and editorial collaboration, patience, love, and cherished companionship, and for saying yes.

Notes

Introduction

1. Aimé Césaire, "Letter to Maurice Thorez," translated by Chike Jeffers, *Social Text 103* 28, no. 2 (Summer 2010): 149–50.

2. Aimé Césaire, *Discourse on Colonialism* (New York: Monthly Review Press, 2000). On the militant and "revolutionary cadences" of this text and its "call for us to plumb the depths of the imagination for a different way forward," see Robin D. G. Kelley's introduction, "A Poetics of Anticolonialism," in the same edition.

3. The letter is obviously more political than literary, yet it's telling that when Césaire critiques the PCF's Eurocentric chauvinism, he calls them "a literary tribe that, concerning everything and nothing, dogmatizes in the name of the party." Césaire is chafing not only at their political and intellectual dogmas; the implication is that these views likewise exclude the literature produced by nonwhite and non-European writers. See Césaire, "Letter to Maurice Thorez," 149.

4. As Brent Edwards has shown, many of the detours in Césaire's reception and circulation pass through the reviews and periodicals (and the critical and scholarly reception, and often overlooking, of said periodicals) produced by young black student collectives, notably those organized by the Nardal sisters in Paris. See Brent H. Edwards, *The Practice of Diaspora: Literature, Translation, and the Rise of Black Internationalism* (Cambridge, MA: Harvard University Press, 2013), 120–29; on *La dépéche africaine* and *La revue du monde noir*, 147–52; on *L'étudiant noir*, 178–86.

5. "Mon corps est né en Amérique, mon cœur est né en Russie, et, aujourd'hui, je me tiens tout honteux entre mes deux patries." Richard Wright, "L'humanité est plus grande que l'Amérique ou la Russie," *Franc-Tireur* December 16, 1948, 1 and 4. The article appears as the inaugural feature of the paper's column "War and Peace" (La Guerre et La Paix). It is based on the speech Wright delivered as his contribution to the founding of the Rassemblement Démocratique Révolutionnaire, a political party founded by Jean-Paul Sartre and David Rousset that hoped to find an alternative "third way" between the French Communist Party's Left and the Gaullist Right. Sartre sought to enlist Wright in organizing the party and growing its appeal, especially among the black intellectual exiles who were beginning to flock to Paris. Founded in 1948, not long before the appearance of this article, the party floundered and was dissolved within a year. Sartre cast his lot with the French Communist Party; Wright, who had already left

in 1944 but openly broke with the Communist Party with his contribution to Richard Crossman's anticommunist anthology *The God That Failed* in 1949, significantly never joined another political party; he traveled to Kwame Nkrumah's Ghana, Bandung, Spain, and London before dying of a sudden illness in Paris in 1960.

6. On the shift by American writers and intellectuals on the Left from the 1930s to the Cold War anti-Stalinist Left and the alignment with the "liberal narrative" of the Cold War, see Thomas Hill Schaub, *American Fiction in the Cold War* (Madison: University of Wisconsin Press, 1991), 3–24.

7. Alan M. Wald, "Cold War Modernity," *Modernism/Modernity* 21, no. 4 (2014): 1017–23.

8. Odd Arne Westad, *The Global Cold War: Third World Interventions and the Making of Our Times* (New York: Cambridge University Press, 2005), 4.

9. See Louis Menand, *The Free World: Art and Thought in the Cold War* (New York: Farrar, Straus & Giroux, 2021), xii. Werner Sollors makes the same point with Richard Wright's *The Outsider* specifically as exemplar: "Avant-garde artists and educators, intellectuals mattered in this world. The very fact that they had been banned (or were still banned) meant that they were important; American intellectuals and artists played a state-supported role which they have not regained in later years." Werner Sollors, *Ethnic Modernism* (Cambridge, MA: Harvard University Press, 2008), 217. The "seriousness" of this attitude can also be measured in the emergence of a discourse surrounding the articulation of a "crisis of Man," a combination of the Cold War's specter of ideological confrontation with the consequences of fascist totalitarianism in the Holocaust and its undermining of confidence in the foundations of Enlightenment values. See Mark Greif, *The Age of the Crisis of Man: Thought and Fiction in America, 1937–1973* (Princeton, NJ: Princeton University Press, 2015).

10. Komozi Woodard cites the Black Convention Movement as signaling the high tide of black nationalism in the United States. He argues that "the politics of black cultural nationalism played a critical role in nationality formation between 1966 and 1976." See Woodard, *A Nation within a Nation: Amiri Baraka (LeRoi Jones) and Black Power Politics* (Chapel Hill: University of North Carolina Press), 259.

11. As Brenda Gayle Plummer notes, "competition between the West and the Soviet bloc underwent transition after Stalin's death, becoming less dangerous to Europeans and North Americans but more lethal to emerging nations." Plummer, *In Search of Power: African Americans in the Era of Decolonization, 1956–1974* (New York: Cambridge University Press, 2013), 2.

12. Raymond Williams, *Politics and Letters: Interviews with New Left Review* (London: New Left Books, 1979), 252.

13. Frantz Fanon, *Black Skin White Masks*, translated by Richard Philcox (New York: Grove Press, 2008), 89. Fanon's emphasis on "lived experience" as opposed to "the fact of blackness," as the title of chapter 5 of *Peau noir, masques blancs* (1952) is rendered in the Charles Lam Markmann translation from 1967, is, of course, of central importance to this study. Doyle Calhoun has noted that Fanon's *noir* and *noirceur* for "blackness" constitutes Fanon's "effort to represent—indeed to *lexicalize*—Blackness in French," pointing out that Fanon "frequently combines noirceur with the possessive adjective, positing Blackness as something the speaking-subject can claim for him- or herself" a shift that provides "a means to rethink, rewrite and resignify Blackness" as an embodied perspective rather than a taxonomical or descriptive adjective. See Doyle Calhoun,

"Fanon's Lexical Intervention: Writing Blackness in Black Skin, White Masks." *Paragraph (Modern Critical Theory Group)* 43 (2): 161.

14. Williams, *Politics and Letters*, 252. The literary and cultural historian Alan Nadel describes "containment culture" as "a privileged American narrative" that "although technically referring to US foreign policy from 1948 until at least the mid-1960s … also describes American life in numerous venues and under sundry rubrics during that period: to the extent that corporate production and biological reproduction, military deployment and industrial technology, televised hearings and filmed teleplays, the cult of domesticity and the fetishizing of domestic security, the arms race and atoms for peace all contributed to the containment of communism, the disparate acts performed in the name of these practices joined the legible agenda of American history as aspects of containment culture." Alan Nadel, *Containment Culture: American Narratives, Postmodernism, and the Atomic Age* (Durham, NC: Duke University Press, 1995), 2–3.

15. Louis Althusser, *Lenin and Philosophy and Other Essays*, trans. Ben Brewster (New York: Monthly Review Press, 1971), 222.

16. Althusser, 222–23 (original emphasis). For the purposes of this study, it does not seem to me necessary to explicate and defend an entire theory of racialized alienation; there is, of course, an extensive literature on the subject. I note that Marx's interest in alienation (and his use of the term) in the *Grundrisse* is clearly oriented around what he calls "the worker's propertylessness" and the fact that "production based on exchange value … is at its base the exchange of *objectified labour* as exchange value for living labour as use value, or, to express this in another way … as alien property: *alienation [Entäusserung]* of labour." The result is that "the reproduction of the worker is by no means posited through *mere labour*, for his property relation is not the result but the presupposition of his labour." Karl Marx, *Grundrisse*, trans. Martin Nicolaus (New York: Penguin, 1993), 514–15, original emphasis. If race is also in some sense a "property," in this case one of social value, and blackness in relation to that system of values is effectively analogous to the situation of propertylessness, then it is easy to see how one can begin to conceive of a reproduction of race that is not the end point of a social process but its ideologically presupposed point of departure. This would have the effect of placing a black writer in a *distinctly alienated* relation to the literary field; it is not hard to see how a self-awareness of this on the part of said writer would then easily become an inescapable admixture—an alienated affect—carried into, *coloring*, if you will, the "internal distance" Althusser evokes. Ultimately, it is not necessary to accept Althusser's or even Marx's accounts (or my own use or misuse of their accounts) to follow the argument of this book. They are compelling and convincing to me, but a looser more impressionistic sense of alienation is sufficient for making sense of the literary history and the readings of individual works that I undertake.

17. I agree with Eric Porter's suggestion in his reassessment of the late midcentury Du Bois, that one of the key insights Du Bois makes, and could make only at that conjuncture, is the possibility of a future marked by an endless global war (whose imperialist logics will always be, at least partially, embedded or expressed as racialist antagonisms), a prognosis that Porter rightly connects to the US-led Global War on Terror, to which there appears to be no end in sight. See Eric Porter, *The Problem of the Future World: W. E. B. Du Bois and the Race Concept at Midcentury* (Durham, NC: Duke University Press, 2010).

18. Some historians have recognized the prescience and lucidity of black writers

with respect to the political and ideological crosscurrents of this era. Nikhil Singh cites Richard Wright and Ralph Ellison as exemplary for instance. See Nikhil Pal Singh, *Black Is a Country: Race and the Unfinished Struggle for Democracy* (Cambridge, MA: Harvard University Press, 2004), 220–21. I am also indebted in my thinking here to Michael Hanchard, who has argued that temporality itself, including struggles over its control and definitions, are central to black diasporic cultures in modernity. See Michael Hanchard, "Afro-Modernity: Temporality, Politics, and the African Diaspora" *Public Culture* 11 (1999): 245–68.

19. Ted Underwood argues that periodization subtends an institutional economy of literary prestige and suggests that the blind spots produced by this bid for distinction might be overcome by the quantitative tools being developed under the rubric of "the digital humanities," which allow to emerge a "gradualist" slope of development (that periodization, he thinks, tends to miss). Although there are merits to these arguments, periodization does continue to matter for the study of African American and Afro-diasporic literatures. The digital tools Underwood imagines applying can complement but never successfully replace a historicist grounding for these works (or any other literature for that matter), which means that understanding the period they emerge in and out of will continue to be a necessary function of good criticism. See Ted Underwood, *Why Literary Periods Mattered: Historical Contrast and the Prestige of English Studies* (Stanford, CA: Stanford University Press, 2013).

20. Fredric Jameson, *The Political Unconscious: Narrative as a Socially Symbolic Act* (Ithaca, NY: Cornell University Press, 1981), 9.

21. Jameson, 52–53. To be clear, I am not arguing that black writers or writing are immune to the ideological forces shaping texts (and the climate for our reception of those texts), as Jameson contends they always are. Rather, I am arguing that the clash between the specific ideological pressures of the postwar period coming from above, and the nascent aesthetic, affective, and political interests of black writers bubbling up from below, produced a clash that necessarily (in a preponderant number of cases) pushed these writers to explore expressive strategies that placed them outside the dominant frameworks, or in Jameson's terms, the "containment strategies," of their historical moment.

22. For a summary of the impact of Warren's *What Was African American Literature?* on the field, see Melissa Asher Daniels and Gregory Laski, "Introduction," *African American Review* 44, no. 4 (2011): 567–70. I have disagreements with Warren's thesis, but this book is naturally, and happily, indebted to his brilliant provocations. See Kenneth W. Warren, *What Was African American Literature?* (Cambridge, MA: Harvard University Press, 2011).

23. Warren, 9.

24. See Stuart Hall, *Cultural Studies, 1983: A Theoretical History*, ed. Jennifer Daryl Slack and Lawrence Grossberg (Durham, NC: Duke University Press, 2016), xi–xii.

25. Stacy I. Morgan, *Rethinking Social Realism: African American Art and Literature, 1930–1953* (Athens: University of Georgia Press, 2004), 303.

26. Vaughn Rasberry, *Race and the Totalitarian Century: Geopolitics in the Black Literary Imagination* (Cambridge, MA: Harvard University Press, 2016), 17.

27. Cedric R. Tolliver, *Of Vagabonds and Fellow Travelers: African Diaspora Literary Culture and the Cultural Cold War* (Ann Arbor: University of Michigan Press: 2019), 3. Tolliver makes a compelling case for the assassination of Patrice Lumumba on Janu-

ary 17, 1961, as a catalytic turning point, rather than the assassination of Malcolm X on February 21, 1965, which is the event my account turns on. For my purposes, I think it is important that the lexical shift in the United States to a popular rhetoric of "Black Power" really consolidates after the latter. Tragically, however, both murders must be added to a much longer list of names (some famous and some far less so) that indelibly shaped and radicalized black politics and literary culture in the 1960s. See Tolliver, 158–84.

28. In addition to Stacy Morgan's *Rethinking Social Realism: African American Art and Literature, 1930–1953* (Athens: University of Georgia Press, 2004) and Michael Denning's *The Cultural Front: The Laboring of American Culture in the Twentieth Century* (New York: Verso, 1996), among the major studies I have in mind are Lawrence Jackson's *The Indignant Generation: A Narrative History of African American Writers and Critics, 1934–1960* (Princeton, NJ: Princeton University Press, 2011), Mary Dudziak's *Cold War Civil Rights: Race and the Image of American Democracy* (Princeton, NJ: Princeton University Press, 2011), and Jacqueline Goldsby's "The Art of Being Difficult: African American Poetry and Painting in the 1940s and 1950s," a lecture delivered at Brigham Young University Humanities Lecture on March 7, 2014, offers glimpses of her forthcoming monograph, *Birth of the Cool: African American Literary Culture of the 1940s and 1950s*. It is notable that *The Norton Anthology of African American Literature*, most recently reedited in 2014, marks this period by positing the coexistence and, it is hinted, evolutionary struggle between the literary modes or rubrics, "realism, naturalism, modernism," with modernism functioning effectively as a triumphant successor stage. Yet this framework is offered rather apologetically, with the editors openly acknowledging the "semantic instability" of their own arrangement and averring that they are deploying these placeholders "as conveniences, points of analytical departure, demanding fuller interrogation." See Henry Louis Gates Jr. and Valerie Smith, eds., *The Norton Anthology of African American Literature*, 3rd ed. (New York: W. W. Norton & Co., 2014), 1355–56.

29. Henry Louis Gates Jr., *Loose Canons: Notes on the Culture Wars* (New York: Oxford University Press, 1992), 122.

30. Claude McKay, *Amiable with Big Teeth*, ed. Jean-Christophe Cloutier and Brent Hayes Edwards (New York: Penguin, 2017). See also Glenda R. Carpio and Werner Sollors, "Five Harlem Short Stories by Zora Neale Hurston," *Amerikastudien/American Studies* 55, no. 4 (2010): 557–60.

31. Here I have in mind especially Brent Edwards, *Epistrophies: Jazz and the Literary Imagination* (Cambridge, MA: Harvard University Press, 2017); Kinohi Nishikawa, "The Archive on Its Own: Black Politics, Independent Publishing, and *The Negotiations*," *MELUS* 30, no. 3 (2015): 176–201; Britt Rusert, "From Black Lit to Black Print: The Return to the Archive in African American Literary Studies," *American Quarterly* 68, no. 4 (2016): 993–1005.

32. The publication history in this case is revealing. Williams finished the book in 1956 and adamantly wanted to call his novel "One for New York," a fitting Blue Period title. When it was finally published by Ace Books in 1960, his publisher insisted on the decidedly more "protest" title, *The Angry Ones*. When the book was reissued in 1996, Williams wrote in the preface: "The title was not and is not mine, which I like to think, called up deeper and more lasting responses. It did this because there was no adjective in it that purported to explain or to make more saleable this book whose original title

was *One for New York.*" John A. Williams, *The Angry Ones* (New York: Old School Books, 1996). Note the importance of affect to Williams, and its opacity to the publishers, who insist that their conscription of him into a canon of "protest" fiction is a sine qua non for his marketability and legibility as a black writer in 1960 but also in 1996.

33. Irving Howe's accusation of racial inauthenticity and Ellison's brilliant response to it in "The World and the Jug" from *Shadow and Act* (1964) is well known; less so but equally revealing is Leslie Fiedler on the same track but from a different angle: "Ellison's invisible protagonist, however convincingly specified, reminds us disconcertingly of Kafka's K., i.e., seems a secondhand version of the black man in America, based on a European intellectual's version of the alienated Jew." See Leslie A. Fiedler, *Waiting for the End: A Portrait of Twentieth-Century American Literature and Its Writers* (New York: Stein and Day, 1970), 107.

34. Raymond Williams, *Marxism and Literature* (New York: Oxford University Press, 1977), 133. The sense in which I use the phrase is very much in agreement with Jonathan Flatley's usage in *Affective Mapping.* His study is focused on melancholy and modernism; I am interested in melancholy as only one part of a broader set of responses by a subset of black writers (many with modernist tendencies). Because Williams's use of the term can be confused with a variety of arguments and ideas about affect, Flatley includes a glossary chapter that usefully explicates this concept in detail and that I am indebted to for my own understanding and usage. See Jonathan Flatley, *Affective Mapping: Melancholia and the Politics of Modernism* (Cambridge, MA: Harvard University Press, 2008), 24–27.

35. The pathbreaking work of Lawrence Jackson is, I believe, the first to note this striking conjunction. Jackson makes this observation mainly to comment on the irony that it should coincide with so many black writers leaving for Europe. See Jackson, *Indignant Generation*, 381.

36. On the foundation of the Black Arts Repertory Theatre/School and the flourishing of the Black Arts Movement around it, see James E. Smethurst, *The Black Arts Movement: Literary Nationalism in the 1960s and 1970s* (Chapel Hill: University of North Carolina Press, 2005), 100–179. On the importance of Malcolm X and his assassination for Baraka and Black Nationalist politics, see Woodard, *Nation within a Nation*, 59–60. See Peniel E. Joseph, *Waiting 'til the Midnight Hour: A Narrative History of Black Power in America* (New York: Holt Paperbacks, 2007), 132. Joseph notes that with the escalation of white violence, the dramatic speeches during the Meredith march and subsequent jockeying with Martin Luther King Jr. and Ralph Abernathy over leadership of the movement effectively "catapulted Stokely into the political space last occupied by Malcolm X." Peniel E. Joseph, *Stokely: A Life* (New York: Basic Civitas Books, 2014), 125.

37. An example of this is Stephanie Brown's study of postwar black fiction, an otherwise excellent book, which is held back too often by its recycling of these tired tropes. See Brown, *The Postwar African American Novel: Protest and Discontent, 1945–1950* (Jackson: University Press of Mississippi, 2011).

38. The special issue was *Phylon* 11, no. 4 (1950), edited by Mozell C. Hill and M. Carl Holman. A good example of the trope I am invoking is represented by N. P. Tillman's choice of title for his contribution to the symposium: "The Threshold of Maturity."

39. See Warren, "Particularity and the Problem of Interpretation," in *What Was African American Literature?* (Cambridge, MA: Harvard University Press, 2012), 44–80.

40. See William J. Maxwell, *F. B. Eyes: How J. Edgar Hoover's Ghostreaders framed African American Literature* (Princeton, NJ: Princeton University Press, 2015). Maxwell also authored one of the best revisionary studies of the interwar black communist literary scene: *New Negro, Old Left: African American Communism between the Wars* (New York: Columbia University Press, 1999).

41. See Mary Helen Washington, "When Gwendolyn Brooks Wore Red," in *The Other Blacklist: The African American Literary and Cultural Left of the 1950s* (New York: Columbia University Press, 2014), 165–203.

42. Kazin levels some of his harshest assessments in a passage leading up to his case against Richard Wright's *Native Son*: "The folly of so many left-wing minds was to assume that artistry was something one added to the concern with those problems, and that what one added to it was nothing more than the quality of one's knowledge and energy. In the end this primitivism sapped both knowledge and energy, for it compelled writers to rely too much upon their emotional resources and thus cheated them. The energy was lost in declamations and that hoarse strident irony which became a traditional feature in left-wing style; the knowledge became less an aroused awareness of the pain of life than a need to arouse others by shocking and indoctrinating them.... It is precisely because Wright himself was so passionately honest and desired to represent the sufferings of his race as forcefully as possible that the unconscious slickness of *Native Son*, its manipulation of terror in a period fascinated by terror, seems so sinister. For Wright was only the child of his generation, and his resources no different in kind from the resources of naturalism and the left-wing conception of life and literature to which, like many Negro writers, he surrendered his thinking because of the general indifference or hostility to Negroes and Negro writing." Alfred Kazin, *On Native Grounds: An Interpretation of Modern American Prose Literature* (New York: Harcourt Brace, 1942), 386. For Walter Rideout, see *The Radical Novel in the United States, 1900–1954: Some Interrelations of Literature and Society* (Cambridge, MA: Harvard University Press, 1956). For James Baldwin's famous critique, see "Everybody's Protest Novel," in *Collected Essays*, ed. Toni Morrison (New York: Library of America, 1998).

43. Peter J. Kalliney, *The Aesthetic Cold War: Decolonization and Global Literature* (Princeton, NJ: Princeton University Press, 2022), 12. I also agree with Kalliney that we ought to "speak less of a debate between metropolitan modernism (or experimental writing, or art for art's sake) and socialist realism and more about the tension between aesthetic autonomy and aesthetic utilitarianism" (10).

44. Elizabeth Alexander, *The Black Interior: Essays* (Minneapolis: Graywolf Press, 2004).

45. John Akomfrah, *The Stuart Hall Project* (London: Smoking Dog Films/Lina Gopaul, 2013).

46. Nathaniel Mackey, *The Paracritical Hinge: Essays, Talks, Notes, Interviews* (Madison: University of Wisconsin Press, 2005), 201.

47. Mackey, 201.

48. Mackey, 201.

49. Mackey is playing a variation on a phrase from William Gass, who said that blue "is the color consciousness becomes when caressed." See William H. Gass, *On Being Blue: A Philosophical Inquiry* (New York: New York Review Books, 1976; NYRB Classics, 2014).

50. Mackey, *Paracritical Hinge*, 201.

51. Richard Wright, *The Outsider* (New York: Library of America, 1991), 511.

52. Teju Cole, *Known and Strange Things: Essays* (New York: Random House, 2016), 147.

53. Cole, 147.

54. Sara Blair, *Harlem Crossroads: Black Writers and the Photograph in the Twentieth Century* (Princeton, NJ: Princeton University Press, 2007), 50. Blair essentially makes this same argument, especially through her magnificent chapter on Ellison and photography. Blair's study is concerned with ranging across the century, however; I want to zero in on DeCarava as emblematic of the midcentury literary period, especially with respect to formal inventiveness and affect.

55. "What Adorno says of Beethoven—that his is 'the most sublime music ever to aim at freedom under continued unfreedom'—is applicable to Miles's ascendant Jacobsean swerve in and out of the confinements of Gershwin's composition and Evans's arrangement. Freedom in unfreedom is flight and this music could be called the most sublime in the history of escape." Fred Moten, "Taste Dissonance Flavor Escape (Preface to a Solo by Miles Davis)," in *Consent Not to Be a Single Being*, vol. 1, *Black and Blur* (Durham, NC: Duke University Press, 2017), 85.

56. Ralph Ellison, *Invisible Man* (New York: Vintage, 1989), 580.

57. Kenneth Warren, *So Black and Blue: Ralph Ellison and the Occasion of Criticism* (Chicago: University of Chicago Press, 2003), 3.

58. Warren, 7.

Chapter One

1. Thelma Golden, "An Interview with Hilton Als Moderated by Thelma Golden," *Glenn Ligon: Stranger*, exhibition catalog (New York: Studio Museum Harlem, 2001), 12.

2. Darby English, *How to See a Work of Art in Total Darkness* (Cambridge, MA: MIT Press, 2010), 133.

3. Golden, "Interview with Hilton," 16.

4. Carly Berwick, "Stranger in America," *Art in America*, no. 5 (May 2011): 124.

5. *Glenn Ligon: Stranger*, 113–14.

6. James Baldwin, *The Cross of Redemption: Uncollected Writings*, ed. Randall Kennan (New York: Vintage, 2011), 8–9.

7. In *Caribbean Discourse*, the chapter entitled "Cross-Cultural Poetics" includes a significant gloss on this very point. "The very specific slogan of the French bourgeoisie in 1789, 'Liberty, Equality, Fraternity,' has tended for a long time to be considered in an absolute way as one of the cornerstones of universal humanism. The irony was that it, in fact, meant that. This is how the positivism of Auguste Comte, in fact, became a religion in South America among an alienated elite." Édouard Glissant, *Caribbean Discourse*, trans. J. Michael Dash (Charlottesville: University of Virginia Press, 1992), 98–99.

8. Chakrabarty notes that "historians have long acknowledged that the so-called 'European age' in modern history began to yield place to other regional and global configurations towards the middle of the twentieth century." The core argument of his book, however, is that this transition has not been mirrored by an accompanying decentering in the historiographic narratives and intellectual frameworks generally held to be authoritative in the West. Dipesh Chakrabarty, *Provincializing Europe: Postcolonial Thought and Historical Difference* (Princeton, NJ: Princeton University Press, 2007), 3.

9. As significant as his fiction may be, and I tend to think the mainstream of our criticism continues undervalue it, one cannot deny the importance of Baldwin's contribution to the genre of the essay. Perhaps I should say "hopefully no longer," since the capacity to neglect Baldwin, even as an essayist, is even recently still quite possible. A striking example is a book about twentieth-century public intellectuals by Edward Mendelson called *Moral Agents: Eight Twentieth-Century American Writers*. These agents turn out to be exclusively male and white, and the book includes chapters devoted to Dwight MacDonald and William Maxwell Jr. without even a mention of Baldwin anywhere in the text, not even in the chapter devoted to Norman Mailer. The book was published in 2015.

10. Michel Fabre, *La rive noire: De Harlem à la Seine* (Paris: Lieu Commun, 1985).

11. Thomas Barbour, "Little Magazines in Paris," *Hudson Review* 4, no. 2 (Summer, 1951): 278–83.

12. José Esteban Muñoz, *Disidentifications: Queers of Color and the Performance of Politics* (Minneapolis, MN: University of Minnesota Press, 2013), 1.

13. José Esteban Muñoz, *Disidentifications*, 18–19. Muñoz gives a wonderful reading of Baldwin's disidentification through the narrative intervention of the character Jimmy at the end of *Just above My Head* (1979). He detects in Jimmy "the subject who stands inside—and, in the most important ways, outside—of fiction, ideology, the 'real.'" I would only add that what it reveals is the persisting will in Baldwin to find a voice and a position outside the confines of the ideological. This fundamentally artistic motivation was forged in and out of Baldwin's blue period, and most of the late fiction struggles to retain the strategic ambiguity and independence of the earlier work. In the 1970s, the historical context no longer favored that approach, and not simply because the politics and ideologies of the moment were more strident. It was also because Baldwin as a person had more sympathy for those positions and more antipathy to the forces opposing them than he had before. See Muñoz, *Disidentifications*, 19–21.

14. As D. Quentin Miller notes, the use of the first-person singular pronoun in "Encounter on the Seine," "A Question of Identity," "Equal in Paris," and "Stranger in the Village" is significant. See D. Quentin Miller "Separate and Unequal in Paris," in *James Baldwin: America and Beyond*, ed. Cora Kaplan and Bill Schwarz (Ann Arbor: University of Michigan Press, 2011), 159–72.

15. See Jackson's chapter "The Negro New Liberal Critic and the Big Little Magazine" in his *Indignant Generation: A Narrative History of African American Writers and Critics, 1934–1960* (Princeton, NJ: Princeton University Press, 2011), 275–96. On the "Harlem Ghetto," see 278–79.

16. Jackson, 278–79.

17. Ralph Ellison's "Harlem Is Nowhere" was written for *Magazine of the Year* in 1949 but not published until decades later because the magazine folded; Ann Petry's "Harlem," for the April 1949 issue of *Holiday*. See Jackson, *Indignant Generation*, 280–81.

18. Jackson, 287.

19. Edmund Wilson had published an essay in the *New Yorker* in November 1948 praising the literary qualities of *Uncle Tom's Cabin*. Jackson suggests that Philip Rahv, the editor of *Partisan Review*, which reprinted Baldwin's essay in 1949, was eager to run a piece attacking a highly esteemed "patrician" critic whom he despised. See Jackson, *Indignant Generation*, 283–87.

20. "He [Baldwin] lightly explained away his conduct by saying, "Zero was here and you were there." Jackson, 286.

21. Although the influence of James on Baldwin has been well established in earlier scholarship, the popularization of the connection has been slower. In 2001, the Irish writer Colm Tóibín called Baldwin "the Henry James of Harlem," a title that hasn't exactly stuck but that attests to a broadening understanding of this relation beyond the academy. See Colm Tóibín, "The Last Witness," *London Review of Books* 23, no. 18 (2001): 15–20.

22. David A. Leeming, "An Interview with James Baldwin on Henry James," *Henry James Review* 8, no. 1 (1986): 47–56.

23. Leeming, 47.

24. Leeming, 56.

25. Cheryl Wall gives a good description of this *métissage*: "[Baldwin] shapes his expression of interiority with a prose style that looks back to the King James Bible, as well as to [Henry] James[,] … to the visionary rhetoric of African American sermons and the laconic ironies of the blues." Cheryl Wall, "Stranger at Home: James Baldwin on What It Means to Be an American," in *James Baldwin: America and Beyond*, ed. Bill Schwarz and Cora Kaplan (Ann Arbor: University of Michigan Press, 2011), 41.

26. The best account of how consciousness is distributed intersubjectively in James's fiction remains Sharon Cameron's indispensable *Thinking in Henry James* (Chicago: University of Chicago Press, 1989).

27. James Baldwin, *Notes of a Native Son* (Boston: Beacon Press, 1957), 18.

28. Baldwin, 19.

29. See Vaughn Rasberry, "'Now Describing You': James Baldwin and Cold War Liberalism," in *James Baldwin: America and Beyond*, ed. Bill Schwarz and Cora Kaplan (Ann Arbor: University of Michigan Press, 2011), 84–105. Schaub's reconstruction of the shift in critical consensus from the interwar to the postwar period is especially pertinent. He also argues that the postwar period sees a turn to inwardness, which he associates with a renewed preference for first-person narration. This claim is somewhat overstated, but we both see writers who are looking for ways to "step outside the public narcosis" and who mark that difference by "locating an inside otherness." Thomas Hill Schaub, *America Fiction in the Cold War* (Madison: University of Wisconsin Press, 1991), 81.

30. Schaub, 87.

31. See Jackson, *Indignant Generation*, 319.

32. The best and most recently compiled source for biographical information on Ottley is Mark A. Huddle's edition of his diaries, *Roi Ottley's World War II: The Lost Diary of an African American Journalist* (Lawrence: University Press of Kansas, 2013). For an overview of Ottley's career, see Huddle's introduction.

33. Huddle, 29.

34. Ottley's former colleague Marvel Cooke wrote the review for the *Amsterdam News*. The title he ran was "Roi Ottley: Prisoner of White Supremacy." Huddle, 29–30.

35. Interestingly, two years before the appearance of Ralph Ellison's novel, Baldwin described "the American Negro in Paris" as "very nearly the invisible man." See Baldwin, *Collected Essays*, 86.

36. Frances Stonor Saunders calls the US intelligence operations devoted to "cultural propaganda," particularly those under the auspices of the Congress for Cultural Freedom between 1950 and 1967, which funded many of these magazines, "the hidden

weapon in America's Cold War struggle." Saunders, *The Cultural Cold War: The CIA and the World of Arts and Letters* (New York: New Press, 2013), 1. See also Hugh Wilford, *The Mighty Wurlitzer: How the CIA Played America* (Cambridge, MA: Harvard University Press, 2009).

37. C. Wright Mills, *The Power Elite* (New York: Oxford University Press, 1956).

38. Martin K. Doudna, *Concerned about the Planet: The* Reporter *Magazine and American Liberalism, 1949-1968* (Greenport, CT: Greenwood Press, 1977), 80-81. Literary contributors to the *Reporter* other than Baldwin included W. H. Auden, Saul Bellow, Ray Bradbury, Malcolm Cowley, Shirley Jackson, Bernard Malamud, Alberto Moravia, V. S. Pritchett, Ignazio Silone, Delmore Schwartz, Wallace Stegner, John Steinbeck, and Robert Penn Warren. Doudna, 82. On Max Ascoli's relatively tepid interest in race circa 1951 when Baldwin is publishing his review, but also his gradually increasing interest in civil-rights in his editorials for the magazine, see Doudna, 104-8.

39. Doudna, 80-81.

40. Baldwin, "The Negro at Home and Abroad," *The Reporter*, November 27, 1951, 36-37.

41. Baldwin, 36.

42. Baldwin, 36.

43. Baldwin, 37.

44. Baldwin's invocation of "Lebensraum" in relation to US race relations and his allusions to the causes and aftermath of Nazism also foreshadow postwar debates over the analogy of African American experiences of US slavery to the experiences of Jews in Hitler's concentration camps prompted by Stanley Elkins's *Slavery: A Problem in American Institutional and Intellectual Life* (1959). For an excellent overview of this debate and the role of African American intellectuals in it (including Baldwin, Richard Wright, and Ralph Ellison), see Richard H. King, *Race, Culture, and the Intellectuals, 1940-1970* (Baltimore: Johns Hopkins University Press, 2004), 151-72.

45. Baldwin, 37.

46. Baldwin, 37.

47. Baldwin, 37.

48. David Leeming, *James Baldwin: A Biography* (New York: Henry Holt, 1994), 104-5.

49. His last piece, "The Projects of Poverty," appeared in the April 1986 issue, although in that case, as in many others, the magazine was reprinting earlier material.

50. James Baldwin, *Collected Essays*, 117.

51. Baldwin, 117.

52. Baldwin, 117.

53. J. H. O'Dell, "Foundations of Racism in American Life," *Freedomways* 4 (1964), 98.

54. Baldwin, *Collected Essays*, 129.

55. Cheryl A. Wall, "Stranger at Home: James Baldwin on What It Means to Be an American," in *James Baldwin: America and Beyond*, ed. Bill Schwarz and Cora Kaplan (Ann Arbor: University of Michigan Press, 2011), 38.

56. Baldwin, *Collected Essays*, 383.

57. Baldwin, "Stranger in the Village," 121.

58. James Baldwin, *Collected Essays*, 7-8.

59. Teju Cole, "Black Body: Reading James Baldwin's *Stranger in the Village*," *New Yorker*, August 19, 2014, reprinted as "Black Body," in *Known and Strange Things: Essays* (New York: Random House, 2016), 3–16.

60. Douglas Field, "What Is Africa to Baldwin? Cultural Illegitimacy and the Step-fatherland," in *James Baldwin: America and Beyond*, ed. Bill Schwarz and Cora Kaplan (Ann Arbor: University of Michigan Press, 2011), 209-28.

61. Leeming, *Biography*, 104-5.

62. James Baldwin, *The Cross of Redemption: Uncollected Writings*, ed. Randall Kennan (New York: Vintage, 2011), 65-69.

63. James Baldwin, *Collected Essays*, 138.

64. Baldwin's Western sublime is worth comparing with Bruce Robbins's notion of the "sweatshop sublime" in which a fictional character has an epiphanic insight into their relationship to the globalized system of capitalist production that undergirds their existence. The analogy to Baldwin's insight here is not perfect, but there is an overlapping area of affect that Robbins touches on, namely the sense of powerlessness to act upon the thing that you willingly or unwillingly benefit from: "Yet at the same time this insight is also strangely powerless. Your sudden, heady access to the global scale is not access to a commensurate power of action *on* the global scale." Bruce Robbins, "The Sweatshop Sublime" *PMLA* 117, no. 1 (2002): 85. The lack of ability to change relations of power, however, is not the same as the lack of ability to change the order of knowledge, and such power is never insignificant.

65. It is interesting to note that Chakrabarty's example in this instance is drawn from literary studies. Chakrabarty, *Provincializing Europe*, 28.

66. Michel Foucault, *The Order of Things: An Archaeology of the Human Sciences* (New York: Vintage, 1994). Another way to emphasize the irony Baldwin is employing here would be to recast Robbins's "sweatshop sublime" as the material history that Baldwin knows intimately (and I would even venture to say embodies corporeally) that undergirds it. Lindon Barrett in his last book was, I believe, attempting to comprehensively render this same accounting in conceptual and historicist terms. I propose that we read Baldwin with Barrett's thinking filling in the landscape, so to speak, from passages such as this one: "While human corporeality emerges at the micropolitical level as a discrete catalogue serving as well as obfuscating the economic and social management of mass populations, at the macropolitical level the transforming and emergent metropoles along the Atlantic coastlines of Europe and the 'New World' forge their exemplary modern profiles by means of the immense surplus values depending on the depletion and the disordering of the political jurisdictions along the Senegambian, Guinean, and west-central African coastlines as well as the stark regimes of enforced labor in the Americas. In the words of the historian Walter Rodney, the peculiarity is the criterion by which almost 'no human suffering was too high to pay for the monetary gain from trade in slaves and from the extension of capitalist production into the New World.' Insofar as racial blackness forms the historical and enabling point of 'dis/integration' for the paradigms of Western modernity and, in this way, seems an eccentricity of the modern, the violent historical forging of the African diasporic communities of the Americas discloses the conceptual impossibility to be, on the contrary, the reported beneficence of modern 'civic animation,' the consolidated macropolitical and micropolitical determinations by which the modern remains viable." Lindon Barrett, *Racial Blackness and the Discontinuity of Western Modernity* (Urbana: University of Illinois Press, 2014), 2.

67. James Baldwin, *Collected Essays*, 118.

68. See Maurice Blanchot, *The Space of Literature* (Lincoln: University of Nebraska Press, 1989), xx.

69. Jackson, *Indignant Generation*, 408.

70. I recognize that this point is debatable, but to give just two examples representing very different political persuasions and investments, consider Eldridge Cleaver's *Soul on Ice* (1968) and Walter White's *A Man Called White* (1948). These seem to me equally good examples of autobiographical works by black writers that were emblematic of the political climate of their times, books that could, and did, command important political and cultural attention in the context of their appearance but that, for different reasons, cannot possibly mobilize or command that same kind of power or attention today. What made Cleaver potent in his own era has, in the long run, made him impotent in another. By all available evidence, Baldwin's autobiographical essays have not followed anything like that trajectory. This chapter has, I hope, made some fresh inroads that give us a convincing way to explain why this is. This book examines the period that comes between White's and Cleaver's books; each, incidentally, offers a good before-and-after snapshot of the affective and political climate that preceded, and then succeeded, the Blue Period, one that shows how distinct, and even stark, the differences between all three of them are.

71. Mark McGurl, *The Novel Art: Elevations of American Fiction After Henry James* (Princeton, NJ: Princeton University Press, 2001), 19, original emphasis. It is telling that there is no discussion in McGurl's book of any fiction by a black author. Obviously, there are many examples of black writers who turned to James as a model (e.g., Baldwin, Wright, Ellison, Mayfield). This only demonstrates how recently in our critical past our canons have remained symptomatically segregated, even in studies pursued by progressively inclined scholars.

72. James Baldwin, *Go Tell It on the Mountain* (New York: Vintage, 2013), 197, emphasis added.

73. This lends weight to the view that Baldwin's title for his essay collection *Notes of a Native Son* contains a double allusion not always recognized: to Richard Wright and to Henry James. James uses the word *naught* or *nought* relatively infrequently in his fiction, and even in his nonfiction, it is appears more frequently in later writings, including *The American Scene* (1907), *Italian Hours* (1909), *A Small Boy and Others* (1913), *Notes of a Son and Brother* (1914), and *Notes on Novelists* (1914), where it appears three times. Of these, I would venture that Baldwin read *Notes of a Son and Brother* and quite possibly also *Notes on Novelists*. This would hint at a further Jamesian homage in the choice of title for his essay collection. For the quote from James, he is quoting a letter from his brother William, who is commenting upon Carlyle's attitude toward religion: "He names God frequently and alludes to the highest things as if they were realities, but all only as for a picturesque effect, so completely does he seem to regard them as circumvented and set at naught by the politicians." Henry James, *Notes of a Son and Brother* (New York: Charles Scribner's, 1914), 201.

74. W. E. B. Du Bois, *Writings*, ed. Nathan Huggins (New York: Library of America, 1986), 494. James Arthur Manigault-Bryant argues that Du Bois's understanding of the "frenzy" is not necessarily as pejorative as it might seem. In his description of "the Pythian Madness" of the worshippers, he sees an ambivalent but ultimately syncretic attempt by Du Bois to reconcile his African heritage and American modernity.

See Manigault-Bryant, "Reimagining the 'Pythian Madness' of Souls: W. E. B. Du Bois's Poetics of African American Faith," *Journal of Africana Religions* 1, no. 3 (2013): 324–47.

75. Ashon T. Crawley, *Blackpentecostal Breath: The Aesthetics of Possibility* (New York: Fordham University Press, 2017), 152.

76. Baldwin, *Go Tell It on the Mountain*, 205.

77. The threshing floor as a metaphor for sorting good from evil, and the saved from the damned, appears in a variety of contexts in the Old and New Testaments; Matthew 3:12 and Isaiah 21:10 seem especially suggestive to John's situation.

78. Baldwin, *Go Tell It on the Mountain*, 209, emphasis added.

79. One could read "The Threshing Floor" as a condensed Dantean journey to the sources of the African American self. Again, much of Lindon Barrett's work would be germane to unpacking the historical, juridical, and semiotic linkages that form the pillars of that netherworld. He would also notice the importance of phonic material and remind us of the revisions and challenges to the very idea of value that the "singing" voice of the illiterate (or simply unworded) life knowledge of the black enslaved posed to the "signing" textual literacy and authority of white masters—not only its challenge to the possibility of value, but the freedom to manifest the needs and desires of the self in terms that make sense of a different valuation of presence, one that "recreates African Americans as in-voiced, rather than onerously em-bodied," for example. His tragic loss will continue to reverberate, but the conversation with his far-reaching ideas has in many ways only just begun. See Lindon Barrett, *Blackness and Value: Seeing Double* (New York: Cambridge University Press, 1999), 114.

80. Richard Wright, *Early Works* (New York: Library of America, 1991), 405.

81. Wright, 406.

82. Baldwin, *Go Tell It on the Mountain*, 203.

83. Baldwin, 210.

84. Baldwin, 211, emphasis added.

85. Maurice Blanchot, *The Book to Come*, trans. Charlotte Mandell (Stanford, CA: Stanford University Press, 2003), 79.

86. Baldwin, *Go Tell It on the Mountain*, 225.

Chapter Two

1. Édouard Glissant, *Sun of Consciousness*, trans. Nathanaël (New York: Nightboat Books, 2020), 23.

2. Édouard Glissant, *Un champ d'îles* (Paris: Instance, 1953).

3. Cahiers d'Art is widely credited with being one of the most important hubs in the diffusion and reception of modern art in postwar France. For more background, see Christian Derouet, ed., *Christian Zervos et Cahiers d'art, Archives de la Bibliothèque Kandinsky* (Paris: Centre Georges Pompidou, 2011). In a review, Chara Kolokytha describes Cahiers as "a monthly bulletin *d'actualité artistique* published in Paris by Christian Zervos and distributed in Europe and overseas. The magazine published ninety-seven issues from 1926 to 1960 collaborating with the most prominent figures in the history of art on an international level, while the same title was used from 1934 onwards to indicate the function of an art gallery and a publishing house; meeting points for contemporary artistic and literary parties for more than three decades." See Kolokytha,

"Christian Zervos et Cahiers d'art, Archives de la Bibliothèque Kandinsky," *Konsthistorisktidskrift* 82, no. 4 (April 2013): 339–42.

4. Édouard Glissant, *La terre inquiète* (Paris: Dragon, 1955).

5. For an overview of Lam's career in this period, see Maria R. Balderrama, ed., *Wifredo Lam and His Contemporaries, 1938–1952* (New York: Studio Museum Harlem, 1992).

6. Magdalena J. Zaborowska, *James Baldwin's Turkish Decade: Erotics of Exile* (Durham, NC: Duke University Press, 2009).

7. John E. Drabinski, *Theorizing Glissant: Sites and Citations* (London: Rowman & Littlefield, 2015), 6.

8. Peter Hallward tracks a deflating political project "from nation to relation" in a chronological reading of the novels starting with *La lézarde*. See Hallward, *Absolutely Postcolonial* (Manchester, UK: Manchester University Press, 2002), 66–126.

9. Glissant, *Sun of Consciousness*.

10. Britton's study "aims to situate Glissant in the context of [Anglophone] postcolonial theory." Her work remains a seminal study of Glissant, but she again reads only the novels against the theory. See Celia Britton, *Édouard Glissant and Postcolonial Theory: Strategies of Language and Resistance* (Charlottesville: University of Virginia Press, 1999). Nesbitt likewise has focused his attention on the novels, particularly the radical politics of *La lézarde*. See Nick Nesbitt, "Early Glissant: From the Destitution of the Political to Antillean Ultra-Leftism," *Callaloo* 36, no. 4 (2013): 933–48; and Nesbitt, *Voicing Memory: History and Subjectivity in French Caribbean Literature* (Charlottesville. University of Virginia Press, 2003). Kullberg has drawn important attention to *Soleil de la conscience* but not to Glissant's other contemporary literary criticism. See Christina Kullberg, *The Poetics of Ethnography in Martinican Narratives: Exploring the Self and Environment* (Charlottesville: University of Virginia Press, 2013). Suzy Cater has produced the most significant breakthrough in rethinking Glissant in the 1950s, but her work is also more oriented toward considering his influence and relations with French authors and figures. Suzy Cater, "A Schizophrenia That Wasn't One: Édouard Glissant and Poetry, Painting and Politics in 1950s Paris," *French Forum* 41, no. 3 (2016): 257–72.

11. Indeed, except for Suzy Cater, there is virtually no commentary on this aspect of Glissant's life and writings, despite the dominant role it played in the formative stages of his literary career. Cater's article focuses on the author's ambiguous avowal of a kind of "schizophrenia" between artistic and political commitment in this period. My own work is necessarily much indebted to hers. Nevertheless, in some respects she doesn't carry her argument far enough, nor does she (in the space of an article) have the room to connect Glissant's literary and art criticism to his other important works from the decade. For understandable reasons, her work is focused on Glissant in relationship primarily to other French poets and critics, whereas I seek to use the same materials to make a point that bridges the concerns and aesthetic practices of French and American black expatriates.

12. This fundamentally utopian valence did not escape the attention of the art world, as Suzy Cater also notes in her article. The art historian and curator Hans Ulrich Obrist says he learned of Glissant's work from the Italian artist Alighiero Boetti during a visit to Rome in 1986. Obrist singles out the global and utopian aspects of Glissant's "archipelic thought" as having a special appeal to his generation of artists and curators. See

prefatory remarks to *Édouard Glissant & Hans Ulrich Obrist: 100 Notes—100 Thoughts No. 038* (Kassel: Documenta [13] Hatje Cantz Verlag, 2011).

13. Daniel Radford describes the father's role as that of a mediator between sugarcane cutters and other workers in the plantation complex. Glissant told Radford that men in his father's position tended to be "colorful, standing out, always on horseback; most of them kept revolvers." Daniel Radford, *Édouard Glissant: Poètes d'aujourd'hui* (Paris: Seghers, 1982), 13.

14. See Philippe Dewitte, *Les mouvements nègres en France: 1919-1939* (Paris: L'Harmattan, 1985); Michael Richardson and Krzysztof Fijalkowski, *Refusal of the Shadow: Surrealism and the Caribbean* (New York: Verso, 1996); Brent Hayes Edwards, *The Practice of Diaspora: Literature, Translation, and the Rise of Black Internationalism* (Cambridge, MA: Harvard University Press, 2003); J. Michael Dash, "Caraïbe Fantôme: The Play of Difference in the Francophone Caribbean," *Yale French Studies*, no. 103 (2003): 93-105. Glissant recalled meeting Breton as a young boy (he was thirteen at the time) at an impromptu gathering near the Lycée Schoelcher. See Celia Britton, "Souvenirs des années 40 à la Martinique: Interview avec Édouard Glissant," *L'esprit créateur* 47, no. 1 (2007): 96-104.

15. On the wider campaign of dissident activity against the Vichy regime in the Antilles, see Eric Jennings, "La dissidence aux Antilles, 1940-1943," *Vingtième siècle, revue d'histoire* 68 (October–December 2000): 55-71.

16. Nick Nesbitt, "Early Glissant: From the Destitution of the Political to Antillean Ultra-Leftism," *Callaloo* 36, no. 4 (2013): 933.

17. Celia Britton, "Souvenirs des années 40 à la Martinique: Interview avec Édouard Glissant," 101-2. Glissant notes that no examples of the journal appear extant. The journal survives in popular memory, however: a street in Lamentin was renamed "rue Franc-Jeu" in 2006. See Britton, 102. It seems likely that Glissant and his friends chose the name Franc-Jeu (which means "fair play") possibly as a nod to the surrealist journal *Le grand jeu*, a short-lived literary review published between 1928 and 1932 by René Daumal, Roger Vailland, and Roger Gilbert-Lecomte with a mischievous bent, but also even more likely as an ironic appropriation and subversion of the title of the Vichy regime's youth journal of the same name; Vichy specifically designated its own "Franc-Jeu" produced in the metropole for distribution in the colonial "outremer." Copies of Vichy's *Franc-Jeu* can be viewed in the digital archives of the Bibliothèque nationale de France (https://catalogue.bnf.fr/ark:/12148/cb32777065k).

18. Glissant and Fanon met in Paris during his first year there in 1946; they would meet again significantly near the end of Fanon's life in July 1961 at a clandestine location in Rome. See David Macey, *Frantz Fanon: A Biography* (New York: Picador, 2000), 118-19; for the meeting in Rome, see 462. For Glissant's account of the Rome meeting, see his "Un nouveau sens de l'humanité pour les pays du Sud," *Antilla* 23 (November–December 1991): 38-39.

19. Ruth Bush has studied the impact of *Présence africaine* as an institution and the degree to which it could exert influence on the cultural field of French and Francophone literary publics. Bush focuses primarily on sub-Saharan African writing, but her quantitative and comparative approach gives an empirical basis for challenging any notion that writers, including Glissant, were simply ignored. I consider her work further later. See Ruth Bush, *Publishing Africa in French: Literary Institutions and Decolonization, 1945-1967* (Liverpool, UK: Liverpool University Press, 2016), 215-16.

20. This figure does not include articles that appeared elsewhere, including work for Bataille's journal *Critique* and for Diop's *Présence africaine*. See Édouard Glissant, "Alejo Carpentier et 'l'Autre Amérique,'" *Critique*, no. 105 (February 1956): 113–19; "Le romancier noir et son peuple: Notes pour une conférence," *Présence africaine*, no. 16 (October–November 1957): 26–31, which I discuss in further detail later. The figure for the total number of pieces in *Lettres nouvelles* is given in Radford, *Poètes d'aujourd'hui*, 21.

21. Christina Kullberg, "Crossroads Poetics," *Callaloo* 36, no. 4 (2013): 968.

22. Romual Blaise Fonkoua calls it Glissant's "récit de voyage à l'envers," or inverted travelogue. Fonkoua Romual Blaise, "Édouard Glissant: Naissance d'une anthropologie antillaise au siècle de l'assimilation," *Cahiers d'études africaines* 35, no. 140 (1995): 798. Christina Kullberg reconstitutes the complex literary and intellectual interchange between French midcentury ethnography and Antillean literature. Christina Kullberg, "Crossroads Poetics," *Callaloo* 36, no. 4 (2013): 968. Likewise, J. Michael Dash reads *Soleil* as a surrealist inflected exercise "so that the travel narrative becomes a voyage of self-discovery," his point of view "as much an insider on the outside as Breton or [Pierre] Mabille in the Caribbean." Dash, "Caraïbe Fantôme," 101.

23. Michel Leiris, *Contacts de civilisations en Martinique et en Guadeloupe*, Collection Race et Société (Paris: UNESCO and Gallimard, 1955). Glissant is referred to in that book as editor of the avant-garde journal *Caravelle* in a chapter devoted to emerging literary and cultural trends in the Antilles (104). See Edouard Glissant, *L'intention poétique* (Paris: Seuil, 1969; repr., Paris: Gallimard, 1997), 121–29, esp. 126. The most thorough accounting of the Glissant-Leiris relationship is provided by Celia Britton, in "Ethnography as Relation: The Significance of the French Caribbean in the Ethnographic Writing of Michel Leiris," *French Studies* 66, no. 1 (2012): 41–53.

24. See Kullberg, "Crossroads Poetics."

25. Glissant, "Michel Leiris, ethnographe," *Les lettres nouvelles* 43 (1956): 609–21.

26. As the book's most recent English translator, Brent Hayes Edwards, points out, Leiris also produced a new preface for the 1951 edition of *Phantom Africa* in which he specifically cited his travels to Ivory Coast in 1945 and to Martinique and Guadeloupe in 1948 as catalysts for his realization "that there is no ethnography or exoticism that can be sustained in the face of the gravity of the social questions posed by the construction of the modern world, and that if contact between men born in different climates is not a myth, it is precisely to the extent that it can be realized through work in common against those in our twentieth-century capitalist society who are the representatives of the old system of slavery." Quoted in Brent Hayes Edwards, *Phantom Africa* (Calcutta: Seagull Books, 2017), 23–24. On further nuances of the 1951 edition and preface, see 55–56.

27. Édouard Glissant, *Poetic Intention*, trans. Nathanaël, with Anne Malena (New York: Nightboat Books, 2010), 16.

28. Édouard Glissant, *Soleil de la conscience* (Paris: Éditions Falaize, 1956), 11. Falaize was an imprint founded by Georges Fall, a French art collector and critic—another reminder of Glissant's connection to that world. Other commentators on this text like Dash have used the Seuil edition, published in 1957. My pagination here always refers to the Falaize 1956 edition. Translations are my own.

29. Glissant, 11.

30. Glissant, 15.

31. Glissant, 11; Dash, "Caraïbe Fantôme," 101.

32. Leiris goes into some detail about the sociological formation of the Antillean intelligentsia, including a racial composition that had been almost exclusively colored or mulatto and male, but after Césaire was being reshaped by the rise of dark-skinned and women writers, poets, and critics. He argues that it is only in the postwar period that they become self-consciously activated and invested in the project of forging an Antillean cultural independence. See Leiris, *Contacts de civilisations*, 116, and 107–10.

33. His friend Maurice Aliker, for example, was one of the founders of Franc-Jeu. The Bibliothèque nationale de France Fonds Édouard Glissant (NAF 28894 46f) holds a letter to their mutual friend Laurent Ortolé dated June 21, 1946, that describes Maurice as the secretary of the group. It's worth noting that the Aliker name is politically significant in Martinique. Pierre Aliker was Aimé Césaire's longtime right-hand man and deputy mayor of Fort-de-France. Pierre's brother André Aliker was a famous journalist, the editor of the communist newspaper *Justice*, and a labor organizer who was murdered in 1934 while working on exposing corruption by wealthy *béké* (white Martinican) landholders. The Alikers are from Le Lamentin, where Glissant banded together with friends to form Franc-Jeu in the 1940s. The film *Aliker* (2009) is a biopic about the life and assassination of André Aliker directed by the Martinican filmmaker Guy Deslauriers with a screenplay by the novelist Patrick Chamoiseau.

34. Glissant, *Soleil de la conscience*, 59.

35. See Gary Wilder, *Freedom Time: Negritude Decolonization, and the Future of the World* (Durham, NC: Duke University Press, 2015). Wilder's book focuses on a recontextualization and recovery of the federating projects put forward by Césaire and Senghor. The absence of Glissant in his narrative suggests the dominance of the reception of Glissant as a poetic writer in the 1950s and 1960s who will emerge only later (after his Deleuzian encounter) as a notable but principally literary theorist.

36. Glissant's friends were militants. We have seen that he was in touch with Fanon, who sent a letter of support to the Front in 1961; they would also meet clandestinely in Rome in 1961. Béville, under the alias "Paul Niger" was a former colonial administrator turned militant who was on the radar of French intelligence. He was killed in 1962 in a freak air crash while trying to clandestinely reenter Guadeloupe. He was also a poet; he published a single collection, *Initiation*, with Seghers in 1954. Marcel Manville was a childhood friend of Fanon—a lawyer by training, he was defending Algerian National Liberation Front fighters and dissidents in court in 1955–1961, a cause that drew the ire of the Secret Armed Organization (OAS by its French initials), which threatened to assassinate him. Fanon would use his apartment in the west of Paris near the Porte de Champerret as a hideout during his stays in the capital. He continued his involvement in anticolonial and labor movements throughout his life and was bringing a suit before the French courts about the October 1961 police massacre of Algerians when he died in 1998. See Nesbitt, "Early Glissant." On Manville's life in these years, see David Macey's *Frantz Fanon: A Biography* (New York: Picador, 2000). On Béville, see Ronald Selbonne, *Albert Béville alias Paul Niger: Une négritude géométrique: Guadeloupe-France-Afrique* (Paris: Ibis Rouge, 2013).

37. The strength of these bonds of friendship can be gleaned from the speech Glissant gave honoring Béville and his comrades after the crash of 1962. See Édouard Glissant, "Discours prononcé par Édouard Glissant au nom de l'Association générale des Étudiants martiniquais à la soirée commémorative d'Albert Béville, Justin Catayée et Roger

Tropos, à Paris Palais de la Mutualité, le 6 juillet 1962," https://www.edouardglissant
.fr/discoursmutualite.html.

38. Glissant, *Soleil de la conscience*, 56.

39. Arthur Rimbaud, *Œuvres complètes* (Paris: Éditions Gallimard, 1963), 220, 244.

40. The *Cahier* was first published by Césaire in Paris in 1939, just before his return
to Martinique, in the surrealist journal *Volontés*. As A. James Arnold and Clayton Eshleman note the influence of Claudel and Rimbaud is more readily perceptible in the 1939
text in part because of Césaire's occasional adoption of Alexandrine lines; they also
note how the "I" of the poem is delayed, not appearing until strophe 25, unlike the subsequent and more commonly available editions where it intrudes earlier. The poem first
appeared in book form in Cuba, published in Havana by Molina y Compañía in 1942 in a
Spanish translation by Lydia Cabrera with a preface by the French Surrealist poet Benjamin Péret and illustrations by Wifredo Lam (Cabrera and Lam were also in turn published by Suzanne and Aimé Césaire in *Tropiques*, nos. 6-7, February 1943, 61-62). But
Césaire substantially continued revising the poem between 1939 and 1947, when it was
published in bilingual editions by Brentano in New York and Bordas in Paris. Césaire
made further changes to yet another revised edition published by Présence africaine in
1956. For this one, Césaire attempted to excise spiritual markers and bring it closer in
line with a socio-political and decolonial vision. The poem remains, as its editors and
most influential commentators (including Maryse Condé, the first to present a complete scholarly analysis of the poem in French in 1978) have always known, a poem of
great tension and ambiguity, insulated by "a zone of incandescence" as Césaire himself called it, that cannot be ideologically categorized. See A. James Arnold and Clayton Eshleman *The Original 1939 Notebook of a Return to the Native Land* (Middletown,
CT: Wesleyan University Press, 2013), xi-xx. On the paratextual importance and impact of Wifredo Lam as illustrator of the *Cahier*, see Richard Watts, "Translating Culture: Reading the Paratexts to Aimé Césaire's *Cahier d'un retour au pays natal*," *TTR* 13,
no. 2 (2000): 29-45.

41. André Breton, "A Great Black Poet," in *Notebook of a Return to the Native Land*,
trans. and ed. Clayton Eshleman and Annette Smith (Middletown, CT: Wesleyan University Press, 2001), xii.

42. Nathanaël notes that Glissant addressed the snow in the essay during a television interview from 1957 and provides an excellent summary: "Glissant identifies the
snow as the propulsive force behind the writing of his first essay. Comparing the im-
pression it sustains to that left by the flame trees of the Caribbean on European tourists
of the day, he insists on the greater weight of the snow for an Antillean, for its permanence in French pedagogy, which imparts the seasons and a displaced geography to the
students of what will soon become its overseas territories—derived from recent status
as colonies. The snow holds in its essence the whole of the colonial enterprise as meton-
ymy." *Sun of Consciousness* (New York: Nightboat Books, 2020), 83.

43. Glissant, *Sun of Consciousness*, 70.

44. "View of the mind. Foam of the city, on the wave, unglimpsed. Whether on the
wave, or in the city, the foam is fragile. It awaits the moment of being tried by the shore,
and until then it struggles to endure on its crest. As for the ferryman of foams, what can
he do in turn, if not endeavor to endure?" Glissant, *Sun of Consciousness*, 78.

45. Pascale Casanova, *The World Republic of Letters* (Cambridge, MA: Harvard University Press, 2004), 122.

46. Casanova, 123.

47. Bush, *Publishing Africa in French*, 216.

48. There is a persistent confusion in bibliographic sources over the correct publication date for *Les Indes*. I believe this is almost certainly due to Glissant's inclusion of the date mark 1955 within the poem—a detail I investigate closely here. Nevertheless, having examined the Falaize edition available in Princeton's Firestone Library, a first edition (Falaize did not have the means to print another) is marked "achevé d'imprimer juillet 1956" and is one of the 750 copies printed on "fleur d'alfa." The printer also indicates that fifty copies of the poem were printed with engraved illustrations by Enrique Zañartu. (Zañartu showed work at Galerie du Dragon and he notably provided illustrations of Dragon's 1972 edition of Pablo Neruda's *La rosa separada*.) For these reasons, I believe the correct date for the first publication to be July 1956.

49. Dominique O'Neill, *The Indies* (Toronto: Éditions du GREF, 1992).

50. O'Neill, *Indies*, 1.

51. Glissant, *Les Indes: Poème de l'une et l'autre terre* (Paris: Éditions Falaize, 1956), 63.

52. We set aside Horatio Nelson Huggins's *Hiroona*, completed before 1895 and first published in 1930, because he was not of African descent. For background on *Hiroona*, see A. James Arnold, ed., *History of Literature in the Caribbean*, vol. 2, *English- and Dutch-Speaking Regions* (Philadelphia: John Benjamins Publishing, 2001), 231.

53. My assertion that Glissant's *Les Indes* is the first epic in Francophone Caribbean poetry is based on the authority of the best surveys of the field. These include F. Abiolo Irele and Simon Gikandi, eds., *The Cambridge History of African and Caribbean Literature*, vol. 2 (New York: Cambridge University Press, 2000); Silvio Torres-Saillant, *An Intellectual History of the Caribbean* (New York: Palgrave Macmillan, 2006); A. James Arnold, *History of Literature in the Caribbean*, vol. 1, *Hispanic and Francophone Regions* (Philadelphia: John Benjamins Publishing, 1994). See especially Jack Corzani, "Poetry before Negritude," in *History of Literature in the Caribbean*, vol. 1, *Hispanic and Francophone Regions*, ed. James A. Arnold (Philadelphia: John Benjamins Publishing, 1994), 465-77. Also see Nick Nesbitt's chapter "Caribbean Literature in French: Origins and Development," in *The Cambridge History of African and Caribbean Literature*, ed. F. Abiolo Irele and Simon Gikandi, 2:643-69.

54. Maryse Condé, "Memories of Reading *Les Indes* for the First Time," trans. Celia Britton, *Callaloo* 36, no. 4 (2013): 867.

55. Nick Nesbitt, *Caribbean Critique: Antillean Critical Theory from Toussaint to Glissant* (Liverpool, UK: Liverpool University Press, 2013), 244.

56. Glissant, *Les Indes*, 44.

57. O'Neill, *Indies*, 66, 74.

58. O'Neill, 75-89.

59. Ezra Pound, *ABC of Reading* (1934; New York: New Directions, 1987), 43-44.

60. Glissant, *Les Indes*, 65.

61. Stephen Halliwell, *The Poetics of Aristotle: Translation and Commentary*, (Chapel Hill: University of North Carolina Press, 1987), 116.

62. Aristotle, *Poetics* (New York: Penguin, 1996), xxx.

63. "We need only remember that the form of history is movement, not just at obvious flash points but, for those who experience it, at all points. History, as we know (experience) it, is under way toward the truths at which it never finally arrives. Historical actors are always, knowingly or (more usually) unknowingly, turning events and

struggling against the counterturns of others." Marshall Brown, *Turning Points: Essays in the History of Cultural Expressions* (Stanford, CA: Stanford University Press, 1997), 28.

64. Paul Ricoeur sees a connection between peripeteia, recognition, and the ipseity of self-recognition that only a narrative identity can confer, one that results from the kind of knowledge produced only when perceiving one's continuity in light of the reversals of experience. *Les Indes* could also be thought of, in this sense, as an attempt to use the epic as a means to produce a narrative identity for the Antillean subject, or just Antillean identity tout court. "It is in this way that personal identity, considered as enduring over time, can be defined as a narrative identity, at the intersection of the coherence conferred by emplotment and the discordance arising from the peripeteia within the narrated action." Paul Ricoeur, *The Course of Recognition*, trans. David Pellauer (Cambridge, MA: Harvard University Press, 2007), 101. The wake is Sharpe's metaphor for the afterlife of slavery, which she argues constitutes the unifying temporality of black life under modernity: "To be *in* the wake is to occupy and to be occupied by the continuous and changing present of slavery's as yet unresolved unfolding." Christina Sharpe, *In the Wake: On Blackness and Being* (Durham, NC: Duke University Press, 2016), 13.

65. Glissant, *Les Indes*, 58; Louis Delgrès (1766–1802) was a Creole born in Saint-Pierre, Martinique, who led an insurgency in Guadeloupe against Napoleon's troops who had come to reimpose slavery on the island. Cornered at Matouba, his band of resistance fighters chose to blow themselves up and inflict casualties rather than surrender. On the historiographic trope of the "primitive" and its haunting return, see Hayden White, *Tropics of Discourse* (Baltimore: Johns Hopkins University Press, 1978), 180.

66. Glissant, *Les Indes*, 18, 14.

67. Glissant, 91.

68. Kathleen Gyssels isolates and analyzes patterns of imagery in close readings of the poems. See her "Scarlet Ibises and the Poetics of Relation: Perse, Walcott and Glissant," *Commonwealth Essays and Studies* 31 (2008): 103–16.

69. Apart from Glissant, the most important legacy of his influence is in the work of Derek Walcott, who would take the Caribbean epic arguably to its greatest heights in *Omeros*. It is interesting that Glissant and Walcott cite the same pair of poets as decisively influential: Aimé Césaire and Saint-John Perse. Walcott memorably compares them in his essay "The Muse of History" as the "Prospero and Caliban" of Antillean poetry. The poetic model of Perse is invoked again in "The Antilles: Fragments of Epic Memory"; both essays for obvious reasons are crucial points of reference for thinking about the form and tradition of epic in a Caribbean context. See Derek Walcott, *What the Twilight Says: Essays* (London: Faber and Faber, 1998), 36–84.

70. The French poet and critic Jacques Charpier (who Suzy Cater reminds us was part of the circle of poets in the art world around Glissant in the 1950s) wrote a monograph on Saint-John Perse published by Gallimard in 1962; Alain Bosquet and Maurice Saillet also produced studies in the mid-1950s and early 1960s. Princeton University Press's Bollingen Series published translations by Denis Devlin, *Exile* (1949); Louise Varèse, *Éloges and Other Poems* (1956); Hugh Chisholm, *Winds* (1956); Wallace Fowlie, *Seamarks* (1958); and Robert Fitzgerald, *Chroniques* (1961). On the diplomatic side, Perse was close to the Kennedys and contributed to Pierre Salinger's *A Tribute to John F. Kennedy* (1964). The point here is to recall the transatlantic consensus promoting and celebrating Perse at the height of the Cold War as a figure of intellectual brilliance and

humanistic excellence. For a young, little-known, Afro-Antillean poet like Glissant to check such a revered figure and implicitly insert himself as the rightful heir to this position in 1956 can be fully appreciated only by recognizing the relative cultural capital available to each within the terms of those early postwar years.

71. Glissant, "Saint-John Perse et les Antilles," *La nouvelle revue française*, no. 278 (February 1976): 73.

72. See Bernadette Cailler, *Conquérants de la nuit nue: Édouard Glissant et l'H(h)istoire antillaise* (Tübingen, Germany: Gunter Narr Verlag, 1988), 40–67.

73. For Perse's influences on Glissant, see Dash, *Édouard Glissant* (New York: Cambridge University Press, 1995) 30–37.

74. Glissant, "Saint-John Perse and the Caribbean," in *Caribbean Discourse* (Charlottesville: University of Virginia Press, 1989), 225–31.

75. Glissant, 227.

76. Glissant, 230, 227.

77. Édouard Glissant, "Carthage," *Lettres nouvelles* 4, no. 43 (1956): 559–63.

78. For commentary on the meanings of these lines in *Anabase* and uses of salt throughout the poem, see Bernard Weinberg, "Saint-John Perse's *Anabase*," *Chicago Review* 15, no. 3 (1962): 83–85.

79. John E. Drabinski, *Glissant and the Middle Passage: Philosophy, Beginning, Abyss* (Minneapolis: University of Minnesota Press, 2019), 45.

80. Édouard Glissant, *Collected Poems*, ed. Jefferson Humphries, trans. Melissa Manolas (Minneapolis: University of Minnesota Press, 2005), 108.

81. See René Galand's chapter devoted to *Winds*, "The Epic of Mankind," in *Saint-John Perse* (New York: Twayne Publishers, 1972), 88–107, 104–5.

82. Saint-John Perse, *Oeuvre poétique I* (Paris: Gallimard, 1953), 121.

83. Saint-John Perse, *Winds*, trans. Hugh Chisholm (New York: Pantheon, 1953).

84. Vijay Prashad, *The Darker Nations: A People's History of the Third World* (New York: New Press, 2007), 32–33.

85. Quoted in Christopher J. Lee's introduction to *Making a World after Empire: The Bandung Moment and Its Afterlives* (Athens: Ohio University Press, 2010), 9. Revisions of Bandung have been plentiful in recent years. I have in mind specifically the collected essays in Lee's *Making a World*, as well as the excellent documentary study of Richard Wright's participation in the conference: Brian Russell Roberts and Keith Foulcher's *Indonesian Notebook: A Sourcebook on Richard Wright and the Bandung Conference* (Durham, NC: Duke University Press, 2016).

86. "I confused a man, love, and marriage with making the revolution," Condé says in an interview with Rebecca Wolff. See Rebecca Wolff, "Interview: Maryse Condé," *BOMB*, July 1, 1999, 74–80.

87. Condé, "Memories of Reading *Les Indes*," 865.

88. Condé, 865.

89. Condé, 866.

90. Maryse Condé, "Autour d'une littérature antillaise," *Présence africaine* 81, no. 1 (1972): 170–71.

91. "And here I am. Face to face with myself. Trapped. For ever. For ever? All this time he's talking. What's he saying? 'It's Spring now in Paris.' Spring? The streetcleaner on the rue de l'Université will have taken off his thick, blue turtleneck sweater that shows under his overalls. Will he have noticed my absence? How will he welcome me

back? Yet another flight! One day I'll have to break the silence. I'll have to explain. What? This mistake, this tragic mistake I couldn't help making, being what I am. My ancestors led me on. What more can I say? I looked for myself in the wrong place. In the arms of an assassin. Come now, don't use big words. Always dramatizing. Spring? Yes, it's Spring in Paris." Maryse Condé, *Hérémakhonon*, trans. Richard Philcox (Washington, DC: Three Continents Press, 1982), 176.

92. Édouard Glissant, *Les Indes*, trans. Dominique O'Neill (Toronto: Éditions du GREF, 1992), 23.

93. Sylvia Wynter, "The Ceremony Must Be Found: After Humanism," *boundary 2* 12–13, no. 1 (1984): 28–29.

94. Wynter, 57.

95. Sylvia Wynter, "Beyond the Word of Man: Glissant and the New Discourse of the Antilles," *World Literature Today* 63, no. 4 (1989): 637–48.

96. Wynter, 639. Nick Nesbitt offers an astute and, I think, convergent analysis of the politics of *La lézarde* in "Early Glissant."

97. Wynter, "Beyond the Word of Man," 643.

98. Wynter, 644.

99. Sylvia Wynter, "1492: A New World View," in *Race, Discourse, and the Origin of the Americas: A New World View* (Washington, DC: Smithsonian Institution Press, 1995), 8, original emphasis. It is, of course, no simple matter to give a comprehensive account of such a far-and-wide-ranging thinker, but it is instructive to note the importance of the pivotal "Copernican" 1492 account that Wynter herself suggests as a kind of summa of her thinking in her extensive interview with David Scott. See David Scott, "The Re-Enchantment of Humanism: An Interview with Sylvia Wynter," *Small Axe* 8 (September 2000): 119–207. The entire interview is relevant, but on 1492 see especially 191–207. Walter Mignolo provides an extensive treatment of Wynter's decolonial epistemic project while likewise reasserting the centrality 1492. See his chapter "Sylvia Wynter: What Does It Mean to be Human?," in *Sylvia Wynter: On Being Human as Praxis*, ed. Katherine McKittrick (Durham, NC: Duke University Press, 2015), 106–23.

100. Wynter, "Beyond the Word of Man," 646.

101. Wynter's role in the critical arguments of the 1960s and 1970s, particularly in debates with Kenneth Ramchand, Kamau Braithwaite, and others, including the 1971 Association for Commonwealth Literature and Language Studies conference in Kingston, Jamaica, are summarized by Norval Edwards in "The Foundational Generation: From *The Beacon* to *Savacou*," in *The Routledge Companion to Anglophone Caribbean Literature*, ed. Michael A. Bucknor and Alison Donnell (New York: Routledge, 2011), 111–23. It's worth noting that her position at Stanford was itself somewhat amphibious (ambiguous) because she was officially a member of the Spanish and Portuguese Department there.

102. This is reflected in the collection of essays from leading scholars responding to her work gathered and edited by Katherine McKittrick, *Sylvia Wynter: On Being Human as Praxis* (Durham, NC: Duke University Press, 2015). It is still too early to be able to clearly discern the reasons for her abrupt and swift "rediscovery" (particularly in the American academy). However, one can speculate that the post-2008 landscape, with its increasing sense of ecological dread, racial tension, and political dysfunction, as well as fracturing consensus over the role of the humanities in the contemporary university, has sharpened interest in Wynter's theories, in particular her more recent

work on "overrepresentation" and "ethnoclass" as aspects of a "coloniality of being" usurping and arrogating the planet's resources to itself in a pattern of "overconsumption on the part of the rich techno-industrial North"—as set out in her 2003 essay "Unsettling the Coloniality of Being/Power/Truth/Freedom: Towards the Human, after Man, Its Overrepresentation—An Argument," *CR: The New Centennial Review* 3, no. 3 (2003): 257–337.

103. Interview conducted on February 6, 1957, and produced by the Office National de Radiodiffusion Télévision Française. The footage of this interview has been archived by the Institut National de l'Audiovisuel, at http://www.ina.fr/video/I05251873 /edouard-glissant-a-propos-des-livres-les-indes-et-soleil-de-la-conscience-video .html.

Chapter Three

1. Jean-Christophe Cloutier has drawn particular attention to the fate of Ann Petry's papers, parts of Ralph Ellison's archive, and, most famously, his recovery of Claude McKay's lost novel, *Amiable with Big Teeth*. See Jean-Christophe Cloutier, *Shadow Archives: The Lifecycles of African American Literature* (New York: Columbia University Press, 2019).

2. Kinohi Nishikawa, "The Archive on Its Own: Black Politics, Independent Publishing, and the *Negotiations*," *MELUS* 40, no. 3 (2015): 177.

3. Anthony Reed, *Freedom Time: The Poetics and Politics of Black Experimental Writing* (Baltimore: Johns Hopkins University Press, 2016), 3.

4. Reed, 3.

5. Reed, 3–4.

6. Werner Sollors argued early on for a "populist modernism" in Amiri Baraka poetics; Aldon Nielsen, Tony Bolden, and Michael North treated black modernist poetics in depth; Geoffrey Jacques, Nathaniel Mackey, and Evie Shockley all chronicled the renegade innovations to poetics made by Afro-modernist poets. Melvin Tolson's *Harlem Gallery* (1965) has garnered long-overdue attention in studies by Matthew Hart and Lena Hill. See Werner Sollors, *Amiri Baraka/LeRoi Jones: The Quest for a Populist Modernism* (New York: Columbia University Press, 1978); Michael North, *The Dialect of Modernism: Race, Language, and Twentieth-Century Literature* (New York: Oxford University Press, 1994); Aldon Lynn Nielsen, *Black Chant: Languages of African-American Postmodernism* (New York: Cambridge University Press, 1997); Tony Bolden, *Afro-Blue: Improvisations in African American Poetry and Culture* (Champaign: University of Illinois Press, 2003); Evie Shockley, *Renegade Poetics: Black Aesthetics and Formal Innovation in African American Poetry* (Iowa City: University of Iowa Press, 2011); Geoffrey Jacques, *A Change in the Weather: Modernist Imagination, African American Imaginary* (Amherst: University of Massachusetts Press, 2009); Nathaniel Mackey, *Discrepant Engagement: Dissonance, Cross-Culturality, and Experimental Writing* (New York: Cambridge University Press, 1993); Matthew Hart, *Nations of Nothing But Poetry: Modernism, Transnationalism, and Synthetic Vernacular Writing* (New York: Oxford University Press, 2010); Lena Hill, *Visualizing Blackness and the Creation of the African American Literary Tradition* (New York: Cambridge University Press, 2014).

7. The original Sanborn maps for Kansas City are held by the Kenneth Spencer Research Library at the University of Kansas. Sanborn maps are large, lithographed street

plans created by the Sanborn Map Company for the purposes of assessing fire insurance for underwriters in US cities. The maps were produced between 1867 and 1961; the Kansas City map showing Vincent O. Carter's neighborhood was produced in 1909. They have been digitized and can be viewed online at https://digital.lib.ku.edu/ku -sanborn/root. The highway system's origins lie in Thomas Harris MacDonald's tenure at the powerful Bureau of Public Roads (1919-1939), but the proximate factors for Eisenhower's Highway Act were war needs (including FDR's concern over finding jobs for returning veterans) and military planning in a Cold War context. See Thomas L. Karnes, *Asphalt and Politics: A History of the American Highway* (Jefferson, NC: McFarland & Co., 2009), esp. 121–31; Tom Lewis, *Divided Highways: Building the Interstate Highways, Transforming American Life* (New York: Viking Penguin, 1997).

8. Joe and Eola Carter's birth year can be definitively ascertained from their appearance in a news report in the *Kansas City Times*, on Wednesday, August 4, 1965, at p. 3, in which each is said to be fifty-seven years old. They were both wounded but successfully defended themselves from a holdup and robbery, during which the assailant was killed when he was pushed from the third-floor balcony.

9. Founded in 1854, Lincoln University was the first historically black university in the United States. Carter enrolled just as Horace Mann Bond, the university's first black president, was beginning his tenure in 1945. Prominent literary alumni at the time of Carter's enrollment included the poets Langston Hughes and Melvin B. Tolson, whose legacy at the university may have influenced Carter's decision to attend. Two other giants whose presence he would have felt strongly on campus were Thurgood Marshall (class of 1930), who in those years was leading the National Association for the Advancement of Colored People's Legal Defense and Educational Fund, and Kwame Nkrumah (class of 1939), whose incarceration for his anticolonial political activism with the United Gold Coast Convention in 1948 would have been a major topic of campus interest and conversation.

10. On the New Literary Club and Vincent O. Carter's time at Lincoln, see his entry in Lincoln University's yearbook, *The 1950 Lion* (Philadelphia: Clark Printing House, 1950).

11. Oliver Franklin, "Notes on Vincent O. Carter '50." Carter didn't talk much about his time at Lincoln with Liselotte Haas, but he often spoke of his affection for a certain "Roscoe." As Franklin notes, Browne was voted most popular professor by the college paper, the *Lincolnian*, in 1947.

12. Herbert R. Lottman, "Preface: The Invisible Writer," in *The Bern Book: A Record of a Voyage of the Mind*, by Vincent O. Carter (New York: John Day Co., 1970), ix.

13. Lottman, x.

14. Lottman's dating may be slightly off here, or there may have been early manuscripts for the novel that circulated. The best evidence for dating *The Primary Colors* is a letter sent by Carter to Lottman dated "Bern, April 3rd, 1970," which references the manuscript in a passage recommending that Lottman encourage his agent "Eileen" to keep pressing the issue with the publisher: "I was very sorry that I didn't have the ms of the Primary Colors ready to give her, it is being freshly typed and is now finished but for the proof reading. Perhaps, if you could communicate your enthusiasm for that book, it might help to arouse her curiosity." In a letter to his mother and dated from Bern on October 16, 1969, Carter mentions having found "a very nice girl who has agreed to type the manuscript of The Primary Colors for practically nothing!" The letter was among

the papers kept by Liselotte Haas and acquired in 2002 by Chip Fleischer at Steerforth Press. Mr. Fleischer kindly sent me a photocopy of the letter.

15. The unpublished manuscript fragment entitled "The Secret" was among the papers kept by Liselotte Haas and acquired in 2002 by Chip Fleischer at Steerforth Press. The autograph copy remains in Mr. Fleischer's possession, and he kindly sent me copies to examine.

16. *Cultural Affairs* was founded in 1968 as a quarterly journal covering the intersection of the arts and public policy in order to promote the influence of the Associated Councils of the Arts, a Rockefeller Foundation–sponsored project to bring American business and arts communities into closer cooperation and to promote publicly funded local arts programs.

17. Ellison fended off criticism of the council in the press and was highly loyal to its chairman Roger Stevens. See Arnold Rampersad, *Ralph Ellison: A Biography* (New York: Vintage, 2008), 426–27.

18. Lottman, "Preface," v.

19. Lottman, ix.

20. Nona Balakian, "Black Odyssey, White World," *New York Times Book Review*, July 21, 1973, 25.

21. Darryl Pinckney, *Out There: Mavericks of Black Literature* (New York: Basic Civitas Books, 2002), xiv.

22. Pinckney, 63–64.

23. After reviewers complained about the novel's opening section, Steerforth cut forty-five pages from the opening, so there are two versions of the novel in circulation: the 2003 hardcover, which faithfully reproduces the manuscript Carter left in Liselotte Haas's care at his death, and the shortened paperback version of 2004. The rest of Vincent Carter's known autograph manuscripts are in the hands of Chip Fleischer at Steerforth and Mr. Oliver Franklin, OBE, of Philadelphia, an amateur collector and bibliophile who is also a graduate of Lincoln and Oxford universities.

24. Whitney Terrell, "At the Crossroads," *New York Times Book Review*, April 20, 2003, 30.

25. Terrell, 30.

26. Terrell, 30.

27. See Kevin Quashie, *The Sovereignty of Quiet: Beyond Resistance in Black Culture* (New Brunswick, NJ: Rutgers University Press, 2012).

28. Vincent O. Carter, *The Bern Book: A Record of a Voyage of the Mind* (New York: John Day Co., 1970), xv.

29. Carter, xv.

30. Carter, xvi.

31. Carter, xvi.

32. An 1897 edition of the Meyers guide to Switzerland can be viewed at the Hathi Trust, at https://catalog.hathitrust.org/Record/006511266. Copies of this edition are widely available in major research libraries.

33. See "Meyer/Bibliographisches Institut," *The Oxford Companion to the Book* (Oxford: Oxford University Press, 2010), http://www.oxfordreference.com/view/10.1093/acref/9780198606536.001.0001/acref-9780198606536-e-3159.

34. Jonathan Wipplinger, "The Racial Ruse: On Blackness and Blackface Comedy in Fin-de-Siècle Germany," *German Quarterly* 84, no. 4 (2011): 463, emphasis added.

35. Carter, *Bern Book*, 4.

36. Carter, 5.

37. Carter, 50, original emphasis.

38. Carter, 50.

39. Carter, 282.

40. Carter archives his own arrival in Bern in a comical, mock-heroic conquistador voice: "And so on June 21st, in the Year of Our Lord, 1953, I, Vincent O. Carter, did sign the register of the Adler Hotel (the Eagle) in the very street through which the prancing steeds had borne the armored knights. The street was the Gerechtigkeitsgasse, which means Street of Justice!" Carter, 71–72. The hotel Carter refers to still operates under the name Hotel zum Goldigen Adler (the Golden Eagle) at 7 Gerechtigkeitsgasse, in Bern.

41. Lisa Colletta, ed., *The Legacy of the Grand Tour: New Essays on Travel, Literature, and Culture* (Lanham: Fairleigh Dickinson University Press, 2015), x.

42. Mikhail Bakhtin, *Problems of Dostoevsky's Poetics* (Minneapolis: University of Minnesota Press, 1984), 185, original emphasis.

43. Carter, *Bern Book*, 176.

44. Claudia Tate, *Psychoanalysis and Black Novels: Desire and the Protocols of Race* (New York: Oxford University Press, 1998), 13.

45. Garnette Cadogan's essays about walking while black are among the best contemporary sources we have for answering this question empirically. See, e.g., "Due North," in *Tales of Two Cities: Stories of Inequality in a Divided New York*, ed. John Freeman (New York: Penguin, 2015), 1–11.

46. Carter, *Bern Book*, 269.

47. Carter, 269.

48. Carter, 271.

49. Susan Buck-Morss, "The Flaneur, the Sandwichman and the Whore: The Politics of Loitering," *New German Critique*, no. 39 (Autumn 1986): 136.

50. The Situationist International was founded in 1957 (the same year Carter finished *The Bern Book*) at Cosio d'Arroscia, Italy, when Asger Jorn a leader of the Movement for an Imagist Bauhaus, and Guy Debord, then a leading member of the Lettrist International, decided to join forces. In their early years, the situationists were by virtue of their antecedents preoccupied more with artistic practice and its theorization. To be fair, they did devote the tenth issue of their journal (1966) to the Algerian Independence Struggle, and Debord expressed solidarity with the wars of decolonization. Nevertheless, the bulk of the Situationist International's theorizations have always had an oblique relation to decolonization, racism, and the history of slavery and colonial violence. Regardless, Debord's years of flânerie and intellectual formation on the Left Bank in the 1950s were available as an experience to him in ways that Carter makes clear were not possible for, or were experienced very differently as, a black writer. For background on the Situationist International, strategy, its relation to Western Marxism, and other struggles, see Peter Wollen, "The Situationist International," *New Left Review*, March 1, 1989, 72–95; Stevphen Shukaitis, "'Theories Are Made Only to Die in the War of Time': Guy Debord and the Situationist International as Strategic Thinkers," *Culture and Organization* 20, no. 4 (2014): 251–68; Tom McDonough, "Unrepresentable Enemies: On the Legacy of Guy Debord and the Situationist International," *Afterall: A Journal of Art, Context and Enquiry*, no. 28 (Autumn–Winter 2011): 42–55; Guy Debord,

Correspondence: The Foundation of the Situationist International (June 1957–August 1960) (Los Angeles: Semiotext[e], 2009); Ken Knabb, ed. and trans., *Situationist International Anthology* (Berkeley, CA: Bureau of Public Secrets, 2006).

51. Buck-Morss, "The Flaneur, the Sandwichman and the Whore," 137.

52. Carter, *Bern Book*, 279.

53. Carter, 294.

54. Carter, 296.

55. Carter, 296.

56. Sugrue's case study is Detroit, but his analysis applies broadly to the urban, industrial cities of the Midwest like Kansas City. See Thomas J. Sugrue, *The Origins of the Urban Crisis: Race and Inequality in Postwar Detroit* (Princeton, NJ: Princeton University Press, 1996), 3–5. On the history of segregation, urbanism, and development in Kansas City, see Sherry Lamb Schirmer, *A City Divided: The Racial Landscape of Kansas City, 1900–1960* (Columbia: University of Missouri Press, 2002). For case studies and essays exploring the "intimate relationship between race and real estate," see Adrienne Brown and Valerie Smith, eds., *Race and Real Estate* (New York: Oxford University Press, 2015). For an administrative and legal history of federal intervention in housing segregation policy and ensuing white flight to the suburbs, see Richard Rothstein, *The Color of Law: A Forgotten History of How Our Government Segregated America* (New York: W. W. Norton & Co., 2017).

57. "Vincent O. Carter to Herbert Lottman Letter nd/1973." This letter was among the papers kept by Liselotte Haas and acquired in 2002 by Chip Fleischer at Steerforth Press. The autograph copy remains in Mr. Fleischer's possession, and he kindly sent me copies to examine.

58. Isabel Wilkerson, *The Warmth of Other Suns: The Epic Story of America's Great Migration* (New York: Vintage, 2010), 10.

59. Farah Jasmine Griffin, *Who Set You Flowin'? The African-American Migration Narrative* (New York: Oxford University Press, 1995), 5.

60. Toni Morrison, "City Limits, Village Values: Concepts of the Neighborhood in Black Fiction," in *Literature and the American Urban Experience: Essays on the City and Literature*, ed. Michael C. Jaye and Ann Chalmers Watts (New Brunswick, NJ: Rutgers University Press, 1981), 37.

61. Morrison, 37.

62. Morrison, 38.

63. Madhu Dubey, *Signs and Cities: Black Literary Postmodernism* (Chicago: University of Chicago Press, 2003), 2.

64. Dubey, 4.

65. Dubey, 236. Morrison's assertion, which Dubey explicitly acknowledges, is in fact: "If anything I do, in the way of writing novels … isn't about the village or the community or about you, then it is not about anything … which is to say, yes, the work must be political." For Morrison's comments in context, see her "Rootedness: The Ancestor as Foundation," in *I Am Because We Are: Readings in Africana Philosophy*, ed. Fred Lee Hord and Jonathan Scott Lee (Amherst: University of Massachusetts Press, 2016), 397–403.

66. In a fuller material history of these transformations, one would go on to include the physical destruction and degradation of the urban landscape in the wake of the riots of the 1960s, as the promise and hope of integration through civil rights wavered and

foundered under the onslaught of political assassinations, prominent cases of police brutality, the loss of employment opportunity brought on by deindustrialization, the flight of capital to less developed countries enabled by free-trade deregulation, and the financialization of markets, as well as improvements in telecommunications technology, packaging, and container shipping. For a political history of these years of transformation, see Manning Marable, *Race, Reform, and Rebellion: The Second Reconstruction and beyond in Black America, 1945-2006*, 3rd ed. (Jackson: University Press of Mississippi, 2007), esp. "The Cold War in Black America, 1945-1954," at 12-37.

67. "The Interstate made long-distance commuting possible, thereby contributing to the 'white flight' that separated races and classes from each other. More often than not, urban planners laid down the roadways in the neighborhoods of African-Americans, Hispanics, and other minorities, people who did not possess the political power to challenge them. In the ensuing years, planners and residents alike found that new highways had the power to divide rather than unite us, and that they could transform a once vibrant neighborhood into a cold, alien landscape." Lewis, *Divided Highways*, xiv.

68. Dubey, *Signs and Cities*, 236.

69. For a publishing and reception history of African American pulp fiction, see Justin Gifford, *Pimping Fictions: African American Crime Literature and the Untold Story of Black Pulp Publishing* (Philadelphia: Temple University Press, 2013). For a remarkable case study, see Kinohi Nishikawa, "The Archive on Its Own: Black Politics, Independent Publishing, and *The Negotiations*," *MELUS* 40, no. 3 (2015): 176-201.

70. I am indebted to Brooks Hefner for bringing this body of work to my attention. I base these observations on the findings he presented in his paper "Popular Literary Production and Radical Genre Revision in African American Newspapers, 1928-1955," delivered at the conference "The Arts in the Black Press during the Age of Jim Crow," Yale University, March 2017.

71. Sonny Gibson, *Kansas City: Mecca of the New Negro* (Kansas City: Self-published, 1997).

72. The booklet appears to have been modeled on *Your Saint Louis and Mine*, a history of black St. Louis published in 1937 by their older brother Ben Young, a self-taught illustrator, amateur historian, and co-owner of the *St. Louis American* newspaper. For the history of the Young family, particularly in relation to these publications, see Antonio F. Holland, *Nathan B. Young and the Struggle over Black Higher Education* (Columbia: University of Missouri Press, 2006), 194-96.

73. See Evelyn Brooks Higginbotham, *Righteous Discontent: The Women's Movement in the Black Baptist Church, 1880-1920* (Cambridge, MA: Harvard University Press, 1993). It's worth noting in this regard that the Youngs devote a large section of *Your Kansas City and Mine* to local church history and prominent clergy members. Throughout the text, it is easily apparent that being active in civic and religious life are often overlapping or even synonymous for men and women alike. William H. Young and Nathan B. Young Jr., eds., *Your Kansas City and Mine* (Kansas City: n.p., 1950).

74. Young and Young, *Your Kansas City and Mine*, iv.

75. A cultural history of the city in this era is presented in John Simonson, *Paris of the Plains: Kansas City from Doughboys to Expressways* (Charleston, SC: History Press, 2010).

76. Most evidence suggests that Carter was proficient enough in German to have

read Grass in 1959; *The Tin Drum* was translated into English in 1961, and we know Carter was actively at work on *The Primary Colors* in the years 1957–1963.

77. Vincent O. Carter, *Such Sweet Thunder* (Hanover, NH: Steerforth Press, 2003), 3.

78. One of the most substantial sources of information for Franklin and *The Call* is the essay dedicated to the paper and its competitors the *St. Louis Argus* and the *St. Louis American* by George Everett Slavens, *The Black Press in the South, 1865–1979*, ed. Henry Lewis Suggs (Westport, CT: Greenwood Press, 1983), 214–56. More detailed information about operations, sales, and marketing is contained in Noel Wilson, "The Kansas City Call and the Negro Market" (PhD diss., University of Illinois, 1971). An important profile of Franklin and the paper is featured in Young and Young, *Your Kansas City and Mine*, 12–13.

79. For the history of that migration, see Nell Irvin Painter, *Exodusters: Black Migration to Kansas after Reconstruction* (New York: W. W. Norton & Co., 1992).

80. Darlene Clark Hine, "Black Professionals and Race Consciousness: Origins of the Civil Rights Movement, 1890–1950," *Journal of American History* 89, no. 4 (2003): 1279–94.

81. Young and Young, *Your Kansas City and Mine*, 13.

82. Wilson, "Kansas City Call," 10.

83. Young and Young, *Your Kansas City and Mine*, 12.

84. Carter, *Such Sweet Thunder*, 49.

85. Carter, 404.

86. See Roy Wilkins, *Standing Fast: The Autobiography of Roy Wilkins* (New York: Da Capo Press, 1994), 64–65.

87. See Sherry Lamb Schirmer, *A City Divided: The Racial Landscape of Kansas City, 1900–1960* (Columbia: University of Missouri Press, 2002), 249.

88. See Wilkins, *Standing Fast*, 65.

89. Carter, *Such Sweet Thunder*, 195–96.

90. Jacqueline Goldsby, *A Spectacular Secret: Lynching in American Life and Literature* (Chicago: University of Chicago Press, 2006), 6.

91. "As gently as I could, I urged Franklin to dilute some of the blood and gore with more serious news." Wilkins, *Standing Fast*, 59–60.

92. Carter, *Such Sweet Thunder*, 198.

93. Carter, 199.

94. Carter, 203.

95. Carter, 201.

96. Carter, 202.

97. Wilkins, *Standing Fast*, 77

98. Carter, *Such Sweet Thunder*, 371.

99. Benedict Anderson, *Imagined Communities: Reflections on the Origin and Spread of Nationalism* (New York: Verso, 1983).

100. Walter Benjamin, *The Writer of Modern Life: Essays on Charles Baudelaire*, trans. Edmund Jephcott, Harry Zohn, Howard Eiland, and Rodney Livingstone (Cambridge, MA: Harvard University Press, 2006), 68.

101. Quoted in Benjamin, 72.

102. Benjamin, 40.

103. See Monroe Dodd, *A Splendid Ride: The Streetcars of Kansas City, 1870–1957* (Kansas City: Kansas City Star Books, 2002), 113.

104. Arthur Lubow, "A Portrait of America That Still Haunts, Decades Later," *New York Times*, June 12, 2020.

105. Roland Barthes, *Image-Music-Text*, trans. Stephen Heath (New York: Hill and Wang, 1977), 182.

Chapter Four

1. Toni Cade Bambara, "Report from Part One," *New York Times Book Review*, January 7, 1973.

2. Gwendolyn Brooks, *Report from Part One* (Detroit: Broadside Press, 1972), 167.

3. Brooks, 167.

4. I have in mind Edwards's succinct description of the performative characteristics of a "gender hierarchy ... that also announces itself anew, in event after event, through appeals to the leader's mystical authority and through the affective complex of anticipation and arrival that is built into the charismatic leadership scenario." Erica R. Edwards, *Charisma and the Fictions of Black Leadership* (Minneapolis: University of Minnesota Press, 2012), xiii.

5. Brooks, *Report from Part One*, 84.

6. Brooks, 84–85.

7. Brooks, 85.

8. Brooks, 85.

9. See Anna Holmes, "The Underground Art of the Insult," *New York Times*, May 17, 2015, 13.

10. Don L. Lee (Haki Madhubuti), "Gwendolyn Brooks: Beyond the Wordmaker— The Making of an African Poet," in *Report from Part One*, by Gwendolyn Brooks (Detroit: Broadside Press, 1972), 17.

11. The Brooks episode was titled "Poet in Bronzeville." First airing on June 27, 1948, *Destination Freedom* offered popularized accounts by and for a black audience about major figures in African American history with unprecedented dignity of representation in the popular medium. In a sign of the Cold War anticommunist turn, in August 1950, Durham was axed and the show's format was repurposed to showcase popular white historical figures instead of black ones. See Richard Durham's *Destination Freedom: Scripts from Radio's Black Legacy, 1948–50*, ed. J. Fred MacDonald (New York: Praeger, 1989), 1–11.

12. J. Saunders Redding, "Cellini-Like Lyrics," *Saturday Review of Literature*, September 17, 1949, reprinted in Stephen Caldwell Wright, ed., *On Gwendolyn Brooks: Reliant Contemplation* (Ann Arbor: University of Michigan Press, 2001), 6–7.

13. Langston Hughes, "Name, Race, and Gift in Common," *Voices*, Winter 1950, 54–56.

14. "Once in a great while there is one good poem mixed in with several mediocre ones. And once in a blue moon a Gwendolyn Brooks turns up!" Langston Hughes to Ray Durem, February 27, 1954, in *The Selected Letters of Langston Hughes*, edited by Arnold Rampersad and David Roessel (New York: Alfred A. Knopf, 2015), 381.

15. Toni Cade Bambara, "Report from Part One," *New York Times Book Review*, January 7, 1973.

16. "Though much has been made of the change in Brooks's consciousness that occurred in 1967 ... her use of Black subjects and concern for Black people permeate her

entire canon as much as her mastery of indirection." Joyce's emphasis on continuity should be understood as part of her concern with "detaching Gwendolyn Brooks's poetry from the branches of the Euro-American poetic tradition and planting it at the root of the Afrocentric one." My interest is not in adjudicating which "tree" Brooks springs from (though it seems to me they are obviously painfully entangled), but rather to examine the immediate soil in which her inspiration grew, a very particular articulation of black vernacular modernity in formation—a moment enmeshed in the politics and material cultural of midcentury America that Brooks sets out to dissect. See Joyce A. Joyce, "The Poetry of Gwendolyn Brooks: An Afrocentric Exploration," in *On Gwendolyn Brooks: Reliant Contemplation*, ed. Stephen Caldwell Wright (Ann Arbor: University of Michigan Press, 2001), 246-53.

17. Adam Green, *Selling the Race: Culture, Community, and Black Chicago, 1940-1955* (Chicago: University of Chicago Press, 2007).

18. Alan M. Wald, "Cold War Modernity," *Modernism/Modernity* 21, no. 4 (2014): 1017-23.

19. The complete list, including the earlier version gathered in her *Scratch Book* diary, is reprinted in its entirety in George E. Kent's biography, *Gwendolyn Brooks: A Life* (Lexington: University Press of Kentucky, 1989), 27-28. Kent notes that she later edited the entry as she mused over whether it should be a monthly or a weekly: "She preferred the weekly and crossed out the outline of contents for the monthly. With something of a flourish, she added 'containing works of high quality only'" (28).

20. See Pierre Bourdieu, *The Field of Cultural Production* (New York: Columbia University Press, 1993), 30-33.

21. Robert Bone and Richard Courage argue that 1931 was the pivotal year when Chicago began to overtake Harlem as the center of the renaissance. See Robert A. Bone and Richard A. Courage, *The Muse in Bronzeville: African American Creative Expression in Chicago, 1932-1950* (New Brunswick, NJ: Rutgers University Press, 2011), 89-94.

22. Jacqueline Goldsby has presented several lectures on the subject, including "A Salon for the Masses: Black Reading Circles during the Chicago Renaissance," the fourteenth annual Kaplan Memorial Lecture at the University of Massachusetts, Amherst, and "The Art of Being Difficult: The Turn to Abstraction in African American Poetry and Painting during the 1940s and 1950s," part of the Humanities Lecture Series at Yale University, delivered March 7, 2014.

23. See Dorothy West, *Where the Wild Grape Grows: Selected Writings, 1930-1950*, ed. Verner D. Mitchell and Cynthia Davis (Amherst: University of Massachusetts Press, 2005), 39-40.

24. The 1944 conference is arguably the culminating peak of the Chicago Popular Front era but also the last occasion of its kind. Bill Mullen observes that the only written record of the meeting made by Margaret Burroughs described all in attendance as falling on a spectrum of the progressive Left to openly communist, but also in her assessment, McCarthyism likely accounted for the event never reoccurring. See Bill Mullen, *Popular Fronts: Chicago and African-American Cultural Politics, 1935-46* (Urbana: University of Illinois Press, 1999), 101-4.

25. Abby Arthur Johnson and Ronald Maberry Johnson, *Propaganda and Aesthetics: The Literary Politics of Afro-American Magazines in the Twentieth Century* (Amherst: University of Massachusetts Press, 1991), 135. The best study of the social and political

background for *Negro Story* is Mullen's *Popular Fronts*. For an excellent study examining the feminist politics of *Negro Story*, see Maureen Convery, "What Is the Negro Woman's Story? *Negro Story* Magazine and the Dialogue of Feminist Voices" (PhD diss., Eastern Michigan University, 2016).

26. See Johnson and Johnson, *Propaganda and Aesthetics*, 136.

27. The debts of these writers to Alice Browning and Fern Gayden are not always appreciated. Bill Mullen rightly points out that their acquisition of Richard Wright's story "Almos' a Man" for the inaugural issue was the least he could do for Gayden, who, in her capacity as a social worker, had helped him and his family secure better lodgings in Chicago a decade earlier. Chester Himes, who was frequently financially insolvent in these years, kept himself going by publishing in *Negro Story*, where almost all his early stories appeared. See Lawrence Jackson, *Chester Himes: A Biography* (New York: W. W. Norton & Co.), 188–91.

28. Pauli Murray, who coined the term *Jane Crow*, though not part of the Chicago circle, is obviously important to Hardison's study and hence my own. I haven't included her in this chapter, but a more expansive version of this study would necessarily seek to take into account her place in the Blue Period. For Ayesha Hardison's use of Murray, see her *Writing through Jane Crow: Race and Gender Politics in African American Literature* (Charlottesville: University of Virginia Press, 2014), 11–19.

29. Leela Gandhi, *Affective Communities: Anticolonial Thought, Fin-de-Siècle Radicalism and the Politics of Friendship* (Durham, NC: Duke University Press, 2005), 6.

30. For Gandhi, who examines turn-of-the-century English metropolitan subjects who align themselves with anticolonial politics, these anti-imperialist subcultures include "sexual dissidence, the struggle for animal rights, (proto-)posthumanist spiritualism and religious heterodoxy, pro-suffrage activism and socialism." See Gandhi, 8–9. I use the phrase "politics of friendship" here by way of reference to Derrida's usage, which is also important to Gandhi's. See Jacques Derrida, "The Politics of Friendship," *Journal of Philosophy* 85, no. 11 (November 1988): 632–44.

31. Frank Marshall Davis, *Livin' the Blues: Memoirs of a Black Journalist and Poet*, ed. John Edgar Tidwell (Madison: University of Wisconsin Press, 2003), 241.

32. Assuming the role of éminence grise, Locke tells Davis, "I tried to integrate the first New Negro generation, and they just wouldn't; only Park Avenue teas and Harlem gin kept them from each other's throats." Davis, 241.

33. Alice C. Browning and Fern Gayden, "A Letter to Our Readers," *Negro Story*, May–June 1944, 1.

34. Browning and Gayden, 1.

35. Browning and Gayden, 1.

36. Anne Meis Knupfer, *The Chicago Black Renaissance and Women's Activism* (Urbana: University of Illinois Press, 2006), 66; Convery, "What Is the Negro Woman's Story?," 17.

37. "Quotes," *Negro Story*, May–June 1944, 63.

38. One of the few exceptions to this is the story "World's End," by the Jamaican writer, journalist, and nationalist political activist Roger Mais. The story is both a pastoral and an allegory of the neglected plight of the rural poor and is set in wartime Jamaica. It was published shortly before his arrest in Kingston in July 1944 on sedition and libel charges for his pamphlet "Now We Know," published in the progressive news-

paper *Public Opinion*, which denounced Churchill's reneging on the promises of Jamaica's constitutional referendum and his imperialist agenda. For a detailed study of Mais and his politics in the 1930s and 1940s, and for the context and outcome of the 1944 trial, see Roxanne Watson, "'Now We Know': The Trial of Roger Mais and Public Opinion in Jamaica, 1944," *Journal of Caribbean History* 46, no. 2 (2012): 183–211.

39. Bill Mullen has extensively catalogued the antifascist and progressive bona fides of the Negro Story circle. See his "Popular Fronts: Negro Story Magazine and the African American Literary Response to World War II," *African American Review* 30, no. 1 (1996): 5–15.

40. Multiple studies, including Mullen, Washington, and Convery, make no mention of this striking and highly significant connection.

41. "Chicago Portraits: A Series of Sketches of Chicago Life," *Negro Story*, May–June 1944, 49–50. See also *Maud Martha* (New York: Harper & Brothers, 1953), 108–12.

42. Brooks, *Maud Martha*. The passing reference to an "underground" abortion practitioner is a reminder that the dilemmas and trials facing women are represented in Brooks's work with singular and unflinching frankness. Her poem about abortion "the mother," which opens with the striking line "Abortions will not let you forget," deeply shocked readers when they encountered it in *A Street in Bronzeville* (New York: Harper and Brothers, 1945). See Lawrence Jackson, *Indignant Generation: A Narrative History of African American Writers and Critics, 1934–1960* (Princeton, NJ: Princeton University Press, 2011), 209–10. Barbara Johnson's essay "Apostrophe, Animation, Abortion" remains the defining critical essay on "the mother," and is easily one of the finest pieces of criticism on Brooks's poetry. See Barbara Johnson, "Apostrophe, Animation, Abortion," *Diacritics* 16, no. 1 (Spring 1986): 28–47.

43. See Ayesha Hardison's chapter "Rereading the Construction of Womanhood in Popular Narratives of Domesticity," in her *Writing through Jane Crow* (Charlottesville: University of Virginia Press, 2014), 144–73.

44. Hardison, 148.

45. Gwendolyn Brooks, "Revision of the Invocation," *Negro Story*, May–June 1945, 77.

46. Evie Shockley, *Renegade Poetics: Black Aesthetics and Formal Innovation in African American Poetry* (Iowa City, IA: University of Iowa Press, 2011), 53.

47. Shockley, 50, original emphasis.

48. Owen Dodson, "Open Letter," *Negro Story*, May–June 1945, 48.

49. Lesley Wheeler, *The Poetics of Enclosure: American Women Poets from Dickinson to Dove* (Knoxville: University of Tennessee Press, 2002), 104.

50. Jackson, *Indignant Generation*, 330.

51. *Oxford English Dictionary Online*, s.v. "kitchenette, n."

52. See Robert Kimball and Linda Berlin Emmet, eds., *The Complete Lyrics of Irving Berlin* (New York: First Applause, 2005), ix.

53. Kimball and Emmet, 196.

54. See Amanda Seligman, "Uptown," *Electronic Encyclopedia of Chicago* (Chicago Historical Society, 2005), http://www.encyclopedia.chicagohistory.org/pages/1293 .html. Uptown was also home to Essanay Studios, an important firm in the American silent film industry. Local realtors may have favored the term *kitchenette* for the units in this area in part for its proximate association with the glamour of the show-business industry. On Essanay Studios in Chicago, see Michael Corcoran and Arnie Bernstein,

Hollywood on Lake Michigan: 100 Years of Chicago & the Movies (Chicago: Lake Claremont Press, 1998), 14-23.

55. See Todd Gitlin and Nanci Hollander, *Uptown: Poor Whites in Chicago* (New York: Harper & Row, 1970).

56. See Thomas Lee Philpott, *The Slum and the Ghetto: Neighborhood Deterioration and Middle-Class Reform, Chicago, 1880-1930* (New York: Oxford University Press, 1978).

57. Nannie H. Burroughs, Charles S. Johnson, John M. Gries, and James Ford, *Negro Housing: A Report of the Committee on Negro Housing* (Washington, DC: President's Conference on Home Building and Home Ownership, 1932), 179-80.

58. Arnold R. Hirsch, *Making the Second Ghetto: Race and Housing in Chicago, 1940-1960* (New York: Cambridge University Press, 1983), 24-25.

59. Brown's novel is an interesting anomaly in the Blue Period. As Mary Helen Washington notes in her introduction to the novel, "Many of the images in Trumbull Park anticipate the aesthetics of protest of the 1960s and 1970s." The novel's nonconformity to the dominant pattern of black postwar writing makes the periodization scheme even more legible. See Frank London Brown, *Trumbull Park* (1959; Lebanon, NH: Northeastern University Press, 2005), 1 and xv-xvi (on the novel's aesthetics differing from those predominant in the 1950s).

60. Fred Moten, *In the Break: The Aesthetics of the Black Radical Tradition* (Minneapolis: University of Minnesota Press, 2003), 1.

61. Moten, 1.

62. How can the "civil rights novel," as Mary Helen Washington calls this genre, exist alongside what I define as the Blue Period works? The civil rights movement was built upon balancing the affect of the old Left of the 1930s and the emerging new Left of the 1960s. Naturally, there were writers, intellectuals, and artists who wanted their work to cross this bridge as well, and they achieved that by borrowing the styles of the 1930s and updating them with the identity nuances of the 1960s. They represent a minor current running parallel to the Blue Period and self-consciously so; tellingly, they are almost always about the absence of a protest movement and speak to a world in which that vocabulary is withheld from both ordinary people and the mainstream of intellectual life in a way unimaginable in the 1930s, or again in the late 1960s and 1970s.

63. See James C. Scott, *Two Cheers for Anarchism* (Princeton, NJ: Princeton University Press, 2012), xx; Robin D. G. Kelley, *Race Rebels: Culture, Politics, and the Black Working Class* (New York: Free Press, 1996), 8-9.

64. Michel de Certeau, *The Practice of Everyday Life* (Berkeley: University of California Press, 1988), xix-xx. Consider the following passage that describes the spatial relation in a way immediately relevant to the context of Brooks's Bronzeville: "Thus a North African living in Paris or Roubaix (France) insinuates into the system imposed on him by the construction of a low-income housing development or of the French language the ways of 'dwelling' (in a house or a language) peculiar to his native Kabylia. He super-imposes them and, by that combination, creates for himself a space in which he can find *ways of using* the constraining order of the place or of the language" (30).

65. Hortense Spillers, "Notes on Brooks and the Feminine," in her *Black, White, and in Color: Essays on American Literature and Culture* (Chicago: University of Chicago Press, 2003), 146-47.

66. Kevin Quashie, *The Sovereignty of Quiet: Beyond Resistance in Black Culture* (New Brunswick, NJ: Rutgers University Press, 2012).

67. Barbara Christian, *Black Feminist Criticism: Perspectives on Black Women Writers* (New York: Teachers College Press, 1986), 176.

68. "Brooks does not solve the problem of Maud's anger or of her silence. Part of this lies in the privateness of Maud's story. Her constant self-analysis and self-consciousness emphasize her solitariness." Mary Helen Washington, "'Taming All That Anger Down': Rage and Silence in Gwendolyn Brooks's *Maud Martha*," *Massachusetts Review* 24, no. 2 (1983): 466.

69. Quashie, *Sovereignty of Quiet*, 55.

70. Virginia Woolf, *Women and Writing*, ed. Michèle Barrett (New York: Harvest Harcourt, 1980), 49–50.

71. Dora Zhang, *Strange Likeness: Description and the Modernist Novel* (Chicago: University of Chicago Press, 2020), 170–71.

72. Ralph Ellison, *Invisible Man* (New York: Vintage, 1989), 354.

73. I borrow the phrase "lyrical surplus" from Fred Moten, who uses it, in part, to gloss a passage from the painter Beauford Delaney's journals during his hospitalization in 1961. The last paragraph of that journal entry is, as it happens, an excellent evocation of Blue Period creativity: "Life in Paris gives me an anonymity and objectivity to release long stored up memories of [the] beauty and sorrows of the difficult work of orchestrating and releasing into a personal form of color and design what seems to me a long apprenticeship to jazz and spiritual songs augmented by the deep hope given to my people in the deep south at home. I gave myself to these experiences devotedly." See Moten, *In the Break*, 37–38.

74. Saul Bellow, *The Adventures of Augie March* (New York: Viking Books, 1953), 1.

75. Brooks, *Maud Martha*, 1.

76. Virginia Woolf, *Mrs. Dalloway* (New York: Harcourt Brace, 1925), 3.

77. Woolf, 17–18.

78. Woolf, 49–50, 174–78.

79. Brooks, *Maud Martha*, 67.

80. Harriet Beecher Stowe, *Uncle Tom's Cabin* (London: John Cassell, 1852), 203–4.

81. Brooks, *Maud Martha*, 122.

82. See D. H. Melhem, *Gwendolyn Brooks: Poetry and the Heroic Voice* (Lexington: University Press of Kentucky, 1987), 84–85.

83. See Lisa Ruddick, *Reading Gertrude Stein: Body, Text, Gnosis* (Ithaca, NY: Cornell University Press, 1990), 17–28.

84. For a reading of "the ordinary" in Gwendolyn Brooks, see Lovia Gyarkye, "The Importance of Being Ordinary," *New Republic*, July 19, 2017, https://newrepublic.com/article/143927/importance-ordinary.

85. Brooks, *Maud Martha*, 67.

86. Mary Helen Washington, *The Other Blacklist: The African American Literary and Cultural Left of the 1950s* (New York: Columbia University Press, 2014), 189.

87. Adam Green, *Selling the Race: Culture, Community, and Black Chicago, 1940–1955* (Chicago: University of Chicago Press, 2007), 132.

88. Benedict Anderson, *Imagined Communities* (New York: Verso, 1983; rep. 2006)

89. Hardison, *Writing through Jane Crow*, 146.

90. Allison Pease, "*Maud* and Its Discontents," *Criticism* 36, no. 1 (1994): 105–7.

91. "When I was twelve or thirteen, I began to be interested in Shakespeare and poets such as Wordsworth and Tennyson and Shelley, the conventional loves of youth, I believe, and first loves, I should say, because I think we all still admire those poets." Gloria Wade Gayles, ed., *Conversations with Gwendolyn Brooks* (Jackson: University Press of Mississippi, 2003), 4. On Brooks's unpublished early poetry notebooks, see Erlene Stetson's chapter "Songs after Sunset (1935-36): The Unpublished Poetry of Gwendolyn Elizabeth Brooks," in Maria K. Mootry and Gary Smith, eds., *A Life Distilled: Gwendolyn Brooks, Her Poetry and Fiction* (Urbana: University of Illinois Press, 1989), 119-27.

92. Melhem, *Gwendolyn Brooks*, 86.

93. Alfred Tennyson, *Maud and Other Poems* (London: Edward Moxon, 1866), 10.

94. Brooks, *Maud Martha*, 176.

95. Francis O'Gorman, "What Is Haunting Tennyson's Maud (1855)?," *Victorian Poetry* 48, no. 3 (2010): 310.

96. Brooks, *Maud Martha*, 146.

97. Brooks, 142.

98. Claudia Rankine, *Citizen: An American Lyric* (Minneapolis: Graywolf, 2014).

99. Brooks, *Maud Martha*, 176.

100. Brooks, 178.

101. Woolf, *Mrs. Dalloway*, 63-64.

102. Washington, *Other Blacklist*, 191.

103. Elizabeth Alexander, *The Black Interior: Essays* (Minneapolis: Graywolf Press, 2004), 19.

104. William Empson, *Some Versions of Pastoral* (New York: New Directions, 1974).

105. See Denning's chapter "The Tenement Thinking: Ghetto Pastorals," in *The Cultural Front: The Laboring of American Culture in the Twentieth Century* (New York: Verso, 1996), 230-55.

106. Michael Gold, "Gertrude Stein: A Literary Idiot," in *Critical Essays on Gertrude Stein*, ed. Michael J. Hoffman (Boston: G. K. Hall, 1986), 76.

107. Quoted in Denning, *Cultural Front*, 230

108. Washington, *Other Blacklist*, 301n9.

109. Washington cites James Smethurst as an authority in establishing Brooks's Popular Front credentials while retaining a "high" modernism, a move crucial in allowing her to fold *Maud Martha* back into the ghetto pastoral. The point remains that Brooks's aesthetic practice fundamentally resists this appropriation, and we ought to change our periodization rather than continue straining categories to the point of diluting their usefulness. See James E. Smethurst, *The New Red Negro: The Literary Left and African American Poetry, 1930-1946* (New York: Oxford University Press, 1999), 164-79.

110. Barbara Foley, *Radical Representations: Politics and Form in US Proletarian Fiction, 1929-1941* (Durham, NC: Duke University Press, 1993), 396.

111. Paule Marshall, "From the Poets in the Kitchen," *Callaloo* 18 (Spring-Summer 1983): 25.

112. Paule Marshall, *Brown Girl, Brownstones* (New York: Feminist Press, 1981), 319.

113. Paule Marshall, "Shaping the World of My Art," *New Letters* 40 (Autumn 1973): 97.

114. Langston Hughes, *Montage of a Dream Deferred* (New York: Henry Holt & Co., 1951).

115. Brooks, *Maud Martha*, 100-101.

116. Washington, afterword to *Brown Girl, Brownstones*, 312.

117. "Is this the kingdom? she whispered, suppressing a laugh … Selina was embarrassed for them." *Brown Girl, Brownstones*, 164–66. For the schooling quote, see Paule Marshall, *Brown Girl, Brownstones* (New York: Feminist Press, 1981), 212.

118. Brooks, *Maud Martha*, 43.

119. Marshall, *Brown Girl, Brownstones*, 303.

120. Marshall, 153–54.

121. Marshall, 213.

122. Marshall, 213.

123. Marshall, 213–14.

124. Eve Kosofsky Sedgwick, "Jane Austen and the Masturbating Girl," *Critical Inquiry* 17, no. 4 (1991): 822.

125. Sedgwick, 829.

126. Marshall, *Brown Girl, Brownstones*, 289.

127. Marshall, 292.

128. See Paule Marshall, *Triangular Road, A Memoir* (New York: Basic Civitas Books, 2010).

129. Brooks, *Maud Martha*, 180.

130. Marshall, *Brown Girl, Brownstones*, 309.

131. Marshall, 310.

132. Marshall, 310.

133. Marshall, 310.

134. Brooks, *Maud Martha*, 163.

135. Ellison, *Invisible Man*, 13.

Chapter Five

1. Thomas Mann, *The Magic Mountain* (New York: A. A. Knopf, 2005), 36–37.

2. Pankaj Mishra, "Whatever Happened to the Novel of Ideas?," *New York Times*, September 20, 2015.

3. Mishra.

4. Mishra.

5. Philip Rahv, "The Cult of Experience in American Writing" (1936), *Partisan Review* 7, no. 6 (1940): 412–24.

6. Richard Wright, *Native Son* (New York: Harper Perennial, 2005), 25.

7. Richard Wright, *Early Works* (New York: Library of America, 1991), 865–66.

8. Morris Dickstein, *Dancing in the Dark: A Cultural History of the Great Depression* (New York: W. W. Norton & Co., 2009), 508–9.

9. Even in 1980 Mary McCarthy could write that "ideas are still today felt to be unsightly in the novel." One of the few recent American books she can think of is John Updike's *The Coup* (1978), which allegedly "bristles with ideas." She also notes sourly that "in the USA, a special license has always been granted to the Jewish novel, which is free to juggle ideas in full view of the public; Bellow, Malamud, Philip Roth still avail themselves of the right, which is never conceded to us goys." There is no mention of any black writer. See Mary McCarthy, *Ideas and the Novel* (New York: Harcourt Brace, 1980), 15, 120, 121.

10. In his essay "Many Thousands Gone," Baldwin calls it "one of the most desper-

ate performances in American fiction." See James Baldwin, *Notes of a Native Son* (New York: Dial, 1963), 38.

11. Mishra, "Whatever Happened to the Novel of Ideas?"

12. Arna Bontemps, review of *The Outsider* by Richard Wright, *Saturday Review*, March 28, 1953, 15-16.

13. The following list is exclusively male. Obviously there are other female scholars or writers who have taken an interest in *The Outsider*, but part of the point of this chapter is precisely to self-examine these masculine investments; this list is illustrative of that persistent pattern.

14. See Vaughn Rasberry, *Race and the Totalitarian Century: Geopolitics in the Black Literary Imagination* (Cambridge, MA: Harvard University Press, 2016); Lawrence Jackson, *Indignant Generation: A Narrative History of African American Writers and Critics, 1934-1960* (Princeton, NJ: Princeton University Press, 2011); Tommie Shelby, "Richard Wright: Realizing the Promise of the West," in *African American Political Thought: A Collected History*, ed. Melvin L. Rogers and Jack Turner (Chicago: University of Chicago Press, 2021), 413-38.

15. Paul Gilroy, *The Black Atlantic: Modernity and Double Consciousness* (Cambridge, MA: Harvard University Press 1993), 159-86.

16. See Cedric Robinson, *Black Marxism: The Making of the Black Radical Tradition* (London: Zed Books, 1983), esp. "Richard Wright and the Critique of Class Theory" at 416-40.

17. Harold Cruse, *The Crisis of the Negro Intellectual* (New York: William Morrow & Co., 1967), 181-89.

18. James Zeigler notes that Wright's unpublished essay "I Choose Exile" was rejected because it was insufficiently in agreement with *Ebony*'s anticommunist line; if it had appeared, "it would have impressed on Wright's readers that his break with Communism did not signal a retreat from his black radical conviction that in the history of Western modernity the punishing impositions of white supremacy and capitalist exploitation have always entailed each other." James Zeigler, *Red Scare Racism and Cold War Black Radicalism* (Jackson: University Press of Mississippi, 2015), 96.

19. Adam Shatz, *Writers and Missionaries: Essays on the Radical Imagination* (New York: Verso, 2023), 131.

20. Wright's "Blueprint for Negro Writing" appeared in *New Challenge* 1 (Fall 1937): 53-65. Its canonical status is cursorily confirmed by its inclusion in major anthologies of African American criticism and literature. See Addison Gayle Jr., ed., *The Black Aesthetic* (Garden City, NY: Doubleday & Co.,1971); Henry Louis Gates Jr. and Nellie Y. McKay were the general editors of *The Norton Anthology of African American Literature*'s first edition in 1996 and second edition in 2003. Henry Louis Gates Jr. and Valerie Smith are the general editors for the 2014 third edition; Angelyn Mitchell, ed., *Within the Circle: An Anthology of African American Literary Criticism from the Renaissance to the Present* (Durham, NC: Duke University Press, 1994); Winston Napier, ed., *African American Literary Theory: A Reader* (New York: New York University Press, 2000).

21. Wright, "Blueprint for Negro Writing," 53.

22. Wright, 58.

23. Wright, 57.

24. Gene Andrew Jarrett, *Deans and Truants: Race and Realism in African American Literature* (Philadelphia: University of Pennsylvania Press, 2011), 118-19.

25. On Wright at the National Negro Congress, see Margaret Walker, *Richard Wright: Daemonic Genius* (New York: Amistad Press, 1988), 71. Walker claimed that the South Side Writers Group did not merely influence but helped draft the text itself: "At least five or six members of the South Side Writers Group contributed to 'Blueprint for Negro Writing': Wright and myself, and possibly Ted Ward, Ed Bland, Russell Marshall, and Frank Marshall Davis. What Wright did was take ideas and suggestions from four or five drafts by others and rewrite them in definite Marxist terms, incorporating strong Black Nationalist sentiments and some cogent expressions on techniques and the craft of writing. He published it as his own, and I remember my surprise on seeing the printed piece" (355–56n18).

26. Wright, "Blueprint," 58–59.

27. Jarrett, *Deans and Truants*, 128.

28. In relation to *Uncle Tom's Children*, see Cheryl Higashida, "Aunt Sue's Children: Re-viewing the Gender(ed) Politics of Richard Wright's Radicalism," *American Literature* 75, no. 2 (2003): 395–425. In relation to *Native Son*, see Barbara Johnson, "The Re(a)d and the Black: Richard Wright's Blueprint," in *Richard Wright: Critical Perspectives Past and Present*, ed. Henry Louis Gates Jr. and Kwame Anthony Appiah (New York: Amistad, 1993), 149–55.

29. Wright's ascent is traced in Hazel Rowley's *Richard Wright: The Life and Times* (Chicago: University of Chicago Press, 2001). Rowley neglects to mention, however, Melvin B. Tolson, who declared Wright's winning of the *Story* magazine competition, "The Biggest Event of 1938 in Black America." See Robert M. Farnsworth, ed., *Caviar and Cabbage: Selected Columns by Melvin B. Tolson from the Washington Tribune, 1937–1944* (Columbia: University of Missouri Press, 1982), 198–200. See Brannon Costello, "Richard Wright's *Lawd Today!* and the Political Uses of Modernism," *African American Review* 37, No.1 (2003): 39–52.

30. On the range of influences shaping the novel's tone, see Arnold Rampersad's foreword to *Lawd Today!*, by Richard Wright (Boston: Northeastern University Press, 1993), v–xi.

31. Costello, "Richard Wright's *Lawd Today!*," 49.

32. Higashida, "Aunt Sue's Children," 398. See Barbara Foley, *Radical Representations*; Michael Denning, *The Cultural Front: The Laboring of American Culture in the Twentieth Century* (New York: Verso, 1996), 230–55; Brian Dolinar, *The Black Cultural Front: Black Writers and Artists of the Depression Era Generation* (Jackson: University of Mississippi, 2012).

33. In turning to questions of feeling and affect rather than philosophical or political categories per se, I follow a trend in recent Wright scholarship. See, e.g., Ernest Julius Mitchell, "Tenderness in Early Wright," in *The Cambridge Companion to Richard Wright*, ed. Glenda Carpio (New York: Cambridge University Press, 2019), 199–216.

34. See *Literary Sisters: Dorothy West and Her Circle, a Biography of the Harlem Renaissance*, Verner D. Mitchell and Cynthia Davis (New Brunswick, NJ: Rutgers University Press, 2011), 130–56.

35. Mitchell and Davis, *Literary Sisters*, 130.

36. Mitchell and Davis, *Literary Sisters*, 147.

37. See Matthew N. Hannah, "Desires Made Manifest: The Queer Modernism of Wallace Thurman's *Fire!!*," *Journal of Modern Literature* 38, no. 3 (2015): 162–80. A touching indication of West's enduring affection is the official notice of Thurman's

death in 1934, which she kept in her papers. MC 676, folder 2.13, Dorothy West Papers, Schlesinger Library, Radcliffe Institute, Harvard University, Cambridge, MA.

38. Mildred Jones, who entertained a complicated courtship with both Dorothy West and Langston Hughes during the famed 1932 voyage to the Soviet Union, was also *Challenge*'s graphic designer, for example. See *Literary Sisters*, 142–46; *Challenge* 1, no. 4 (March 1934), masthead.

39. *Literary Sisters*, 150.

40. According to West, Marian Minus edited Wright's work and "did quite a bit for him" generally. See *Literary Sisters*, 150.

41. Wallace Thurman to Dorothy West, September 2, 1934, in an afterword by Adelaide M. Cromwell, in Dorothy West, *The Living Is Easy* (Old Westbury, NY: Feminist Press, 1982), 355.

42. See Earle V. Bryant, *Byline, Richard Wright: Articles from the Daily Worker and New Masses* (Columbia: University of Missouri Press, 2014).

43. Richard Wright to Langston Hughes, May 29, 1937, in Rowley, *Life and Times*, 135.

44. West described the situation in a 1983 interview: "I financed it. I was the editor. I was the everything. When the Chicago group tried to take it away from me, that was the end of the magazine.... I have a certain strength and I said no. They couldn't do anything without me. So that was the last issue." Rowley, *Life and Times*, 137.

45. Margaret Walker, emotionally entangled with Wright herself, noted that Minus "dressed mannishly and looked lesbian in a male fashion." Walker, *Daemonic Genius*, 91.

46. Langston Hughes to Dorothy West, n.d. [1937], MC 676, folder 10.3, Dorothy West Papers, Schlesinger Library, Radcliffe Institute, Harvard University, Cambridge, MA.

47. Higashida, "Aunt Sue's Children," 416.

48. Higashida, 419.

49. Richard Wright, "Blueprint for Negro Literature," draft, p. 14, Richard Wright Papers, Beinecke Rare Book and Manuscript Library, Yale University, New Haven, CT, in Higashida, "Aunt Sue's Children," 422n13.

50. Minus allowed Wright to court her in Chicago before outing herself as a lesbian in New York. In a footnote, Rowley cites a piece of correspondence between Ralph Ellison and Wright that appears to suggest Wright may have felt shamed or pressured by becoming a joke in the eyes of his peers. See Rowley, *Life and Times*, 134.

51. Marian Minus, "Present Trends in Negro Literature," *Challenge* 2, no. 1 (1937): 9–11.

52. Minus, 9.

53. Minus, 11.

54. See Eugene C. Holmes, "Problems Facing the Negro Writer Today," *New Challenge*, Fall 1937, 69–75; Allyn Keith, "A Note on Negro Nationalism," *New Challenge*, Fall 1937, 65–69. My suggestion that Keith is Edward Bland is based on a comparison of the argument and style to his "Racial Bias and Negro Poetry," *Poetry* 63, no. 6 (March 1944): 328–33. Bland, considered a luminary on the South Side literary scene, was killed in the Battle of the Bulge in 1944.

55. *New Challenge*, Fall 1937, 3.

56. John F. Callahan and Marc C. Connor, eds., *The Selected Letters of Ralph Ellison* (New York: Random House, 2019), 108. In the same letter, Ellison tellingly employs

the Ortega y Gasset phrase "living in the heights of one's time," clearly linking the two through his reading of Wright's "Blueprint."

57. "The long isolation of the Negro artist ended with the advent of the WPA projects." Walker, *Daemonic Genius*, 78.

58. Wright was "formulating principles that he clarified in 'Blueprint for Negro Writing' two years later." Michel Fabre, *The Unfinished Quest of Richard Wright*, trans. Isabel Barzun (Urbana: University of Illinois Press, 1993), 118; "Editorial," *New Challenge* 1 (Fall 1937): 3; Henry Hart, ed., *American Writers Congress* (New York: International Publishers, 1935), 178–79, emphasis added.

59. Richard Wright, *American Hunger* (New York: Harper & Row, 1977), 94–98.

60. André Malraux, *Man's Fate*, trans. Haakon M. Chevalier (New York: Modern Library, 1961), 352.

61. Wright, "Blueprint," 61.

62. Typescript draft of "Blueprint," JWJ MSS 3, box 5, folder 76, James Weldon Johnson Memorial Collection, Richard Wright Papers, Beinecke Rare Book and Manuscript Library, Yale University, New Haven, CT.

63. Wright, "Blueprint," 65.

64. Typescript draft of "Blueprint," Richard Wright Papers.

65. Houston Baker Jr. argued that a black feminine "remainder" eluded Wright in his manifesto. Perhaps it was merely suppressed. See Houston Baker Jr. *Workings of the Spirit: The Poetics of Afro-American Women's Writing* (Chicago: University of Chicago Press: 1991), 121.

66. Richard Wright, *White Man Listen!* (New York: Doubleday & Co., 1957), 17.

67. Richard Wright Papers, JWJ MSS 3 Box 5, folder 76.

68. Wright, *American Hunger*, 135; Richard Wright, *Later Works* (New York: Library of America, 1991), 763.

69. For a description of the Kronstadt moment by Fischer and its relation to the anticommunist turn in Lionel Trilling and Whittaker Chambers, see Michael Kimmage, *The Conservative Turn: Lionel Trilling, Whittaker Chambers, and the Lessons of Anti-Communism* (Cambridge, MA: Harvard University Press, 2009), 79–80.

70. Matthew M. Briones, "Call-and-Response: Tracing the Ideological Shifts of Richard Wright through His Correspondence with Friends and Fellow Literati," *African American Review* 37, no. 1 (2003): 53–64.

71. Fabre, *Unfinished Quest*, 230.

72. See William J. Maxwell, *F. B. Eyes: How J. Edgar Hoover's Ghostreaders Framed African American Literature* (Princeton, NJ: Princeton University Press, 2015).

73. Fabre, *Unfinished Quest*, 230.

74. Fabre, 230–31.

75. See Rasberry, *Race and the Totalitarian Century*.

76. Mark Christian Thompson, *Black Fascisms: African American Literature and Culture between the Wars* (Charlottesville: University of Virginia Press, 2007), 153. Among the interwar writers whom Thompson argues are attracted to fascism in this period are George Schuyler, Claude McKay, and Zora Neale Hurston.

77. Thompson, 153.

78. Rasberry, *Race and the Totalitarian Century*, 345.

79. Rasberry, 87–90. Rasberry calls this "the Bildung of Jim Crow as a mode of negative education" in totalitarianism and gives an excellent reading of the scene in which

young Richard must face the cross-examination by Pease and Reynolds at the optometrist's office as effectively a show trial in which truth has ceased to matter, and regardless of one's answer, one will be found guilty and be punished. He also notes the affinity of his own views to those of JanMohamed, whose far-reaching analysis is rooted in Lacanian and Heideggerian readings. See Abdul JanMohamed, *The Death-Bound-Subject: Richard Wright's Archaeology of Death* (Durham, NC: Duke University Press, 2005).

80. Rowley, *Life and Times*, 187.

81. Ayesha Hardison, *Writing through Jane Crow: Race and Gender Politics in African American Literature* (Charlottesville: University of Virginia Press, 2014), 27.

82. Quoted in Rowley, *Life and Times*, 188.

83. See Hardison, *Writing through Jane Crow*, 25–53. Paul Gilroy had already initiated this debate in his chapter on Wright in *The Black Atlantic* in 1993, but apparently without knowledge of *Black Hope*, as he makes no reference to it in his arguments. See Gilroy, *Black Atlantic*, 173–86.

84. Hardison, *Writing through Jane Crow*, 29.

85. Hardison, 49–50.

86. Quoted in Rowley, *Life and Times*, 228.

87. Rowley, *Life and Times*, 228.

88. Rowley, 250.

89. See Dayo F. Gore, *Radicalism at the Crossroads: African American Women and the Cold War* (New York: New York University Press, 2012).

90. Hilton Als reviewing a revival of *Trouble in Mind*, directed by Irene Lewis for the Washington's Arena Stage in DC in fall 2011 and starring E. Faye Butler as Wiletta, observed: "'I want to be an actress!' Wiletta says, repeatedly. The play is about how she can't be, not in 1955, not here. But she refuses to leave the stage. Or to listen to her director.... she's the last woman standing, as sturdy as a dream." See Hilton Als, "Black and Blue: A New Look at Alice Childress," *New Yorker*, October 10, 2011, 132–33.

91. See Barbara Foley, "A Dramatic Picture ... of Woman from Feudalism to Fascism: Richard Wright's Black Hope," in *Richard Wright in a Post-Racial Imaginary*, ed. Alice Mikal Craven, William E. Dow, and Yoko Nakamura (New York: Bloomsbury Academic, 2014), 113–28. "The pivotal actions performed by Maud, Lily, and Ollie in the plot of *Black Hope* suggest the rationale for Wright's chosen title: if the 'hope' of all oppressed people consists in the egalitarian future that Freddie imagines ... then women ... will figure centrally in this liberatory project. We will recall Wright's statement to Reynold's that he wishes his novel-in-progress to "reveal in a symbolic manner the potentially strategic position, socially and politically, which women occupy in the world today." Women were—at least "potentially"—the vanguard of antifascism (127–28). In the same chapter, after noting the many demeaning and abused female characters in Wright's fiction, Foley states that "Maud Hampton is, arguably, the most complex character to appear in Wright's entire *oeuvre*" (121).

92. Hardison, *Writing through Jane Crow*, 42.

93. Hardison, 260–61.

94. *New Masses*, June 17, 1941, quoted in Fabre, *Unfinished Quest*, 224. The idea for a Double V campaign was first articulated by twenty-six-year-old James G. Thompson, a black cafeteria worker at a Cessna Aircraft Corporation plant in Wichita, Kansas. He wrote a letter to the *Pittsburgh Courier* in January 1942 suggesting the idea: "The V for victory sign is being displayed prominently in all so-called democratic countries which

are fighting for victory over aggression, slavery, and tyranny. If this V sign means that to those now engaged in this great conflict, then let we colored Americans adopt the double VV for a double victory. The first V for victory over our enemies from without, the second V for victory over our enemies from within. For surely those who perpetuate these ugly prejudices here are seeking to destroy our democratic form of government just as surely as the axis forces." See Patrick S. Washburn, "*The Pittsburgh Courier's Double V Campaign in 1942," History Division of the Association for Education in Journalism Annual Convention* (East Lansing: Michigan State University, August 1981), 3.

95. Fabre, *Unfinished Quest*, 226.

96. Quoted in Rowley, *Life and Times*, 254–55.

97. The torture of Abner Louima in New York Police Department custody in 1997 and Jon Burge's reign of terror in Chicago being a few of the many notorious examples. See Laurence Ralph, *The Torture Letters: Reckoning with Police Violence* (Chicago: University of Chicago Press, 2020).

98. Richard Wright, *The Man Who Lived Underground* (New York: Library of America, 2021), 37.

99. Wright, 52.

100. Jacques Derrida, "Living On," trans. James Hulbert, in *Parages*, ed. John P. Leavey (Stanford, CA: Stanford University Press, 2011), 124–25.

101. Derrida, 221, original emphasis.

102. Mackey describes the "paracritical hinge" as "a door permitting flow between disparate modes of articulation." See Nathaniel Mackey, *The Paracritical Hinge: Essays, Talks, Notes, Interviews* (Madison: University of Wisconsin Press, 2005), 16.

103. Wright, *Man Who Lived Underground*, 62.

104. Wright, 63.

105. Wright, *Man Who Lived Underground*, 171.

106. See Jay Garcia, *Psychology Comes to Harlem: Rethinking the Race Question in Twentieth-Century America* (Baltimore: Johns Hopkins University Press, 2012), 59–64.

107. Quoted in Fabre, *Unfinished Quest*, 273.

108. See Guirdex Masse, "A Diasporic Encounter: The Politics of Race and Culture at the First International Congress of Black Writers and Artists" (PhD diss., Emory University, 2014). Nadia Ellis devotes her chapter "The Fraternal Agonies of Baldwin and Lamming" to the dynamics between attendees of the congress. See Ellis, *Territories of the Soul: Queered Belonging in the Black Diaspora* (Durham, NC: Duke University Press, 2015), 62–94.

109. "The US State Department was not the only governmental organization to take an interest in what was being said at the Sorbonne, and a declaration of support for the FLN could easily have led to Fanon's arrest." David Macey, *Frantz Fanon: A Biography* (New York: Picador, 2000), 283.

110. Macey, 291.

111. According to Rowley, Wright appears to have been suspicious of Lamming's "animated conversation" with his wife Ellen and gone into a fit of jealousy that distanced the two men. See Rowley, *Life and Times*, 478–79.

112. Macey, *Frantz Fanon*, 280.

113. Quoted in Macey, 280.

114. Macey, 280.

115. At the time, Wright was writing the manuscript for *Savage Holiday* and attend-

ing to business concerning the imminent publication of *The Outsider*, published later in March. See Toru Kiuchi and Yoshinobu Hakutani, *Richard Wright: A Documented Chronology, 1908-1960* (Jefferson, NC: McFarland & Co., 2014), 281-82.

116. "Écoute homme blanc!, de Richard Wright," *El Moudjahid*, August 3, 1959, in Frantz Fanon, *Écrits sur l'aliénation et la liberté*, ed. Khalfa and Young (Paris: Éditions de la Découverte, 2015), 524-26. Reviews in *El Moudjahid* were typically unsigned. Alice Cherki attributes the review to Fanon and notes that his feelings toward Wright had cooled over time, unlike his appreciation for Chester Himes who he talked about in his conference lectures in Tunis.

117. Fanon, 526.

118. Richard Wright, *Black Power: Three Books from Exile* (New York: HarperCollins, 2010), 634, emphasis added.

119. Fanon develops these theories in the chapters "Spontaneity: Its Strength and Weakness" and "The Pitfalls of National Consciousness" in *The Wretched of the Earth*. It is striking the extent to which the popular reception of Fanon misreads or selectively reads this work. Fanon's famous theory of violence is merely the first chapter. The rest of the book is largely devoted to a meticulous sociological and class-based analysis of how revolutionary movements are betrayed, co-opted, and defeated largely at the hands of the indigenous bourgeoisie. The history of postindependence Africa tragically bears out the extraordinary accuracy and almost prophetic power of this diagnosis. See Fanon, *The Wretched of the Earth* (New York: Grove Press, 1968), 107-205.

120. We'll never know what might have been if Wright hadn't gotten suddenly gravely ill and died in 1960 (Fanon following in like fashion only a year later). Wright did appear at the time of his death to be gaining an increasing interest in the growing US involvement in Vietnam. In March 1960, he told his friend Magrit de Sablonière, "So far as the Americans are concerned, I'm worse than a Communist, for my work falls like a shadow across their policy in Asia and Africa." His last public talk at the American Church in Paris on November 8, 1960, specifically mentioned Vietnam. See Rowley, *Life and Times*, 511.

121. I acknowledge that my descriptions of Fanon's philosophical positions can be contested as oversimplified. There is an important suite of debates about how to read the ambiguities and ambivalences in Fanon's texts that has animated poststructuralism, postcolonial studies, black studies, and Afropessimist thought. These issues were already the source of much debate in the 1980s. Homi Bhabha's influential reading suggested that in his divided psyche, "it is as if Fanon is fearful of his most radical insights"; and Henry Louis Gates Jr. cautioned against any ahistorical reading that would skip over "the exceptional instability of Fanon's own rhetoric." Homi Bhabha, "Remembering Fanon" *New Formations*, Spring 1987, 121; Henry Louis Gates Jr. "Critical Fanonism" *Critical Inquiry* 17 (Spring 1991), 470. In *Whither Fanon?* (2018) David Marriott offers a summation and synthesis of the traces of Fanon across the major black thinkers (including Ato Sekyi-Otu, Lewis R. Gordon, C. L. R. James, Achille Mbembe, Fred Moten, David Scott, Jared Sexton, Frank Wilderson III, and Sylvia Wynter) who have been responding to Fanon since the late 1960s. For incisive critiques of the gendered imbalance of this list, and its implications for this discourse, see also T. Denean Sharpley-Whiting, *Frantz Fanon: Conflicts and Feminisms* (Lanham, MD: Rowman & Littlefield, 1998); Michelle Wright, *Becoming Black: Creating Identity in the African Diaspora* (Durham, NC: Duke University Press, 2004), 111-35. I attempt to read Fanon faithfully and contextu-

ally while also accepting, and even welcoming, Marriott's acutely subversive claim that "to read Fanon is to know a thought that is not yet." David Marriott, *Whither Fanon? Studies in the Blackness of Being* (Stanford, CA: Stanford University Press, 2018), 363.

122. Fanon, *Écrits sur l'aliénation et la liberté*, 589–90.

123. I'm concerned here with *The Outsider*, but the other obvious example from this period is *Savage Holiday*, arguably the work that takes the case study model to its most extreme, even dedicated to serial murderer Clinton Brewer. Paula Rabinowitz has argued that Wright is particularly influenced in this period (he had just gone to Argentina to make the *Native Son* picture) by film noir and that the latent pulp modernism of his writing from the 1940s becomes increasingly noirish. This is a very compelling thesis, and although I partly agree that it applies to *The Outsider*, it is even more in evidence in the otherwise unpalatable *Savage Holiday*. See Paula Rabinowitz, *Black, White and Noir: America's Pulp Modernism* (New York: Columbia University Press, 2002).

124. "La bibliothèque de Frantz Fanon" is edited and presented with an introduction by Jean Khalfa. See Fanon, *Écrits sur l'aliénation et la liberté*, 587–90.

125. Fanon, 633–34.

126. Frantz Fanon, *Black Skin, White Masks*, trans. Richard Philcox (1952) (New York: Grove Press, 2008), 139.

127. Fanon, 196.

128. Fanon, 190.

129. Consider a passage of especially pertinent interest from "Tradition and Industrialization," Wright's contribution to the First Negro Writer's Conference: "Tragic and lonely and all too often misunderstood are these men of the elite. The West hates and fears that elite and I must, to be honest, say that the instincts of the West that prompts that hate and fear are, on the whole, correct. For this elite in Asia and Africa constitutes islands of free men, the FREEST MEN IN ALL THE WORLD TODAY. They stand poised, nervous, straining at the leash, ready to go, with no weight of the dead past clouding their minds, no fear of foolish customs benumbing their consciousness, eager to build industrial civilizations." Richard Wright, "Tradition and Industrialization: The Plight of the Tragic Elite in Africa," *Présence africaine*, nos. 8–10 (June–November 1956): 347–60, at 356.

130. See Lewis R. Gordon, *Bad Faith and Antiblack Racism* (Atlantic Highlands, NJ: Humanities Press, 1995).

131. Fanon, *Black Skin, White Masks*, 206.

132. Lewis R. Gordon, *Fanon and the Crisis of European Man: An Essay on Philosophy and the Human Sciences* (New York: Routledge, 1995), 10.

133. These are *L'oeil se noie* and *Les main parallèles*, both from 1949. As the editors note, both plays can be read as Nietszchean dramas of personal conscience, and the dialogues essentially build toward a young, alienated man's decision to act or revolt or suffer the pain of the refusal of the world. See Fanon, *Écrits sur l'aliénation et la liberté*, 15–64.

134. Fanon, xi.

135. Quoted in Rowley, *Life and Times*, 407.

136. In their collage of rhetorical energies and engagements, they resemble one of the other great Blue Period books of the midcentury, C. L. R. James's *Mariners, Renegades and Castaways: The Story of Herman Melville and the World We Live In* (1953; Hanover, NH: University Press of New England, 2001) written while awaiting deporta-

tion from Ellis Island for alleged communist subversion, which likewise attempts to deprovincialize blackness by insisting on the already-diasporic proletarian mythopoesis gifted to the American imaginary by Melville. See Joseph Keith's excellent *Unbecoming Americans: Writing Race and Nation from the Shadows of Citizenship: 1945–1960* (New Brunswick, NJ: Rutgers University Press, 2013).

137. See Jonathan Flatley, *Affective Mapping: Melancholia and the Politics of Modernism* (Cambridge, MA: Harvard University Press, 2008).

138. "For Europe, for ourselves and for humanity, comrades, we must make a new start, develop a new way of thinking, and endeavor to create a new man." Fanon, *Wretched of the Earth*, 239.

139. See Manning Marable, *Malcolm X: A Life of Reinvention* (New York: Viking, 2011), 96.

140. Richard Wright, *The Outsider* (New York: Library of America, 1991), 775.

141. Musil's novel was never completed and published in German between 1930 and 1943. It did not appear in English until 1953. Obviously, my argument is not that Wright is inspired by Musil's character, but rather that he bears a narratological and formal affinity with him—a coincidence that I think speaks to Wright's "native" effort, if you will, to produce a black novel of ideas. Ulrich's cynical pessimism is made clear early in the novel: "'It doesn't matter what one does,' the Man Without Qualities said to himself, shrugging his shoulders. 'In a tangle of forces like this it doesn't make a scrap of difference.'" Robert Musil, *The Man without Qualities* (New York: Picador, 1979), 1:8.

142. Barrett died tragically in 2008, before he could complete work on his last manuscript. Hortense Spillers, in a review of his final work, says, "The 'conceptual impossibility of racial blackness' is so enabling and throws so long and grave and supraordinate a shadow athwart Western sociopolitical, geographical, economic, material, phantasmatic, and psychic procedures that Barrett is saying that it far outweighs, ironically, any other repertoire of ways and means." See Spillers, "Racial Blackness and the (Dis)continuity of Western Modernity by Lindon Barrett (review)," *Modernism/Modernity* 23, no. 1 (2016): 251–55. For Barret, black subjectivity is the "problem" that disrupts but also—in its efforts to, as Fred Moten would say, "regulate" it—enables the sense-making of Western modernity in the first place. The black novel of ideas, necessarily rooted in black subjectivity and intellectual counter-production would almost by definition, by these lights, operate as the "paracritical hinge … a door permitting flow between disparate modes of articulation" that irrupts as an impossibility for thought that nevertheless exists and thus remains at the margin where it is neglected but also, for precisely this reason, remains useful. Mackey, *Paracritical Hinge*, 16; Lindon Barrett, *Racial Blackness and the (Dis)continuity of Western Modernity*, ed. Justin A. Joyce, Dwight McBride, and John Carlos Rowe (Urbana: University of Illinois Press, 2014).

143. There exists by now a copious literature on the racist construction of Enlightenment modernity. For a concise assessment of the impact of the development of black literature in response to each of these founding pillars of Western thought see, Henry Louis Gates Jr., *Figures in Black: Words, Signs, and the "Racial" Self* (New York: Oxford University Press, 1988).

144. "There is not now nor has there ever been a free zone or quiet place from which the discourse of so-called Africanist figures, intellectuals, writers, thinkers, or scholars might issue. And this can be shown to be the case in general." Nahum D. Chandler, *X: The Problem of the Negro as a Problem for Thought* (New York: Fordham University Press,

2014), 14. Chandler's project, like Barrett's, revises, and supplements both the late Foucault and Derrida by re-centering racial blackness as the discursive presupposition and (through chattel slavery, the material and labor condition) of Western modernity. Cross Damon wants to do the opposite, to dissolve the racial question and transcend its limitations on his subjectivity. Yet in doing so, paradoxically the novel must adopt a form, a literary protocol that reasserts something very like Chandler's radical critique, that is, a total and immanent critique of Western modernity from the perspective of the black outsider to it, which is after all what Wright said he was setting out to do.

145. See Keith, *Unbecoming Americans*.

146. Keith, 67.

147. This is from Kierkegaard's *The Concept of Anxiety*, which Wright would have read in Walter Lowrie's 1944 Princeton University Press translation *The Concept of Dread*. See also Floyd W. Hayes III, "The Concept of Double Vision in Richard Wright's *The Outsider*," in *Existence in Black: An Anthology of Black Existential Philosophy*, ed. Lewis R. Gordon (New York: Routledge, 1997), 173–84, at 175.

148. Wright, *The Outsider*, 395.

149. Wright, 396.

150. Wright, 421.

151. Wright, 375.

152. Ralph Ellison, *Invisible Man* (New York: Vintage, 1989), 265–66.

153. Adorno's "Words from Abroad" appears in Theodor W. Adorno, *Notes to Literature*, ed. Rolf Tiedemann, trans. Shierry Weber Nicholsen (New York: Columbia University Press, 1991), 1:192. Nicholsen translates Adorno's *Erde* as "earth," "a language without earth," but "soil" seems closer to me in the relevant sense, e.g., "on foreign soil." In the same essay, Adorno notes in passing that "Benjamin sometimes adopted this implicit hostility to foreign words when he called philosophical terminology a pimp language" (1:190). It feels rather apt to describe Cross Damon, in Benjamin's sense, as speaking a pimp's language throughout most of the novel.

154. Wright, *The Outsider*, 382.

155. Wright, 385.

156. JanMohamed, *Death-Bound-Subject*, 43.

157. JanMohamed, 389.

158. Wright, *The Outsider*, 396.

159. Wright, 419.

160. Wright, 401.

161. Wright, 411.

162. Wright, 426.

163. Wright, 446.

164. In her essay "Mama's Baby, Papa's Maybe: An American Gramma Book," Spillers writes: "Before the 'body' there is 'flesh,' that zero degree of social conceptualization that does not escape concealment under the brush of discourse or the reflexes of iconography." Hortense J. Spillers, *Black, White and in Color: Essays on American Literature and Culture* (Chicago: University of Chicago Press, 2003), 206.

165. Luce Irigaray, *The Sex Which Is Not One*, trans. Catherine Porter (Ithaca, NY: Cornell University Press, 1985), 111. It is also possible that Wright had in mind Sartre's description of the uses of the viscous: "The slimy substance, like pitch, is an aberrant

fluid. The slimy reveals itself as essentially ambiguous because its fluidity exists in slow motion. There is a sticky thickness in its liquidity. It presents itself as a phenomena in the process of becoming … for the soft is only an annihilation which is stopped half-way; soft is what furnishes us with the best image of our own destructive [and constructive] power and its limitations." Jean-Paul Sartre, *Being and Nothingness: A Phenomenological Essay on Ontology*, trans. Hazel Barnes (New York: Washington Square Press, 1956), 775.

166. See Rabinowitz, *Black, White and Noir*. There is, however, one film that Rabinowitz doesn't mention, and that is Carol Reed and Graham Greene's *The Third Man* (1949), starring Orson Welles, which shares obvious thematic concerns and notably the famous Ferris wheel scene, which I think Wright directly alludes to (in addition to *King Lear*) in Ely Houston's speech about "the *third* man" who "feels toward those two men as those two men feel towards the masses of people … He's playing the same game, but on a much smaller scale…. He kill's em, and with no more compunction than if he were killing flies." Wright, *The Outsider* (New York: HarperCollins, 1953), 357.

167. Wright, *The Outsider*, 415.

168. Mary Douglas, *Purity and Danger* (New York: Routledge, 2002), 2.

169. Douglas, 485. The list goes on at some length beyond what is quoted here.

170. See Farah Jasmine Griffin, *Who Set You Flowin'? The African-American Migration Narrative* (New York: Oxford University Press, 1995).

171. Wright, *The Outsider*, 500.

172. Lionel Trilling, "A Tragic Situation," *The Nation*, April 7, 1945, 391–92. See also Fabre, *Unfinished Quest*, 279.

173. For an excellent overview of the politics of Trilling's navigation of midcentury ideology, his relation to Judaism, and an argument for the novel's prescient projection of a rightward shift in postwar Jewish intellectual life, see Michael Kimmage, "Lionel Trilling's 'The Middle of the Journey' and the Complicated Origins of the Neo-Conservative Movement," *Shofar* 21, no. 3 (2003): 48–63.

174. Wright's card also indicates that the same year he was reading André Gide's novels, Dostoyevsky's *The Gambler*; Henry Green's *Party Going*; and Robert Graves's *Goodbye to All That*. Borrowers Cards, A–Z; 1922–1961; box 43, Sylvia Beach Papers, Manuscripts Division, Department of Rare Books and Special Collections, Princeton University Library, Princeton, NJ.

175. Kiuchi and Hakutani, *Richard Wright*, 156.

176. Of particular interest as applied to Wright and his affective community, but also to the politics of black masculinity writ large, is the following passage from Derrida's famous essay on the subject: "Again Montaigne on his friendship with La Boetie: 'In truth, the name of brother is a beautiful and delectable one, and for this reason we made it, he and I, our alliance.' These exclusions of the feminine would have some relation to the movement that has always 'politicized' the model of friendship at the very moment one tries to remove this model from an integral politicization. The tension here is within politics itself. It would be necessary to analyze all discourses that reserve politics and public space for man, domestic and private space for woman." Jacques Derrida, "The Politics of Friendship," *Journal of Philosophy* 85, no. 11 (November 1988): 642.

177. Kiuchi and Hakutani, *Richard Wright*, 157.

178. Kiuchi and Hakutani, 212.

179. James Baldwin, *Nobody Knows My Name* (New York: Dial Press, 1961), 191–92.

180. Keith, *Unbecoming Americans*, 135.

181. Wright, *The Outsider*, 587.

182. The role of Central Intelligence Agency patronage in US and European cultural circles in the Cold War is widely known and no longer disputed. It's worth pointing out that Wright detested and was infuriated by the US government's surveillance and meddling in his life. Interestingly, he appears to have found out about the Congress for Cultural Freedom's CIA connection well before the program's cover was blown by *Ramparts* in 1967. When Richard Crossman asked Wright to contribute to a new volume, Wright castigated him for producing government propaganda and refused. See Rowley, *Life and Times*, 520.

183. Wright, *The Outsider*, 590.

184. See Rowley, *Life and Times*, 92–93.

185. Rowley, 92.

186. Goldsby writes about these artists in her forthcoming book; she has previously discussed these ideas in "The Art of Being Difficult: The Turn to Abstraction in African American Poetry and Painting during the 1940s and 1950s," a lecture delivered at Brigham Young University on March 7, 2014.

187. Wright, *The Outsider*, 590–91.

188. Wright, 574.

189. Wright, 751.

190. Wright, 756.

191. Wright, 763.

192. Wright, 840.

193. Wright, 840.

194. Zora Neale Hurston, *Dust Tracks on a Road*, ed. Robert Hemenway (Urbana: University of Illinois Press, 1984).

195. Daphne A. Brooks, "'Sister, Can You Line It Out?': Zora Neale Hurston and the Sound of Angular Black Womanhood," *Amerikastudien/American Studies* 55, no. 4 (2010): 623.

196. Hortense J. Spillers, "Mama's Baby, Papa's Maybe: An American Grammar Book," *Diacritics* 17, no. 2 (1987): 64–81, at 80.

197. This excavation and critique of masculinist ideology, as Roland Murray has observed, was already being undertaken by black male writers like John Edgar Wideman in *The Lynchers* (1973) and John Oliver Killens in *The Cotillion; or, One Good Bull Is Half the Herd* (1971), texts that are often neglected when we consider the response and dissent to this tendency. See Roland Murray, *Our Living Manhood: Literature, Black Power, and Masculine Ideology* (Philadelphia: University of Pennsylvania Press, 2007).

198. Richard Wright, *Later Works* (New York: Library of America, 1991), 364.

199. Wright, 365.

200. Adorno, *Notes to Literature*, 1:54.

Conclusion

1. "Il nous fait tout à coup respirer un air nouveau, précisément parce que c'est un air qu'on a respiré autrefois, cet air plus pur que les poètes ont vainement essayé de faire régner dans le Paradis et qui ne pourrait donner cette sensation profonde de renouvelle-

ment que s'il avait été respiré déjà, car les vrais paradis sont les paradis qu'on a perdus." Marcel Proust, *À la recherche du temps perdu* (Paris: Gallimard, 1927), 2:12.

2. George Lamming, *The Pleasures of Exile* (Ann Arbor: University of Michigan Press, 1992), 24.

3. Lamming, 261.

4. Farah Jasmine Griffin, "Hunting Communists and Negroes in Ann Petry's *The Narrows*," in *Revising the Blueprint: Ann Petry and the Literary Left*, ed. Alex Lubin (Jackson: Mississippi University Press, 2007), 137.

5. Wright Morris, "The Complexity of Evil," *New York Times Book Review*, August 16, 1953, 27–28. Incidentally, if one were truly looking for midcentury "mulatto" Molly Blooms, one would do better to look for them in the pages of the Trinidadian writer Sam Selvon's *The Lonely Londoners*, another quintessentially Blue Period novel. Set among the first wave of Caribbean emigrants to England, Selvon's West Indian creolization of Joyce (as well as a host of other canonical writers) has long been a source of interest to scholars of postcolonial and modernist studies alike. One of the most perceptive and original accounts of the stylistics in Selvon's novel can be found in Jean-Jacques Lecercle, "Three Accounts of Literary Style," *CR: The New Centennial Review* 16, no. 3 (2016): 151–71. For an example of the perspective from Joyce studies, see Kiron Ward, "Hypercanonical Joyce: Sam Selvon's *The Lonely Londoners*, Creative Disaffiliation, and the Global Afterlives of Ulysses," *Textual Practice* 36, no. 2 (2022): 326–47.

6. On the narrative tensions and affordance of exploring interracial desire in writing from this period, including Petry's, see Tyler T. Schmidt, *Desegregating Desire: Race and Sexuality in Cold War American Literature* (Jackson: University Press of Mississippi, 2013).

7. Nadia Ellis, *Territories of the Soul: Queered Belonging in the Black Diaspora* (Durham, NC: Duke University Press, 2015), 66, 82.

8. Niyi Osundare, "Half a Century Later," *Journal of the African Literature Association* 1, no. 1 (2006): 250–57.

9. Osundare, 250.

10. Alioune Diop is yet another example of a figure who sought to create a space for thinking about blackness and its place in the world outside of the confines of the geopolitics of the day. As Peter Kalliney notes: "Présence Africaine is probably the most resolutely nonaligned intellectual venue of the midcentury period … Alioune Diop, its founding editor, puts it very bluntly in the opening line of the magazine's first editorial statement: "This review is not under the bidding of any philosophical or political ideology.'" Peter J. Kalliney, *The Aesthetic Cold War: Decolonization and Global Literature* (Princeton, NJ: Princeton University Press, 2022), 33.

11. Arguably the best oral-history account of the origins and development of *Présence africaine* from 1947 through the early 1990s is Bennetta Jules-Rosette's interview with Christiane Yandé Diop and the Malagasy poet Jacques Rabemananjara. See Bennetta Jules-Rosette, *Black Paris: The African Writers' Landscape* (Urbana: University of Illinois Press, 1998), 43–48.

12. Osundare, "Half a Century Later," 256.

13. Osundare, 256.

14. Baldwin's "Princes and Powers" appears in James Baldwin, *Collected Essays* (New York: Library of America, 1998), 152.

15. "Take Me to the Water," in Baldwin, *Collected Essays*, 383.

16. "Alas, Poor Richard," in Baldwin, 257–58.

17. Édouard Glissant, "Note sur une 'Poésie Nationale' chez les peuples noirs," *Les lettres nouvelles* 4, no. 36 (March 1956): 393.

18. Aimé Césaire, "Sur la poésie nationale," *Présence africaine* 1, nos. 165–66 (2002): 223. The essay was originally published in *Présence africaine* 2, no. 4 (October–November 1955): 39–41.

19. "Princes and Powers," in Baldwin, *Collected Essays*, 169.

20. Baldwin, 169.

21. Hughes's politics were admirably and even heroically constant. The author of *Scottsboro Limited* never renounced his militant leftist convictions despite the McCarthy hearings and HUAC and their attacks on him personally. He never forgave their efforts to destroy, discredit, and throw into disarray the left Popular Front culture he loved and was so deeply instrumental in fostering.

22. Arnold Rampersad, *The Life of Langston Hughes*, vol. 2, *1914-1967, I Dream a World* (New York: Oxford University Press, 2002), 409.

23. Rampersad, *I Dream a World*, 410.

24. Anatole Broyard, *Kafka Was the Rage: A Greenwich Village Memoir* (New York: Vintage, 1997), 31. For an overview of Broyard's social and literary circles during this period, see Lawrence Jackson, *Indignant Generation: A Narrative History of African American Writers and Critics, 1934-1960* (Princeton, NJ: Princeton University Press, 2011), 291–96.

25. For an overview of Umbra, especially in relationship to the New York poetry scene, see Daniel Kane, *All Poets Welcome: The Lower East Side Poetry Scene in the 1960s* (Berkeley: University of California Press, 2003), 79–90. For an excellent assessment of the poetics and politics of Umbra, see Jon Panish, "'As Radical as Society Demands the Truth to Be': Umbra's Racial Politics and Poetics," in *Don't Ever Get Famous: Essays on New York Writing after the New York School*, ed. Daniel Kane (Champaign, IL: Dalkey Archive Press, 2006), 80–114.

26. Quoted in Kane, *All Poets Welcome*, 82.

27. Kane, 82.

28. Amiri Baraka, *The Autobiography of LeRoi Jones/Amiri Baraka* (New York: Scribner, 1984), 199.

29. "The crowd of dudes I was hanging with had swollen, it seemed that that place on Cooper Square became a meeting place for a certain kind of black intellectual during that period. But it was not just a casual circle anymore, there was clearly something forming, something about to come into being. We sat around trying to talk it and coax it into being. I met Max Stanford, from Philly, who'd recently moved to New York. I didn't know it at first, but Max was with the Revolutionary Action Movement (RAM), which had just formed. Larry Neal became a part of that group. Larry, clean as blue wind, would sit in and contribute to those discussions of what was going on in the world, who were we in it, what was the role of the black artist. What should our art be? Larry was a poet, and he too had come up out of Philly and was also, unbeknownst to me, with RAM." Baraka, 198.

30. Baraka, 200.

31. Hettie Jones, *How I Became Hettie Jones* (New York: Grove Press, 1996), 222.

32. Baraka, *Autobiography of LeRoi Jones/Amiri Baraka*, 197.

33. At least publicly. Privately, things were much messier. Hettie Cohen paints a

very different portrait of the immediate period after the assassination, which depicts a rather more pathetic and stumbling Baraka than the persona he projects founding the Black Arts Repertory Theatre/School and parading across 125th Street heroically with Sun Ra. "All that spring of 1965, Roi came home to read his mail, change his clothes, and makes sorrowful love, comparing his situation to that of Jomo Kenyatta, who'd left an English wife to lead the Kenyan people. He'd fumble around his neglected desk; I knew he wasn't writing." Jones, *How I Became Hettie Jones*, 223.

34. Baraka, *Autobiography of LeRoi Jones/Amiri Baraka*, 201.

35. On the convergence of black radical movements and the Algerian revolution, see Elaine Mokhtefi, *Algiers, Third World Capital: Black Panthers, Freedom Fighters, Revolutionaries* (London: Verso, 2018).

36. For Cabral's role and impact on black radical movements in the United States, see the notes recorded by the Africa Information Service from his meeting with leaders on his visit to the United States in October 20, 1962, published as "Connecting the Struggles: An Informal Talk with Black Americans," in *Return to the Source: Selected Speeches of Amílcar Cabral* (New York: Monthly Review Press, 1974), 75–92. For an insider's assessment of this militant phase of the black freedom struggle, see Muhammad Ahmad [Maxwell Stanford Jr.], *We Will Return in the Whirlwind Black Radical Organizations, 1960–1975* (Chicago: Charles H. Kerr, 2007).

37. Che's guerilla theories are a central focus of Régis Debray's *La révolution dans la révolution? Lutte armée et lutte politique en Amérique latine* (Paris: Maspero, 1967). On Debray's relaying of *foco* theory, and for a compelling and concise periodization and analysis of the objective historical determinants of the late 1960s, see Fredric Jameson, "Periodizing the 60s," *Social Text*, nos. 9–10 (Spring–Summer 1984): 178–209.

38. Che Guevara, from his *Message to the Tricontinental* (Havana: Executive Secretariat of the Organization for Solidarity of the Peoples of Africa, Asia, and Latin America, 1967), as quoted in Michelle D. Paranzino "'Two, Three, Many Vietnams': Che Guevara's Tricontinental Revolutionary Vision," in *The Tricontinental Revolution: Third World Radicalism and the Cold War*, ed. R. Joseph Parrott and Mark Atwood Lawrence, Cambridge Studies in US Foreign Relations (Cambridge: Cambridge University Press, 2022), 298.

39. For a substantial definition of *Third Worldism*, see Robert Malley, *The Call from Algeria: Third Worldism, Revolution, and the Turn to Islam* (Berkeley: University of California Press, 1996), 2–5. The English-language release of Chris Marker's 1977 film *Le fond de l'air est rouge* was *A Grin without a Cat*. A more literal translation would be something like "The Atmosphere Is Red." The subtitle of the film is "Scenes from the Third World War (1967–1977)."

40. The best and, for now, only extensive source of biographical information on Smith is LeRoy S. Hodges Jr., *Portrait of an Expatriate: William Gardner Smith, Writer* (Westport, CT: Greenwood Press, 1985).

41. "No figure embodied the contradictions of democracy and the ironies of the Allied war effort more poignantly than the Negro Soldier." Vaughn Rasberry, *Race and the Totalitarian Century: Geopolitics in the Black Literary Imagination* (Cambridge, MA: Harvard University Press, 2016), 29.

42. Quoted in Robert A. Bone, *The Negro Novel in America* (New Haven, CT: Yale University Press, 1965), 176. See William Gardner Smith, "The Negro Writer: Pitfalls and Compensations," *Phylon* 11, no. 4 (1950): 297–303.

43. Smith, 303.

44. Smith, 303.

45. G. F. Eckstein (C. L. R. James), "Two Young American Writers," *Fourth International* (March–April 1950), 56.

46. Some of this neglect seems not entirely benign. Smith's obituary in the *Times* (not unlike Wright's) is extremely laconic and careless. It misleadingly describes his first novel and typos mar the 1963 book, which also loses its article: "From that experience, he wrote his first book, 'The Last of the Conquerors,' about the problems of black Americans in Germany.... He also wrote three novels, 'Anger at Innocence,' 'South Street' and 'Stain Face' all on the subject of race." See "William Gardner Smith, Author And Newspaperman, Dies at 47," *New York Times*, November 8, 1974, 42.

47. See Tyler Stovall, "The Fire This Time: Black American Expatriates and the Algerian War," *Yale French Studies* 98 (Fall 2000): 182–200. Kristin Ross writes that Smith's novel "kept a trace of the event alive during the thirty years when it had entered a 'black hole' of memory." See Ross, *May '68 and Its Afterlives* (Chicago: University of Chicago Press 2002), 44.

48. Jean-Luc Einaudi's research put a spotlight on Maurice Papon and his coordination of Jewish deportations while police prefect in the Gironde between 1942 and 1944, in addition to his role in the massacre of Algerians in October 1961 and the killing of French Communist Party members demonstrating against right-wing terrorist violence by the Secret Armed Organization in 1962. Papon was eventually indicted in 1998 for crimes against humanity relating to his involvement in the deportation of Jews to Auschwitz; he was never held responsible for his role in the killing of Algerians or communists. See Jean-Luc Einaudi, *La bataille de Paris, 17 octobre 1961* (Paris: Seuil, 1991). On French state censorship, see Fabrice Riceputi, *La bataille d'Einaudi: Comment la mémoire du 17 octobre 1961 revint à la République* (Neuvy-en-Champagne, France: Éditions le Passager Clandestin, 2015).

49. See Paul Gilroy, *Against Race: Imagining Political Culture beyond the Color Line* (Cambridge, MA: Harvard University Press, 2000), 316–26, at 323. Gilroy's assessment is challenged by Alexa Weik von Mossner, who argues persuasively that the novel enacts a "critical and reflexive cosmopolitanism" that Gilroy underappreciates in his reading. See Alexa Weik von Mossner, "Confronting *The Stone Face*: The Critical Cosmopolitanism of William Gardner Smith," *African American Review* 45, nos. 1–2 (2012): 167–82.

50. William Gardner Smith, *The Stone Face* (New York: Farrar, Straus and Co., 1963), 7.

51. Smith, 171–72.

52. In Agamben's terms (by way of Benjamin's essay on "bare life" that Agamben is riffing on), the novel discloses the logic of (fascist) sovereignty that establishes its racialist nomos precisely through the juridical linkage "of the rule of law over the living" so that it will "exist and cease to exist alongside bare life." Giorgio Agamben, *Homo Sacer: Sovereign Power and Bare Life*, trans. Daniel Heller-Roazen (Stanford, CA: Stanford University Press, 1998), 65.

53. Smith, *Stone Face*, 195–96. The insistence on the dehumanizing aspects of torture techniques marks another rapprochement with Fanon. But it also has a wider set of implications in its foreshadowing of the use of torture as a major instrument of military prosecution in the Cold War's many "dirty wars," and post-2001 in the US-led led Global War on Terror. Indeed, it has been shown that the "counterinsurgency" and

"pacification" methods developed and deployed by the French in Algeria (notably by Roger Trinquier and Paul Aussaresses) formed the template for the Central Intelligence Agency's Phoenix program in Vietnam and for various military juntas throughout Central and Latin America, notably Argentina and Chile, which appear to have received training directly from the French, much as the School of the Americas offered US training in the same inhumane "techniques" to client authoritarian regimes seeking to uproot any leftist opposition to their rule. Before Gillo Pontecorvo's *Battle of Algiers* (1966), one of the only other representations of torture in Algeria was Jean-Luc Godard's *Le petit soldat*, completed in 1960 but censored in France until 1963, making it a compelling text to consider alongside *The Stone Face*. The important point is that the use of torture was not a response or a reaction to terrorism. It was, as Marnia Lazreg, has shown, "the direct outcome of *guerre révolutionnaire* (revolutionary-war) theory, elaborated by a number of (colonial) military officers in the 1950s." See Marnia Lazreg, *Torture and the Twilight of Empire: From Algiers to Baghdad* (Princeton, NJ: Princeton University Press, 2008), 15. I am convinced that Smith's deliberate inclusion of the description of the tactics of French military torture is informed through his journalistic contacts at high levels. In other words, he understood and was trying to give expression to this important and still deeply misunderstood or mischaracterized aspect of anti-insurgent warfare as conducted by the Western powers primarily on postcolonial sites and on the bodies of postcolonial subjects.

54. On Levinas, see his *Totality and Infinity: An Essay on Exteriority*, trans. Alphonso Lingis (Dordrecht, Netherlands: Kluwer Academic Publishers, 1991).

55. Smith, *Stone Face*, 202.

56. Smith, 205–6.

57. "In the postwar world, struggles for African American freedom and decolonization were not just mutually analogous. They were directly engaged with one another as components of a wider offensive against the citadels and far corners of the imperial structure of racial capitalism." John Munro, *The Anticolonial Front: The African American Freedom Struggle and Global Decolonization, 1945–1960* (New York: Cambridge University Press, 2017), 311.

58. I have argued for reading *The Stone Face* as epitomizing the "anticolonial novel." See Jesse McCarthy, "Form and the Anticolonial Novel: William Gardner Smith's *The Stone Face*," *Novel* 55 (1): 61–94.

59. Smith, *Stone Face*, 212.

60. Smith, 213.

61. William Gardner Smith, *Return to Black America* (Englewood Cliffs, NJ: Prentice-Hall, 1970), 4.

62. David Scott, *Conscripts of Modernity: The Tragedy of Colonial Enlightenment* (Durham, NC: Duke University Press, 2004), 210.

63. Sigmund Freud, *Civilization and Its Discontents* (New York: W. W. Norton, 2010).

64. Fisk was an important site of Demby's self-fashioning as a young black writer. He noted in his 2008 interview with Giovanna Micconi that "many of the Harlem Renaissance survivors still taught there. Aaron Douglas was there, Arna Bontemps was the librarian, John Work was the choral music director and was in charge of the Fisk Jubilee choir." William Demby and Giovanna Micconi, "Ghosts of History: An Interview with William Demby," *Amerikastudien/American Studies* 56, no. 1 (2011): 125–26.

65. Demby and Micconi, 123. Demby's connection to Rossellini, and through Citto

Masselli to Michelangelo Antonioni, is clearly an important line of reciprocal influence that merits further study. I would note in passing the important echo in scenic construction between the ending of *The Catacombs* and the famous scene with Ingrid Bergman in the Naples Archeological Museum in Rossellini's *Viaggio in Italia* (1954). More broadly, the aesthetic suturing of American jazz to postwar Italian film is a cultural matrix of which Demby is both a contributor and a symptomatic example.

66. Demby and Micconi, 133.

67. William Demby, *The Catacombs* (New York: Pantheon Books, 1965), 13.

68. Demby, 15; Demby and Micconi, "Ghosts of History," 134.

69. Sharon Patricia Holland, *The Erotic Life of Racism* (Durham, NC: Duke University Press, 2012). Especially relevant here is Holland's observation that racism as a lived quotidian experience (which it certainly is for Doris) is socially intimate, interpersonal, "erotic," even as it is violently abstractionist, interpolating subjects into imposed historical narratives they have no say in.

70. Demby and Micconi, "Ghosts of History," 134.

71. Sara Marzioli, "The Subterranean Performance of History between Harlem and Rome in William Demby's *The Catacombs*," *African American Review* 47, nos. 2–3 (2014): 422.

72. Demby (whose father worked in the oil industry) was keen to underscore Algeria's far-reaching geopolitical implications, noting that it anticipated "the rise of the Muslim world and of its appropriation of the sources of oil that would condition Western history. You could feel that the war was not just an anti-colonial war, but that oil had much to do with it. It involved the plane crash of Enrico Mattei and the oil companies I was familiar with. All of this was discussed in Rome, in the gossip underneath the surface of café talk.... The church, the Communist party, and the CIA—these were the people who were financing history." Demby and Micconi, "Ghosts of History," 135.

73. Demby mentions De Chirico as an early enthusiasm in his interview: "At least once a week I'd go to the Carnegie Museum, which was almost ten or twelve miles away from home, to wander through the galleries and gaze for hours at the works of the Italian artists, modernists like Giorgio de Chirico. Demby and Micconi, 124. On De Chirico's self-conception of his "metaphysical" architectural paintings, see a more recently discovered autograph essay, "Giorgio De Chirico," trans. Ara H. Merjian, *Grey Room*, no. 44 (Summer 2011): 86–89; Ara H. Merjian, *Giorgio de Chirico and the Metaphysical City: Nietzsche, Modernism, Paris* (New Haven, CT: Yale University Press, 2014).

74. Marzioli, "Subterranean Performance of History," 418–19.

75. See Demby, *Catacombs*, 3, 210–11. Rotella's involvement with lettrism and the *nouveau réalistes* provides a possible connection to the situationists and the circulation of ideas in these vanguard circles about the relationship between mediation, capitalism, and spectacle, concerns that Demby places at the forefront of his novel. On the vanguard art-world connections of these groups, see Craig J. Saper, *Networked Art* (Minneapolis: University of Minnesota Press, 2001), 163.

76. Guy Debord, *The Society of the Spectacle*, trans. Donald Nicholson-Smith (Brooklyn, NY: Zone Books, 1994).

77. See James C. Hall, *Mercy Mercy Me: African-American Culture and the American Sixties* (New York: Oxford University Press, 2001), 175. There are obviously tensions between Hall's periodization project and my own. His is a cultural history deeply invested in literature; mine a literary history deeply invested in culture. I continue to think the

first half of the decade bears some qualitative differences with the second. No period-ization is ever going to be clear-cut; Hall's work and my own ought to be considered complementary Venn diagrams over an area of commonly held interests, not rival ac-counts.

78. Hall, 175–76, original emphasis.

79. Demby, *Catacombs*, 10.

80. Demby, 189.

81. Demby, 199.

82. Demby, 199–200.

83. Demby, 179, original emphasis.

84. Daniel J. Boorstin, *The Image: A Guide to Pseudo-Events in America* (New York: Vintage, 1992).

Bibliography

Adorno, Theodor W. *Notes to Literature: Volume One*. Edited by Rolf Tiedemann. Translated by Shierry Weber Nicholsen. New York: Columbia University Press, 1991.

Agamben, Giorgio. *Homo Sacer: Sovereign Power and Bare Life*. Translated by Daniel Heller-Roazen. Stanford, CA: Stanford University Press, 1998.

Ahmad, Muhammad [Maxwell Stanford Jr.]. *We Will Return in the Whirlwind: Black Radical Organizations, 1960-1975*. Chicago: Charles H. Kerr, 2007.

Alexander, Elizabeth. *The Black Interior: Essays*. Minneapolis: Graywolf Press, 2004.

Als, Hilton. "Black and Blue: A New Look at Alice Childress." *New Yorker*, October 10, 2011, 132-33.

Althusser, Louis. *Lenin and Philosophy and Other Essays*. Translated by Ben Brewster. New York: Monthly Review Press, 1971.

Anderson, Benedict. *Imagined Communities: Reflections on the Origin and Spread of Nationalism*. New York: Verso, 1983.

Aristotle. *Poetics*. New York: Penguin, 1996.

Arnold, James A., ed. *History of Literature in the Caribbean*. Vol. 1, *Hispanic and Francophone Regions*. Philadelphia: John Benjamins Publishing, 1994.

———. *History of Literature in the Caribbean*. Vol. 2, *English- and Dutch-Speaking Regions*. Philadelphia: John Benjamins Publishing, 2001.

Baker, Houston, Jr. *Workings of the Spirit: The Poetics of Afro-American Women's Writing*. Chicago: University of Chicago Press, 1991.

Bakhtin, Mikhail. *Problems of Dostoevsky's Poetics*. Edited and translated by Caryl Emerson. Minneapolis: University of Minnesota Press, 1984.

Balakian, Nona. "Black Odyssey, White World." *New York Times*, July 21, 1973, 25.

Balderrama, Maria R., ed. *Wifredo Lam and His Contemporaries, 1938-1952*. New York: Studio Museum Harlem, 1992.

Baldwin, James. *Collected Essays*. Edited by Toni Morrison. New York: Library of America 1998.

———. *The Cross of Redemption: Uncollected Writings*. Edited by Randall Kennan. New York: Vintage, 2011.

———. *Go Tell It on the Mountain*. New York: Vintage, 2013.

———. "The Negro at Home and Abroad." *The Reporter*, November 27, 1951, 36–37.

———. *Nobody Knows My Name*. New York: Dial Press, 1961.

———. *Notes of a Native Son*. Boston: Beacon Press, 1957.

Bambara, Toni Cade. "Report from Part One." *New York Times Book Review*, January 7, 1973, 1.

Baraka, Amiri. *The Autobiography of LeRoi Jones/Amiri Baraka*. New York: Scribner, 1984.

Barbour, Thomas. "Little Magazines in Paris." *Hudson Review* 4, no. 2 (Summer 1951): 278–83.

Barret, Lindon. *Blackness and Value: Seeing Double*. New York: Cambridge University Press, 1999.

———. *Racial Blackness and the (Dis)continuity of Western Modernity*. Edited by Justin A. Joyce, Dwight McBride, and John Carlos Rowe. Urbana: University of Illinois Press, 2014.

Barthes, Roland. *Image-Music-Text*. Translated by Stephen Heath. New York: Hill and Wang, 1977.

Bellow, Saul. *The Adventures of Augie March*. New York: Viking Books, 1953.

Benjamin, Walter. *The Writer of Modern Life: Essays on Charles Baudelaire*. Translated by Edmund Jephcott, Harry Zohn, Howard Eiland, and Rodney Livingstone. Cambridge, MA: Harvard University Press, 2006.

Berwick, Carly. "Stranger in America." *Art in America*, no. 5 (May 2011): 124–25.

Bhabha, Homi. "Remembering Fanon." *New Formations*, Spring 1987, 118–24.

Blair, Sara. *Harlem Crossroads: Black Writers and the Photograph in the Twentieth Century*. Princeton, NJ: Princeton University Press, 2007.

Blaise, Fonkoua Romual. "Édouard Glissant: Naissance d'une anthropologie antillaise au siècle de l'assimilation." *Cahiers d'études africaines* 35, no. 140 (1995): 797–818.

Blanchot, Maurice. *The Space of Literature*. Lincoln: University of Nebraska Press, 1989.

———. *The Book to Come*. Translated by Charlotte Mandell. Stanford, CA: Stanford University Press, 2003.

Bland, Edward. "Racial Bias and Negro Poetry." *Poetry* 63, no. 6 (March 1944): 328–33.

Bolden, Tony. *Afro-Blue: Improvisations in African American Poetry and Culture*. Champaign: University of Illinois Press, 2003.

Bone, Robert A. *The Negro Novel in America*. New Haven, CT: Yale University Press, 1965.

Bone, Robert A., and Richard A. Courage, eds. *The Muse in Bronzeville: African American Creative Expression in Chicago, 1932–1950*. New Brunswick, NJ: Rutgers University Press, 2011.

Bontemps, Arna. "The Outsider by Richard Wright." *Saturday Review*, March 28, 1953, 15–16.

Boorstin, Daniel J. *The Image: A Guide to Pseudo-Events in America*. New York: Vintage, 1992.

Bourdieu, Pierre. *The Field of Cultural Production*. New York: Columbia University Press, 1993.

Breton, André. "A Great Black Poet." In *Notebook of a Return to the Native Land*, translated and edited by Clayton Eshleman and Annette Smith, ix–xix. Middletown, CT: Wesleyan University Press, 2001.

Briones, Matthew M. "Call-and-Response: Tracing the Ideological Shifts of Richard

Wright through His Correspondence with Friends and Fellow Literati." *African American Review* 37, no. 1 (Spring 2003): 53–64.

Britton, Celia. *Édouard Glissant and Postcolonial Theory: Strategies of Language and Resistance*. Charlottesville: University of Virginia Press, 1999.

———. "Ethnography as Relation: The Significance of the French Caribbean in the Ethnographic Writing of Michel Leiris." *French Studies* 66, no. 1 (January 2012): 41–53.

———. "Souvenirs des années 40 à la Martinique: Interview avec Édouard Glissant." *L'esprit créateur* 47, no. 1 (Spring 2007): 96–104.

Brooks, Daphne A. "'Sister, Can You Line It Out?': Zora Neale Hurston and the Sound of Angular Black Womanhood." *Amerikastudien/American Studies* 55, no. 4 (2010): 617–27.

Brooks, Gwendolyn. *Annie Allen*. New York: Harper & Brothers, 1949.

———. "Chicago Portraits: A Series of Sketches of Chicago Life." *Negro Story* 1, no. 1 (May–June 1944): 49–53.

———. *In the Mecca*. New York: Harper & Row, 1968.

———. *Maud Martha*. New York: Harpers & Brothers, 1953.

———. *Report from Part One*. Detroit: Broadside Press, 1972.

———. *Report from Part Two*. Chicago: Third World Press, 1996.

———. "Revision of the Invocation," *Negro Story*, May–June 1945, 77–78.

———. *A Street in Bronzeville*. New York: Harper & Row, 1945.

Brown, Adrienne, and Valerie Smith, eds. *Race and Real Estate*. New York: Oxford University Press, 2015.

Brown, Frank London. *Trumbull Park*. Lebanon, NH: Northeastern University Press, 2005.

Brown, Marshall. *Turning Points: Essays in the History of Cultural Expressions*. Stanford, CA: Stanford University Press, 1997.

Brown, Stephanie. *The Postwar African American Novel: Protest and Discontent, 1945–1950*. Jackson: University Press of Mississippi, 2011.

Browning, Alice C., and Fern Gayden. "Letter to Our Readers." *Negro Story*, May–June 1944, 1.

Broyard, Anatole. *Kafka Was the Rage: A Greenwich Village Memoir*. New York: Vintage, 1997.

Bryant, Earle V. *Byline, Richard Wright: Articles from the* Daily Worker *and* New Masses. Columbia: University of Missouri Press, 2014.

Buck-Morss, Susan. "The Flaneur, the Sandwichman and the Whore: The Politics of Loitering." *New German Critique*, no. 39 (Autumn 1986): 99–140.

Burroughs, Nannie H., Charles S. Johnson, John M. Gries, and James Ford. *Negro Housing: A Report of the Committee on Negro Housing*. Washington, DC: President's Conference on Home Building and Home Ownership, 1932.

Bush, Ruth. *Publishing Africa in French: Literary Institutions and Decolonization, 1945–1967*. Liverpool, UK: Liverpool University Press, 2016.

Cabral, Amílcar. "Connecting the Struggles: An Informal Talk with Black Americans." In *Return to the Source: Selected Speeches of Amílcar Cabral*, 75–92. New York: Monthly Review Press, 1974.

Cadogan, Garnette. "Due North." In *Tales of Two Cities: Stories of Inequality in a Divided New York*, edited by John Freeman, 1–11. New York: Penguin, 2015.

Cailler, Bernadette. *Conquérants de la nuit nue: Édouard Glissant et l'H(h)istoire antillaise*. Tübingen, Germany: Gunter Narr Verlag, 1988.

Calhoun, Doyle. "Fanon's Lexical Intervention: Writing Blackness in *Black Skin, White Masks*." *Paragraph (Modern Critical Theory Group)* 43, no. 2 (2020): 159–78.

Callahan, John F., and Marc C. Connor, eds. *The Selected Letters of Ralph Ellison*. New York: Random House, 2019.

Cameron, Sharon. *Thinking in Henry James*. Chicago: University of Chicago Press, 1989.

Carpio, Glenda R., and Werner Sollors. "Five Harlem Short Stories by Zora Neale Hurston" *Amerikastudien/American Studies* 55, no. 4 (2010): 557–60.

Carter, Vincent O. *The Bern Book: A Record of a Voyage of the Mind*. New York: John Day Co., 1970.

———. *Such Sweet Thunder*. Hanover, NH: Steerforth Press, 2003.

Casanova, Pascale. *The World Republic of Letters*. Cambridge, MA: Harvard University Press, 2004.

Cater, Suzy. "A Schizophrenia That Wasn't One: Édouard Glissant and Poetry, Painting and Politics in 1950s Paris." *French Forum* 41, no. 3 (Winter 2016): 257–72.

Césaire, Aimé. *Notebook of a Return to the Native Land*. Translated and edited by Clayton Eshleman and Annette Smith. Middletown, CT: Wesleyan University Press, 2001.

———. *Discourse on Colonialism*. Translated by Joan Pinkham. New York: Monthly Review Press, 2000.

———. "Letter to Maurice Thorez." Translated by Chike Jeffers. *Social Text 103* 28, no. 2 (Summer 2010): 145–52.

———. *The Original 1939 Notebook of a Return to the Native Land*. Edited and translated by A. James Arnold and Clayton Eshleman. Middletown, CT: Wesleyan University Press, 2013.

———. "Sur la poésie nationale" *Présence africaine* 1, nos. 165–66 (2002): 221–23.

Chakrabarty, Dipesh. *Provincializing Europe: Postcolonial Thought and Historical Difference*. Princeton, NJ: Princeton University Press, 2007.

Chandler, Nahum D. *X: The Problem of the Negro as a Problem for Thought*. New York: Fordham University Press, 2014.

Christian, Barbara. *Black Feminist Criticism: Perspectives on Black Women Writers*. New York: Teachers College Press, 1986.

Cloutier, Jean-Christophe. *Shadow Archives: The Lifecycles of African American Literature*. New York: Columbia University Press, 2019.

Cole, Teju. "Black Body: Reading James Baldwin's Stranger in the Village." *New Yorker*, August 19, 2014.

———. *Known and Strange Things: Essays*. New York: Random House, 2016.

Colletta, Lisa, ed. *The Legacy of the Grand Tour: New Essays on Travel, Literature, and Culture*. Lanham, MD: Fairleigh Dickinson University Press, 2015.

Condé, Maryse. "Autour d'une littérature antillaise." *Présence africaine* 81, no. 1 (1972): 170–71.

———. *Hérémakhonon*. Translated by Richard Philcox. Washington, DC: Three Continents Press, 1982.

———. Interview with Rebecca Wolff. *BOMB*, July 1, 1999, 74–80.

———. *I Tituba: Black Witch of Salem*. Translated by Richard Philcox. Charlottesville: University of Virginia Press, 2009.

———. "Memories of Reading *Les Indes* for the First Time." Translated by Celia Britton. *Callaloo* 36, no. 4 (Fall 2013): 865–68.

———. *Le cœur à rire et à pleurer: Souvenirs de mon enfance*. Paris: Éditions Robert Laffont, 1999.

———. *Tales from the Heart: True Stories from My Childhood*. Translated by Richard Philcox. New York: Soho Press, 2001.

Convery, Maureen. "What Is the Negro Woman's Story? *Negro Story* Magazine and the Dialogue of Feminist Voices." PhD diss., Eastern Michigan University, 2016.

Corcoran, Michael, and Arnie Bernstein, *Hollywood on Lake Michigan: 100 Years of Chicago & the Movies*. Chicago: Lake Claremont Press, 1998.

Corzani, Jack. "Poetry before Negritude." In *History of Literature in the Caribbean*, vol. 1, *Hispanic and Francophone Regions*, edited by James A. Arnold, 465–77. Philadelphia: John Benjamins Publishing, 1994.

Costello, Brannon. "Richard Wright's *Lawd Today!* and the Political Uses of Modernism." *African American Review* 37, no. 1 (2003): 39–52.

Crawley, Ashon T. *Blackpentecostal Breath: The Aesthetics of Possibility*. New York: Fordham University Press, 2017.

Crossman, Richard, ed. *The God that Failed*. New York: Harper & Brothers, 1949.

Cruse, Harold. *The Crisis of the Negro Intellectual*. New York: William Morrow & Co., 1967.

Dadié, Bernard Binlin. *An African in Paris*. Translated by Karen C. Hatch. Urbana: University of Illinois Press, 1994.

———. *The City Where No One Dies*. Translated by Janis Alene Mayes. Washington, DC: Three Continents Press, 1986.

———. *One Way: Bernard Dadié Observes America*. Translated by Jo Patterson. Urbana: University of Illinois Press, 1994.

Dash, J. Michael. "Caraïbe Fantôme: The Play of Difference in the Francophone Caribbean." *Yale French Studies*, no. 103 (2003): 93–105.

———. *Édouard Glissant*. New York: Cambridge University Press, 1995.

Davis, Frank Marshall. *Livin' the Blues: Memoirs of a Black Journalist and Poet*. Edited by John Edgar Tidwell. Madison: University of Wisconsin Press, 2003.

Debord, Guy. *Correspondence: The Foundation of the Situationist International (June 1957–August 1960)*. Translated by Stuart Kendall. Los Angeles: Semiotext(e), 2009.

———. *The Society of the Spectacle*. Translated by Donald Nicholson-Smith. Brooklyn, NY: Zone Books, 1994.

Debray, Régis. *La révolution dans la révolution? Lutte armée et lutte politique en Amérique latine*. Paris: Maspero, 1967.

De Certeau, Michel. *The Practice of Everyday Life*. Berkeley: University of California Press, 1988.

Demby, William. *The Catacombs*. New York: Pantheon Books, 1965.

Denning, Michael. *The Cultural Front: The Laboring of American Culture in the Twentieth Century*. New York: Verso, 1996.

Derouet, Christian, ed. *Christian Zervos et Cahiers d'art, Archives de la Bibliothèque Kandinsky*. Paris: Centre Georges Pompidou, 2011.

Derrida, Jacques. "Living On." In *Parages*, translated by James Hulbert and edited by John P. Leavey, 103–91. Stanford, CA: Stanford University Press, 2010.

———. "The Politics of Friendship." *Journal of Philosophy* 85, no. 11 (November 1988): 632–44.

Dewitte, Philippe. *Les mouvements nègres en France: 1919-1939*. Paris: L'Harmattan, 1985.

Dickstein, Morris. *Dancing in the Dark: A Cultural History of the Great Depression*. New York: W. W. Norton & Co., 2009.

Dodd, Monroe. *A Splendid Ride: The Streetcars of Kansas City, 1870-1957*. Kansas City: Kansas City Star Books, 2002.

Dodson, Owen. "Open Letter" *Negro Story*, May–June 1945, 48.

Dolinar, Brian. *The Black Cultural Front: Black Writers and Artists of the Depression Era Generation*. Jackson: University of Mississippi, 2012.

Doudna, Martin K. *Concerned about the Planet: The* Reporter *Magazine and American Liberalism, 1949-1968*. Greenport, CT: Greenwood Press, 1977.

Douglas, Mary. *Purity and Danger: An Analysis of Concepts of Pollution and Taboo*. New York: Routledge, 2002.

Drabinski, John E., and Marisa Parham, eds. *Theorizing Glissant: Sites and Citations*. London: Rowman & Littlefield, 2015.

Dubey, Madhu. *Signs and Cities: Black Literary Postmodernism*. Chicago: University of Chicago Press, 2003.

Du Bois, W. E. B. *Writings*. Edited by Nathan Huggins. New York: Library of America, 1986.

Dudziak, Mary. *Cold War Civil Rights: Race and the Image of American Democracy*. Princeton, NJ: Princeton University Press, 2011.

Edwards, Brent H. *Epistrophies: Jazz and the Literary Imagination*. Cambridge, MA: Harvard University Press, 2017.

———. *The Practice of Diaspora: Literature, Translation, and the Rise of Black Internationalism*. Cambridge, MA: Harvard University Press, 2003.

Edwards, Erica R. *Charisma and the Fictions of Black Leadership*. Minneapolis: University of Minnesota Press, 2012.

Edwards, Norval. "The Foundational Generation: From *The Beacon* to *Savacou*." In *The Routledge Companion to Anglophone Caribbean Literature*, edited by Michael A. Bucknor and Alison Donnell, 111–23. New York: Routledge, 2011.

Einaudi, Jean-Luc. *La bataille de Paris, 17 octobre 1961*. Paris: Seuil, 1991.

Ellis, Nadia. *Territories of the Soul: Queered Belonging in the Black Diaspora*. Durham, NC: Duke University Press, 2015.

Ellison, Ralph. *Invisible Man*. 1952; New York: Vintage, 1989.

———. *Shadow and Act*. New York: Random House, 1964.

Empson, William. *Some Versions of Pastoral*. New York: New Directions, 1974.

English, Darby. *How to See a Work of Art in Total Darkness*. Cambridge, MA: MIT Press, 2010.

Fabre, Michel. *La rive noire: De Harlem à la Seine*. Paris: Lieu Commun, 1985.

———. *The Unfinished Quest of Richard Wright*. Translated by Isabel Barzun. 1973; Urbana: University of Illinois Press, 1993.

Fanon, Frantz. *Black Skin, White Masks*. Translated by Richard Philcox. 1952; New York: Grove Press, 2008.

———. *Écrits sur l'aliénation et la liberté*. Edited by Jean Khalfa and Robert Young. Paris: Éditions de la Découverte, 2015.

———. *Toward the African Revolution: Political Essays*. Translated by Haakon Chevalier. New York: Grove Press, 1969.

———. *The Wretched of the Earth*. Translated by Constance Farrington. New York: Grove Press, 1968.

Farnsworth, Robert M. ed. *Caviar and Cabbage: Selected Columns by Melvin B. Tolson from the Washington Tribune, 1937–1944*. Columbia: University of Missouri Press, 1982.

Fiedler, Leslie A. *Waiting for the End: A Portrait of Twentieth-Century American Literature and Its Writers*. New York: Stein and Day, 1970.

Field, Douglas. "What Is Africa to Baldwin? Cultural Illegitimacy and the Stepfatherland." In *James Baldwin: America and Beyond*, edited by Cora Kaplan and Bill Schwarz, 209–28. Ann Arbor: University of Michigan Press, 2011.

Flatley, Jonathan. *Affective Mapping: Melancholia and the Politics of Modernism*. Cambridge, MA: Harvard University Press, 2008.

Foley, Barbara. "A Dramatic Picture ... of Woman from Feudalism to Fascism: Richard Wright's Black Hope." In *Richard Wright in a Post-Racial Imaginary*, edited by Alice Mikal Craven, William E. Dow, and Yoko Nakamura, 113–28. New York: Bloomsbury Academic, 2014.

———. *Radical Representations: Politics and Form in US Proletarian Fiction, 1929–1941*. Durham, NC: Duke University Press, 1993.

Foucault, Michel. *The Birth of Biopolitics: Lectures at the Collège de France, 1978–1979*. Translated by Graham Burchell. New York: Picador, 2008.

———. *The Order of Things: An Archaeology of the Human Sciences*. Translated by Alan Sheridan. New York: Vintage, 1994.

Freud, Sigmund. *Civilization and Its Discontents*. New York: W. W. Norton, 2010.

Galand, René. *Saint-John Perse*. New York: Twayne Publishers, 1972.

Gandhi, Leela. *Affective Communities: Anticolonial Thought, Fin-de-Siècle Radicalism and the Politics of Friendship*. Durham, NC: Duke University Press, 2005.

Garcia, Jay. *Psychology Comes to Harlem: Rethinking the Race Question in Twentieth-Century America*. Baltimore: Johns Hopkins University Press, 2012.

Gass, William H. *On Being Blue: A Philosophical Inquiry*. New York: New York Review Books, 1976; NYRB Classics, 2014.

Gates, Henry Louis, Jr. "Critical Fanonism." *Critical Inquiry* 17 (Spring 1991): 457–70.

———. *Figures in Black: Words, Signs, and the "Racial" Self*. New York: Oxford University Press, 1988.

———. *Loose Canons: Notes on the Culture Wars*. New York: Oxford University Press, 1992.

Gates, Henry Louis, Jr., and Nellie Y. McKay, eds. *The Norton Anthology of African American Literature*. New York: W. W. Norton & Co., 1996.

———. *The Norton Anthology of African American Literature*. 2nd ed. New York: W. W. Norton & Co., 2003.

Gates, Henry Louis, Jr., and Valerie Smith, eds. *The Norton Anthology of African American Literature*. 3rd ed. New York: W. W. Norton & Co., 2014.

Gayle, Addison, Jr., ed. *The Black Aesthetic*. Garden City, NY: Doubleday & Co., 1971.

Gayles, Gloria Wade, ed. *Conversations with Gwendolyn Brooks*. Jackson: University Press of Mississippi, 2003.

Gibson, Sonny. *Kansas City: Mecca of the New Negro*. Kansas City: Self-published, 1997.

Gifford, Justin. *Pimping Fictions: African American Crime Literature and the Untold Story of Black Pulp Publishing*. Philadelphia: Temple University Press, 2013.

Gilroy, Paul. *Against Race: Imagining Political Culture beyond the Color Line*. Cambridge, MA: Harvard University Press, 2000.

———. *The Black Atlantic: Modernity and Double Consciousness*. Cambridge, MA: Harvard University Press, 1993.

Gitlin, Todd, and Nanci Hollander. *Uptown: Poor Whites in Chicago*. New York: Harper & Row, 1970.

Glissant, Édouard. "Alejo Carpentier et 'l'Autre Amérique,'" *Critique*, no. 105 (February 1956): 113–19.

———. *Caribbean Discourse*. Translated by J. Michael Dash. Charlottesville: University of Virginia Press, 1992.

———. "Carthage." *Lettres nouvelles* 4, no. 43 (1956): 559–63.

———. *Collected Poems*. Edited by Jefferson Humphries and translated by Melissa Manolas. Minneapolis: University of Minnesota Press, 2005.

———. "Discours prononcé par Édouard Glissant au nom de l'Association Générale des Étudiants Martiniquais à la soirée commémorative d'Albert Béville, Justin Catayée et Roger Tropos, à Paris Palais de la Mutualité, le 6 juillet 1962." Édouard Glissant: Une pensée archipélique. https://www.edouardglissant.fr/discoursmutualite.html.

———. *Les Indes: Poème de l'une et l'autre terre*. Paris: Éditions Falaize, 1956.

———. *The Indies*. Translated by Dominique O'Neill. Toronto: Éditions du GREF, 1992.

———. "Michel Leiris, ethnographe." *Les lettres nouvelles* 43 (1956): 609–21.

———. *Soleil de la conscience* Paris: Éditions Falaize, 1956.

———. *La terre inquiète*. Paris: Éditions du Dragon, 1955.

———. "Le romancier noir et son peuple: Notes pour une conférence," *Présence africaine*, no. 16 (October–November 1957): 26–31.

———. *L'intention poétique*. Paris: Seuil, 1969; repr., Paris: Gallimard, 1997.

———. "Note sur une 'Poésie Nationale' chez les peuples noirs." *Les lettres nouvelles* 4 no. 36 (March 1956): 391–97.

———. *Poetic Intention*. Translated by Nathanaël with Anne Malena. New York: Nightboat Books, 2010

———. "Saint-John Perse et les Antillais." *La nouvelle revue française*, no. 278 (February 1976): 73–78.

———. *Sun of Consciousness*. Translated by Nathanaël. New York: Nightboat Books, 2020.

———. *Un champ d'îles*. Paris: Instance, 1953.

———. "Un nouveau sens de l'humanité pour les pays du Sud," *Antilla* 23 (November–December 1991): 38–39.

Gold, Michael. "Gertrude Stein: A Literary Idiot." In *Critical Essays on Gertrude Stein*, edited by Michael J. Hoffman, 76–78. Boston: G. K. Hall, 1986.

Golden, Thelma. *Glenn Ligon: Stranger*. Exhibition catalog. New York: Studio Museum Harlem, 2001.

———. "An Interview with Hilton Als Moderated by Thelma Golden," *Glenn Ligon: Stranger*, 12-16.

Goldsby, Jacqueline. *A Spectacular Secret: Lynching in American Life and Literature.* Chicago: University of Chicago Press, 2006.

Gordon, Lewis R. *Bad Faith and Antiblack Racism.* Atlantic Highlands, NJ: Humanities Press, 1995.

———. *Fanon and the Crisis of European Man: An Essay on Philosophy and the Human Sciences.* New York: Routledge, 1995.

Gore, Dayo F. *Radicalism at the Crossroads: African American Women and the Cold War.* New York: New York University Press, 2012.

Green, Adam. *Selling the Race: Culture, Community, and Black Chicago: 1940-1955.* Chicago: University of Chicago Press, 2007.

Greif, Mark. *The Age of the Crisis of Man: Thought and Fiction in America, 1937-1973.* Princeton, NJ: Princeton University Press, 2015.

Griffin, Farah Jasmine. "Hunting Communists and Negroes in Ann Petry's *The Narrows*." In *Revising the Blueprint: Ann Petry and the Literary Left*, edited by Alex Lubin, 137-49. Jackson: Mississippi University Press, 2007.

———. *Who Set You Flowin'? The African-American Migration Narrative.* New York: Oxford University Press, 1995.

Gyarkye, Lovia. "The Importance of Being Ordinary." *New Republic*, July 19, 2017. https://newrepublic.com/article/143927/importance-ordinary.

Gyssels, Kathleen. "Scarlet Ibises and the Poetics of Relation: Perse, Walcott and Glissant." *Commonwealth Essays and Studies* 31 (2008): 103-16.

Hall, James C. *Mercy Mercy Me: African-American Culture and the American Sixties.* New York: Oxford University Press, 2001.

Hall, Stuart. *Cultural Studies, 1983: A Theoretical History.* Edited by Jennifer Daryl Slack and Lawrence Grossberg. Durham, NC: Duke University Press, 2016.

Halliwell, Stephen. *The Poetics of Aristotle: Translation and Commentary.* Chapel Hill: University of North Carolina Press, 1987.

Hallward, Peter. *Absolutely Postcolonial: Writing between the Singular and the Specific.* Manchester, UK: Manchester University Press, 2002.

Hanchard, Michael. "Afro-Modernity: Temporality, Politics, and the African Diaspora." *Public Culture* 11 (1999): 245-68.

Hannah, Matthew N. "Desires Made Manifest: The Queer Modernism of Wallace Thurman's *Fire!!*." *Journal of Modern Literature* 38, no. 3 (Spring 2015): 162-80.

Hardison, Ayesha. *Writing Through Jane Crow: Race and Gender Politics in African American Literature.* Charlottesville: University of Virginia Press, 2014.

Hart, Henry, ed. *American Writers Congress.* New York: International Publishers, 1935.

Hart, Matthew. *Nations of Nothing But Poetry: Modernism, Transnationalism, and Synthetic Vernacular Writing.* New York: Oxford University Press, 2010.

Hayes, Floyd W., III. "The Concept of Double Vision in Richard Wright's The Outsider." In *Existence in Black: An Anthology of Black Existential Philosophy*, edited by Lewis R. Gordon, 173-84. New York: Routledge, 1997.

Higashida, Cheryl. "Aunt Sue's Children: Re-viewing the Gender(ed) Politics of Richard Wright's Radicalism" *American Literature* 75, no. 2 (2003): 395-425.

Higginbotham, Evelyn Brooks. *Righteous Discontent: The Women's Movement in the Black Baptist Church, 1880-1920.* Cambridge, MA: Harvard University Press, 1993.

Hill, Lena. *Visualizing Blackness and the Creation of the African American Literary Tradition* New York: Cambridge University Press, 2014.

Hine, Darlene Clark. "Black Professionals and Race Consciousness: Origins of the Civil Rights Movement, 1890–1950." *Journal of American History* 89, no. 4 (2003): 1279–94.

Hirsch, Arnold R. *Making the Second Ghetto: Race and Housing in Chicago, 1940–1960.* New York: Cambridge University Press, 1983.

Hodges, LeRoy S., Jr. *Portrait of an Expatriate: William Gardner Smith, Writer.* Westport, CT: Greenwood Press, 1985.

Holland, Antonio F. *Nathan B. Young and the Struggle over Black Higher Education.* Columbia: University of Missouri Press, 2006.

Holland, Sharon Patricia. *The Erotic Life of Racism.* Durham, NC: Duke University Press, 2012.

Holmes, Anna. "The Underground Art of the Insult." *New York Times*, May 17, 2015, 13.

Holmes, Eugene C. "Problems Facing the Negro Writer Today." *New Challenge*, Fall 1937, 69–75.

Huddle, Mark A., ed. *Roi Ottley's World War II: The Lost Diary of an African American Journalist.* Lawrence: University Press of Kansas, 2013.

Hughes, Langston. "Letter to Dorothy West." Dorothy West Papers, 1937, n.d., MC 676, folder 10.3, Schlesinger Library, Radcliffe Institute, Harvard University, Cambridge, MA.

———. *Montage of a Dream Deferred.* New York: Henry Holt, 1951.

———. "Name, Race, and Gift in Common." *Voices*, Winter 1950, 54–56.

Hurston, Zora Neale. *Dust Tracks on a Road.* Edited by Robert Hemenway. Urbana: University of Illinois Press, 1984.

Irele, Abiola F., and Simon Gikandi, eds. *The Cambridge History of African and Caribbean Literature.* Vol. 2. New York: Cambridge University Press, 2000.

Irigaray, Luce. *The Sex Which Is Not One.* Translated by Catherine Porter. Ithaca, NY: Cornell University Press, 1985.

Jackson, Lawrence. *Chester Himes: A Biography.* New York: W. W. Norton & Co., 2017.

———. *The Indignant Generation: A Narrative History of African American Writers and Critics, 1934–1960.* Princeton, NJ: Princeton University Press, 2011.

Jacques, Geoffrey. *A Change in the Weather: Modernist Imagination, African American Imaginary.* Amherst: University of Massachusetts Press, 2009.

James, C. L. R. *Mariners, Renegades and Castaways: The Story of Herman Melville and the World We Live In.* 1953; Hanover, NH: University Press of New England, 2001.

———., under pseudonym G. F. Eckstein. "Two Young American Writers." *Fourth International* (March–April 1950): 53–56.

James, Henry. *Notes of a Son and Brother.* New York: Charles Scribner's, 1914.

Jameson, Fredric. *The Political Unconscious: Narrative as a Socially Symbolic Act.* Ithaca, NY: Cornell University Press, 1981.

———. "Periodizing the 60s." *Social Text*, nos. 9–10 (Spring–Summer 1984): 178–209.

JanMohamed, Abdul. *The Death-Bound-Subject: Richard Wright's Archaeology of Death.* Durham, NC: Duke University Press, 2005.

Jarrett, Gene Andrew. *Deans and Truants: Race and Realism in African American Literature.* Philadelphia: University of Pennsylvania Press, 2011.

Jennings, Eric. "La dissidence aux Antilles, 1940–1943." *Vingtième siècle, revue d'histoire* 68 (October–December 2000): 55–71.

Johnson, Abby Arthur, and Ronald Maberry Johnson, eds. *Propaganda and Aesthetics: The Literary Politics of Afro-American Magazines in the Twentieth Century*. Amherst: University of Massachusetts Press, 1991.

Johnson, Barbara. "Apostrophe, Animation, Abortion," *Diacritics* 16, no. 1 (Spring 1986): 28–47.

———. "The Re(a)d and the Black: Richard Wright's Blueprint." In *Richard Wright: Critical Perspectives Past and Present*, ed. Henry Louis Gates Jr. and Kwame Anthony Appiah, 149–55. New York: Amistad, 1993.

Jones, Hettie. *How I Became Hettie Jones*. New York: Grove Press, 1996.

Jones, LeRoi (Amiri Baraka). *The Dead Lecturer: Poems*. New York: Grove Press, 1964.

Joyce, Joyce A. "The Poetry of Gwendolyn Brooks: An Afrocentric Exploration." In *On Gwendolyn Brooks: Reliant Contemplation*, edited by Stephen Caldwell Wright, 246–53. Ann Arbor: University of Michigan Press, 2001.

Julcs-Rosette, Bennetta. *Black Paris: The African Writers' Landscape*. Urbana: University of Illinois Press, 1998.

Kahn, Ashley. *Kind of Blue: The Making of the Miles Davis Masterpiece*. New York: Da Capo Press, 2001.

Kalliney, Peter J. *The Aesthetic Cold War: Decolonization and Global Literature*. Princeton, NJ: Princeton University Press, 2022.

Kane, Daniel. *All Poets Welcome: The Lower East Side Poetry Scene in the 1960s*. Berkeley: University of California Press, 2003.

Karnes, Thomas L. *Asphalt and Politics: A History of the American Highway*. Jefferson, NC: McFarland & Co., 2009.

Kazin, Alfred. *On Native Grounds: An Interpretation of Modern American Prose Literature*. New York: Harcourt Brace, 1942.

Keith, Allyn. "A Note on Negro Nationalism." *New Challenge*, Fall 1937, 65–69.

Keith, Joseph. *Unbecoming Americans: Writing Race and Nation from the Shadows of Citizenship, 1945–1960*. New Brunswick, NJ: Rutgers University Press, 2013.

Kelley, Robin D. G. "A Poetics of Anticolonialism." In *Discourse on Colonialism*, 7–28. New York: Monthly Review Press, 2000.

———. *Race Rebels: Culture, Politics, and the Black Working Class*. New York: Free Press, 1996.

Kent, George E. *Gwendolyn Brooks: A Life*. Lexington: University Press of Kentucky, 1989.

Kimball, Robert, and Linda Berlin Emmet, eds. *The Complete Lyrics of Irving Berlin*. New York: First Applause, 2005.

Kimmage, Michael. *The Conservative Turn: Lionel Trilling, Whittaker Chambers, and the Lessons of Anti-Communism*. Cambridge, MA: Harvard University Press, 2009.

———. "Lionel Trilling's 'The Middle of the Journey' and the Complicated Origins of the Neo-Conservative Movement." *Shofar* 21, no. 3 (Spring 2003): 48–63.

King, Richard H. *Race, Culture, and the Intellectuals, 1940–1970*. Baltimore: Johns Hopkins University Press, 2004.

Kiuchi, Toru, and Yoshinobu Hakutani, eds. *Richard Wright: A Documented Chronology, 1908–1960*. Jefferson, NC: McFarland & Co., 2014.

Knabb, Ken, ed. and trans. *Situationist International Anthology*. Berkeley, CA: Bureau of Public Secrets, 2006.

Knupfer, Anne Meis. *The Chicago Black Renaissance and Women's Activism*. Urbana: University of Illinois Press, 2006.

Kolokytha, Chara. "Christian Zervos et Cahiers d'art, Archives de la Bibliothèque Kandinsky." *Konsthistorisktidskrift* 82, no. 4 (April 2013): 339–42.

Kullberg, Christina. "Crossroads Poetics." *Callaloo* 36, no. 4 (Fall 2013): 968–82.

———. *The Poetics of Ethnography in Martinican Narratives: Exploring the Self and Environment*. Charlottesville: University of Virginia Press, 2013.

Lamming, George. *In the Castle of My Skin*. Ann Arbor: University of Michigan Press, 1991.

———. *The Pleasures of Exile*. Ann Arbor: University of Michigan Press, 1992.

Lazreg, Marnia. *Torture and the Twilight of Empire: From Algiers to Baghdad*. Princeton, NJ: Princeton University Press, 2008.

Lecercle, Jean-Jacques. "Three Accounts of Literary Style." *CR: The New Centennial Review* 16, no. 3 (Winter 2016): 151–71.

Lee, Christopher J., ed. *Making a World after Empire: The Bandung Moment and Its Afterlives*. Athens: Ohio University Press, 2010.

Lee, Don L. (Haki Madhubuti). "Gwendolyn Brooks: Beyond the Wordmaker—The Making of an African Poet." In *Report from Part One*, by Gwendolyn Brooks, 13–30. Detroit: Broadside Press, 1972.

Leeming, David A. "An Interview with James Baldwin on Henry James." *Henry James Review* 8, no. 1 (Fall 1986): 47–56.

———. *James Baldwin: A Biography*. New York: Henry Holt, 1994.

Leiris, Michel. *Contacts de civilisations en Martinique et en Guadeloupe*. Collection Race et Société. Paris: UNESCO and Gallimard, 1955.

———. *Phantom Africa*. Translated by Brent Hayes Edwards. Calcutta: Seagull Books, 2017.

Levinas, Emmanuel. *Totality and Infinity: An Essay on Exteriority*. Translated by Alphonso Lingis. Dordrecht, Netherlands: Kluwer Academic Publishers, 1991.

Lewis, Tom. *Divided Highways: Building the Interstate Highways, Transforming American Life*. New York: Viking Penguin, 1997.

Lincoln University. *The 1950 Lion*. Philadelphia: Clark Printing House, 1950.

Lottman, Herbert R. "Preface: The Invisible Writer." In *The Bern Book: A Record of a Voyage of the Mind*, by Vincent O. Carter, v–xi. New York: John Day Co., 1970.

Lubow, Arthur. "A Portrait of America That Still Haunts, Decades Later," *New York Times*, June 12, 2020.

MacDonald, J. Fred, ed. *Richard Durham's Destination Freedom: Scripts from Radio's Black Legacy, 1948–50*. New York: Praeger, 1989.

Macey, David. *Frantz Fanon: A Biography*. New York: Picador, 2000.

Mackey, Nathaniel. *Discrepant Engagement: Dissonance, Cross-Culturality, and Experimental Writing*. New York: Cambridge University Press, 1993.

———. *The Paracritical Hinge: Essays, Talks, Notes, Interviews*. Madison: University of Wisconsin Press, 2005.

Malley, Robert. *The Call from Algeria: Third Worldism, Revolution, and the Turn to Islam*. Berkeley: University of California Press, 1996.

Malraux, André. *Man's Fate*. Translated by Haakon M. Chevalier. New York: Modern Library, 1961.

Manigault-Bryant, James Arthur. "Reimagining the 'Pythian Madness' of Souls: W. E. B. Du Bois's Poetics of African American Faith," *Journal of Africana Religions* 1, no. 3 (2013): 324–47.

Mann, Thomas. *The Magic Mountain*. New York: A. A. Knopf, 2005.

Marable, Manning. *Malcolm X: A Life of Reinvention*. New York: Viking, 2011.

———. *Race, Reform, and Rebellion: The Second Reconstruction and Beyond in Black America, 1945–2006*. Jackson: University Press of Mississippi, 2007.

Marriott, David. *Whither Fanon? Studies in the Blackness of Being*. Stanford, CA: Stanford University Press, 2018.

Marshall, Paule. *Brown Girl, Brownstones*. 1959; New York: Feminist Press, 1981.

———. "From the Poets in the Kitchen." *Callaloo* 18 (Spring–Summer 1983): 22–30.

———. "Shaping the World of My Art." *New Letters* 40 (Autumn 1973): 97–112.

———. *Triangular Road, A Memoir*. New York: Basic Civitas Books, 2010.

Marx, Karl. *Grundrisse*. Translated by Martin Nicolaus. New York: Penguin, 1993.

Marzioli, Sara. "The Subterranean Performance of History between Harlem and Rome in William Demby's The Catacombs." *African American Review* 47, nos. 2–3 (2014): 417–29.

Masse, Guirdex. "A Diasporic Encounter: The Politics of Race and Culture at the First International Congress of Black Writers and Artists." PhD diss., Emory University, 2014.

Maxwell, William J. *F. B. Eyes: How J. Edgar Hoover's Ghostreaders Framed African American Literature*. Princeton, NJ: Princeton University Press, 2015.

———. *New Negro, Old Left: African-American Writing and Communism between the Wars*. New York: Columbia University Press, 1999.

McCarthy, Jesse. "Form and the Anticolonial Novel: William Gardner Smith's The Stone Face." *Novel: a Forum on Fiction* 55 (1): 61–94.

McCarthy, Mary. *Ideas and the Novel*. New York: Harcourt Brace, 1980.

McDonough, Tom. "Unrepresentable Enemies: On the Legacy of Guy Debord and the Situationist International." *Afterall: A Journal of Art, Context and Enquiry*, no. 28 (Autumn–Winter 2011): 42–55.

McGurl, Mark. *The Novel Art: Elevations of American Fiction after Henry James*. Princeton, NJ: Princeton University Press, 2001.

McKay, Claude. *Amiable with Big Teeth*. Edited by Jean-Christophe Cloutier and Brent Hayes Edwards. New York: Penguin, 2017.

Melhem, D. H. *Gwendolyn Brooks: Poetry and the Heroic Voice*. Lexington: University Press of Kentucky, 1987.

Menand, Louis. *The Free World: Art and Thought in the Cold War*. New York: Farrar, Straus & Giroux, 2021.

Mendelson, Edward. *Moral Agents: Eight Twentieth-Century American Writers*. New York: New York Review Books, 2015.

Merjian, Ara H. *Giorgio de Chirico and the Metaphysical City: Nietzsche, Modernism, Paris*. New Haven, CT: Yale University Press, 2014.

Micconi, Giovanna. "Ghosts of History: An Interview with William Demby." *Amerikastudien/American Studies* 56, no. 1 (2011): 125–26.

Mignolo, Walter. "Sylvia Wynter: What Does It Mean to Be Human?" In *Sylvia Wynter: On Being Human as Praxis*, edited by Katherine McKittrick, 106–23. Durham, NC: Duke University Press, 2015.

Miller, Quentin D. "Separate and Unequal in Paris." In *James Baldwin: American and Beyond*, edited by Cora Kaplan and Bill Schwarz, 159–72. Ann Arbor: University of Michigan Press, 2011.

Mills, C. Wright. *The Power Elite*. New York: Oxford University Press, 1956.

Minus, Marian. "Present Trends in Negro Literature," *Challenge* 2, no. 1 (1937): 9–11.

Mishra, Pankaj. "Whatever Happened to the Novel of Ideas?" *New York Times*, September 20, 2015, 31.

Mitchell, Angelyn ed. *Within the Circle: An Anthology of African American Literary Criticism from the Renaissance to the Present*. Durham, NC: Duke University Press, 1994.

Mitchell, Ernest Julius. "Tenderness in Early Wright." In *The Cambridge Companion to Richard Wright*, edited by Glenda Carpio, 199–216. New York: Cambridge University Press, 2019.

Mitchell, Verner D., and Cynthia Davis. *Literary Sisters: Dorothy West and Her Circle, A Biography of the Harlem Renaissance*. New Brunswick, NJ: Rutgers University Press, 2011.

Mokhtefi, Elaine. *Algiers, Third World Capital: Black Panthers, Freedom Fighters, Revolutionaries*. London: Verso, 2018.

Mootry, Maria K., and Gary Smith, eds. *A Life Distilled: Gwendolyn Brooks, Her Poetry and Fiction*. Urbana: University of Illinois Press, 1989.

Morgan, Stacy I. *Rethinking Social Realism: African American Art and Literature, 1930–1953*. Athens: University of Georgia Press, 2004.

Morris, Wright. "The Complexity of Evil." *New York Times Book Review*, August 16, 1953, 27–28.

Morrison, Toni. *Beloved*. New York: Vintage, 2004.

———. "City Limits, Village Values: Concepts of the Neighborhood in Black Fiction." In *Literature and the American Urban Experience: Essays on the City and Literature*, edited by Michael C. Jaye and Ann Chalmers Watts, 35–44. New Brunswick, NJ: Rutgers University Press, 1981.

———. "Rootedness: The Ancestor as Foundation." In *I Am Because We Are: Readings in Africana Philosophy*, edited by Fred Lee Hord and Jonathan Scott Lee, 397–403. Amherst: University of Massachusetts Press, 2016.

Moten, Fred. *Consent Not to Be a Single Being*. Vol. 1, *Black and Blur*. Durham, NC: Duke University Press, 2017.

———. "Taste Dissonance Flavor Escape (Preface to a Solo by Miles Davis)." In *Black and Blur*. Durham, NC: Duke University Press, 2017.

———. *In the Break: The Aesthetics of the Black Radical Tradition*. Minneapolis: University of Minnesota Press, 2003.

Mullen, Bill V. *Popular Fronts: Chicago and African-American Cultural Politics, 1935–46*. Urbana: University of Illinois Press, 1999.

———. "Popular Fronts: Negro Story Magazine and the African American Literary Response to World War II." *African American Review* 30, no. 1 (1996): 5–15.

Muñoz, José Esteban. *Disidentifications: Queers of Color and the Performance of Politics*. Minneapolis: University of Minnesota Press, 2013.

Munro, John. *The Anticolonial Front: The African American Freedom Struggle and Global Decolonization, 1945-1960*. New York: Cambridge University Press, 2017.

Murray, Roland. *Our Living Manhood: Literature, Black Power, and Masculine Ideology*. Philadelphia: University of Pennsylvania Press, 2007.

Musil, Robert. *The Man without Qualities*. Vol. 1. New York: Picador, 1979.

Nadel, Alan. *Containment Culture: American Narratives, Postmodernism, and the Atomic Age*. Durham, NC: Duke University Press, 1995.

Napier, Winston, ed. *African American Literary Theory: A Reader*. New York: New York University Press, 2000.

Nesbitt, Nick F. *Caribbean Critique: Antillean Critical Theory from Toussaint to Glissant*. Liverpool, UK: Liverpool University Press, 2013.

———. "Caribbean Literature in French: Origins and Development." In *The Cambridge History of African and Caribbean Literature*, edited by Abiola Irele and Simon Gikandi, 2:643-69. New York: Cambridge University Press, 2000.

———. "Early Glissant: From the Destitution of the Political to Antillean Ultra-Leftism." *Callaloo* 36, no. 4 (2013): 932-48.

———. *Voicing Memory: History and Subjectivity in French Caribbean Literature*. Charlottesville: University of Virginia Press, 2003.

Nielsen, Aldon Lynn. *Black Chant: Languages of African-American Postmodernism*. New York: Cambridge University Press, 1997.

Nishikawa, Kinohi. "The Archive on Its Own: Black Politics, Independent Publishing, and *The Negotiations*." *MELUS* 30, no. 3 (2015): 176-201.

North, Michael. *The Dialect of Modernism: Race, Language, and Twentieth-Century Literature*. New York: Oxford University Press, 1994.

Obrist, Hans Ulrich. *Édouard Glissant & Hans Ulrich Obrist*. 100 Notes—100 Thoughts No. 38. Kassel: Documenta (13) Hatje Cantz Verlag, 2011.

O'Dell, J. H. "Foundations of Racism in American Life." *Freedomways* 4 (1964): 98-99.

O'Gorman, Francis. "What Is Haunting Tennyson's Maud (1855)?" *Victorian Poetry* 48, no. 3 (2010): 293-312.

Osundare, Niyi. "Half a Century Later." *Journal of the African Literature Association* 1, no. 1 (2006): 250-57.

Ottley, Roi. *Roi Ottley's World War II: The Lost Diary of an African American Journalist*. Edited and with an introduction by Mark A. Huddle. Lawrence: University Press of Kansas, 2013.

Painter, Nell Irvin. *Exodusters: Black Migration to Kansas after Reconstruction*. New York: W. W. Norton & Co., 1992.

Panish, Jon. "'As Radical as Society Demands the Truth to Be': Umbra's Racial Politics and Poetics." In *Don't Ever Get Famous: Essays on New York Writing after the New York School*, edited by Daniel Kane, 80-114. Champaign, IL: Dalkey Archive Press, 2006.

Paranzino, Michelle D. "'Two, Three, Many Vietnams': Che Guevara's Tricontinental Revolutionary Vision." In *The Tricontinental Revolution: Third World Radicalism and the Cold War*, edited by R. Joseph Parrott and Mark Atwood Lawrence, 276-303. Cambridge Studies in US Foreign Relations. Cambridge: Cambridge University Press, 2022.

Pease, Allison. "*Maud* and Its Discontents." *Criticism* 36, no. 1 (1994): 101-7.

Peniel, E. Joseph. *Stokely: A Life*. New York: Basic Civitas Books, 2014.

———. *Waiting 'til the Midnight Hour: A Narrative History of Black Power in America.* New York: Holt Paperbacks, 2007.

Perse, Saint-John. *Oeuvre Poétique I.* Paris: Gallimard, 1953.

———. *Winds.* Translated by Hugh Chisholm. New York: Pantheon, 1953.

Philpott, Thomas Lee. *The Slum and the Ghetto: Neighborhood Deterioration and Middle-Class Reform, Chicago, 1880–1930.* New York: Oxford University Press, 1978.

Pinckney, Darryl. *Out There: Mavericks of Black Literature.* New York: Basic Civitas Books, 2002.

Porter, Eric. *The Problem of the Future World: W. E. B. Du Bois and the Race Concept at Midcentury.* Durham, NC: Duke University Press, 2010.

Pound, Ezra. *ABC of Reading.* New York: New Directions, 1987.

Prashad, Vijay. *The Darker Nations: A People's History of the Third World.* New York: New Press, 2007.

Proust, Marcel. *À la recherche du temps perdu.* Vol. 2. Paris: Gallimard, 1927.

Quashie, Kevin. *The Sovereignty of Quiet: Beyond Resistance in Black Culture.* New Brunswick, NJ: Rutgers University Press, 2012.

Rabinowitz, Paula. *Black, White, and Noir: America's Pulp Modernism.* New York: Columbia University Press, 2002.

Radford, Daniel. *Édouard Glissant: Poètes d'aujourd'hui.* Paris: Seghers, 1982.

Rahv, Philip. "The Cult of Experience in American Writing." *Partisan Review* (1936) 7, no. 6 (1940): 412–24.

Ralph, Laurence. *The Torture Letters: Reckoning with Police Violence.* Chicago: University of Chicago Press, 2020.

Rampersad, Arnold. *The Life of Langston Hughes.* Vol. 2, *1914–1967, I Dream a World.* New York: Oxford University Press, 2002.

———. *Ralph Ellison: A Biography.* New York: Vintage, 2008.

Rampersad, Arnold, and David Roessel, eds. *The Selected Letters of Langston Hughes.* New York: Alfred A. Knopf, 2015.

Rankine, Claudia. *Citizen: An American Lyric.* Minneapolis: Graywolf, 2014.

Rasberry, Vaughn. "'Now Describing You': James Baldwin and Cold War Liberalism." In *James Baldwin: America and Beyond,* edited by Bill Schwarz and Cora Kaplan, 84–105. Ann Arbor: University of Michigan Press, 2011.

———. *Race and the Totalitarian Century: Geopolitics in the Black Literary Imagination.* Cambridge, MA: Harvard University Press, 2016.

Redding, J. Saunders. "Cellini-Like Lyrics." *Saturday Review of Literature,* September 17, 1949.

Reed, Anthony. *Freedom Time: The Poetics and Politics of Black Experimental Writing.* Baltimore: Johns Hopkins University Press, 2016.

Riceputi, Fabrice. *La bataille d'Einaudi: Comment la mémoire du 17 octobre 1961 revint à la République.* Neuvy-en-Champagne, France: Éditions le Passager Clandestin, 2015.

Richardson, Michael, and Krzysztof Fijalkowski. *Refusal of the Shadow: Surrealism and the Caribbean.* New York: Verso, 1996.

Ricoeur, Paul. *The Course of Recognition.* Translated by David Pellauer. Cambridge, MA: Harvard University Press, 2007.

Rideout, Walter. *The Radical Novel in the United States, 1900-1954: Some Interrelations of Literature and Society*. Cambridge: Harvard University Press, 1956.

Rimbaud, Arthur. *Œuvres complètes*. Paris: Éditions Gallimard, 1963.

Roberts, Brian R., and Keith Foulcher, eds. *Indonesian Notebook: A Sourcebook on Richard Wright and the Bandung Conference*. Durham, NC: Duke University Press, 2016.

Robbins, Bruce. "The Sweatshop Sublime." *PMLA* 117, no. 1 (2002): 84-97.

Robinson, Cedric. *Black Marxism: The Making of the Black Radical Tradition*. London: Zed Books, 1983.

Rodney, Walter. *A History of the Upper Guinea Coast, 1585-1800*. Oxford, UK: Clarendon, 1970.

Ross, Kristin. *May '68 and Its Afterlives*. Chicago: University of Chicago Press, 2002.

Rothstein, Richard. *The Color of Law: A Forgotten History of How Our Government Segregated America*. New York: W. W. Norton & Co., 2017.

Rowley, Hazel. *Richard Wright: The Life and Times*. Chicago: University of Chicago Press, 2001.

Ruddick, Lisa. *Reading Gertrude Stein: Body, Text, Gnosis*. Ithaca, NY: Cornell University Press, 1990.

Rusert, Britt. "From Black Lit to Black Print: The Return to the Archive in African American Literary Studies." *American Quarterly* 68, no. 4 (2016): 993-1005.

Salih, Tayeb. *Season of Migration to the North*. Translated by Denys Johnson-Davies. New York: NYRB Classics, 2009.

Saper, Craig J. *Networked Art*. Minneapolis: University of Minnesota Press, 2001.

Sartre, Jean-Paul. *Being and Nothingness: A Phenomenological Essay on Ontology*. Translated by Hazel Barnes. New York: Washington Square Press, 1956.

Saunders, Frances Stonor. *The Cultural Cold War: The CIA and the World of Arts and Letters*. New York: New Press, 2013.

Schaub, Thomas Hill. *American Fiction in the Cold War*. Madison: University of Wisconsin Press, 1991.

Schirmer, Sherry Lamb. *A City Divided: The Racial Landscape of Kansas City, 1900-1960*. Columbia: University of Missouri Press, 2002.

Schmidt, Tyler T. *Desegregating Desire: Race and Sexuality in Cold War American Literature*. Jackson: University Press of Mississippi, 2013.

Schneider, Ute. "Meyer/Bibliographisches Institut." In *The Oxford Companion to the Book*, edited by Michael F. Suarez, SJ, and H. R. Woudhuysen, 929. New York: Oxford University Press, 2010.

Scott, David. *Conscripts of Modernity: The Tragedy of Colonial Enlightenment*. Durham, NC: Duke University Press, 2004.

———. "The Re-enchantment of Humanism: An Interview with Sylvia Wynter." *Small Axe*, no. 8 (September 2000): 119-207.

Scott, James C. *Two Cheers for Anarchism*. Princeton, NJ: Princeton University Press, 2012.

Sedgwick, Eve Kosofsky. "Jane Austen and the Masturbating Girl." *Critical Inquiry* 17, no. 4 (1991): 818-37.

Selbonne, Ronald. *Albert Béville alias Paul Niger: Une négritude géométrique: Guadeloupe-France-Afrique*. Paris: Ibis Rouge, 2013.

Seligman, Amanda. "Uptown." *The Electronic Encyclopedia of Chicago* (Chicago Historical Society), 2005. http://www.encyclopedia.chicagohistory.org/pages/1293 .html.

Selvon, Sam. *The Lonely Londoners*. London: Allan Wingate, 1956.

Sharpe, Christina. *In the Wake: On Blackness and Being*. Durham, NC: Duke University Press, 2016.

Sharpley-Whiting, T. Denean. *Frantz Fanon: Conflicts and Feminisms*. Lanham, MD: Rowman & Littlefield, 1998.

Shatz, Adam. *Writers and Missionaries: Essays on the Radical Imagination*. New York: Verso, 2023.

Shelby, Tommie. "Richard Wright: Realizing the Promise of the West." In *African American Political Thought: A Collected History*, edited by Melvin L. Rogers and Jack Turner, 413–38. Chicago: University of Chicago Press, 2021.

Shockley, Evie. *Renegade Poetics: Black Aesthetics and Formal Innovation in African American Poetry*. Iowa City: University of Iowa Press, 2011.

Shukaitis, Stevphen. "'Theories Are Made Only to Die in the War of Time': Guy Debord and the Situationist International as Strategic Thinkers." *Culture and Organization* 20, no. 4 (2014): 251–68.

Simonson, John. *Paris of the Plains: Kansas City from Doughboys to Expressways*. Charleston, SC: History Press, 2010.

Singh, Nikhil. *Black Is a Country: Race and the Unfinished Struggle for Democracy*. Cambridge, MA: Harvard University Press, 2004.

Smethurst, James E. *The Black Arts Movement: Literary Nationalism in the 1960s and 1970s*. Chapel Hill: University of North Carolina Press, 2005.

———. *The New Red Negro: The Literary Left and African American Poetry, 1930–1946*. New York: Oxford University Press, 1999.

Smith, William Gardner. *The Last of the Conquerors*. New York: Farrar, Strauss & Co., 1948.

———. "The Negro Writer: Pitfalls and Compensations" *Phylon* 11, no. 4 (1950): 297–303.

———. *Return to Black America*. Englewood Cliffs, NJ: Prentice-Hall, 1970.

———. *The Stone Face*. New York: Farrar, Straus & Co., 1963

Sollors, Werner. *Amiri Baraka/LeRoi Jones: The Quest for a Populist Modernism*. New York: Columbia University Press, 1978.

———. *Ethnic Modernism*. Cambridge, MA: Harvard University Press, 2008.

Spillers, Hortense. *Black, White, and in Color: Essays on American Literature and Culture*. Chicago: University of Chicago Press, 2003.

———. "Mama's Baby, Papa's Maybe: An American Grammar Book" *Diacritics* 17, no. 2 (1987): 64–81.

———. "Review of Racial Blackness and the (Dis)continuity of Western Modernity by Lindon Barrett." *Modernism/Modernity* 23, no. 1 (2016): 251–55.

Stovall, Tyler. "The Fire This Time: Black American Expatriates and the Algerian War." *Yale French Studies* 98 (Fall 2000): 182–200.

Stowe, Harriet Beecher. *Uncle Tom's Cabin*. London: John Cassell, 1852.

Suggs, Henry Lewis, ed. *The Black Press in the South, 1865–1979*. Westport, CT: Greenwood Press, 1983.

Sugrue, Thomas J. *The Origins of the Urban Crisis: Race and Inequality in Postwar Detroit*. Princeton, NJ: Princeton University Press, 1996.

Tate, Claudia. *Psychoanalysis and Black Novels: Desire and the Protocols of Race*. New York: Oxford University Press, 1998.

Tennyson, Alfred. *Maud and Other Poems*. London: Edward Moxon, 1866.

Terrell, Whitney. "At the Crossroads." *New York Times Book Review*, April 20, 2003.

Thiong'o, Ngũgĩ wa. *A Grain of Wheat*. New York: Penguin Classics, 2012.

Thompson, Mark Christian. *Black Fascisms: African American Literature and Culture between the Wars*. Charlottesville: University of Virginia Press, 2007.

Tóibín, Colm. "The Last Witness." *London Review of Books* 23, no. 18 (September 2001): 15-20.

Tolliver, Cedric. R. *Of Vagabonds and Fellow Travelers: African Diaspora Literary Culture and the Cultural Cold War*. Ann Arbor: University of Michigan Press, 2019.

Torres-Saillant, Silvio. *An Intellectual History of the Caribbean*. New York: Palgrave Macmillan, 2006.

Trilling, Lionel. *The Liberal Imagination*. New York: Viking Press, 1950.

———. *The Middle of the Journey*. 1947; New York: New York Review Books, 2002.

———. "A Tragic Situation." *The Nation*, April 7, 1945, 391-92.

Underwood, Ted. *Why Literary Periods Mattered: Historical Contrast and the Prestige of English Studies*. Stanford, CA: Stanford University Press, 2013.

Walcott, Derek. *What the Twilight Says: Essays*. New York: Faber and Faber, 1998.

Wald, Alan M. "Cold War Modernity." *Modernism/Modernity* 21, no. 4 (November 2014): 1017-23.

Walker, Margaret. *For My People*. New Haven, CT: Yale University Press, 1942.

———. *Richard Wright: Daemonic Genius*. New York: Amistad Press, 1988.

Wall, Cheryl A. "Stranger at Home: James Baldwin on What It Means to Be an American." In *James Baldwin: America and Beyond*, edited by Bill Schwarz and Cora Kaplan, 35-52. Ann Arbor: University of Michigan Press, 2011.

Ward, Kiron. "Hypercanonical Joyce: Sam Selvon's *The Lonely Londoners*, Creative Disaffiliation, and the Global Afterlives of Ulysses." *Textual Practice* 36, no. 2 (2022): 326-47.

Warren, Kenneth W. "Particularity and the Problem of Interpretation." In *What Was African American Literature?*, 44-80. Cambridge, MA: Harvard University Press, 2012.

———. *So Black and Blue: Ralph Ellison and the Occasion of Criticism*. Chicago: University of Chicago Press, 2003.

———. *What Was African American Literature?* Cambridge, MA: Harvard University Press, 2012.

Washburn, Patrick S. "*The Pittsburgh Courier*'s Double V Campaign in 1942," *History Division of the Association for Education in Journalism Annual Convention*. East Lansing: Michigan State University, August 1981.

Washington, Mary Helen. *The Other Blacklist: The African American Literary and Cultural Left of the 1950s*. New York: Columbia University Press, 2014.

———. "When Gwendolyn Brooks Wore Red." In *The Other Blacklist: The African American Literary and Cultural Left of the 1950s*, 165-203. New York: Columbia University Press, 2014.

———. "Taming All That Anger Down: Rage and Silence in Gwendolyn Brooks' *Maud Martha*." *Massachusetts Review* 24, no. 2 (1983): 453-66.

Watson, Roxanne. "'Now We Know': The Trial of Roger Mais and Public Opinion in Jamaica, 1944." *Journal of Caribbean History* 46, no. 2 (2012): 183-211.

Watts, Richard. "Translating Culture: Reading the Paratexts to Aimé Césaire's *Cahier d'un retour au pays natal.*" *TTR* 13, no. 2 (2000): 29–45.

Weik von Mossner, Alexa. "Confronting *The Stone Face:* The Critical Cosmopolitanism of William Gardner Smith." *African American Review* 45, nos. 1–2 (2012): 167–82.

Weinberg, Bernard. "Saint-John Perse's *Anabase.*" *Chicago Review* 15, no. 3 (1962): 75–124.

West, Dorothy. *The Living Is Easy.* Old Westbury, NY: Feminist Press, 1982.

——. *Where the Wild Grape Grows: Selected Writings, 1930–1950.* Edited by Verner D. Mitchell and Cynthia Davis. Amherst: University of Massachusetts Press, 2005.

Westad, Odd Arne. *The Global Cold War: Third World Interventions and the Making of Our Times.* New York: Cambridge University Press, 2005.

Wheeler, Lesley. *The Poetics of Enclosure: American Women Poets from Dickinson to Dove.* Knoxville: University of Tennessee Press, 2002.

White, Hayden. *Tropics of Discourse.* Baltimore: Johns Hopkins University Press, 1978.

Wilder, Gary. *Freedom Time: Negritude Decolonization, and the Future of the World.* Durham, NC: Duke University Press, 2015.

Wilford, Hugh. *The Mighty Wurlitzer: How the CIA Played America.* Cambridge, MA: Harvard University Press, 2009.

Wilkerson, Isabel. *The Warmth of Other Suns: The Epic Story of America's Great Migration.* New York: Vintage, 2010.

Wilkins, Roy. *Standing Fast: The Autobiography of Roy Wilkins.* New York: Da Capo Press, 1994.

Williams, John A. *The Angry Ones.* New York: Old School Books, 1996.

Williams, Raymond. *Marxism and Literature.* New York: Oxford University Press, 1977.

——. *Politics and Letters: Interviews with New Left Review.* London: New Left Books, 1979.

Wilson, Noel. "The Kansas City Call and the Negro Market." PhD diss., University of Illinois, 1971.

Wipplinger, Jonathan. "The Racial Ruse: On Blackness and Blackface Comedy in 'Fin-de-Siècle' Germany." *German Quarterly* 84, no. 4 (2011): 457–76.

Wollen, Peter. "The Situationist International." *New Left Review*, March 1, 1989, 72–95.

Woodard, Komozi. *A Nation within a Nation: Amiri Baraka (LeRoi Jones) and Black Power Politics.* Chapel Hill: University of North Carolina Press, 1999.

Woolf, Virginia. *Mrs. Dalloway.* New York: Harcourt Brace, 1925.

——. *Women and Writing.* Edited by Michèle Barrett. New York: Harvest Harcourt, 1980.

Wright, Michelle. *Becoming Black: Creating Identity in the African Diaspora.* Durham, NC: Duke University Press, 2004.

Wright, Richard. *American Hunger.* New York: Harper & Row, 1977.

——. *Black Power: Three Books from Exile.* New York: HarperCollins, 2010.

——. "Blueprint for Negro Writing." *New Challenge* (Fall 1937): 53–65.

——. *Early Works.* New York: Library of America, 1991.

——. "L'humanité est plus grande que l'Amérique ou la Russie." *Franc-Tireur*, December 16, 1948, 1–4.

——. Introduction to *In the Castle of My Skin*, by George Lamming, v–viii. New York: McGraw-Hill, 1953.

———. *Later Works*. New York: Library of America, 1991.

———. *Lawd Today!* Lebanon, NH: Northeastern Library of Black Literature, 1993.

———. *The Man Who Lived Underground*. New York: Library of America, 2021.

———. *Native Son*. New York: Harper Perennial, 2005.

———. *The Outsider*. New York: HarperCollins, 1953.

———. *The Outsider*. New York: Library of America, 1991.

———. "Tradition and Industrialization: The Plight of the Tragic Elite in Africa," *Présence africaine*, nos. 8–10 (June–November 1956): 347–60.

Wright, Stephen Caldwell, ed. *On Gwendolyn Brooks: Reliant Contemplation*. Ann Arbor: University of Michigan Press, 2001.

Wynter, Sylvia. "Beyond the Word of Man: Glissant and the New Discourse of the Antilles." *World Literature Today* 63, no. 4 (1989): 637–48.

———. "The Ceremony Must Be Found: After Humanism." *boundary* 2 12–13, no. 1 (1984): 19–70.

———. "1492: A New World View." In *Race, Discourse, and the Origin of the Americas: A New World View*, edited by Vera Lawrence Hyatt and Rex Nettleford, 5–57. Washington, DC: Smithsonian Institution Press, 1995.

———. "Unsettling the Coloniality of Being/Power/Truth/Freedom: Towards the Human, after Man, Its Overrepresentation—An Argument." *CR: The New Centennial Review* 3, no. 3 (2003): 257–337.

Young, William H., and Nathan B. Young Jr., eds. *Your Kansas City and Mine*. Kansas City: n.p., 1950.

Zaborowska, Magdalena. *James Baldwin's Turkish Decade: Erotics of Exile*. Durham, NC: Duke University Press, 2009.

Zeigler, James. *Red Scare Racism and Cold War Black Radicalism*. Jackson: University Press of Mississippi, 2015.

Zhang, Dora. *Strange Likeness: Description and the Modernist Novel*. Chicago: University of Chicago Press, 2020.

Index

Achille, Louis T., 166
Adams, Henry, 33
Adorno, Theodor, 187, 220n55, 260n153
Adventures of Augie March, The (Bellow), 123
affective communities, 107
Affective Communities (Gandhi), 111
affective mapping, 171
Affective Mapping (Flatley), 218n34
African American studies, 7–9, 69
African in Paris, An (*Un nègre à Paris*) (Dadié), 190
Afro-Asian Conference, 63
Afro-Diasporic studies, 69
Against Race (Gilroy), 202
Agamben, Giorgio, 203, 266n52
Akomfrah, John, 13
"Alas, Poor Richard" (Baldwin), 194
Alexander, Elizabeth, 13, 132
alienage, 173
alienation. *See* black alienation
Aliker, Maurice, 230n33
Allied Arts Guild, 110
"Almos' a Man" (Wright), 113–14, 245n27
Als, Hilton, 18–19, 255n90
Alston, Charles, 8
Althusser, Louis, 6, 136–37, 215n16
Ambassadors, The (James), 24–25, 165
American Hunger (Wright), 154
Americans, The (Frank), 102
American Writers Congress, 154

Amiable with Big Teeth (McKay), 8
Anabase (Perse), 60–61
Angry Ones, The (Williams), 9, 217n32
"Anniad, The" (Brooks), 106
Annie Allen (Brooks), 8, 106–7, 116–17, 196
anticolonialism, 2–3, 63, 111, 185, 199, 203–4, 245n30. *See also* decolonization
antifascism, 113, 153
Appiah, Kwame Anthony, 192
Ariel (Plath), 133
Aristotle, 57
Armstrong, Louis, 9–10
Arnold, A. James, 231n40
Arrivants, The (Braithwaite), 55
"Art of Fiction, The" (James), 23–24
Art of the Novel, The (James), 183
Asante, Molefi, 192
Ascoli, Max, 26–27
Ask Your Mama (Hughes), 196
Associated Councils of the Arts, 74
Aswell, Edward, 156–57
Attaway, William, 110
Austen, Jane, 140
"Autobiographical Notes" (Baldwin), 32
"awoman," 178

Bacon, Francis, 66
Baker, Houston, Jr., 254n65
Bakhtin, Mikhail, 81
Balakian, Nona, 75

Baldwin, James: on Africa, 32–33; background on, 20–21, 29; cultural authority of, 20–22, 31–32, 34–35, 70–71; and encounter narrative, 33–34; and Glissant, 44, 48–49, 63; and Henry James, 23–25, 36–37, 165, 222n21, 225n73; and Lebensraum, 28, 223n44; and novel of ideas, 143; paintings inspired by, 18–19; and protest fiction, 11–12; and *Reporter*, 26–27; sexuality of, 29; and Western sublime, 33, 224n64, 224n66; and Wright, 21, 23, 25, 39, 182, 194–95; on writing in 1950s, 19–20. *See also* black interiority; gothicism; negation; prophetic speech; *and specific works*

Bambara, Toni Cade, 104, 107

Bandung Conference, 32

Baraka, Amiri, 10, 105, 191, 197–99, 264n29, 264n33. *See also* Jones, LeRoi

"bare life," 203, 266n52

Barrett, Lindon, 173, 224n66, 226n79, 259n142, 259n144

Barthes, Roland, 46, 102

Baudelaire, Charles, 101

Bearden, Romare, 183

Bellow, Saul, 123, 143, 145

Beloved (Morrison), 67

Benjamin, Walter, 101

Bennett, Lerone, 105

Berlin, Irving, 117

Bern Book, The (Carter), 69, 71, 73, 75–86, 89, 101, 165

Béville, Albert, 50, 230n36

"Beyond the Word of Man" (Wynter), 66

Bhabha, Homi, 257n121

Bitzius, Albert, 79

black alienation, 5–7, 30–33, 49–54, 64–65, 86, 137–40, 146–49, 166–75, 202–3, 215n16. *See also* lived experience; melancholy; racism

"Black Art" (Baraka), 197

Black Arts Movement, 8, 105, 134

Black Boy (Wright), 155, 157, 160, 164–65, 167, 169, 181, 186–87

Black Church, 31, 33, 37–41

black colonial ghetto, 52

Black Convention Movement, 214n10

blackface minstrelsy, 78–79

black flâneurism, 82–84, 101

black folklore, 148

Black Hope (Wright), 158–60, 164, 255n91

black intellection, 36

black interiority, 9, 12–13, 30, 36–41, 108, 116, 120–35, 160–65, 172–73, 183–87

black isolation, 154–55, 158, 162–63, 187

Black Jacobins, The (James), 204

Black Marxism (Robinson), 146

black masculinity, 169–70

Black Metropolis (Cayton and Drake), 118, 132, 160

black nationalism, 9, 106, 148–49, 152–54, 161, 214n10

"Black Odyssey, White World" (Balakian), 75

"Black Panther" (Hughes), 197

Black Panther Party, 196

Black Power, 10, 108, 216n27

black powerlessness, 35, 135

black press, 88, 90–102, 109–10, 150–51. *See also specific newspapers*

black protest writing, 75

black religious practices, 37–39

black revolution, 56, 64, 104–5, 171, 196–99, 202–4, 208. *See also* radicalism

Black Salt, The (*Le sel noir*) (Glissant), 60–61

Black Skin, White Masks (Fanon), 6, 167, 169–71

Black Spider, The (Gotthelf), 79

black student life, 49

black subjectivity, 12–13, 25, 33, 49, 84, 119–22, 129, 152, 166, 202–3

black writing. *See* black alienation; black press; ethnography; experimentalism; ghetto pastoral; gothicism; melancholy; negation; paraliterature; Paris; prophetic speech; urban space; *and specific writers*

Blair, Sara, 15, 220n54

Blair, Thomas L., 192

Blakely, Henry, 110

Blanchot, Maurice, 34, 40

Bland, Aldon, 110, 113

Bland, Edward, 110, 112, 153, 252n25, 253n54

"Blue in Green" (Mackey), 14
Blue Period (Davis), 13
"Blueprint for Negro Writing" (Wright), 39, 146–50, 152–56, 158, 160–61, 252n25
"Blue Room" (Davis), 13
Bond, Horace Mann, 237n9
Bone, Robert, 109, 244n21
Bonnefoy, Yves, 46
Bontemps, Arna, 146
Boorstin, Daniel, 208
Bosquet, Alain, 233n70
Bourdieu, Pierre, 35–36
Boyers, Robert, 75
Braithwaite, Kamau, 55
Breton, André, 45, 52, 55–56
"Bright and Morning Star" (Wright), 152
Britton, Celia, 44, 227n10
Bronzeville, 110–11, 113, 247n64
Brooks, Cleanth, 23
Brooks, Gwendolyn: background on, 109; and black liveliness, 133; and black revolution, 104–5, 108, 114–15; and communism, 11; criticism of, 106–7; and James, 127–29; and kitchenette, 119, 122, 125–26, 132; and Marshall, 135–37; and modernist description, 122–26, 129–33; poetry of, 106–7, 114–16, 119, 133, 243n16; and reappropriating media images, 128–29; and resistance, 119–20, 138, 185; and scholarship, 120, 133–34; and small literary magazines, 110, 114–17; and Tennyson, 129–30; and Woolf, 121, 125–26, 131–32; and Wright, 158. *See also* black interiority; experimentalism; gender; ghetto pastoral; *Negro Story*; *and specific works*
Brown, Frank London, 119, 247n59
Brown, Oscar, Jr., 107
Browne, Roscoe Lee, 73
Brown Girl, Brownstones (Marshall), 9, 108, 134–42, 190
Browning, Alice C., 110, 112–13, 117, 245n27
Brown v. Board of Education, 32
Broyard, Anatole, 197

Buck-Morss, Susan, 83–85
Burnett, Whit, 110
Burroughs, Margaret, 244n24
Burroughs, Nannie H., 118
Bush, Ruth, 54, 228n19

Cabral, Amílcar, 199
Cabrera, Lydia, 231n40
Cahier d'un retour au pays natal (Césaire), 52, 55–56, 231n40
Cahiers d'Art, 42, 226n3
Cailler, Bernadette, 59
Calhoun, Doyle, 214n13
Camus, Albert, 49
Cantos (Pound), 57
Caribbean Discourse (Glissant), 43, 47, 53, 60, 66–67, 220n7
Carmichael, Stokely, 10, 197, 218n36
Carpio, Glenda, 8
Carter, Vincent O.: background on, 71–75, 88, 237nn8–9; and Buddhism, 85; correspondence of, 87–88; criticism of, 75–77; cultural authority of, 70–71, 79–82; and double-voicing, 81–82; and Ellison, 85; as flâneur, 82–84; and humor, 80–81, 84, 86; and Joyce, 88, 93; and self-imposed exile, 69–70, 102–3. *See also* black alienation; Kansas City
"Carthage" (Glissant), 60–61
Casanova, Pascale, 53–54
Castle, The (Kafka), 169
Catacombs, The (Demby), 188, 200, 204–9, 267n65
Cater, Suzy, 44, 46, 227nn10–12
Cayton, Horace R., 118, 132, 156, 160, 164, 181
"Ceremony Must Be Found, The" (Wynter), 66
Césaire, Aimé, 1–4, 44–46, 50–52, 55–56, 64, 166, 192–95, 201, 213nn3–4, 230nn32–33, 233n69. *See also specific works*
Césaire, Suzanne, 45–46
Chakrabarty, Dipesh, 20, 33, 220n8
Challenge, 150–51, 153
Chandler, Nahum, 173, 259n144
Charpier, Jacques, 233n70

Cherki, Alice, 257n116
Chicago Defender, 94
"Chicago Portraits" (Brooks), 113–14
Chicago Renaissance, 109–10, 152–53, 244n21. *See also* Popular Front
Childress, Alice, 160
Chosen Place, the Timeless People, The (Marshall), 206–7
Christian, Barbara, 120, 134
Citizen (Rankine), 131
"City Limits, Village Values" (Morrison), 89–90. *See also* "village values"
City Where No One Dies, The (La ville où nul ne meurt) (Dadié), 190
civil rights movement, 12, 90, 94, 98, 119, 193, 198, 240n66, 247n62. *See also* black alienation; lynching; racism; segregation; slavery
Clarke, John Henrik, 105
Cleaver, Eldridge, 225n70
Cloutier, Jean-Christophe, 8, 236n1
Cohen, Hettie, 199, 264n33
Cold War: background on, 5; black writing and, 3–4, 6, 20, 32, 34–35, 44, 86, 146, 172–73, 178, 200–201, 206; and domestic sphere, 132; liberal narrative of, 25; and literary criticism, 4; "modernity," 5, 108; propaganda, 222n36; surveillance, 11–12, 262n182; and temporality, 85
Cole, Teju, 15, 32
Coleman, Ornette, 196
Colored American Magazine, 150
Columbus, Christopher, 56, 65–68
Committee on Negro Housing, 118
communism, 1–4, 11–12, 45, 109, 151–52, 155–57, 161, 173, 182. *See also* Marxism; Popular Front
Communist Control Act, 156
Condé, Maryse, 44, 56, 64–65, 67, 234n91
Conference of Negro-African Writers and Artists, 32
Congress of Black Writers and Artists, 46
Conrad, Earl, 110
Conscripts of Modernity (Scott), 204
Convery, Maureen, 112
Cooke, Marvel, 160

"Copernican," 235n99
Costello, Brannon, 149
Cotillion; or, One Good Bull Is Half the Herd, The (Killens), 262n197
Couch, William, 110, 112
Courage, Richard A., 109, 244n21
Crawley, Ashon, 37
Crisis, 98
Crogman, Ada, 98
Crossman, Richard, 156, 213n5, 262n182
"crossroads poetics," 47
Cruse, Harold, 146
"Cult of Experience in American Writing, The" (Rahv), 143–44
Cunningham, Margaret Danner, 105, 110

Dadié, Bernard Binlin, 190
Dale, Thelma, 160
Danner, Margaret, 105, 110
Dark Legend (Wertham), 164
Dash, J. Michael, 43, 49, 59–60, 66
Davis, Ben, 151
Davis, Cynthia, 150
Davis, Frank Marshall, 110–12, 252n25
Davis, George, 164
Davis, Miles, 13–14, 187, 220n55
Dead Lecturer, The (Baraka), 198
de Beauvoir, Simone, 175
Debord, Guy, 84, 206, 239n50
Debray, Régis, 199
DeCarava, Roy, 14–15, 220n54
de Certeau, Michel, 120, 247n64
décollage, 206
decolonization, 2, 12, 32, 44, 84, 199–200. *See also* anticolonialism
Defender, 110
Delaney, Beauford, 248n73
Deleuze, Gilles, 43, 53
Delgrès, Louis, 56, 58
Demby, William, 188, 191, 200, 204–9
Denning, Michael, 37, 108, 133, 149
Depestre, René, 192, 194
Derrida, Jacques, 162–63, 259n144, 261n176
desegregation, 200
Dessalines, Jean-Jacques, 56
Destination Freedom, 106–7, 243n11

Dickstein, Morris, 145
Different Drummer, A (Kelley), 70
Diop, Alioune, 46, 54, 166, 192, 263n10
Diop, Christiane Yandé, 192
disalienation, 168, 170–72, 202–3
Discours antillais (*Caribbean Discourse*)
    (Glissant), 43, 47, 53, 60, 66–67, 220n7
Discourse on Colonialism (Césaire), 2
disidentification, 21–22
Divine Days (Forrest), 70
Dodson, Owen, 116
Dolinar, Brian, 149
Dorn, Ed, 198
Dos Passos, John, 149
double-voicing, 81–82
Douglas, Mary, 179
Drabinski, John, 61
Drake, St. Clair, 118, 132, 181
Dubey, Madhu, 89–91
Du Bois, W. E. B., 6, 37, 48–49, 98, 180,
    195, 215n17, 225n74
Dumayet, Pierre, 68
Dunfords Travels Everywheres (Kelley), 70
Durham, Richard, 106–7
"Dusk of Dawn" (Du Bois), 195
Dust Tracks on a Road (Hurston), 185

Ebony, 110, 128, 251n18
Éditions du Dragon, 42, 55
Edwards, Brent, 9, 213n4, 229n26, 243n4
Edwards, Erica, 105
Einaudi, Jean-Luc, 266n48
Eliot, T. S., 60, 117, 149
Ellis, Nadia, 191
Ellison, Ralph: and Associated Coun-
    cils of Arts, 74; on black isolation, 154;
    and black vernacular culture, 176; and
    description, 122; and Federal Writers'
    Project, 26; and hibernation, 85–86,
    191; and Marshall, 135, 137, 141–42;
    and novel of ideas, 145–46, 184; and
    small literary magazines, 111; and
    Wright, 156, 175–76, 182, 253n50
elusion, 134, 137–39
Empson, William, 133
Encarta Africana (Gates and Appiah), 192
"Encounter on the Seine" (Baldwin), 26

epistemologies of unbelonging, 173
Ernst, Max, 45
Ervin, Hazel Arnett, 189
Eshleman, Clayton, 231n40
"Ethics of Living Jim Crow, The"
    (Wright), 147
ethnography, 31–32, 47–51, 60, 78–82
Europe '51, 205
Evans, Walker, 160
"Everybody's Protest Novel" (Baldwin),
    21, 23, 25
experimentalism, 69–70, 77, 81, 108, 110,
    114–15, 120–33, 197–98
Expression, 110

Fabre, Michel, 21, 154, 156, 161
Fanon, Frantz, 6, 44–46, 147, 166–
    72, 185, 193, 203, 214n13, 228n18,
    257nn119–21
Federal-Aid Highway Act, 90
Federal Writers' Project, 26
Fiction of the Fifties (Gold), 19–20
Fiedler, Leslie, 218n33
Field, Douglas, 33
Field of Islands, A (*Un champ d'îles*) (Glis-
    sant), 42
"Fire and Cloud" (Wright), 38–40
Fire Next Time, The (Baldwin), 75
First Congress of Black Writers and Art-
    ists, 166, 191–95
Fischer, Louis, 156
Flatley, Jonathan, 171, 218n34
Fleischer, Chip, 76–77, 238n23
Foley, Barbara, 11, 134, 149, 160, 255n91
Ford, Nick Aaron, 113
Forrest, Leon, 70, 77
Foucault, Michel, 33, 48, 65, 206,
    259n144
Franc-Jeu, 46, 51–52, 228n17, 230n33
Frank, Robert, 102
Franklin, Chester Arthur, 94–99
Franklin, Clara, 94–95
Freedom Time (Wilder), 50
"From the Poets in the Kitchen" (Mar-
    shall), 135
Front des Antillais et Guyanais pour l'Au-
    tonomie, 50

Frost, Robert, 117
Fuller, Hoyt, 105

Galand, René, 62
Gallimard, 43
Gandhi, Leela, 107, 111, 245n30
Garcia, Jay, 164
Garvin, Vicki, 160
Gass, William, 219n49
Gates, Henry Louis, Jr., 8, 192, 257n121
Gayden, Fern, 110, 112, 152, 245n27
gender, 104–17, 120–21, 127–32, 135–36, 160. *See also* black powerlessness; patriarchy; resistance
George, Stefan, 187
ghetto pastoral, 37, 108, 133–34, 179, 249n109
Gibson, Sonny, 91, 93
Gilroy, Paul, 13, 146, 202, 266n49
Glissant, Édouard: and *antillanité*, 43; background on, 42–43, 45–46, 67; and Baldwin, 44, 48–49, 63; and Condé, 64–65; and creolization, 42–43, 66; and "cross-cultural poetics," 20; cultural authority of, 32, 47–48, 70–71; and Fanon, 228n18, 230n36; and First Congress of Black Writers and Artists, 166, 192; on human imagination, 57–59, 62; and opacity, 43; and Paris, 44, 51–53; and Perse, 59–62, 233n70; and "schizophrenia," 227nn10–11; and scholarship, 42–44, 47, 51; and snow, 53, 68, 231n42; and Wynter, 64–67. *See also* black student life; ethnography; Franc-Jeu; Front des Antillais et Guyanais pour l'Autonomie; prophetic speech; translations; *and specific works*
gnōsis, 57–58
God That Failed, The (Crossman), 156, 213n5
Gold, Herbert, 19
Gold, Michael, 133, 149
Goldsby, Jacqueline, 97, 109, 183
Gordon, Lewis, 170
Gore, Dayo F., 160
Go Tell It on the Mountain (Baldwin), 10, 21, 29, 36–38, 40

gothicism, 36–39
Gotthelf, Jeremias, 79
Gourfain, Joyce, 183
Goveia, Elsa, 65
Grain of Wheat, A (Thiong'o), 190
Grand Parade, The (Mayfield), 9, 119
Grass, Günter, 93
Gratiant, Georges, 45
Green, Adam, 107, 109, 128
Greene, Graham, 261n166
Griffin, Farah Jasmine, 89, 180, 189
Guattari, Félix, 43, 53
Guevara, Che, 200
Guillén, Nicolás, 55, 151

Hall, James, 206–7
Hall, Stuart, 7, 13
Hallward, Peter, 43
Hanchard, Michael, 216n18
Hansberry, Lorraine, 119
Happersburger, Lucien, 29
Hardison, Ayesha, 109, 111, 114, 128–29, 159–60, 245n28
Harlem Crossroads (Blair), 15
Harlem Gallery (Tolson), 196
"Harlem Ghetto, The" (Baldwin), 22
"Harlem in Nowhere" (Ellison), 164
Harlem Renaissance, 8, 147, 244n21
Harlot's Ghost (Mailer), 201
Harper's, 29–30, 127–28
Heath, Malcolm, 57
Hefner, Brooks, 241n70
Hegel, Georg, 146, 173
Hemingway, Ernest, 84
Henderson, David, 197
Hérémakhonon (Condé), 65, 234n91
Herzog (Bellow), 143
"He Seen It In the Stars" (Himes), 113
Higashida, Cheryl, 149, 152
Himes, Chester, 111, 113, 156, 245n27, 257n116
Hine, Darlene Clark, 94
Hirsch, Arnold, 118–19
Hoetis, Themistocles, 23
Holiday, Billie, 14
Holland, Sharon, 205
Holmes, Eugene C., 153

Hoover, J. Edgar, 11, 156
Hopkins, Pauline, 150
"How Bigger Was Born" (Wright), 158
Howe, Irving, 218n33
"How It Feels to Be Colored Me" (Hurston), 18
Hughes, Langston, 107, 136, 151, 196–97, 237n9, 264n21
humanism, 59, 65–66, 220n7
Hume, David, 173
humor, 80
Humphrey, Hubert, 27
Hunter-Gault, Charlayne, 198
Hurston, Zora Neale, 8, 18, 110, 161, 185–86, 254n76

I, Tituba (Condé), 67
"I Choose Exile" (Wright), 251n18
imagined communities, 128
"In a Cozy Kitchenette Apartment," 117–18
inequality of ignorance, 33
Internal Security Act, 173
Interracial South Side Cultural Conference, 110
interstate highways, 90, 241n67
In the Castle of My Skin (Lamming), 10, 188–89
In the Mecca (Brooks), 196
"Into the Wild Blue Yonder" (Scott), 113
invagination, 162–63
Invisible Man (Ellison), 8–10, 15–16, 85, 122, 135–46, 175–76, 184, 190
"Invisible Writer, The" (Lottman), 74–75
Irele, Abiola, 192
Irigaray, Luce, 178
"I Tried to Be a Communist" (Wright), 156

Jackson, Lawrence, 22–23, 35, 146, 218n35, 245n27
James, Cyril Lionel Robert, 181–82, 201, 204, 258n136
James, Henry, 23–25, 35–37, 41, 121, 125, 127–29, 165, 222n21
James, William, 126, 225n73
Jameson, Fredric, 7, 216n21

Jane Crow, 111, 129, 159, 245n28. *See also* gender; Jim Crow; racism; segregation; slavery
JanMohamed, Abdul, 157, 177, 254n79
Jarrett, Gene A., 148
Jefferson, Thomas, 36, 173
Jet, 110, 128
Jim Crow, 71, 88, 96, 99, 111, 144, 157, 189, 254n79. *See also* Jane Crow; racism; segregation; slavery
John Reed Club, 150, 154
Johnson, Charles S., 118
Johnson, Fenton, 112
Johnson, John H., 110, 128
Johnson Publishing, 107, 128–29
Jones, Claudia, 160
Jones, LeRoi, 10, 104–5, 197. *See also* Baraka, Amiri
Jorn, Asger, 239n50
Joseph, Peniel E., 218n36
Joyce, James, 13, 88, 93, 122, 149
Joyce, Joyce Ann, 107
Just above My Head (Baldwin), 221n13

Kafka, Franz, 169, 197, 218n33
Kalliney, Peter J., 12, 219n43, 263n10
Kansas City, 91–102
Kansas City (Gibson), 91, 93
Kansas City Call, 94–98, 102
Kansas City Sanborn Insurance Maps, 71–72
Kansas City Star, 96
Kant, Immanuel, 173
Kazin, Alfred, 11, 219n42
Keith, Allyn, 153
Keith, Joseph, 173, 182
Kelley, Robin D. G., 120
Kelley, William Melvin, 70, 77
Kennedy, John F., 207–8
Kent, George E., 244n19
Khalfa, Jean, 167–69
Kierkegaard, Soren, 146, 173, 175, 182
Killens, John, 105, 262n197
Kind of Blue (Davis), 187
King, Martin Luther, Jr., 75, 169, 193, 208
kitchenette, 117–19, 122, 125–26, 132, 135, 179, 246n54

"kitchenette building" (Brooks), 119
"kitchen-sink realism," 179–80
Knupfer, Anne Meis, 112
Kolokytha, Chara, 226n3
Kronstadt moment, 156, 161
Kullberg, Christina, 44, 47, 227n10

L'Afrique fantôme (*Phantom Africa*) (Leiris), 48, 229n26
La lézarde (*The Ripening*) (Glissant), 43, 46, 66–67
Lam, Wilfredo, 42, 45, 231n40
Lamming, George, 166, 188–89, 256n111
Lange, Dorothea, 160
Last of the Conquerors (Smith), 200–201
La terre inquiète (*The Troubled Earth*) (Glissant), 42
Laude, Jean, 46
La ville où nul ne meurt (*The City Where No One Dies*) (Dadié), 190
Lawd Today! (Wright), 149
Le bateau ivre (Rimbaud), 57
Le coeur à rire et à pleurer (*Tales from the Heart*) (Condé), 64
Le Discours antillais (*Caribbean Discourse*) (Glissant), 43, 47, 53, 60
Lee, Don L., 106
Lee, Russell, 159–60
Leeming, David A., 24, 29, 33
Léger, Alexis, 59
Leiris, Michel, 45–48, 229n26, 230n32
Les damnés de la terre (Fanon), 168
Le sel noir (*The Black Salt*) (Glissant), 60–61
Les Indes (Glissant), 43–44, 46–47, 55–68, 232n48, 233n64
Les lettres nouvelles, 46, 48, 54, 60, 194
L'espace littéraire (Blanchot), 34
"L'ethnographe devant le colonialisme" (Leiris), 48
L'Étranger (*The Stranger*) (Camus), 49
"Let's Go Visiting" (Bland), 113
Letter from a Birmingham Jail (King), 75
"Letter to Maurice Thorez" (Césaire), 1–2
Levenson, Michael, 121
Lévi-Strauss, Claude, 45, 48, 60
Lewis, Ida, 104

Lewis, Norman, 183
Lewis, Tom, 90
LGBTQ+, 110–11, 146, 150–51, 153
Liberal Imagination, The (Trilling), 11, 23
liberalism (US), 20, 25–27, 29, 123
Libretto for the State of Liberia (Tolson), 196
Ligon, Glenn, 18–19
Lincoln University in Pennsylvania, 73, 237n9
literature, space of, 33–34
lived experience, 4, 6, 156, 169, 214n13. *See also* black alienation
"Living On" (Derrida), 162–63
Llorens, David, 105
Locke, Alain, 111–12, 148
loitering, 84–85
Lonely Londoners, The (Selvon), 263n5
Lottman, Herbert R., 73–76, 87, 237n14
Louverture, Toussaint, 56
Lumumba, Patrice, 199, 203, 216n27
Lycée Schoelcher, 45
Lynchers, The (Wideman), 262n197
lynching, 97
Lyotard, Jean-François, 206

Mackey, Nathaniel, 14, 163, 219n49
Madhubuti, Haki, 106
Magic Mountain, The (Mann), 143
Mailer, Norman, 201–2
Mais, Roger, 245n38
Malcolm X, 10, 172, 193, 197–99, 208, 216n27
Malraux, André, 154
Man Called White, A (White), 225n70
Manigault-Bryant, James Arthur, 225n74
Mann, Thomas, 143
Man's Fate (Malraux), 154
Manville, Marcel, 50, 230n36
Man Who Lived Underground, The (Wright), 160, 162–63
Man without Qualities, The (Musil), 172, 259n141
March on Washington for Jobs and Freedom, 207–8
Marie-Joseph, Cosnay, 50

Mariners, Renegades, and Castaways (James), 182, 258n136
Markmann, Charles Lam, 214n13
marriage, 136–37
Marriott, David, 257n121
Marshall, Paule, 9, 108, 134–42, 206–7
Marshall, Russell, 252n25
Marshall, Thurgood, 237n9
Martinique, 45, 47, 50–51
Marxism, 1–2, 12, 84, 110–11, 146, 148–49, 160, 184, 200, 215n16. *See also* communism
Marzioli, Sara, 205–6
Masson, André, 45
"Maud" (Tennyson), 129–30
Maud Martha (Brooks), 9–10, 104, 108, 113, 117, 120–21, 123–42, 158–59, 246n42, 249n109
Maugée, Aristide, 45
Maugham, Somerset, 127–28
Mawsim al-Hijrah ilâ al-Shamâl (*Season of Migration to the North*) (Salih), 190
Maximin, Daniel, 192
Maxwell, William J., 11, 156
Mayfield, Julian, 9, 119
McCarran-Walter Act, 173, 182
McCarthy, Mary, 23, 250n9
McGurl, Mark, 35–36, 225n71
McKay, Claude, 8, 254n76
melancholy, 53, 80, 84–86, 102–3, 128, 153, 189, 218n34. *See also* black alienation
Melhem, D. H., 126, 129
"Memories of My Grandmother" (Wright), 163–64
Menand, Louis, 5
Mendelson, Edward, 221n9
Ménil, René, 45
Meredith, James, 198
Merleau-Ponty, Maurice, 168
Meyer, Joseph, 78–79
Meyers Konversations-Lexikon, 78–79
Meyers Reisebücher, 78
"Michel Leiris, ethnographe" (Glissant), 48
Middle of the Journey, The (Trilling), 181
Mignolo, Walter, 235n99
"migration narrative," 88–90, 180

Mills, C. Wright, 26
Milner, Ron, 105
Minus, Marian, 110, 150–53, 253n50
Mishra, Pankaj, 143–46
Mitchell, Verner, 150
modernist description, 121–25
Monroe, Harriet, 109
Montage of a Dream Deferred (Hughes), 196
Mont-Saint Michel and Chartres (Adams), 33
Moral Agents (Mendelson), 221n9
Morejón, Nancy, 192
Morgan, Stacy, 8, 109
Morris, Wright, 189
Morrison, Toni, 67, 90, 101, 240n65
Moten, Bennie, 102
Moten, Fred, 119, 248n73, 259n142
"mother, the" (Brooks), 246n42
Moudjahid, El, 167, 257n116
Moveable Feast, A (Hemingway), 84
Mrs. Dalloway (Woolf), 121, 124–26, 131–32, 134
Mullen, Bill, 11, 109, 112, 114, 244n24, 245n27
Muñoz, José Esteban, 21–22, 221n13
Munro, John, 203
Murray, Albert, 70
Murray, Pauli, 245n28
Murray, Roland, 262n197
"Muse of History, The" (Walcott), 233n69
Music Box Revue, 117–18
Musil, Robert, 143, 172–73, 259n141

NAACP, 95–96, 98, 169
Nadeau, Maurice, 46, 54
Nadel, Alan, 215n14
Naked and the Dead, The (Mailer), 201
Narrows, The (Petry), 9–10, 189–90
National Liberation Front, 166–67
National Negro Congress, 148
National Urban League, 118
Native Son (Wright), 21, 23, 25, 144–45, 149, 158–59, 161, 167, 219n42
Nausea (Sartre), 179
Neal, Larry, 198, 264n29

negation, 14, 19, 36–37, 41, 83, 129, 147, 149–50, 155, 176

négritude, 52, 64, 166, 171

"Negro at Home and Abroad, The" (Baldwin), 25–29

Negro Digest, 110

"Negro in Literature, The," 10

"Negro in Paris, The" (Baldwin), 26–27

Negro Story, 107–8, 110–17, 245n27

"Negro Writer, The" (Smith), 200

"Negro Writer and His World, The" (Lamming), 166

Negro Youth Photo Script, 110

Nesbitt, Nick, 44, 50

New Challenge, 110, 147, 149–51, 153–54

Newton, Huey, 196

New Vistas, 110

New World A-Coming (Ottley), 26

Niger, Paul, 50, 230n36

Nishikawa, Kinohi, 9, 69

Nkrumah, Kwame, 204, 237n9

No Green Pastures (Ottley), 26–29

Non-Aligned Movement, 63

No Name in the Street (Baldwin), 193

normativity, 108, 134, 137–39

Norton Anthology of African American Literature, The, 217n28

Notebook of a Return to the Native Land (Césaire), 2

"Note on Negro Nationalism, A" (Keith), 153

Notes of a Native Son (Baldwin), 26, 32, 225n73

Notes of a Son and a Brother (James), 37

"Note sur une 'Poésie Nationale' chez les peuples noirs" (Glissant), 194

"Not My People's War" (Wright), 161

Novum Organum (Bacon), 66

Obrist, Hans Ulrich, 227nn10–12

Of Human Bondage (Maugham), 127–28

O'Hara, Frank, 198

Olsen, Tillie, 133–34

Olson, Charles, 198

O'Meally, Robert, 18

Omeros (Walcott), 55

O'Neill, Dominique, 43, 55, 63

One Way (*Patron de New York*) (Dadié), 190

On Native Grounds (Kazin), 11

"Open Letter" (Dodson), 116

Organization of Solidarity with the Peoples of Africa, Asia, and Latin America, 199–200

Ortega y Gasset, José, 154, 254n56

Osundare, Niyi, 192–93

Ottley, Roi, 26–29

"Our Humanity Is Greater Than America or Russia" (Wright), 2–3

Outsider, The (Wright), 4, 10, 14, 141, 146–47, 155, 157, 160, 165–66, 170–87, 214n9, 251n13, 261n166

"Out There" (Pinckney), 75–76

Paalen, Wolfgang, 42

Padmore, Dorothy, 182

Padmore, George, 182

painting, 18–19

Pan-African movement, 2, 182

Panther and the Lash (Hughes), 196–97

Papon, Maurice, 266n48

paraliterature, 91–92

Paris, 44, 51–54, 65

patriarchy, 120–21, 127–28, 151–52. *See also* gender

Patron de New York (*One Way*) (Dadié), 190

Pease, Allison, 129

Péret, Benjamin, 231n40

periodization, 1–2, 7–9, 58–59, 69, 71, 90, 108, 145, 147, 196, 202, 216n19

péripétie, 57–58, 233n64

periplum, 57

Perse, Saint-John, 59–63, 233nn69–70

Petry, Ann, 9, 189–90

Phantom Africa (*L'Afrique fantôme*) (Leiris), 48, 229n26

Philcox, Richard, 6

Pichette, Henri, 46

Pinckney, Darryl, 75–76

Plath, Sylvia, 133

Pleasures of Exile, The (Lamming), 189

Plummer, Brenda Gayle, 214n11

Poetics (Aristotle), 57

Poetics of Relation, The (Glissant), 43
Poetry, 105
Popular Front, 4, 11, 38, 108–10, 112–17, 150, 159–60, 244n24. *See also* Chicago Renaissance; communism
Porter, Eric, 215n17
Portrait of a Lady, The (James), 128
Portrait of the Artist as a Young Man (Joyce), 88
postcolonialism, 43, 204
poststructuralism, 43–44
Pound, Ezra, 57
Prashad, Vijay, 63
Preface to a Twenty Volume Suicide Note (Baraka), 198
Présence africaine, 46, 54, 166, 192, 194, 228n19, 263n10
"Present Trends in Negro Literature" (Minus), 153
Primary Colors, The (Carter), 74, 76, 87–88, 237n14. See also *Such Sweet Thunder* (Carter)
"Princes and Powers" (Baldwin), 32, 193
"Problems Facing the Negro Writer Today" (Holmes), 153
proletarian literature, 4, 11–12, 134, 149
prophetic speech, 40–41, 48, 51–53, 56, 60, 62, 67
Proust, Marcel, 164–65, 189
Pryor, Richard, 18
pseudo-events, 208
"Psychiatry Comes to Harlem" (Wright), 164
psychogeography, 84
pulp fiction, 91
pulp modernism, 178–79, 258n123

Quashie, Kevin, 77, 120–21

Rabinowitz, Paula, 178–79, 258n123, 261n166
racialization, 22, 34, 36, 81–85, 131, 146, 171–72
racism: as bad faith, 170; Baldwin's views on, 28; and black consciousness, 194–95; and blackface, 78–79; and blacklisting, 147; comparative studies of, 26–31; "erotic life of," 205; and experimentalism, 69–70; internalized, 83; and literary tropes, 125–27, 130–31, 133; and redlining, 90, 119; and violence, 96–98. *See also* black alienation; civil rights movement; Jane Crow; Jim Crow; lynching; segregation; slavery
"Racism and Culture" (Fanon), 166
Radford, Daniel, 228n13
radicalism, 4, 45, 54, 105, 108, 198. *See also* black revolution
Radical Novel in America, The (Rideout), 11
Rahv, Philip, 143–45, 221n19
Raisin in the Sun, A (Hansberry), 119
Rampersad, Arnold, 74, 196–97
Rankine, Claudia, 131
Rasberry, Vaughn, 8, 25, 28, 146, 157–58, 254n79
Redding, J. Saunders, 107
Redmond, Eugene, 198
Reed, Anthony, 70
Reed, Carol, 261n166
Reed, Ishmael, 77, 197
Reporter, 26–27
Report from Part One (Brooks), 104, 106–7
Report from Part Two (Brooks), 106
resistance, 2, 119–20, 137–38, 140–41, 167, 185, 190
Return to Black America (Smith), 204
"Revision of the Invocation" (Brooks), 114–15
Revolt of the Masses, The (Ortega y Gasset), 154
Rhav, Philip, 23
Ricoeur, Paul, 233n64
Rideout, Walter, 11
Rimbaud, Arthur, 52–53, 57, 231n40
Ripening, The (La lézarde) (Glissant), 43, 46
Robbins, Bruce, 224n64, 224n66
Robeson, Paul, 147
Robinson, Cedric, 146
Rockefeller, Nelson, 27
Rodney, Walter, 224n66
"Rootedness" (Morrison), 89

Ross, Kristin, 202, 266n47
Rossellini, Roberto, 205
Rosskam, Ed, 159-60
Rotella, Mimmo, 206
Rousset, David, 213n5
Rowley, Hazel, 158-59, 164, 253n50, 256n111
Ruddick, Lisa, 126
Rusert, Britt, 9

Saillet, Maurice, 233n70
Salih, Tayeb, 190
Sartre, Jean-Paul, 23, 48, 146, 168-69, 175, 179, 213n5, 260n165
Saunders, Frances Stonor, 222n36
Savage Holiday (Wright), 258n123
Schaub, Thomas, 25, 222n29
Schuyler, George, 254n76
Scott, Bessie, 113
Scott, David, 204, 208
Scott, James C., 120
Scottsboro Limited (Hughes), 196, 264n21
Seale, Bobby, 196
Season in Hell, A (Rimbaud), 52-53
Season of Migration to the North (*Mawsim al-Hijrah ilâ al-Shamâl*) (Salih), 190
Second Black Writer's Conference, 104-5, 107-8
"Secret, The" (Carter), 74, 238n15
Sedgwick, Eve Kosofsky, 139-40
segregation, 26, 90, 92, 100, 102, 108, 113, 118, 154, 175. *See also* Jane Crow; Jim Crow; racism; slavery
"Self as Journey, The" (Baldwin), 24-25, 165
Selvon, Sam, 263n5
Senghor, Leopold, 50, 193
Sense and Sensibility (Austen), 140
Sentimental Journey (Sterne), 80-81
Seven League Boots, The (Murray), 70
Shakespeare, William, 33
Sharpe, Christina, 57
Shatz, Adam, 147
Shelby, Tommie, 146
Shockley, Evie, 116
Signs and Cities (Dubey), 89-91

Situationist International, 239n50
Situations (Sartre), 169
slavery, 56, 61, 67, 92, 229n26, 259n144. *See also* Jane Crow; Jim Crow; racism; segregation
Smethurst, James, 11, 249n109
Smith, Bessie, 33
Smith, Valerie, 134
Smith, William Gardner, 200-204, 266n46
Smith Act, 173
So Black and Blue (Warren), 16
Société de Culture Africaine, 46
Soleil de la conscience (Glissant), 42-44, 46-55, 61, 68, 227n10
Sollors, Werner, 8, 214n9, 236n6
Something Else!!!! (Coleman), 196
Sontag, Susan, 75
Soul on Ice (Cleaver), 225n70
Souls of Black Folk, The (Du Bois), 37
South Side Writers Group, 110-11, 148-51, 153, 252n25
Soyinka, Wole, 192
Spillers, Hortense, 120, 178, 186, 259n142, 260n164
Spyglass Tree, The (Murray), 70
Stanford, Maxwell Curtis, Jr., 198
Stark, Inez Cunningham, 110
Stein, Gertrude, 126, 133
Sterne, Laurence, 80-81
Stevens, Wallace, 117
Stone Face, The (Smith), 200-204, 266n53
Story, 110
Stovall, Tyler, 202
Stowe, Harriet Beecher, 21, 23, 125, 149
Stranger, The (*L'Étranger*) (Camus), 49
"Stranger in the Village" (Baldwin), 18, 21, 26, 28-35, 48, 70, 80, 195
Street, The (Petry), 189
Street in Bronzeville, A (Brooks), 106, 108, 117, 119, 196, 246n42
Stuart Hall Project, The, 13
Such Sweet Thunder (Carter), 71-72, 74, 76-77, 86-90, 93-102, 238n23. See also *Primary Colors, The* (Carter)

Sugrue, Thomas J., 87
Survey Graphic Number, The (Locke), 148
"sweatshop sublime," 224n64, 224n66

Tales from the Heart (Le coeur à rire et à pleurer) (Condé), 64
"Talking It Over" (Wilkins), 98
Tate, Claudia, 82
Taylor, Eleanor Ross, 133
Taylor-Burroughs, Margaret, 110
Tennyson, Alfred, 129-30
Terrell, Whitney, 77
Their Eyes Were Watching God (Hurston), 110, 161
There Is a Tree More Ancient Than Eden (Forrest), 70
Thésée, Lucie, 45
Thiong'o, Ngũgĩ wa, 190
Third Man, The, 261n166
Thomas, Lorenzo, 197
Thompson, Mark Christian, 157
Thorez, Maurice, 1-2
Three Lives (Stein), 126
"Threshing Floor, The" (Baldwin), 36-38, 40, 226n79
Thurman, Wallace, 150-51
Till, Emmett, 189
Tin Drum, The (Grass), 93
Tóibín, Colm, 222n21
Tolliver, Cedric, 8, 216n27
Tolson, Melvin B., 196, 237n9
Tomkins, Grace, 110
Totalitarian Century, The (Rasberry), 25
Touré, Askia Muhammad, 197
Toward the African Revolution, 167
"Tradition and Industrialization" (Wright), 166, 258n129
Train, Whistle, Guitar (Murray), 70
translations, 43, 49, 55, 60
travel writing, 80-82
Tricontinental Conference, 200
Trilling, Lionel, 11, 23, 127, 181
Tristes Tropiques (Lévi-Strauss), 48
"Trolley, New Orleans (1955)" (Frank), 102
Tropiques, 45-46, 52, 55-56

Troubled Earth, The (La terre inquiète) (Glissant), 42
Trouble in Mind (Childress), 160, 255n90
Truman, Harry S., 91, 200
Trumbull Park (Brown), 119, 247n59
12 Million Black Voices (Wright), 159-60, 167, 169

Umbra, 197-99
Un champ d'îles (A Field of Islands) (Glissant), 42
Uncle Tom's Cabin (Stowe), 21, 23, 38, 41, 125, 149, 221n19
Uncle Tom's Children (Wright), 151, 167
Underwood, Ted, 216n19
Un nègre à Paris (An African in Paris) (Dadié), 190
urban space, 89-90, 118-19, 138

Variety, 117
Vents (Winds) (Perse), 60-63
"village values," 89-93, 101

Wahl, Jean, 46
Walcott, Derek, 55, 233n69
Wald, Alan, 5, 108
Walker, Margaret, 110, 154, 252n25
Wall, Cheryl, 32, 222n25
Wallace, David Foster, 143
Ward, Theodore, 110, 252n25
Warren, Kenneth, 7, 10-11, 16
Warshow, Robert, 22
Washington, Mary Helen, 11, 108-9, 114, 120, 123, 127, 132-36, 189, 247n59, 247n62
Webb, Constance, 181-82
Weik von Mossner, Alexa, 266n49
Well-Wrought Urn, The (Brooks), 23
Wertham, Fredric, 164
West, Dorothy, 26, 110, 147, 150-52, 253n44
Westad, Odd Arne, 5
West Indies, 55-66
West Indies Ltd. (Guillén), 55
"Whatever Happened to the Novel of Ideas?" (Mishra), 143

Wheatley, Phillis, 36
Wheeler, Lesley, 116–17
White, Hayden, 204, 206
White, Walter, 225n70
white flight, 90
White Man Listen! (Wright), 167–68
Whiter Fanon? (Marriott), 257n121
"Why I Stopped Hating Shakespeare"
   (Baldwin), 33
Wideman, John Edgar, 262n197
Wilder, Gary, 50, 230n35
Wilkerson, Isabel, 88
Wilkins, Roy, 98–100
Williams, Eric, 167
Williams, John A., 9, 217n32
Williams, Raymond, 5, 10, 218n34
Williams, William Carlos, 117, 124
Wilson, Edmund, 23, 221n19
Winds (*Vents*) (Perse), 60–63
Wing, Betsy, 43
Wipplinger, Jonathan, 78–79
"With Malice toward None" (Ford), 113
"Women and Fiction" (Woolf), 121
"Women in the Dynamics of Contempo-
   rary Development" (Morejón), 192
Woodard, Komozi, 214n10
Woodruff, Hale, 8
Woolf, Virginia, 121, 124–26, 131–32, 134
"Word from Writer Directly to Reader,
   A" (Baldwin), 19
"World and the Jug, The" (Ellison),
   218n33
World Republic of Letters, The (Casanova),
   53–54
"World's End" (Mais), 245n38
Wretched of the Earth, The (Fanon), 172,
   257n119
Wright, Ellen, 74
Wright, Richard: and Baldwin, 21, 23, 25,
   39, 189, 194–95; and black masculin-
   ity, 169, 186, 261n176; and black ver-
   nacular culture, 175–76; and Brooks,
   158; and communism, 150–51, 155–57,
   160–61, 213n5; death of, 257n119; and

documentary realism, 4, 159–60; and
Ellison, 156, 171, 175, 182, 253n50; and
Fanon, 166–72, 185, 257n116; and fascism, 157–58; and Federal Writers'
Project, 26; and Gates, 192; and Hurston, 110, 175, 185–86; and ideological unveiling, 180–81; and intellectual
friendships, 181–82; and literary form,
157–58, 170–71, 173, 176; and Minus,
150–51, 253n50; and modernization
theory, 184–85; and nonalignment,
3–4, 201; and novel of ideas, 144–46,
164, 172, 175, 179–80, 184–86; in Paris,
21; and Popular Front, 38–40; and
Proust, 165; and psychoanalysis, 164–
65, 176–77; and scholarship, 159, 164;
and small literary magazines, 110–11,
113, 150–51; and Wertham, 164; and
women, 151–53, 155, 159–61, 164, 176–
80, 183–84, 186, 254n65; and World
War II, 161. *See also* black alienation;
black isolation; black nationalism;
Marxism; negation; *and specific works*
Writing through Jane Crow (Hardison),
159
Wynter, Sylvia, 44, 64–68, 235n99,
235nn101–2

Yacine, Kateb, 46
Yonnondio (Olsen), 134
Young, Andrew, 198
Young, Ben, 241n70
Young, Nathan B., Jr., 91–93, 241n73
Young, Robert, 167
Young, William H., 91–93, 241n73
Your Kansas City and Mine (Young and
   Young), 91–93, 241n73
Your Saint Louis and Mine (Young),
   241n72

Zañartu, Enrique, 55
Zeigler, James, 251n18
Zervos, Christian, 42
Zhang, Dora, 121